D1789396

STATE FORMATION IN EUROPE, 843–1789

State Formation in Europe, 843–1789 follows the formation and development of the European state from the division of the Carolingian Empire to the French Revolution.

The book's primary focus is on Europe's patterns of internal and external development in comparison to political organization in other parts of the world. By analysing Europe as a single unit, rather than dividing it into nation states, it reveals the broader historical connections within the Continent. Bagge takes the reader through a discussion of how kingdoms evolved into states, introducing the influence of the Church and the town on these state structures. The relationship between state, Church and town is traced to explain how these different power struggles played out and why the territorial state became the dominant form of organization. Finally, the book clarifies why Europe developed in this way and the global consequences of this development.

By observing Europe through the perspective of the rest of the world, readers gain insight into trends common to the whole Continent while crossing the traditional border between the Middle Ages and early modern period. This book is essential reading for students studying medieval and early modern political history, state formation and Europe in a global context.

Sverre Håkon Bagge was Professor at the University of Bergen from 1991 to 2012. His books in English include: *Society and Politics in Snorri Sturluson's* Heimskringla (1991); *Kings, Politics, and the Right Order of the World in German Historiography, c. 950–1150* (2002); *Cross and Scepter: The Rise of the Scandinavian Kingdoms from the Vikings to the Reformation* (2014).

STATE FORMATION IN EUROPE, 843–1789

A Divided World

Sverre Håkon Bagge

Routledge
Taylor & Francis Group

LONDON AND NEW YORK

First published 2019
by Routledge
2 Park Square, Milton Park, Abingdon, Oxon OX14 4RN

and by Routledge
52 Vanderbilt Avenue, New York, NY 10017

Routledge is an imprint of the Taylor & Francis Group, an informa business

British Library Cataloguing in Publication Data
A catalogue record for this book is available from the British Library

Library of Congress Cataloging-in-Publication Data
Names: Bagge, Sverre, 1942- author.
Title: State formation in Europe, 843-1789 : a divided world / Sverre Hêakon Bagge.
Description: Abingdon, Oxon ; New York, NY : Routledge, 2019. | Includes bibliographical references. |
Identifiers: LCCN 2019005252 (print) | LCCN 2019011555 (ebook) | ISBN 9780429196829 (ebook) | ISBN 9780367185640 (hardback : alk. paper) | ISBN 9780367185626 (pbk. : alk. paper) | ISBN 9780429196829 (ebk.)
Subjects: LCSH: Europe--History--476-1492. | Europe--History--1492-1648. | Europe--History--1648-1789. | State, The--Origin.
Classification: LCC D104 (ebook) | LCC D104 .B28 2019 (print) | DDC 940.1--dc23
LC record available at https://lccn.loc.gov/2019005252

ISBN: 978-0-367-18564-0 (hbk)
ISBN: 978-0-367-18562-6 (pbk)
ISBN: 978-0-429-19682-9 (ebk)

Typeset in Bembo
by Taylor & Francis Books

To the memory of Jacques Le Goff

CONTENTS

PREFACE

This book has its origins in an almost lifelong interest in European history, although, previously, my research has mainly dealt with limited parts and epochs of it, notably the Scandinavian countries in the Middle Ages. The Centre for Medieval Studies at the University of Bergen, of which I was the director 2002–12 and the many colleagues and visitors there were an important source of inspiration. My retirement in 2012 offered new opportunities to deal with larger topics and address a more general audience, which then resulted in the present book. I am very grateful to Gunner Lind and Gerd Althoff and three anonymous reviewers who have read the whole text and given good advice. I dedicate the book to the memory of Jacques Le Goff, a great historian who was never afraid of addressing the big questions and of whom I have many fond memories.

Thanks also to Chris Given-Wilson, Zoe Opačić, Martyn Rady, John Watts and Hilde de Weert for help and advice. Finally, it has been a great pleasure to work with Routledge in the final phase; my best thanks to Lydia, Morwenna, Zoe, Susan, Megan, Christina and Gail.

INTRODUCTION

> Today we take the state for granted. We grumble about its demands; we complain that it is encroaching more and more on what used to be our private concerns, but we can hardly envisage life without it. In the world today, the worst fate that can befall a human being is to be stateless … This was not always so. There were periods – not long ago as historians measure time – when the state did not exist, and when no one was concerned that it did not exist.[1]

With these words, the American historian Joseph Strayer draws our attention to one of the most fundamental changes in the Western world – and, by implication, also the rest of the world – the formation of the state, which he dates to between 1100 and 1600, with the thirteenth century as a particularly crucial period. Although there can hardly be any doubt about the importance of Strayer's observation, both the chronology and the character of European state formation have been subject to extensive debate.

What do we mean by the term state? The definition of a state in contemporary international law is based on the Treaty of Montevideo of 1933: a state must have a permanent population, well-defined borders, a government and a capacity to honour international obligations. By contrast, there are no demands regarding the quality of government, internal sovereignty, impersonal bureaucracy, etc., which play a major part in the discussion of the origins of the state and of European state formation in the Middle Ages and the early modern period. The borders of many of the new states were the result of the divisions of territories between colonial powers, without consideration of linguistic and cultural homogeneity. Despite – or rather because of – the arbitrary character of these borders, the United Nations and other international bodies insist on their permanence, fearing that concessions on this point would endanger the whole system.[2]

If we turn to the scholarly literature, we find widely different uses of the term. To social anthropologists, any larger territory governed by one or a body of rulers is a state, in contrast to localized tribal society.[3] Historians tend to have stricter definitions, including some amount of bureaucratization and a distinction between private and public, the monopoly of violence and a legislative authority. Concerning Europe in the period that is the subject of the present book, early modernists generally have a more restrictive attitude than medievalists, although there are differences among the latter regarding the term and its use.[4] In this context, however, it is important to note that different uses of the term do not necessarily correspond to different opinions about the historical reality. In the following, the term will be used in a relatively loose sense. In accordance with the Montevideo definition, considerable attention will be paid to the elementary meaning of a territory formally governed by one ruler, whereas the degree of 'stateness' regarding internal conditions will be subject to a separate discussion.

Strayer's book summarizes the thought of a school of medievalists in Britain and the USA reaching back to the early twentieth century, a school that had rejected the picture of the dark Middle Ages current in the Renaissance and the Enlightenment as well as the Romantic view of the exotic Middle Ages often to be found in the nineteenth century.[5] The Middle Ages were the period when the European state was formed, not only in the sense that the modern division of the continent into separate political units took place at the time but also that the origins of their basic institutions can be traced back to this period. Although mostly dealing with individual states, these scholars had a stronger focus on the institutional aspect and regarded the development of law and administration as an attempt to solve the practical problems of government and the distribution of power. Thus, the Middle Ages laid the foundation for the modern state, far more so than classical antiquity or even the Renaissance had. State formation therefore represented a clear progress, replacing ruthless warlords in mutual competition with predictable government and the rule of law, or at least marking the beginning of a development in this direction. Strayer himself can hardly be accused of idealizing medieval government but he had a strong sense of government as an alternative to chaos.[6] Southern was more fascinated by the intellectual and cultural achievements of the Middle Ages but had a similar understanding of the practical aspects of government as Strayer.[7] This view can to some extent be understood against the background of English history. England was 'a much governed country' in the Middle Ages – probably the 'most governed' in Europe – and several of the medieval institutions, like Parliament, still exist in the twenty-first century. However, this is not the only explanation; Strayer's main field was French history, to which he made a number of important contributions, including his biography of King Philip IV. Within the social sciences, this approach has a parallel in Max Weber's studies of the emergence of the rational and impersonal European state, in contrast to the dominance of personal links and charisma in earlier ages.[8]

A reaction against this interpretation began in the 1970s.[9] Interest turned towards social and cultural history and the history of the common people, women, the poor and marginal, history from below rather than above. The trend can easily be illustrated by the space allotted to political history compared to other fields in general overviews, such as *The New Oxford History of England* and, somewhat less, *The New Cambridge Medieval History*, compared to their predecessors. The difference between the past and the present was more strongly emphasized and a negative view of the state became prominent. There has been a renaissance for early medieval history, which has often appeared in a more positive light: pre-state society was also able to solve conflicts; the introduction of public justice and royal government were more in the interest of the elites than the common people. The rise of the history of mentality, post-modernism and deconstructionism represented a reaction against the idea of progress in previous research.[10]

These tendencies were partly anticipated by previous French and German traditions. The French *Annales* School originally had a strong focus on social history. Thus, the state and even more traditional political history have a subordinate place in Fernand Braudel's monumental *La Mediterranée* (1949) and local studies on social and economic history largely replaced political history during the following period. Later, the history of mentality resulted in a number of important studies dealing with social ideas, political behaviour and royal ideology.[11] However, this school tended to emphasize the similarity rather than the difference between the Middle Ages and the early modern period, referring to the whole period until the French Revolution as the Old Regime (*l'ancien régime*). Moreover, the increasing importance of social history as a result of the influence of the *Annales* School and Marxism has led to a stronger focus on the social consequences – often the negative ones – of the development of the state. Both traditions have been influenced by social anthropology and have in turn influenced international scholarship, including the English-speaking world.[12]

German historiography for a long time had a strong focus on the imperial power in the period until the thirteenth century, in contrast to the decline and dissolution in the following period, thus, on the rise and decline of the state. More recently, a new perspective has been introduced, focusing on personal relationships rather than institutions and questioning the idea of state building under the Ottonians and their successors.[13] To some extent, this perspective was anticipated in the inter-war period by Theodor Mayer's 'Personenverbandstaat' and Otto Brunner's 'Herrschaft',[14] as well as by Percy Ernst Schramm's studies of the rituals of rulership.[15] There is still a strong emphasis on cultural factors, political thought as well as symbols and rituals.[16] Regarding the use of the term 'state' for the medieval period, there has been some uneasiness among German and Austrian scholars, as illustrated by the big volume of papers from a conference in Vienna in 2007 about the early medieval state.[17]

Politically, the development of the European Union has questioned the idea of the national state as the logical conclusion to a development going back to the Middle Ages and the early modern period. By contrast, there has been a new interest in the Holy Roman Empire,[18] as well as a stronger emphasis on the difference between the contemporary state and its medieval and early modern predecessors. Admittedly, this is not a totally new approach; the focus on political division was usually combined with an awareness of the cultural unity of Europe.

Whereas the importance of the European state has been reduced after 1945, the opposite is the case with the rest of the world, where the number of states increased from 51 to 193 during the post-war period and some kind of a national state for the first time in history became the normal political organization all over the world. This development formed the background of Charles Tilly's project on European state formation. When and why did the state become the normal political unit in Europe and how could this development be used as a model for the new states in other parts of the world?[19] In practice, this latter aim proved difficult to achieve and the main importance of Tilly's and his collaborators' work lies in their interpretation of the European development.

Tilly's understanding of European state formation is succinctly expressed in the statement 'War made the state and vice versa.'[20] States were formed through military competition, in particular through the military revolution in the early modern period: the formation of large armies and navies, equipped with more advanced weapons, and large and complex fortifications, led to higher taxation, increased bureaucracy and increased interference from the states in the lives of their subjects. A logical consequence of this emphasis was to date the formation of the state to the early modern period; there were no real states in the Middle Ages. Tilly here continues the tradition from German scholars like Otto Hintze and Norbert Elias, who in different ways regarded the European state as an epochal novelty.[21]

Tilly later developed his theories in a separate monograph, covering the period 990–1990.[22] Here he introduces the distinction between coercion and capital, the former characterizing agrarian states, the latter urban ones, although the most successful states are combinations of the two. Tilly agrees with the Marxists in emphasizing the oppressive character of the state but does not regard it as an instrument of the landowning aristocracy.[23] On the contrary, the state is an independent variable, dominating and controlling its inhabitants, including the aristocracy. A series of other scholars followed in Tilly's footsteps, partly developing his theories, partly modifying them.[24] Tilly also had considerable influence on the great project on state formation funded by the European Science Foundation, 1988–92. However, there have also been reactions against Tilly's exclusive focus on war as the driving force in state formation.[25] In a recent discussion of state formation, in a global rather than European perspective, Francis Fukuyama emphasizes the weakness of the European states rather than their strength and pays greater attention to the development of civilian institutions.[26] While Fukuyama follows Tilly in mainly focusing on the early modern period, the gradual formation of the nation state in the Middle Ages is a central theme in Michael Mann's analysis of social power.[27] The European state has also played an important part in the discussion about why Europe came to dominate the world during the last few centuries.[28]

From a historical point of view, tracing the ancestry of the state back to the early Middle Ages is relevant whether we believe in its transformation by the European Union or not. Recent developments have made us more aware of the various forms a state could take and the difference between the classical national state and its earlier predecessors. Not only the Holy Roman Empire but also a number of other units form a reminder of this. The national state is no longer the obvious political unit it was when Strayer wrote 50 years ago. Europe no longer has the central place it then had in historical research and teaching. Concerning the former, however, a comparison with the rest of the world increases the importance of the political division of Europe and its origins – there is no other example of an area of similar size being divided in this way. Concerning the latter, a history of Europe over a period of a thousand years must inevitably imply some comparison with other parts of the world, despite the obvious difficulty in gaining sufficient knowledge of these areas. Fortunately, a number of works have appeared recently which make comparison easier.

Geographically, the present book is confined to Western Christendom, i.e. the part of the continent that adhered to Roman Catholicism in the Middle Ages and was later divided between this religious adherence and that of Protestantism. 'Europe' is simply a short and convenient, although not quite correct term for this unit. As the focus will be on common features or at least variations within a common culture, of which religion is an important expression, the European Continent in a strictly geographical sense, covering the whole area west of the Ural, would be too large and complex to handle over nearly a thousand years.

During this long period, we are dealing with great changes, which, however, would seem to be minor compared to the ones that took place between 1789 and today. In 650, the population of Europe is estimated at around 11 million, which increased to around 130–40 million in 1750. In 2014, it was 520 million.[29] In the late eighteenth century, there was hardly any industry according to modern definitions of the term; with the exception of a few, rather primitive machines, all work was carried out by the muscular force of humans or animals. Land transport could not be faster than a horse could run and sea transport, although faster, was limited by the strength and directions of winds and streams. The average life expectancy was around 30 years, against 70–80 today in the Western world; this of course mainly because of the high child mortality; people surviving until adulthood might expect a further 20–40 years, largely depending on social status. Politically, there was no democracy in the modern sense. The existing states were ruled either by absolute kings or by small elites controlling the representative institutions. The state provided only very few of the services we expect from it today, such as education, health care, transport and control of the safety and welfare of its inhabitants. The state system itself has also changed significantly during the last 200 years, from more than 400 units in 1789 to only 25 after 1870, followed by new increases in 1918–20 and in the period after 1989. Finally, the sovereign European state, whose origins have been traced to various dates between the thirteenth century and 1648, has had its independence reduced as the result of the European Union and may possibly, at some point in the future, be replaced by the United States of Europe.

Despite these changes, there is much to suggest that the medieval and early modern period were crucial to the development of the state we know today. First, there is more continuity in the European state system than it would immediately seem, in a way that makes the continent unique or almost unique in a global context. Second, existing differences between various European countries can to some extent be traced back to the period before 1789. And third, despite the immediate impression of the period 843–1789 as static compared to the following one, important changes took place, which largely serve to explain what happened later. While Western Christendom in the mid-ninth century was a marginal area compared to the great civilizations in the Mediterranean (the Arab Empire), India and China, Europe in 1789 had for a long time dominated the Baltic and Mediterranean Seas, had taken possession of most of America and established colonies in Asia (mainly India), Africa and Oceania. Internally, military technology, bureaucracy, finance and political thought and debate had reached a level of complexity and sophistication far beyond what existed in the ninth century. Thus, the history of European state formation during this period forms an important part of the explanation of the dominance of European or more correctly Western civilization (including the USA) which has characterized the last two centuries, although we may now be approaching its end.

It may be objected to this time limit that it omits the period when the greatest changes in the European state system took place and when European superiority over the rest of the world was firmly established. Apart from practical considerations – length and the author's greater knowledge of the earlier period – the period before 1800 has the advantage of presenting Europe at a stage before its superiority became obvious and before the breakthrough of modern industrialism and mass democracy. There can be no doubt about the importance of the latter period for European dominance, but it is a greater challenge to trace the trends in this direction in the earlier period.

The main aim of the following is to discuss the European state as a phenomenon, not the individual states. The book will therefore deal briefly with many great events that have played an important part in historical literature. Instead, it will focus on the general patterns of the internal development of the European state, building on the tradition of bureaucratic and administrative history as well as ideological and cultural features. Of course, it will also be necessary to deal specifically with various individual states, which makes it difficult to avoid that some of the Great Powers, notably England and France, receive particular attention. These countries also have the advantage of illustrating the two main types of government: constitutionalism and absolutism. The attempt at tracing the characteristic features of the European state logically leads to a comparison with political organizations in other parts of the world. Here the contrast between European division and the great empires, notably China, becomes an important issue. Why was Europe divided and what were the consequences of this division? This in turn leads to a discussion of the reasons for the European dominance of the rest of the world which seems to have been well under way in the late eighteenth century.

Second, the book will be less exclusively focused on administrative and bureaucratic history than many previous accounts, including intellectual history, courtly culture and the difference between absolutist and constitutional government. It will also include state-like organizations like the Church and the city, both of which were of crucial importance for the development of the European state system. Finally, without neglecting the importance of warfare for state formation, it will maintain that this factor worked in a different way from the formation of the great empires; it was more important for internal development than for the formation of territories. By contrast, the latter was to a considerable extent the result of legal and ideological factors: the rise of dynasties.

The following discussion will be divided into three main sections, based on themes rather than chronology. The first section (Chapter 1) will focus on the division of Europe into separate states and the importance of war and military competition in this. The second (Chapters 2 and 3) deals with the main features of the internal development of the European state, while the final section (Chapters 4, 5, 6) takes its point of departure in the changes introduced in the early sixteenth century: the Renaissance, the Reformation and the European expansion to other parts of the world. The focus will then be on the difference between the various states, notably between absolutist and constitutional ones, and the reasons for this difference. This section will mainly focus on the early modern period, although some of the differences will be traced back to the Middle Ages.

Notes

1 Strayer, *On the Medieval Origins*, p. 3.
2 Østerud, 'State Formation'.
3 For example, Service, *Primitive Social Organization* and *Origins of State and Civilization*; Fried, *The Evolution of Political Society* and Diamond, *Guns, Germs and Steel*, pp. 265–92.
4 See e.g. the discussions between Johannes Fried and Hans-Werner Goetz about the Carolingian state and between Susan Reynolds and Rees Davies about the use of the term for the Middle Ages as a whole: Fried, 'Der karolingische Herrschaftsverband' and '*Gens* und *regnum*'; Goetz, 'Zum politischen Denken', pp. 113–16, 170–3 and 183–9; Reynolds, 'The Historiography' and 'There Were States'; Davies, 'The Medieval State'. Whereas the former discussion seems to be about the character of the Carolingian Empire, the latter is mainly about terminology, without any profound difference of opinion about the historical reality.
5 Cantor, *Inventing the Middle Ages*, pp. 48–78, 245–86, 337–70, with references to scholars like F.W. Maitland, Charles Homer Haskins, R.W. Southern and, of course, Strayer.
6 Ibid., pp. 277–83.
7 Southern, *Medieval Humanism*, pp. 206–33, on Henry I's government and *Western Society and the Church*, pp. 100–33, on the development of papal government.
8 Weber, *Wirtschaft und Gesellschaft*.
9 Iggers, *New Directions*; Freedman and Spiegel, 'Medievalisms Old and New'.
10 Cf., in particular, Foucault's studies on justice, opening with the destruction of Damien's body in the eighteenth century and continuing with the total control of the soul in contemporary justice in *Surveiller et punir*. However, I tend to share Pinker's surprise at the paradox that the present age, which, according to a number of criteria, represents a clear progress compared to earlier periods, has been subject to such criticism by a number of intellectuals; see Pinker, *Enlightenment Now*, pp. 395–409.
11 For example, Duby, *Les trois ordres*; Le Goff, *Saint Louis*.

12 Burke, *History and Social Theory* and *Varieties of Cultural History*; Geary, 'Living with Conflicts', and Koziol, 'Begging Pardon and Favour'. Bartlett, in *England 1075–1225*, pays considerably more attention to factions, personal alliances and political culture than does traditional constitutional historiography.

13 Althoff, *Freunde, Verwandte und Getreue: Kaiser Otto III; Spielregeln*; Keller, *Zwischen Regionaler Begrenzung*; Reuter, *Germany*.

14 Mayer, 'Die Ausbildung', and Brunner, *Land und Herrschaft*.

15 Schramm, 'Die Krönung in Deutschland'; *Der König von Frankreich; Geschichte des englischen Königtums*, etc.

16 Skinner, *The Foundations* and *Visions of Politics*, vols II, III; Blanning, *Culture of Power* and *Pursuit of Glory*; Althoff, *Die Macht der Rituale*, cf. also Buc, *The Dangers of Ritual*. For a general discussion of the new trends, not confined to the question of the state, see Freedman and Spiegel, 'Medievalisms Old and New'.

17 Pohl and Wieser, *Der frühmittelalterliche Staat*, where the term 'Staatlichkeit' frequently occurs, although there are also a number of examples of 'Staat'. Nevertheless, 'Staat' in German is used in a more restricted sense than English 'state', as pointed out by Jussen, 'The King's Two Bodies Today', p. 107.

18 For example, Scales, *The Shaping*; Wilson, *The Holy Roman Empire*, pp. 655–86.

19 Tilly, 'Reflections'.

20 Tilly, *Coercion*, p. 67.

21 Weber, *Wirtschaft und Gesellschaft*; Hintze, *Staat und Verfassung*; Elias, *Zivilisation*, vol. II, pp. 123–311.

22 Tilly, *Coercion*.

23 Anderson, *Passages* and *Lineages* form examples of this interpretation.

24 Downing, *The Military Revolution*; Tallett, *War and Society*; Ertman, *The Birth of Leviathan*; Hui, *War and State Formation*; Nexon, *The Struggle for Power*; Hoffman, *Why Did Europe?*

25 Spruyt, *The Sovereign State*.

26 Fukuyama, *Origins*, pp. 229–89, 402–57.

27 Mann, *The Sources of Social Power*, pp. 416–49.

28 Tilly, *The Formation*; Hui, *War and State Formation*; Morris, *War*; Hoffman, *Why Did Europe?*

29 The numbers are based on statistics for the whole of Europe, with deduction of the countries outside Western Christendom, notably Russia. Russia was very sparsely populated in 1750; its total population was probably less than that of France, which is estimated at 20 million. This and a little more for the other non-western countries thus have to be deducted from the 163 million inhabitants of Europe as a whole.

1

THE FORMATION OF THE EUROPEAN STATE SYSTEM

In a pamphlet published in 1637, the Jesuit Guido Aldeni reported that his Chinese friends, when told about the many kings in Europe, asked how Europeans could avoid war. Aldeni's answer was that the problem was less than it seemed, because the kings were related by marriage and, if a war broke out, the pope might intervene to stop it.[1] We do not know whether the Chinese were convinced by these arguments, but in any case, modern historians and social scientists have to admit that they were right in their assumption: the division of Europe did lead to almost constant war and competition. However, modern scholars also tend to think that this competition was a dynamic element, which forms part of the explanation for Europe's later supremacy.

In trying to explain this division, we first have to note that great empires are not the normal political organization of world civilizations, i.e. the parts of the world characterized by intensive agriculture, urbanization, social stratification and organized government. It goes without saying that societies of hunters and gatherers are not organized as empires. Permanent settlement, agriculture and a certain population density are necessary for the formation of states and empires, which, within Eurasia, are mainly to be found in a zone stretching across the Continent, mostly between around 20 and 40 degrees north, 'the lucky latitudes', as Ian Morris calls them. This area has a temperate climate and is the home of 50 out of 56 edible plants and 9 out of 14 large mammals domesticated by humans.[2] The corresponding latitudes to the south might have had similar advantages, at least climatically, but they cover much less land, respectively in South America, South Africa and Australia, divided by large stretches of sea.

To the extent that we can talk about a 'normal' pattern among historical civilizations, it must be periods of empire alternating with periods of division. This applies to India, the Middle East and the Mediterranean region. Thus, both China and Europe are exceptions, China forming a great empire during most of its history since 221 BC and Europe being divided into various numbers of political units since AD 843 at the latest.

Terrain and ecology are often used to explain this feature of Europe.[3] The Alps, the Pyrenees and the Carpathians form strong barriers between north and south. The great plain north of the Alps would seem easier to unite, but a number of rivers, mostly going from south to north, create problems for the movements of armies. In the early Middle Ages, large parts of this area were also covered by forest, which, of course, increased the difficulty. However, nor should the geographical difficulties in China be underestimated; China is actually more mountainous than Europe.[4] More important is the fact that it was apparently more densely populated, with a large part living in the fertile areas along the rivers Yang-Zse-Kiang and Hoangho. Rivers had a similar importance in Europe, particularly in the flat areas north of the Alps but there were more of them, so that the population was more dispersed. Moreover, rice, the main staple in southern China, yields more than grain and thus allows a greater population density than in Europe. Finally, it has been pointed out that China covered a smaller area than Europe – China, at the time of unification, was significantly smaller than it is today. Nevertheless, China was far from easy to unite; the conquerors had to cross high mountains and numerous rivers, whereas Europe north of the Alps would seem relatively easy to cross.[5]

A less distant example of unification is the Roman Empire which covered the lands around the Mediterranean combined with parts of Western Europe. If the Romans had not conquered this area, it would have been easy to find reasons why it could never have been united; the lands along the northern coast of the Mediterranean are extremely mountainous and the whole area was never united again after the fall of the Empire. The original core area of the Empire, Italy, was one of the most divided parts of Europe until the nineteenth century. When the Romans nevertheless managed to conquer the Mediterranean area, the explanation must be sought in their superior military tactics and organization: heavily armed and armoured as well as trained and disciplined infantry,[6] and, above all, in the political field. Although they were ruthless in war, they were also able to make defeated enemies into allies that could be used for new conquests.

Once united, however, the Empire had the advantage of the sea as a communication area, where provisions for Rome and other great cities could be transported on ships, armies could be moved to conquer new areas and crush rebellions and cultural exchange could take place. By contrast, no such line of communication existed between the inland parts of the European Continent north of the Alps, which became the centre of medieval and early modern Europe. Admittedly, Europe as it developed during the Middle Ages, had a northern parallel to the Mediterranean, namely, the North and Baltic Seas. Here, however, the sailing season was shorter and the surrounding areas less densely populated.

Actually, both these seas became European in the Middle Ages and most of the following period – the Ottoman dominance of the eastern Mediterranean in the sixteenth and parts of the seventeenth century was the main exception – but in a different way from the Roman period. The dominant forces were divided, partly in different states and partly in cities or leagues of cities. This points to an important difference between the Roman Empire and its successors in the following period, not only the competition between states but also the greater independence of merchants and city communities.

Most large empires seem to have been formed by nomads or warlike peoples in the highlands or outskirt areas invading wealthy and densely populated agricultural regions. This applies to the Persian, Arab, Mongol and Ottoman Empires. It does not directly apply to the Romans, although they were clearly less culturally and economically advanced than the peoples they conquered, first, various peoples in Italy, including Etruscans and Greeks, then the countries in the Eastern Mediterranean. China shows a somewhat similar pattern. The principality of Qin, which carried out the unification of China, was relatively poor and situated on the outskirts of the cluster of competing countries. China was divided into a number of petty principalities over a period of around 1000 years (c. 1200–220 BC). A gradual reduction of the number of polities took place during this period, until only seven were left between 475 and 221.[7] Finally, one of them, the Qin, conquered the others and founded the first imperial dynasty, which was shortly afterwards (202) replaced by the Han. The unification of China was extremely bloody. There were almost continuous wars between 770 and 221. Up to 8–20 per cent of the population was mobilized in the army, against 1 per cent in Rome and even less in early modern Europe. The casualties were apparently also enormous, estimated at up to 450,000 in a single battle. Although the sources may exaggerate, this nevertheless suggests a different scale than in Europe, where the Romans are said to have lost 50,000 men in their greatest defeat, the Battle of Cannae in 216 BC.

As we are dealing with a culturally homogeneous area with almost constant competition, it is difficult to explain Qin's victory by specific technological or organizational differences; nor can the final victory of one principality be regarded as inevitable, although the intensity of the competition makes this more likely than in the case of Europe. The main factor would seem to be better organization and larger armies, which was developed gradually, notably from the mid-fourth century.[8] Once the country had been united under the Qin and Han dynasties (221 BC–AD 220), later divisions always proved temporary, despite a period of more than 300 years between the fall of Han and the rise of Sui and Tang from 581.

Turning to Europe after the fall of the Roman Empire, we can identify one factor that made the emergence of a great empire unlikely, namely, the absence or relative absence of invasions. After the Germanic invasions that led to the fall of the Roman Empire in the west, no invaders managed to conquer large parts of Europe. Magyars and Slavs formed kingdoms in East Central Europe and Scandinavian Vikings raided large parts of the British Isles and the Continent but did not permanently change the political geography of any larger part. The Mongols invaded Poland and Hungary in the thirteenth century and caused considerable damage, but withdrew quickly. They only made a lasting impact further east, destroying Kievan Rus, while modern Russia, centred on the principality of

Moscow, developed partly in alliance and partly in conflict with the Mongols. Finally, the Ottomans posed a serious threat in the late fifteenth and early sixteenth centuries, but by that time, European fortifications and military technology had been sufficiently developed to limit their advance to the Balkan area. Thus, neither conquest from the outside nor defence against such a conquest led to the formation of a European empire. Europe could enjoy the luxury of a number of units competing with and fighting each other without risking conquest from outside.

The relative absence of invasions may be explained partly by the distance from the core area of the nomads in Central Asia and partly by the poverty of early medieval Europe. The Eastern Mediterranean and the Middle East were more attractive areas, at least until the thirteenth century. Nevertheless, these factors are hardly sufficient to explain why Europe did not become a great empire; we also have to examine the actual formation of political units after the fall of the Roman Empire in the west. This will also address the second big question raised by the comparison: how and why was there a system of relatively stable smaller units rather than fluctuations between larger and smaller ones? And what explains the actual divisions between the European kingdoms?

After the fall of the Roman Empire, there would seem to have been an open future. Admittedly, the Roman provinces of the western parts of Europe, Italy, Spain, Gaul and England, might form a point of departure but with the partial exception of Gaul, all of these underwent radical changes in the following period. There also seem to have been few existing divisions within the new areas that were eventually included in Western Christendom. Thus, the formation of the later state system began in the early Middle Ages. If we want a precise date, the treaty of Verdun in 843, which divided the Carolingian Empire between the three sons of Louis the Pious, seems the most obvious. Admittedly, it was later replaced by several other treaties and there was no awareness at the time that this was a permanent division, nor did the three units much resemble states in the modern sense. However, the division between the two main powers on the Continent, France and Germany, became permanent. Later conquests and/or conversion to Christianity led to the establishment of new kingdoms.

In explaining these developments, we must first eliminate a factor that has played a considerable part in earlier historiography and has seen some revival after the Fall of Communism in 1989, namely, the idea of the state as the expression of national identity.[9] As we shall see, national ideas were not without importance in the medieval and early modern period, but they are not able to explain the origins of states. Taking the most obvious expression of national identity, language, there are relatively few language groups in Europe which only partly correspond to national borders. The three main Indo-European language groups are Romance, Germanic and Slavonic, distributed respectively in the south and west, the centre and north and the north and east. In addition, there is Celtic in the west, parts of Britain and France, and Baltic in Northern Germany and along the Baltic Sea, now confined to Lithuania and Latvia. Finally, there are the non-Indo-European languages

Basque in the Pyrenees and Finno-Ugric in Finland, Estonia and Hungary. The languages are localized in a way that in many cases led to the dominance of one language or language group – although mostly with considerable differences between dialects. However, states were created from above, not from below, so to the extent that language was important, it was that of elites. Besides, the liturgical and administrative language was often Latin, which reduced the importance of linguistic differences.

By contrast, terrain would seem an obvious factor. There are also some clear examples of this. The Pyrenees form a natural border between France and the Spanish kingdoms, although even this border was disputed. The Alps separate Italy from the areas to the north, but this did not prevent the German and French kings from interfering in Italy and, from the sixteenth century, together with the king of Spain, dominating most of the peninsula. Further north, both Hungary and Bohemia had core areas in the form of lowland protected by mountains, whereas Poland lacks this and had more changing borders.

The sea can divide as well as unite. It is striking that the earliest and most stable borders are to be found along the Atlantic coast. Later, the middle zone, along the Rhine and the other great rivers as well as across the Alps, became the most divided, whereas the Eastern zone, dominated by the kingdoms of Poland, Bohemia and Hungary and larger German principalities like Saxony and Prussia, was in an intermediate position.[10] Whereas the Atlantic coast formed an efficient border, the situation was different in the Mediterranean and the North and Baltic Seas. The original borders between the Scandinavian countries were established at a time when the most important military power was sea power; therefore, the southern part of what is now Sweden plus most of the surrounding islands belonged to Denmark, while Norway got hold of a sea empire to the north and west.[11] Aragon established a sea empire from the thirteenth century onwards in the Mediterranean, and England expanded across the sea to Ireland and across the Channel to France.

Nevertheless, terrain explains relatively little. Most of the central part of the European Continent consists of flat land, increasingly cultivated from the last centuries of the first millennium onwards, with no obvious divisions in the terrain. In the south, the Iberian and Apennine peninsulas are both mountainous, but the former developed strong kingdoms which were eventually reduced to two, whereas the latter became one of the most divided parts of Europe. Similarly, France and Germany are topographically fairly similar but politically different; France united under one king and Germany divided into around 400 principalities. Moreover, the most divided parts of Germany were not the forested and mountainous parts in the south and east, but the intensely cultivated ones in the west and the centre. Further north, the highly divided Low Countries present the same picture. Thus, rather than being determined by topography, the borders must be the results of some kind of human activity, the most obvious of which is warfare. However, as will be shown in the following, dynasties and group formation are even more important factors.

Warfare and state formation: from the age of invasions to the eighteenth century

Arguing that war was the driving force in the formation of the European state, Charles Tilly points to the existence of around 1,000 states in medieval Europe which were eventually reduced to 25. However, he fails to examine the chronology of this process, which, as we shall see, does not support his argument. Comparing China until the formation of the Empire in 221 BC with Europe in the early modern period, Victoria Hui also points to warfare as the main factor determining the development in both places. Nevertheless, while continuous warfare over around 1,000 years in China led to the gradual reduction of political units until the whole area had become one empire, nothing similar happened in Europe. Hui explains this with the inefficiency of the latter.[12] War became too costly in Europe, because of the extensive use of mercenaries and the merchants and technicians who profited from selling new types of arms to the competing rulers. This explanation seems paradoxical. Whereas apparently no technological change took place in China, only organizational ones, the changes over a similar period in Europe, both organizational but above all technological, were enormous and increased the costs of waging war manifold. Would this not lead to a faster and even more drastic reduction of political units than in China?

We can distinguish between four phases in the military development of medieval and early modern Europe.[13] During the first phase, warfare was highly mobile and fortifications mostly simple, although the large empires of the Carolingians and the Ottonians were based on great and well-organized military forces, in particular, heavily armed and armoured infantry. Fortifications were also important, partly remains from the Roman period, partly new constructions.[14] People in East Central Europe used light cavalry, whereas the Scandinavians fought on foot and above all at sea. Slavs and Magyars made quick raids into Christian countries and returned with their booty before their enemies could mobilize against them, while the Viking ships had the same effect: large enemy armies suddenly appearing out of the great seas, as expressed in contemporary chronicles. Socially, sea warfare and infantry combined with light cavalry indicate relatively little difference between elite and people, at least less than later, although we should not underestimate the wealth and status of the aristocracy in the Carolingian Empire and its successors. During this phase, the defenders also had less advantage over the attackers. Although fortifications did exist, they needed far larger forces for their defence than their counterparts in later ages.[15] This was also a period when kingdoms and principalities were relatively vaguely defined, and borders could change easily.

During this period, the political map of Europe was created in its main outlines. The permanent division of the Carolingian Empire into the kingdoms of Germany and France is usually dated to around 900. The division was originally the result of the fact that Louis the Pious left three sons, who all claimed a part of his heritage. In the following period, the territorial divisions would seem to have been a direct consequence of the number of sons the previous ruler left at his death but eventually, it became the norm that one son inherited the whole of his father's realm. This led to the permanent division between the kingdoms in the west and east which became France and Germany. The development was gradual, but an important factor was the change of dynasties in both realms; in France in 987 and in Germany in 911. Three kingdoms in Scandinavia, Denmark, Norway and Sweden, and three in East Central Europe, Poland, Bohemia and Hungary, emerged between the late ninth and early eleventh century. They all developed dynasties which lasted until the fourteenth century. Anglo-Saxon England, which had for a long time been divided into separate kingdoms, was united by King Alfred of Wessex (870–99). This was a direct consequence of the Viking attacks, which destroyed most of the petty kingdoms in the country. Alfred defeated the Vikings and, together with his successors, united most of the country. Alfred's successors ruled the country until the eleventh century, when it was conquered first by Cnut of Denmark (1017) and then by William the Conqueror (1066).

Scotland developed as a kingdom from the mid-ninth century, having been converted to Christianity in the previous period. The later dynasty traced its ancestry back, directly or indirectly, to Kenneth MacAlpin, of whom very little is known. Linguistically, the country was divided between the Gaelic-speaking north and the English-speaking south; in the latter area, there was no sharp distinction between England and Scotland. By contrast, Ireland never became really united under one ruler.[16] There were many kings, respectively of superior, intermediate and lower rank. The superior king, ruling the whole country had little actual power and the office was often vacant. Nor was there any proper dynasty and the rules of succession were vague. This made Ireland vulnerable to external interference. The first Scandinavian Vikings arrived in Ireland in 795 and from 841, they had a permanent stronghold in Dublin and the area around it. Later, this area was conquered by the English and formed a starting-point for the conquest of the whole island in the sixteenth and seventeenth centuries.

The fact that defenders had little advantage over attackers may partly explain the importance of this period for the formation of the European state system. However, the new kingdoms were not solely the result of warfare. The division of the Carolingian Empire was not peaceful, but its basic principle was dynastic rights. The formation of new kingdoms on the European periphery may at least partly have been the results of struggles between various local chieftains about which we know little but also of friendship and alliances with European rulers, particularly the German king. Above all, the introduction of Christianity is a crucial factor. The Church created permanent institutions which strengthened the power of the king. Christianity was introduced partly by missionaries from Christian countries, notably England and Germany, and partly by indigenous rulers who had been converted abroad. Politically, the rise of Germany as a great power in the tenth century was a particularly important factor. Political pressure from Germany was an incentive for the kings of the neighbouring countries, Denmark and the three kingdoms in East Central Europe, to convert, while at the same time, Germany was not strong enough to conquer these countries.

The transition from the first to the second phase in the military development was least partly a response to the various invasions of Europe from the seventh century onwards, the Arabs in the south and the Scandinavians and Slavs in the north and east. The introduction of the stirrup was important for the development of cavalry with heavy armour, fighting with lances to charge at the enemy, instead of as earlier with bows and arrows or light spears that were thrown. Castles were built for defensive purposes during the invasions in the post-Carolingian period and eventually developed into very elaborate constructions, partly through the adaptation of the superior fortification technology of the Byzantines and the Arabs which became known to the Europeans during the Crusades. From the eleventh century onwards, stone castles gradually became the norm, which gave the defenders a significant advantage over the attackers.

There are many examples of the superiority of heavy cavalry and castles over the previous military technology, including the German victories over Hungarians and Slavs in the tenth century and the Norman Conquest of England in 1066. However, the main examples of conquests or spectacular victories during this phase are to be found on the outskirts of Western Christendom, in the Baltic area, Spain, Southern Italy and the Eastern Mediterranean, including Byzantium and Palestine. The importance of the military technology in this is open to discussion. Most probably, it was decisive in the Baltic area which was conquered through the establishment of castles and fortified towns. Heavy cavalry also had some success during the Crusades in Palestine and the eastern Mediterranean, Sicily and Southern Italy and Spain. It was normally superior in pitched battles on flat ground but was vulnerable to numerically superior light cavalry in mountainous terrain and on marches. However, in the Mediterranean and the Middle East, the enemies had a well-developed fortification technology; as a matter of fact, the European technology was largely the result of influence from these countries. They also had well-trained armies and competent commanders. The most important strategic advantage the Europeans gained in the Mediterranean in the crusading period was dominance at sea. On land, the First Crusade (1096–99) was a spectacular victory, but mainly because the enemy was unprepared and, in addition, weakened by internal division. The conquest of Constantinople in 1204 would hardly have taken place without the struggle over the succession to the Byzantine throne. Once the Ottomans had taken control of the Eastern Mediterranean in the fifteenth century, the Europeans were repeatedly defeated.

By contrast, they were more successful in Southern Italy, Sicily and Spain. Knights from Normandy in northern France, descendants of Scandinavians settled there in the early ninth century, conquered Southern Italy and Sicily from the Arabs and the Byzantines in the late eleventh and early twelfth centuries. The success of the Normans can be explained both by the division of their enemies and the decline of the Byzantine Empire, which at the time had controlled parts of Sicily and Southern Italy, as well as with their alliance with the pope, but an important factor is also their qualities as warriors, notably their ferocity. The Christian conquest of Spain began when the Caliphate of Cordoba dissolved in

1031 and was divided into separate units.[17] In the following period, a number of smaller Christian kingdoms became united through marriage alliances and dynastic succession and eventually conquered most of Muslim Spain. After the mid-thirteenth century, only the Muslim kingdom of Granada in the south-east remained, sheltered by high mountains and generally difficult terrain. It was eventually conquered in 1492. Most of the new territories became parts of Castile. Portugal conquered Lisbon in 1147, which remained a border town until 1250, when the coast of the Algarve was conquered, and Lisbon became the capital. In the east, Aragon conquered the area around Valencia (1238) and the Balearic Islands (1229–32), both of which became kingdoms in a personal union with the crown of Aragon. Aragon continued its expansion with conquests or attempts at conquest of Sicily, Sardinia and parts of Greece. The conquest of Spain is often depicted as a continuous crusade, but the reality is more complex; there were also alliances across the religious borders and rivalry between the various Christian powers. Nevertheless, the crusading ideology clearly contributed to the success of the conquest.

Armies now became smaller and more professionalized, which had important social consequences. An aristocratic elite formed the core of the military forces, while the rest of the population consisted of peasants in various ways subordinated to the aristocracy. Castles could be used as defence against external enemies but also to control the peasants. Infantry did not disappear from the armies but became less important. Castles could thus be an instrument for kings or conquerors to secure control of territories. Eventually, however, they largely worked in the opposite direction. The castellan might make himself independent, and a country might in this way be divided into smaller principalities governed from castles. This happened to a greater or lesser extent in France, parts of Germany, the Low Countries and Italy. Kings and other lords gave land with or without castles to their subordinates as fiefs, i.e. not as permanent property, but as temporary possessions to hold on behalf of the lord, in return for service, normally of a military kind.

The development of heavy cavalry thus had obvious consequences for state formation, strengthening the power of the aristocracy and weakening that of the king. However, the differences between the various European countries show that there is no automatic correlation between military technology and political organization. English military technology was largely similar at the time, which did not prevent this country from developing a strong state and a government with extensive judicial powers. In Scandinavia and East Central Europe, where the new technology was introduced in the twelfth and particularly the thirteenth century, the aristocracy increased its power at the cost of the king, but this did not lead to a division of these countries into petty principalities. Of the older kingdoms, France and Germany used basically the same military technology but were politically very different. Both countries were dominated by strong princes and nobles who controlled larger or smaller territories from their castles, but while these rulers became largely independent in Germany, they became increasingly subordinated to the king in France.

Despite the superiority of defence over attack, however, some major changes between the main powers of Europe took place in the thirteenth century. In the previous period, France had mainly been ruled by a number of territorial lords under the formal supremacy of the king. One of these lords, Duke William of Normandy, had conquered England in 1066 and one of his successors, King Henry II (1154–89), had through marriage got hold of a number of fiefs that amounted to more than half the territory of the kingdom. In 1202–06, King Philip II Augustus of France managed to conquer Normandy and in the following period, his successors conquered large parts of southern France, partly from the English but mainly through participation in the Crusades against the Albigensian heretics in southern France. At about the same time, a marriage alliance united the Norman Kingdom of Southern Italy and Sicily with Germany. The Emperor Frederick II ruled both territories but had his main focus on the south. His and his successors' struggles against the papacy and a long interregnum after his death (1250–72) led to a substantial reduction of the imperial power in Germany which now became divided into around 400 smaller units, ruled by secular or clerical princes or independent cities. Thus, for most of the time until the unification of Germany in 1870, France was the strongest power on the European Continent. Admittedly, the difference between the two countries should not be exaggerated. France was far from the centralization that characterized the country from the Revolution onwards and Germany still retained some common institutions, including the Emperor and the Diet (*Reichstag*).

There is no clear military explanation of the changes that took place during the second period; the technology and organization were the same on both sides, although greater or lesser skill of the commanders cannot be excluded. The most decisive factor was probably the ability to gain adherents. There were normally no firm loyalties and there were legitimate claims on both sides. Philip Augustus could intervene against King John of England with the argument that he was his feudal overlord and in this way make John's vassals join his own cause. German vassals felt little loyalty to a ruler who was abroad all the time and were in addition under pressure from the pope who had excommunicated Frederick and his successors.

The third phase shows the revival of the infantry, which is expressed in the spectacular English victories over numerically superior French armies during the Hundred Years War (1337–1453), such as Crecy (1346), Poitiers (1356) and Agincourt (1415). The war itself had its background in the remaining English fiefs in southern France, which both kings regarded as an anomaly; they both wanted direct control of them.[18] The development of stronger bows, first, crossbows, then longbows, increased the importance of the infantry. In the fourteenth century, an arrow had a range of nearly 300 yards when shot by a skilled archer and could pierce mail but not plate from around 100 yards. A skilled archer could fire ten to twelve shots in the minute with a longbow but only one or two with a crossbow.[19] However, the victories mentioned above are not evidence of a general superiority of infantry over cavalry. Infantry cannot force cavalry to fight, nor can it win by attacking first.[20] In order to succeed, the English commanders had to find an advantageous position and entice the enemy to attack, while at the same time avoiding the danger of being surrounded and besieged, which would force them to surrender because of lack of provisions. In this respect, the Swiss, who had the strongest infantry in the later Middle Ages, had some advantages over the English, as a force of pikemen was more mobile than one of archers, if sufficiently trained and disciplined. Despite a number of victories of infantry over heavy cavalry, however, there is no evidence of the superiority of larger political units over smaller, nor of the decline of the military aristocracy. Still, castles were the key to military success and the mobility of the cavalry an important factor. When France established a new army towards the end of the war, in the fifteenth century, it was still dominated by cavalry. The war ended with the French conquest of all English possessions in the country with the exception of Calais.

Once more, the outcome of the war is not exclusively determined by military factors. The English successes in the fifteenth century were not only the result of Henry V's military genius but also of chaos and internal division in France. From the Peace of Troyes (1420) onwards, the war also became a French civil war, as Henry married the daughter of the King of France and his son from this marriage, Henry VI, born in 1422, was presented as the legitimate heir to the throne, whereas Charles VII, son of the previous French king Charles VI, was said to have been the result of his mother's affair with her husband's brother. Despite some setbacks in the beginning, however, Charles eventually gained the support of the majority of the people. An important factor in this was Joan of Arc (Jeanne d'Arc),[21] a young peasant girl who arrived at the court of Charles VII in Chinon in 1429, claiming to have received a message from God to save France from the English and establish Charles as the lawful king. Having convinced the king and his supporters, she was given the command of a troop of soldiers and won some spectacular victories. Most importantly, she was able to relieve Orléans from the English siege and to have Charles crowned in Reims, which at the time was in the zone controlled by the English and their French allies. The coronation actually became a turning-point; royal coronation had great prestige in France and thus gave Charles an advantage over his English rival. Although Joan was soon after-wards (1430–31) captured and burnt as a heretic, her brief career shows the importance of popular reactions against the English invaders and the use of religion and divine revelation for patriotic purposes,[22] although the decisive change in King Charles' fortune was that the majority of the aristocracy began to support him, partly because they saw their interests best served in this way and partly because of the long tradition of lawful, dynastic kingship.[23]

The fourth phase introduced the most revolutionary changes and is rightly referred to as the military revolution. This included the introduction of firearms, first, the arquebus, then the musket and, above all, the cannon. Such arms were used already in the fourteenth century but only became really effective in the fifteenth. As demonstrated by the French victory at the end of the Hundred Years War in 1450–53, and the fall of Constantinople in 1453, cannons had now become strong enough to make medieval castles obsolete. Whereas earlier, their walls could easily be defended against largely superior forces and the means to conquer them were complicated and often unsuccessful, they could now be destroyed by a sufficient amount of artillery.[24] This introduced a short period of superiority for offensive forces and some spectacular conquests of formerly strong castles. However, it did not take long before the balance was restored. A new fortification technology, developed by Italian engineers in the early sixteenth century, resulted in walls able to withstand artillery. The tall and relatively thin medieval walls were replaced by lower and more massive bastions covered with sand, which reduced the power of the cannon balls. The shape of the bastions was also highly irregular, in order to make it more difficult to aim the cannons correctly.

Drill and strict discipline were introduced around 1600 – the great pioneer was Prince Maurice of Orange, the Dutch leader in the war of independence against Spain. This corresponded to the need for coordinated action and for firing as quickly as possible. The muskets took considerable time to load, but the soldiers were trained to do this as quickly as possible and at the same time. When the first line had fired, they moved to the back, so that the next line could do the same, and so forth. The strength of an army with muskets depended on how quickly it could fire; consequently, greater speed in firing would compensate for numerical inferiority. In addition, men were needed for fighting at short range, where guns could not be used. Therefore, soldiers with firearms were supplemented by pikemen, according to the Swiss model. The introduction of the bayonet from the late seventeenth century abolished this distinction, allowing the musketeers to fight at close range as well. In addition to these changes, the size of armies changed significantly. Whereas late medieval armies rarely counted more than 10,000 men, they might number more than 100,000 in the sixteenth and seventeenth centuries. This was partly a matter of increased competition; size was of course crucial to military success, but also has to do with the increasing size and sophistication of fortifications, which necessitated large armies to conduct a siege.

Steady improvement in this field continued in the following period. The most spectacular example is the 'iron ring' around the exposed frontiers of France under Louis XIV, constructed under the leadership of the great military architect, Vauban (1633–1707). Vauban was educated in mathematics, which he applied to his engineering. His fortifications are still to be seen in many parts of France, for instance, Briançon in the south-east, which protected the border towards Savoy. The cost of the project was enormous, nearly 10 per cent of the total expenditure in the period 1665–96.[25] It may, however, have been worth the price; despite repeated French defeats in the Low Countries during the War of the Spanish Succession, allied forces never crossed the French border in this area. Moreover, the systematic construction of stronger and fewer fortifications reduced the number of men necessary to man them and thus made possible a substantial increase in the field army.[26]

The Spanish were the pioneers in the military revolution.[27] The tactical unit in the Spanish army was the *tercio*, an infantry formation consisting of pikemen, swordsmen and arquebusiers or musketeers in a mutually supportive formation, in theory, up to 3,000 soldiers, although it was usually less than half this size. The

Spanish infantry army was developed during the war against Granada, 1481–92, and later during the wars in Italy. It was subject to strong discipline and was regarded as the best army in Europe in the sixteenth and well into the seventeenth century, when it was eventually surpassed by the French. The proud Spanish nobles who served as officers accepted leaving their horses and leading their men on foot.

The use of cannons contributed to the French reconquest of the English possessions in 1450–53 and some smaller political entities succumbed, notably some Italian city states, but otherwise, the number of political units remained as before and there were no great changes in the borders between them. Thus, in the period 1500–1789, the European powers had larger armies and better military equipment than at any time before and fought one another with greater costs and intensity. Nevertheless, the results were minor. Not only did most powers continue to exist – Poland and some Italian city states are the main exceptions – but most them had approximately the same borders by the end of the period as in the beginning. This not only applies to the major kingdoms but also to the around 400 German petty states. Thus, the obvious advantages the new military technology gave to larger and wealthier units had few practical consequences.

The state made war but war did not make the state

Returning to Hui's comparison between China and Europe, the paradox pointed out above has not become less after the previous survey. Whereas China, with apparently the same military technology throughout the period, underwent a radical change in political organization, Europe experienced an equally radical change in military technology with surprisingly few changes in political division. Even more paradoxical: the period of the greatest military changes was also the period with the least changes in political units and their borders. Hui's claim, that European military equipment was costlier than the Chinese and the political organizations less efficient, does not give an adequate explanation for this. There is no doubt that military equipment during the fourth phase was many times costlier than during the previous ones, but this would mean that only the strongest units could make use of it, which in turn should have led to a drastic reduction of them. When this did not happen, it is obvious that Hui's and Tilly's explanation is wrong: war was not the driving force in the formation of the European state system.

Tilly's argument about the reduction from 1,000 to 25 states between 990 and 1870 suggests a parallel to, for instance, the likelihood of newborn animals of various species to reach adulthood. Often only a few achieve this, while the rest disappear without trace. The analogy therefore suggests that the survival of a state was a rare occurrence, something only the strongest were able to achieve; in other words, that we are dealing with a parallel to Darwin's survival of the fittest. In the case of European state formation, however, the territory remains the same and the unsuccessful states do not disappear, but become building material for their successful counterparts, in many cases, influencing them considerably and/or retaining much of their own character.

Tilly never specifies exactly what he regards as a state or how he arrives at the numbers respectively of 1,000 and 500, but he clearly regards the various fiefs in which large parts of continental Europe were divided as states.[28] There may be some arguments in favour of this, although what characterizes this period is rather a division of authority between the higher and the lower levels. There is no sovereign state; the king is the highest authority, but his territory includes a number of more or less independent vassals and princes. The Peace Treaty of Westphalia of 1648 is often regarded as the precise date when the European state system came into existence, including the around 400 German territories. Strictly speaking, this is not true; the only formal recognition of this kind in the treaty concerned the independence of the Dutch Republic from Spain. By contrast, the emperor was still regarded as the head of the German principalities, although this superiority had limited practical importance, as had already been the case for centuries.[29]

An objection may be raised to the thesis about continuity that a kingdom in the twelfth or thirteenth century is not necessarily identical with a state and that the title of the ruler does not necessarily correspond to the importance of his realm. The answer to the former objection is that continued existence over several centuries is a fairly strong criterion of statehood. Whatever the limitations in power and efficiency, it shows that more than the will of individual rulers is involved. Concerning the latter objection, we can point to the example of Navarra, which was an independent kingdom until it was joined with France but was insignificant compared to the principalities of Saxony, Brandenburg or Savoy and above all to the Dutch Republic. However, this is an exception and not the rule. Most kingdoms were larger and more important than other principalities and the rulers of the most successful of the latter, Brandenburg and Savoy, actually managed to become kings, later (1815) also the Dutch stadholder. More importantly, although both kingdoms and other principalities might expand at the cost of their neighbours, there is hardly a single example of a state formed by a continuous struggle between independent princes within a particular area resulting in one of them conquering the others. The only possible examples of this are the earliest phases of the history of the new kingdoms in the north and east, of which very little is known. In the better-known cases that come closest to Tilly's suggestion, the unification of Germany under the leadership of Prussia (1866–70) and of Italy under the leadership of Savoy (1859–70), the unification would not have happened without a considerable popular movement in its favour. In the case of Germany, the unification also took the form of a union between the princes who retained considerable independence.

In its main features, the European state system seems to have been formed between the division of the Carolingian Empire and around 1200. At the latter date, there were fifteen kingdoms in Europe: England, Scotland, France, Castile, Aragon, Portugal, Navarra, Sicily, Germany, Poland, Bohemia, Hungary, Denmark, Norway and Sweden. Only two new kingdoms were added between 1200 and the new kingdoms that emerged after the dissolution of the Holy Roman

Empire in 1806, namely, Prussia (1701) and Sardinia (1720). In addition, both city republics and principalities ruled by princes without the royal title may be regarded as states. In the twelfth century, such units included most of the middle zone from the division of the Carolingian Empire: the Low Countries, Burgundy, Savoy, Provence and the many city republics of northern and central Italy, some of which eventually came to form large territorial units.

Of the fifteen kingdoms in the twelfth century, seven still existed as fully independent units with their own rulers in 1648, namely, England, France, Castile, Portugal, Denmark, Sweden and Poland, which probably suggests that kingdoms were more likely to survive than units without a king.[30] Germany may also be added, as its ruler, the emperor, was of course represented at the conference. However, so were also several of his subordinate princes. The disappearance of the other units was mainly the result of marriage alliances and hereditary succession. England had repeatedly tried to conquer Scotland but without success. The eventual union between the two countries was the result of King James VI of Scotland inheriting the English throne after the death of the childless Elizabeth I in 1603. The union between Denmark and Norway was the result of a series of dynastic marriages from the early fourteenth century onwards, which led to King Oluf of Denmark inheriting Norway from his father in 1380. For a time, the union also included Sweden, which, however, broke out and elected its own king in 1521–23. A series of dynastic marriages led to the reduction of the number of Spanish kingdoms, ending with the one between Isabella of Castile and Ferdinand of Aragon in 1469, which resulted in the union between the two countries in 1479. A part of Navarra was conquered by Castile in 1515 and the rest was joined with France in a personal union when its king, Henry of Bourbon, became king of France in 1589. It was annexed to France in 1620. Sicily joined Aragon in a personal union in 1301 after a rebellion against the French dynasty of Anjou. The later union of the Kingdom of Naples with Sicily in 1443 was the result of war but had a basis in a hereditary claim. Portugal was joined with Spain in 1580 when Philip II became the nearest heir to the throne of this country, but the Portuguese rebelled against Spain in 1640. Most of the kingdoms that entered personal unions were not merged into one but retained their separate institutions while being united under one ruler. Thus, marriage was a more important factor in the formation of the European state system than warfare. Concerning territories whose rulers were not kings, we find that the consolidation of some kingdoms, notably France, led to a reduction of them, whereas those in Germany and the Low Countries became more independent than before.

The main example of the importance of marriage is the formation of the Habsburg Empire. In 1439, the Habsburgs gained the imperial throne as the result of the extinction of the Luxembourg dynasty, but the new emperor, Frederick III (1439–93), achieved little because his hereditary lands were small, and the imperial title gave honour but little power. His son Maximilian (1493–1519) greatly improved the situation by marrying Maria, heiress to the wealthy principality of Burgundy (1477). Although he lost part of Burgundy to Louis XI of France,

Maximilian now controlled the richest area of Northern Europe, as Burgundy was in a personal union with the Low Countries. Moreover, Maximilian's son Philip married Joanna of Castile and a series of unexpected deaths then made Philip's son and Maximilian's grandson, Charles, heir to the Spanish throne in 1516. Three years later, Charles was elected Holy Roman Emperor. In 1556, he was succeeded by his son Philip as king of Spain and by his younger brother Ferdinand as Holy Roman Emperor. As Ferdinand was already king of Bohemia and Hungary, these countries were now joined with the Empire. Most of Hungary was conquered by the Turks in 1541 but reconquered in the late seventeenth century. Thus, over a few generations, the Habsburgs had changed from a mediocre dynasty in southern Germany to the most powerful rulers of Europe, as expressed in the family motto: 'Bella gerunt alii, tu felix Austria, nube' ('Others wage war; you, Happy Austria, marry!'). There is no example of a similar success as the result of war. The importance of the imperial title in this was that it gave the necessary prestige to achieve these honourable marriages.

In contrast to other parts of the world, such as the Arab and Ottoman states and empires, there are relatively few examples in Europe of kingdoms formed by conquest. The Norman kingdoms in Sicily and Southern Italy are one important example and the new principalities in the Baltic area another. In both cases, the conquest was directed at an area where the inhabitants had another religion than Christianity, which made it easier to legitimate the conquest and to recruit soldiers by granting religious privileges. Spain is a similar example, although here the conquest was carried out by existing states which expanded in this way. England is also an example of successful conquest, which, in addition, had a profound influence on its government, but the English kingdom had existed for more than a century before and the conqueror claimed to be the rightful heir of a king who had no direct descendants. Thus, despite the importance of warfare for the relationship between states as well as their internal development, it is not the main explanation for their formation.

In the Middle Ages, there was only one possible candidate to carry out the political unification of a country, namely, its lawful ruler, the king. The development of sovereign states was in most places the result of the victory of the king over the territorial princes, not of an open competition between the princes in which one of them won. In most cases, this was a gradual process, expressed in the formation of legal and political institutions, which will be discussed later. Moreover, if we compare the areas controlled by states in 1500 and 1900, instead of the number of states, the picture becomes very different. Most of the 400–500 states were German principalities which existed continually from the late thirteenth century until 1806.[31] Thus, the size of the typical European state is not 1/400 or 1/500 of the whole continent; most of the twenty-five states in the nineteenth century could trace their origins back to the Middle Ages; the number 400/500 is strictly confined to Germany, with the addition of some Italian units. We are therefore not dealing with an intense competition in which only the fittest survived, but rather with a high probability of survival, not only for relatively strong units but also for units whose ruler could easily walk from one end of his country to the other in less than a day. Thus, the unfittest seem to have been as likely to survive as the fittest.[32] States in the seventeenth and eighteenth centuries were not faced with the alternatives of modernization or extinction. Most old-fashioned and inefficient states continued to exist as before, as can be illustrated by the anecdote about Bismarck when asked what he would do if he knew that the Last Judgement was imminent. He answered that then he would move to Mecklenburg, for there everything happened 200 years after everywhere else. Mecklenburg was Prussia's neighbour but, despite its inefficiency, continued to exist as an independent principality until the reorganization of Northern Germany in 1866.

The number of German petty states was reduced to around forty in the early nineteenth century, under Napoleon and at the Congress of Vienna (1814–15), and the rest became subordinated to the larger German Empire in 1870.[33] Thus, there was no significant reduction of the number of states during the most intensive phase of competition between them in the sixteenth and seventeenth centuries, accompanied by the greatest changes in military technology and organization. There is no doubt that European states made war, but little to suggest that war made the state, at least not that the actual states owed their existence to war.

This conclusion can be developed further by a comparison with other parts of the world, which underwent a similar technological revolution as Europe, expressed in the term Gunpowder Empires. Although beginning their expansion before the arrival of gunpowder, the Ottomans made use of the new technology in their conquest of Constantinople (1453) and Egypt (1517) and greatly increased their empire in the period after 1450, until it included the Balkans as far north as Serbia and Hungary, and the southern and eastern shores of the Mediterranean and Mesopotamia. Further east, the Moghuls invaded India and founded a large empire which remained until the British conquest from the mid-eighteenth century onwards. The different results of the introduction of the same military technology, notably the difference between the dramatic changes that took place in other parts of the world compared to the limited ones in Europe, clearly indicate that other factors must have played an important part.

An all-European empire does not seem to have been a realistic option since the dissolution of the Carolingian Empire. Admittedly, the territory ruled by Charles V (1519–56), comprising Spain with its American possessions, the Low Countries, large parts of Italy and Germany as well as Bohemia and Hungary, would seem to have come close, encircling the other continental great power, France. However, Charles' empire was too composite and weak financially to have been able to conquer the rest of Europe; his aims were dynastic and largely defensive, and his possessions were divided between his son and his brother after his death. Later attempts, by Napoleon and Hitler, came closer, although in both cases, great powers outside the continent of Western Europe, Britain, Russia and in the latter case, the United States, were able as well as willing to prevent it.

When the most primitive of the four periods was apparently the most successful regarding foreign conquest, while the military revolution had limited consequences, the explanation is clearly not that the former technology was more efficient than the latter. The main explanation lies in the importance of legitimacy and dynastic succession. Territories were not up for grabs by the strongest power; they were subject to dynastic rights and could more easily be won by marriage than by war. With this as the point of departure, let us examine the attitudes of European war leaders and what we may call the rules of the game of medieval and early modern warfare. Why did they fight, what were their aims and to what extent were their actions determined or limited by rules?

War within the family: politics and diplomacy

First, we have to conclude that the lack of success was not the result of lack of ruthlessness. The terrorization of the civilian population did not begin with the invention of strategic bombing in the twentieth century, but was probably a standard element of warfare as far back as we have records of it. The cruelty reached a climax in the sixteenth and seventeenth centuries, mainly because of the increased size of the armies. The French conquest of Brescia in 1512 gives an example.[34] Brescia had revolted against the French during their war against Venice in order to join the Venetians. It was attacked by a French army and ordered to surrender. Trusting in the arrival of a Spanish army nearby, the leaders of the city refused, thus opening themselves liable to be sacked in the case of defeat, which was what actually happened. A local citizen gives the following description:

> My soul all but leaves me when I think about it. There was no security in convents or other holy places ... In those three days they inflicted every kind of torment on the wretched inhabitants, men and women, to force them to reveal the hiding place of their money and valuables. Every dishonourable violence was used on women, and throughout the city, day and night, one heard nothing but the most wretched cries of the miserable ... or of women resisting those who were trying to rape them ... Day and night, I would see nothing but desperate gentlemen and citizens, stripped of their clothing, tied, beaten on their genitals, placed with their feet over fire, with bits of wood driven into their teeth or having their mouths poked into with a stick or a knife above the tongue ... until, unable to talk or using signs, they would show themselves ready to disclose the places of their hidden valuables.

Another eyewitness adds:

> A number of priests were burned alive. The nobleman Cristoforo Guaineri had his arms cut off and died on burning coal. A rich merchant named Antonio was flayed alive. Two of my brothers, Ottobono and Girolamo, and Ottobono's son Angelo, were strung up by their hands and only escaped death by paying out 90 gold pieces.

On the other hand, there are the norms of chivalry between the princes and leaders.

Froissart ends his colourful and dramatic account of the Battle of Poitiers with an idyllic scene:

> That evening the Prince of Wales gave a supper for the King of France and most of the captured counts and barons. The king and the most prominent French nobles were placed at a high table, 'lavishly provided'. The prince himself served at the table, 'refusing to sit down with so mighty a prince and so brave a soldier'. He kneeled before him saying: 'Beloved sire, do not make such a poor meal, even though God has not been willing to heed your prayers today … In my opinion, you have good cause to be cheerful … for today you have won the highest renown as a warrior.'[35]

Froissart comments that all who were present thought that the Prince had spoken nobly and to the point. 'Their esteem for him increased and it was generally agreed that in him they would have the most chivalrous lord and master if he was granted life to go in the same auspicious way.'

Was the Black Prince really so humble or was the scene an attempt to gain even greater glory from his military victory? Or was it simply invented by Froissart?[36] In any case, it gives some impression of the medieval and early modern attitude to warfare, on the one hand, the ruthless cruelty to the ordinary civilian population, who had their crops and houses burnt and were tortured and plundered by soldiers, on the other, the idea of a pan-European elite whose members fought one another in a similar way as sportsmen compete today. Froissart is the perfect spokesman for this class, celebrating their military deeds as well as their common values and their respect or even friendship for their adversaries. This chivalrous scene is also an expression of one of Froissart's central values, which occurs in other passages of his work, including his account of the surrender of Calais.

In 1346–47, Edward III spent a long time and much effort and money on the siege of Calais until the town finally surrendered after ten months. The king's anger at the stubbornness of his enemies had increased during the siege and he now wanted his revenge. However, his men pleaded with him: the burghers of Calais had only done their duty out of loyalty to their king. If they were to be punished for this, how could Edward expect his men to sustain sieges to defend his towns or castles? Finally, Edward agreed to pardon most of the burghers but still demanded that six of them be delivered up to him for punishment. Six of the wealthiest and most distinguished burghers volunteered to save their compatriots and turned up before the king – the scene has been immortalized in the famous sculpture by Rodin. In the meantime, Queen Philippa, who was pregnant, had arrived. She interceded for the six and finally secured their pardon.

Most probably, Froissart, like other contemporary writers, often exaggerated the chivalry, in this as well as other episodes;[37] nor should we forget that the main motive for saving the lives of aristocratic prisoners was to gain ransom from them.

Nevertheless, this story, as well as Froissart's engagement in the question of ethics and chivalry in war, does illustrate an important issue in the period. As we shall see, the traditional rules of chivalry had come under attack in the fourteenth century, in both England and France, regarding internal enemies. However, the same logic would imply that they should continue to be practised towards external ones. The introduction of the laws of treason implied that the rebels had become more than just the king's personal enemies; they were enemies of the state, represented by the king. At the same time, this meant that enemies outside the country came in a different category: they were not traitors, because they did not owe loyalty to the king of England, but to another king, towards whom they owed the same obligations as his own subjects owed to him.

The rules referred to by Froissart eventually became generally applied. Thus, after the Battle of Poltava, in 1709, the victorious Russians invited the Swedish higher officers to dinner, while at the same time the captive Ukrainians, who were regarded as rebels, were tortured to death.[38] Ransom of prisoners continued to be practised but in the eighteenth century, they were regarded as prisoners of the state, not of individual officers or commanders. In some cases, the sums needed for the ransom of prisoners of various ranks were agreed upon between the warring parties, or general rules about the ransom were introduced.[39] Eventually, when national armies replaced mercenaries, similar rules were also applied to the civilian population, which was largely protected, while the fighting took place between soldiers in uniform, in accordance with Clausewitz's principle of 'true war'.[40] By contrast, ruthless terror was applied against rebels, as by the English in Scotland in 1746 and in Ireland in 1798 and by the French in Corsica in the 1750s and 1760s. Fortunately for the Americans, the English decided to treat them as lawful enemies during the War of Independence of 1776–83.

This change may have something to do with greater sensitivity to human suffering, of which there are also some other examples in the eighteenth century, but practical considerations are probably more important. Wars were fought to conquer land and the winners wanted to receive them intact, not to have them laid waste by soldiers. Plundering meant that the profit went to the soldiers, while a disciplined army would allow the general and his king to use enemy terrain to finance his war. A prominent example of this is Frederick II's occupation of Saxony during the Seven Years War (1756–63). Saxony financed around 30 per cent of the Prussian war effort and was ruthlessly exploited.[41] Nevertheless, the Prussian occupation was less harmful than seven years of plundering by a mercenary army a hundred years earlier.

The rules of chivalry give the impression of a mutual respect between European rulers that seems to differ from the ruthless competition in China. To what extent did they also determine strategy and tactics? In the autumn of 1524, King Francis I of France had led his army into northern Italy to fight his greatest enemy, Charles V, king of Spain and Holy Roman Emperor.[42] Two options presented themselves, either to attack the remains of the imperial army in Lodi, which was led by two able generals, but demoralized after a long retreat, short of provisions and hit by

disease, or to attack the strongly fortified town of Pavia. Most of Francis' councillors recommended the first option, whereas his old childhood friend Bonnivet
voted for the second, as this would be the more honourable. Francis was persuaded
by him and began the siege of Pavia in October. The city was strongly defended
and several direct attacks were repelled. The siege lasted during the winter, with
cold and heavy rain. The French generals suggested giving up the siege, but once
more Bonnivet appealed to honour and persuaded the king to remain. Then, on 3
February 1525, a Spanish army arrived to relieve Pavia. Francis now had the enemy
on both sides, but preferred to remain in the same position. When the relieving
army started to move, it was met by the strong French artillery and suffered heavy
losses. Francis sensed victory and attacked, followed by his cavalry. However, he
was careless, moving in front of his own artillery, which was forced to stop
shooting. This turned the battle. The relieving army attacked with arquebuses and
soldiers from the garrison attacked from behind. Francis found himself alone
between enemy lines. He fought heroically until at last, bloody and half-naked, he
delivered his glove to the enemy in sign of surrender.

Technologically, Francis' army represented a mixture between old and new, as
did also the king himself. He was a ruthless player in the political game, allying
with Protestants and Turks against Catholic princes, while persecuting the Protestants in his own country. At the same time, he loved honour and chivalry to the
extent that he let honour influence his strategy and ultimately lead him to captivity. Characteristically, in the letter he wrote to his mother immediately after having
been taken captive, he says: 'I have nothing left except my honour and my life.'

Francis was treated respectfully by his captors, in accordance with his rank, but
was closely guarded. The Italian historian Francesco Guicciardini, who at the time
held a prominent position in the papal administration, gives a detailed account of
the event.[43] Learning of the victory, Charles V, Holy Roman Emperor and king of
Spain, was of course delighted but showed a praiseworthy moderation for such a
young man – Charles was 25 years old at the time, born in 1500. He did not sound
the church bells or let the *Te Deum* be sung, because his victory was over another
Christian king. Charles was then faced with the difficult question of how to exploit
his victory. Guicciardini constructs a great deliberation scene, with two councillors
giving radically different advice. Both agree that there are three different options:
(1) setting Francis free without imposing any conditions; (2) setting him free on
harsh conditions; and (3) keeping him permanently in captivity with endless
negotiations. The Bishop of Osma, Charles' confessor, argues in favour of the first
option, the Duke of Alba in favour of the third. The emperor does not decide
immediately, but ponders over the issue. Then Francis is taken ill and seems about
to die. Charles has all the time wanted to see him and now decides to do so. A
friendly conversation takes place between the two rulers and Francis eventually
recovers. Now the advisors tell Charles that he is bound by honour to set Francis
free. Charles finds it necessary to respect this, but he also wants to exploit his victory. He therefore forces Francis to sign a peace treaty on strict terms, including the
cession of Burgundy and Milan, full control over Artois and Flanders, which at the

time were ruled by Charles V but claimed by Francis, and full independence for Charles, Duke of Bourbon, one of the greatest French princes who had rebelled against Francis and fought against him at Pavia. Francis is released but replaced by his two sons, both boys, who will remain in captivity until the peace conditions are fulfilled. Charles' decision leads to violent protests from most of his councillors, including the grand chancellor, Mercurio di Gattinara, who even refuses to sign the treaty. Most of them do not believe that Francis will keep his promises, which proves correct. Immediately after his release, he got the pope to annul his promises, because they had been obtained by force, formed the League of Cognac together with the pope and some other princes and prepared for war against Charles.

The way Guicciardini renders the episode is characteristic of his pessimistic approach to contemporary politics: politicians act spontaneously and irrationally, instead of analyzing the issue properly and drawing the logical conclusion. It is an open question whether Guicciardini himself favoured the first or the third option, but there is no doubt that he regarded the second as the worst. Guicciardini's account may not be an exact report on what actually happened but gives a glimpse of the complicated negotiations. According to other sources, Francis trusted in his personal charm to get a favourable deal from the younger, less experienced and less impressive Charles V. His journey to Spain became a triumph during which he played on his ability to impress the people he met, so much so that he was put in isolation when he arrived in Madrid, which in turn resulted in his illness.

A modern observer might immediately wonder why Charles' conditions were regarded as so outrageous. After all, Francis had suffered a crushing defeat and was totally at the mercy of his enemy. If it had been in another place of the world, like China, he might have been executed, but this was of course out of the question in Europe. He was not only kept in honourable and mostly comfortable captivity but most of his kingdom would be intact; in addition to Milan, he only had to give up one province of France, admittedly a wealthy one, which had only fairly recently come under the king's control. However, Burgundy held a special importance for both princes. It had for a long time been a part of the kingdom of France, although rarely been ruled directly by the king, and had been brought back in the possession of the crown by Louis XI in 1477. It belonged to Charles V's hereditary lands and formed a part of the principality in which he had grown up and with which he identified more than with any of his many other possessions. An argument in favour of Francis' point of view was further that Charles had not conquered Burgundy and had no possibility of doing so – he had no money left to pay for an army after the expedition to Italy. Whereas the previous negotiations between the captive John II of France and Edward III of England mainly dealt with areas that the English had conquered or were able to conquer, Charles V now tried to exploit his victory to gain entirely new territories. This seems to have been unusual; the contemporary expectation was that Charles would release Francis in return for a huge ransom.[44]

Norms and interests

The negotiations over Francis' release proved to be an episode; the war continued, interrupted by occasional peace treaties until 1559, when Francis' and Charles' successors concluded the Peace of Cateau-Cambrésis What did they fight about? Admittedly, wealthy regions were at stake. Cambrésis was the richest country in Europe, with the advantage that its wealth largely consisted of ready money, which could easily be transported and used for various purposes. The second richest, the Low Countries, were also involved and had the same advantages. Nevertheless, wealth was hardly the main motive. The wars cost far more than the participants could hope to gain by conquest. Both France and Spain went bankrupt many times during the sixteenth century. A more important motive was honour and, above all, rights. The wars did not take place between sovereign units in a state of anarchy but in a situation not fundamentally different from the one prevailing within each country, between various contestants competing to have their claims recognized. The targets for wars were not chosen according to value or strategic interests but according to legal claims. When Charles VIII invaded Southern Italy in 1494, he had a legal claim going back to his relative René, who had unsuccessfully claimed Naples and Sicily as the heir of the Angevins. In a similar way, his successor Louis XII claimed Milan in 1499 because he could trace his ancestry back to Isabella of Valois, who married Gian Galeazzo Visconti, son of the duke of Milan, in 1368.[45] The Visconti had been replaced by the Sforza in 1450. When Louis inherited the French throne in 1498 at the sudden death of Charles VIII without issue, he attacked Milan in the following year, claiming that he was the rightful heir and the Sforza were usurpers. As the successor of these rulers, Francis fought to keep or regain these possessions.

Admittedly, strategic considerations were also part of the picture and the line between them and the legal claims are not always easy to draw. An important motive was fear of other rulers planning attacks or growing too strong. During the period of the Reformation, religion played an important part, although modified by other considerations. The Catholic king of France normally supported the German Protestants in order to limit the emperor's power and on occasions even concluded alliances with the Turks. Finally, it may be suggested that war was an aim in itself, apart from gains and losses. In peacetime, hunting was the most prestigious royal sport, but war was even more prestigious. What could be nobler and more challenging, particularly for a young man, ruling a great country and with great resources at his disposal, than to distinguish himself in the most dangerous and difficult of all sports, fighting in person as the leader of a great army against an enemy of equal skill and status? There are many celebrations of war from the Middle Ages and the early modern period, including the following by the poet Bertrand de Born from the twelfth century:

> I tell you that I find no such savor in eating butter and sleeping, as when I hear cried 'On them!' and from both sides hear horses neighing through their

head-guards, and hear shouted 'To aid! To aid!' and see the dead with lance truncheons, the pennants still on them, piercing their sides.[46]

Francis' behaviour at Pavia and on other occasions points in the same direction. Instead of seeking an easy victory against a demoralized army, he chooses the honourable option of attacking a strongly fortified town and when this seems to fail, he regards it as dishonourable to give up. A number of other rulers behaved in the same way, although there were clearly different attitudes, including that of war as a necessary evil. Wars clearly did not aim at conquest of the enemy country or creating an all-European empire; in Hoffman's terminology, they were 'tournaments', aiming at prestige in competition with some external enemy of equal size.[47]

Considering the size of the two opposing parties in this war, it would seem to have been a desperate struggle by the king of France to avoid being absorbed by the overwhelming power of the Habsburgs, the rulers of Spain and its American Empire, Southern Italy, Germany, the Low Countries, Bohemia and parts of Hungary. However, there is little to suggest that this is the correct picture.[48] The Habsburg Empire was not sufficiently unified and had too many enemies to be able to conquer France. Nor was the war to any significant extent conducted on French soil. It would seem that Francis I's main target was Italy and that he was more often the aggressor than Charles V, who had a number of interests in other regions, including the struggle against the Ottomans, who in periods were allied with France. As is evident from the negotiations in connection with Francis' captivity, both rulers were also extremely concerned with honour and claims based on hereditary rights.

A central issue in early modern wars was succession to the throne. There were three such wars in the eighteenth century, respectively over the Spanish, Polish and Austrian successions. The first was essentially a great coalition of the enemies of Louis XIV's France to prevent a further expansion of France, which, as we have seen, ended with a compromise. The second was an attempt to limit the Russian influence in Poland which failed, but gave France some territory in Italy. The third was the most dramatic, almost leading to the dissolution of the Austrian Empire (1740–48).

Charles VI of Austria (1711–40) had no son, only daughters, whereas succession to the Holy Roman Empire was agnatic. By contrast, there were a number of more distant relatives who might agree to divide the Empire between them. The Hungarians openly discussed the possibility of electing a king from another dynasty. To prevent this, Charles in 1713 proclaimed the Pragmatic Sanction, asserting the indivisibility of the Empire and the right of female succession to the throne in the absence of a male heir, and had it accepted by the estates of all Austrian, Bohemian and Hungarian lands and by the European powers. However, as soon as Charles was dead, the 'scrabble for Austria' began. Frederick II of Prussia invaded Silesia late in 1740, thus introducing the War of the Austrian Succession (1740–48). In the Treaty of Nymphenburg of May 1741, France and Spain recognized Charles Albert, Duke of Bavaria, as Holy Roman Emperor and his claim to most of the

Habsburg hereditary lands. The treaty was later joined by Saxony, Savoy-Piedmont and Prussia during its periods of war with Austria.

Charles' heir was his daughter, Maria Theresa, aged 23, who responded to the challenge with formidable energy and courage, mobilizing armies, negotiating with enemies and allies, and who finally managed to save the unity of the Empire, despite having to accept the loss of Silesia. In the most desperate situation, she appealed to the Hungarian nobility, previously not particularly friendly to the Emperor. She arrived in Pressburg (now Bratislava), the capital of Hungary at the time, dressed in Hungarian national costume and with the Hungarian flag over her head. The Hungarians were impressed, but demanded more than she was willing to give them: full independence. After a further emotional appeal, dressed for mourning and in tears, with the crown of St Stephen on her head and with the almost newborn Joseph (later Joseph II) on her lap, she succeeded in her appeal and received the troops she asked for. In addition, she received subsidies from Britain, which also joined the war, and gradually managed to improve the military situation. Despite a number of French victories, the war ended in 1748 with status quo; the Austrian Empire remained intact, except for Silesia. Charles Albert of Bavaria died in 1745 and was succeeded as emperor by Maria Theresa's husband, Francis Stephen, who in turn was succeeded by their son Joseph, at his death in 1765, while Maria Theresa was the actual ruler.

If Austria's enemies had carried out their original plans, it would have led to a major transformation of the map of Europe, the extinction of one of the three great powers of Western and Central Europe. Even without Maria Theresa, however, it might be suggested that this was after all an unlikely outcome; it was generally difficult to arrive at an acceptance of a drastic change of territory in contemporary great power politics. In any case, it is impossible to imagine a crisis like the one in 1740 if Charles VI had been succeeded by a son; the dynastic principle was too strong at the time. It was also strong enough to aid Maria Theresa, despite the fact that she was technically not the legitimate heir to the Roman Empire.

Frederick II of Prussia fought three wars over Silesia (1740–42, 1744–45 and 1756–63). The reason was the immense strategic and probably also economic importance of this region. It extended the borders of Prussia to the south in a way that enabled Prussian forces to threaten both Vienna and Prague. It separated Saxony from Poland, which of course made it extremely attractive to the duke of Saxony who was also king of Poland. One of Frederick's motives for the invasion was to prevent a Saxon conquest. Silesia covered around 40,000 square km or around one-third of England and had one million inhabitants, which then increased the Prussian population by 50 per cent. It was also the wealthiest province of Austria with a productive agriculture, plenty of mineral resources and a famous textile industry. By conquering Silesia, Prussia took the step from being a medium-sized principality to the main rival of the emperor within the German realm.[49] By Frederick's standards, Francis I was a military dilettante, wandering around to find an adversary of sufficient status to fight him, whereas Frederick had organized his army as well as the rest of his country down to the minutest detail in order to be able to fight a prolonged war. Frederick's concept of honour was also different from that of Francis; it was the honour of the state rather than that of the king as a person. Frederick did not expose himself to danger on the battlefield to show his heroism but because he found it necessary for strategic reasons. Moreover, what distinguished him from his adversaries was his skill as a military organizer rather than as a general in the field.[50] Although Frederick was exceptional even in the eighteenth century, the comparison between the two rulers does indicate a trend in the direction of clearer strategic thinking.

As we have seen, the principles of hereditary succession and legitimate rights played an important part in the conflict between Francis I and Charles V. Dynastic connections also to some extent determined the alliance system. Spain and the Empire were normally allies as long as they were both ruled by the Habsburgs (1516–1700), whereas the same happened with France and Spain, once they both were ruled by the Bourbons (1700–1792). The dynastic principle was also fundamental in the peace negotiations that ended the great wars of the following period. Peace negotiations during the Thirty Years War started in 1644, when delegates from the various parties met in Osnabrück and Münster, the Protestants in the former, the Catholics in the latter. The religious divisions at the time were sufficiently sharp to make a common conference impossible. Even so, there is a dramatic contrast between the slaughter, cruelty and misery caused by the war going on at the same time and the elegantly dressed diplomats with their wigs and laces and plumed hats assuring each other in eloquent Latin, French or Spanish of their peaceful intentions and respect for the other party's interests. Legal rights played a very important part in the negotiations. Although it was recognized that conquest might create a right, the delegates consistently avoided drawing any conclusions from this principle; some legal basis had to be found.[51] Without bringing an end to European wars, it settled conditions in Germany for a long time and established a certain balance of power in Europe. The Peace Treaty of Westphalia of 1648 is often regarded as the precise date when the European state system came into existence, including the around 400 German territories. Strictly speaking, this is not true; the only formal recognition of this kind in the treaty concerned the independence of the Dutch Republic from Spain. By contrast, the emperor was still regarded as the head of the German principalities, although this superiority had limited practical importance, as had already been the case for centuries.[52]

At the peace conference of Utrecht in 1713, we can study the development of European diplomacy since 1648. There was no division between Catholics and Protestants; there was some basic agreement among the negotiators and a good personal relationship between them, as between the English Lord Bolingbroke and the French Marquis Torcy, both clever diplomats. There was little mention of general principles, which had played such an important part in 1648, but rather an attempt from all or at least most parties to reach solutions that might be mutually acceptable and prevent a renewal of the war. To some extent, the principle of a balance of power had replaced the strong focus on established rights.

Without going into details about the negotiations, a minor issue may be used for illustration, namely, the question of what was going to happen to the two Wittelsbach electors, the duke of Bavaria and the archbishop of Cologne, who had fought with France against the emperor and were therefore regarded as traitors. Louis XIV tried his best to obtain a favourable settlement for them, despite the fact that the alliance with them had been of little value to him. He emphasized that he had pledged his word to aid them and addressed Queen Anne of England in person for their sake. The English had already compromised themselves by negotiating with the French behind the back of their allies[53] and were not inclined to provoke the emperor by acting on behalf of people he regarded as traitors, but were eventually willing to some concessions because of French pressure. As Bolingbroke put it, it was necessary to do something for 'the Elector of Bavaria, whose interest the old gentleman [Louis XIV] has ... as much at heart as it is possible to believe'.[54] Various projects were proposed but all rejected by the emperor. In the end, the two princes had to resign themselves to the status quo; they were reinstated as imperial princes. As a whole, the conference must be regarded as reasonably successful; it had kept the Spanish Empire largely intact but secured its separation from France as well as establishing a barrier between France and the Dutch Republic in the form of the Austrian Netherlands.

Of course, peace conferences are occasions for politeness, diplomatic language and references to virtues and legal principles. Nevertheless, some of these declarations correspond to actual behaviour. This applies above all to the dynastic principle. In the same way as the right of property and inheritance was a fundamental principle of law in the individual countries, the right of a dynasty to a certain principality or kingdom was fundamental in international politics. Two objections made to the importance of norms in early modern international politics are that Francis I broke his oath to Charles V at the Peace of Madrid and that Frederick II conquered Silesia without a legal claim.[55] The answer to this is, first, that the fact that norms are disobeyed does not mean that they do not exist and, second, that Francis had what his contemporaries regarded as a valid reason, namely, that the pope had declared that his oath was forced and consequently null and void. Concerning Frederick II, he might argue that the absence of a legitimate heir made the division of a composite monarchy legitimate. Although there are strategic explanations for the great alliance against him in the Seven Years War, both its size and its duration seem an argument that he was considered to have acted against the rules and was regarded as dangerous for that reason. Thus, the fundamental principle of early modern international politics was not the integrity of the state but the rights of the dynasty. In the same way as hereditary property was the basis of law within the various European countries, the right of a dynasty to rule a particular country was fundamental in international law. Crises of succession opened up possibilities for expansion based on more or less convincing claims, while an open challenge of the rights of a generally recognized heir was difficult to maintain.

The strongest argument in favour of the importance of norms is the continued existence of the around 400 German principalities. Of course, there are also some political reasons for this. Germany was a kind of buffer between two strong states, France and Habsburg Austria. During the Thirty Years War, France had fought Austria to prevent the emperor from taking control of Germany. In the following period, the emperor had some authority and influence in the area, while his main field of expansion was towards the south, the Ottoman Empire, eventually also the east, with the division of Poland. From a French point of view, the German principalities were too weak and divided to form a threat but might of course form a tempting aim for expansion, as particularly the Rhineland was both a wealthy area and situated close to the French border. Louis XIV made some attempts at expansion here, but experienced opposition from England as well as from the Dutch Republic. However, when the three eastern powers could agree about the division of Poland, it would not be inconceivable that some similar deal might have been made over Germany. Political considerations clearly played a part, but it is difficult to dismiss the importance of established rights.

The attitude of the German princes themselves may be illustrated by the following quotation from the French delegates, D'Avaux and Servien, at the peace conference of Westphalia to Cardinal Mazarin:

> We are obliged, by what little knowledge we have of the disposition of the princes of Germany, to represent to Your Eminence that it is very different from that of the princes of Italy, the latter, being very intelligent and well-advised, approving of, and wishing for, everything that may contribute to make them independent ... but these [the German princes] are much more affected by love of their fatherland and cannot approve of foreigners dismembering the Empire, no matter what hope of gain we hold out to them, preferring ... the substance of the body of which they are members to the advantage that each of them can obtain privately through the division of the Empire.[56]

The norms in this case are based on the dynastic principle which in contemporary Europe was fundamental concerning the relationship between individuals as well as states. Although politically a fairly weak assembly of states, it was governed by rules about the princes' hereditary rights, which, if broken, might lead to sanctions against the culprit under the leadership of the emperor (*Reichsexekution*). Militarily, this was not particularly effective, but there was a general acceptance of mutual rights, which served to preserve the system as such despite occasional transgressions of the rules.[57] As indicated by the quotation, there was also some sense of national identity in Germany despite the political division.[58]

We can here point to the general argument for ordinary people to adhere to norms. If asked whether they would follow the norm if it cost them their life, most people would probably say no. However, in most cases it does not cost one's life to follow the norm, but perhaps only some inconvenience, which may be cancelled by the risk of not following the norm. In other words, the existence of a norm means an extra cost in performing certain actions which at least in some cases makes people inclined to follow it. The difference between individuals and states is that the former are ruled by a superior authority whereas the latter are not. Still, in the same way as the idea of the state as absolutely sovereign was slow to develop, the same applies to the idea of anarchy between states. Typically, early modern wars were wars of succession. A succession presented an opportunity to add to one's territory on the basis of more or less legitimate claims and in some cases, such as Frederick II's conquest of Silesia, with no claim at all, but a situation where the lack of a legitimate successor to the imperial title made it possible to grab a piece of the empire's possessions. In addition, honour was still important but eventually in a somewhat different form. To Francis I, like his medieval predecessors, honour was very personal, linked to his own performance in battle and his rights as a member of a particular dynasty. To Richelieu, Louis XIV and Frederick II, honour was more linked to the state as an abstract entity. The state had to defend its territory and interests to be respected by other states.

The existence of norms in such cases nevertheless has some connection with the principle of a balance of power that had gradually developed. A territory or a country would normally belong to a certain kindred or dynasty. If a claimant could show a connection to this dynasty, he might be opposed by others with similar claims and might have to fight for his claim. The importance of norms is expressed in the fact that an actor trying to expand his power against the norms is more dangerous than one who has a legitimate claim. The others will suspect the former of turning against themselves the next time, while the latter may be believed to be content by having his claim recognized. The other actors would therefore be likely to unite against any actor that tried seriously to disturb the balance. Consequently, the existence of the norms in question has some connection to the contemporary political situation, a number of relatively stable units in mutual competition, none of which was likely to establish a power monopoly or risk extinction. All would want to extend their power and territory but no one would want any of the others to do so. Consequently, there would always be a majority in favour of the status quo.

It may be objected to this conclusion that once France had got an efficient government after the Revolution, it embarked on a series of wars of conquest which for a time radically changed the map of Europe. The answer to this is that these military successes were largely the results of ideological change: the mobilization of the French people to fight for the nation and its freedom, and the rejection of dynastic rights which led to changes of government as well as political borders, the extinction of the Holy Roman Empire and the suppression of a large number of German principalities, including the ecclesiastical ones. From a military point of view, a European continent dominated by France would not have been impossible in the period following the decline of the Habsburg Empire, but it would have necessitated both a more efficient state and the rejection of the dynastic principle. Thus, Hui is correct in pointing to inefficiency as a factor, to which, however, the dynastic principle should be added, combined with the principle of the balance of power. This latter was strengthened after the French defeat in 1814–15 and has played an important part in great power politics until the present.[59]

Finally, let us consider the two cases of states that disappeared, namely, the Italian city states and Poland. Both had in common that they lacked dynasties. The city republics were mostly suppressed or replaced by princes. Southern Italy and Sicily had well-established dynasties with links to others, notably that of Spain, which in periods led to personal unions with this country. Poland was a kingdom from the early eleventh century onwards but the monarchy was defined as elective in 1569. In contrast to most other elective kingdoms, Poland eventually became really elective, with no preference for the son of the previous king. The king's power was also greatly reduced in the eighteenth century. This does not mean that the lack of a dynasty was the only explanation for the partition but it may have made it easier to achieve; it would create no dangerous precedent for the established dynasties. It would also have seemed to be a breach of the principle of the balance of power; under normal circumstances, powers like Britain and France would probably have reacted against it, but as it took place in 1793 and 1795, during the period of the French Revolution, neither of them had any possibility to interfere. The internal development of Poland, including the partition, will be discussed later.

The first step towards the partition of Poland was taken at the initiative of Frederick II of Prussia in 1772 who wanted to extend the coastline of his country and to join two of the three main parts of which it consisted. Another consideration, common to Austria and Prussia, was to limit the influence of Russia, which largely controlled Poland. Catharine the Great of Russia was therefore less in favour of the partition but found it necessary to accept it. Maria Theresa of Austria had moral objections but agreed. As Frederick put it: 'Catherine and I are simply brigands; but I wonder how the Queen-Empress managed to square her confessor … She wept as she took, and the more she wept, the more she took.'[60] Frederick here gives an apt characterization of the three rulers. He was himself a power politician with limited respect for norms and established rights. Russia represented a different political culture, a more absolutist regime where, however, the dynasty was of little importance. The emperor elected his own successor and did not necessarily pick his nearest heir. Moreover, Russia was a new power with little reason to respect the traditional rights of the established rulers. By contrast, Maria Theresa was a traditional monarch, who, in addition, had fought like a lioness for the possessions of her dynasty and in order to prevent the partition of her empire.

Conclusion

Guido Aldeni may sound naïve and he was obviously wrong when dismissing the problem of the many kings in Europe to his Chinese hosts. Nevertheless, the kinship between the European rulers was not without importance and the European state system was formed by marriage more than by war, despite the fact that great changes took place in military technology and organization and that most kings spent a greater part of their incomes on war than on any other purpose. Nor has the importance of war for state formation been dealt with fully in this chapter; it remains to examine its effect on the internal development of the states. Concerning external matters, however, we must conclude that the main phase in the development of the European state system was the period before around 1200, when almost all of the later kingdoms came into existence. Admittedly, a European in the eighteenth century would hardly have found much that was familiar if he or she had been able to return to the thirteenth century. The reason for this, however, is not primarily the division between the states but their internal conditions. Thus, state formation is far more than the division of the continent between a number of kings; laying claims to a particular territory, distinct from that of other kings, was only a first step; the most important was to gain the loyalty and support of its inhabitants, notably the leading ones, whose power might rival that of the king. This process will form the theme of the next part of the book.

Notes

1 Quoted in Tilly, *Coercion*, p. 128.
2 Diamond, *Guns*, pp. 180–91; Morris, *War*, pp. 75–81.
3 For example, Kennedy, *Rise and Fall*, pp. 17–18 and Ferguson, *Civilization*, pp. 36–7.
4 Hoffman, *Why Did Europe?*, pp. 109–12.
5 Hui, *War and State Formation*, pp. 90–3.
6 Keegan, *The Mask of Command*, pp. 33–40 and *A History of Warfare*, pp. 258–73.
7 For this and the following, see Hui, *War and State Formation*, pp. 50–108 and Fukuyama, *The Origins*, pp. 98, 110–16.
8 Parker, *The Military Revolution*, p. 2–3; Hui, *War and State Formation*, pp. 64–108.
9 Geary, *The Myth of Nations*, pp. 24–40.
10 These divisions form the basis for Stein Rokkan's attempt to explain European state formation and the differences between the various countries, which is thought-provoking, although not entirely convincing (Rokkan, 'Dimensions of State-Formation and Nation-Building').
11 Bagge, *Cross and Scepter*, pp. 28–31.
12 Hui, *War and State Formation*, pp. 109–67.
13 On medieval and early modern warfare, see Verbruggen, *The Art of Warfare*; Contamine, *War in the Middle Ages*; Keegan, *A History of Warfare*, and McNeill, *The Pursuit of Power*.
14 Bachrach, *Warfare in Tenth-Century Germany*.
15 Bartlett, *The Making of Europe*, pp. 65–70.
16 For the following, see Duffy, *Ireland*, pp. 16–80.
17 For this and the following, see MacKay, *Spain in the Middle Ages*, pp. 15–78.
18 Cuttino, *English Diplomatic Administration*, pp. 1–28.
19 Finer, 'The Role of the Military', p. 104.
20 Rogers, *War Cruel and Sharp* pp. 348–84, on the Poitiers campaign.
21 Warner, *Joan of Arc*, pp. 13–33.
22 Housley, 'Sanctified Patriotism', pp. 233–5.
23 Henneman, 'The Military Class'; Krynen, *L'Empire du roi*, pp. 296–338.
24 McNeill, *The Pursuit of Power*, pp. 82–100.
25 Meyer, 'State, Roads, War', pp. 110–12.
26 Parker, *The Military Revolution*, pp. 42–3.
27 For the following, see McNeill, *The Pursuit of Power*, pp. 79–143 and Kennedy, *The Rise and Fall*, pp. 31–115.

28 Tilly, *Coercion*, p. 45.
29 Osiander, *The State System*, pp. 78–9; Wilson, *The Holy Roman Empire*, pp. 127–8; Croxton, *Westphalia*, pp. 351–62. See also Nexon, *The Struggle for Power*, pp. 265–88, who has a similar understanding of the Peace Treaty itself, although attaching greater importance to the Reformation as a factor in state formation than I do.
30 Blockmans, *Power*, pp. 66–8; Watts, *The Making of Polities*, p. 97.
31 Cf. Spruyt, *The Sovereign State*, p. 157.
32 Tilly, *Coercion*, pp. 28 and 65, admits that the development was not regular but does not really discuss the problem of 'the survival of the unfittest'. By contrast, Spruyt, *The Sovereign State*, pp. 32–3 and 156–8, quite correctly uses this observation as a counter-argument against Tilly's conclusion.
33 Tilly, *Coercion*, p. 45.
34 Martinez, *Furies*, pp. 56–64.
35 Froissart, *Chronicles*, pp. 143–4.
36 There is at least an alternative version, according to which Edward did not dine with the king because he was attending to Sir James Audley who had been mortally wounded (Taylor, *Chivalry*, p. 181).
37 Froissart, *Chronicles*, pp. 106–9. Froissart's source is Jean le Bel who wrote around ten years after the event. The episode has been much discussed by historians. Sumption, *Trial by Battle*, pp. 581–2 accepts the story. By contrast, Moeglin, 'Eduard III et les six bourgeois', pointing to a number of parallel examples, concludes that Edward demanded the public humiliation of the citizens of Calais, not their execution. See also Taylor, *Chivalry*, p. 198.
38 Englund, *Poltava*, pp. 278–9, 339–40.
39 Contamine, 'Ransom and Booty', pp. 190–3.
40 Keegan, *A History of Warfare*, pp. 3–12.
41 Clark, *Iron Kingdom*, pp. 198–201; Blanning, *Frederick the Great*, pp. 203–7, 262–3.
42 For the following, see Lang, *François I*, pp. 340–52.
43 Guicciardini, *History of Italy*, pp. 348–67.
44 Rodriguez-Salgado, 'The Habsburg-Valois Wars', p. 383.
45 Collins, *Early Modern France*, p. 193.
46 Bertrand de Born, in Kehew, *Lark in the Morning*, pp. 144–5.
47 Hoffman, *Why Did Europe?*, pp. 21–34.
48 Rodriguez-Salgado, 'The Habsburg-Valois Wars', pp. 377–400.
49 Clark, *Iron Kingdom*, pp. 194–5; Blanning, *Frederick the Great*, p. 185.
50 According to Blanning, *Frederick the Great*, p. 281, he was an indifferent general but a brilliant warlord. Other scholars, including Clark, *Iron Kingdom*, pp. 198–210, have a more positive view of him as a general. Frederick won around half of the battles he fought during the Seven Years War, which seems quite impressive, considering that in most cases he was numerically inferior.
51 Osiander, *The States System*, pp. 49–50.
52 Parker, *The Thirty Years' War*; Osiander, *The State System*, pp. 78–9; Burkhardt, *Der Dreissigjährige Krieg*, pp. 198–204; Wilson, *The Holy Roman Empire*, pp. 127–8. See also Nexon, *The Struggle for Power*, pp. 265–88, who has a similar understanding of the Peace Treaty itself, although attaching greater importance to the Reformation as a factor in state formation than I do.
53 This was partly the result of the Tories replacing the Whigs in the British government in 1710 but above all of the death of the Austrian emperor and the succession of Charles VI, who was also the candidate to the Spanish throne (1711). Consequently, by supporting Charles' candidacy, the English risked creating the same situation as they wanted to avoid, the union of Spain with one of the greatest powers on the Continent.
54 Osiander, *The States System*, p. 118.
55 Hui, *War and State Formation*, pp. 158–9.
56 Osiander, *The States System*, p. 38.

57 Ibid., pp. 48–9.
58 See Scales, *The Shaping*, pp. 526–38, and Wilson, *The Holy Roman Empire*, pp. 1–15, for a discussion of this.
59 Kissinger, *World Order*, pp. 59–82, with particular reference to Metternich and Bismarck.
60 Blanning, *Frederick the Great*, p. 294.

2

THE FOUNDATION AND DEVELOPMENT OF EUROPEAN MONARCHY

'War made the state and the state made peace,' says Ian Morris, changing Charles Tilly's famous dictum.[1] Morris' main examples of this are the great empires, particularly the Roman and the Chinese. There were limits to how much an empire could grow. When the Romans had conquered most of what was then regarded as the civilized world, it was costly and unproductive to attempt to conquer thinly populated countries along the borders. The great empires created peace by crushing their enemies and then shaped the conditions for an organized and relatively wealthy society, with trade, communications, roads, circuses, baths, books and institutions of learning. Both Rome and China had strong armies, but their aim was to defend the borders, not to extend them.[2]

As we have seen, war did not make the state in Europe but there is no doubt that the state made war. To the extent that war made the state, it was unsuccessful war. The state was not the result of conquest but of continuous mobilization against one or more enemies, which in turn necessitated greater and more professional armies, technological innovation and the development of a professional bureaucracy. This meant that the way to state formation was not to crush rival powers within the borders but to gain their support and use them against external enemies. Although this did not prevent rebellion, civil wars or rivalry between kings and their subjects, there was no way in which a ruler could suppress his population solely by means of military power, not even in the age of absolutism when kings commanded large and professional armies. The following discussion will deal with the various means of a military, legal, administrative, religious and cultural character, by which the European states were built.

What was a state?

As we have seen, most of the political units that participated in the inter-European competition in the period 1500–1800 had their origins in the Middle Ages. In an elementary sense, the European state system can therefore be traced back to around

1200. Nevertheless, the resemblance between these units and their descendants in the seventeenth and eighteenth centuries is open to discussion. Traditionally, the main criteria for a state have been sovereignty and institutionalization. The state has no superior; externally, it exists in a situation of anarchy, whereas internally, all its inhabitants owe obedience to its government, which has a monopoly of violence and the right to legislate. In principle, all inhabitants are directly subject to the state; there are no separate parts with their own rules or their own demands of loyalty and obedience, except as the result of delegation from the government of the state. Moreover, loyalty and obedience are owed to an institution, not to individual persons. In modern democracies, the government of the state in principle gets its power from all the inhabitants in the country; it is supposed to take care of their interests and is accountable to them for its actions. Thus, the politicians and bureaucrats governing the state do not act as individual persons but on behalf of the community. They are only entitled to act in this way as long as they hold office and there is a sharp distinction between what they can do as public officers and as private individuals.

Concerning the first criterion, the situation is less clear in practice than in principle, even today. Most modern European states are not sovereign,[3] because they belong to the European Union and are subject to rules laid down by its central institutions, which, however, they are also able to influence. 'Conglomerate states', which are said to be characteristic, particularly of the early modern period, still exist today. The clearest examples are Belgium and Switzerland, which are actually coalitions of largely independent parts. Great Britain is a union between four countries with various degrees of independence, which has increased recently. In addition, there are also other units with a special status, like the Channel Islands and the Isle of Man. Similar conditions apply in Spain. This does not mean that there are no differences in this respect between the contemporary state and its earlier predecessors, but it does mean that we should be cautious about dismissing earlier versions, which differ from the strict model of the sovereign state.

There was of course no international organization deciding which units might be regarded as states in the Middle Ages and the early modern period. It is therefore difficult to specify the exact number of states at various periods between the thirteenth and the eighteenth century. In principle, it was an important criterion that the ruler had the title of king; as we have seen, only two rulers succeeded in obtaining the title between the thirteenth century and 1806. Nevertheless, many of the German principalities, like Saxony, Bavaria and Prussia, must be considered states according to most definitions of the term. Their princes controlled their territory in the same way as kings in other countries and, despite their formal subordination to the emperor, they were free to conduct their internal and external policy and might even wage war against the emperor. By contrast, smaller territories were less independent and in practice largely subordinated to stronger neighbours, either the emperor or the rulers of larger principalities.

Nor did the fact that two countries had the same king mean that they were merged into one political unit. In principle, the union king was supposed to rule in the same way as his predecessors before the union. Thus, Scotland, Aragon, Bohemia and Hungary should be listed as independent kingdoms in 1648, as should Portugal during the union with Spain, 1580–1640. By contrast, Norway was clearly subordinated to Denmark after 1536. In practice, however, unions mostly resulted in some superiority of the stronger country where the king had his main residence. Aragon became subordinated to Castile after the War of the Spanish Succession, Scotland joined a closer union with England in 1707 in which the two parliaments were merged, and both Bohemia and Hungary had their independence reduced. Nevertheless, there are many intermediate stages between full sovereignty and dependence on another kingdom which once more makes it difficult to specify an exact number of states.

Concerning the second criterion, institutionalization, until the thirteenth century and even longer, European states seem to have been less developed than their counterparts in many other areas, such as Byzantium, the Arab kingdoms and, above all, China. The kings were far from having a monopoly of violence; they had no taxes, no standing armies and no professional bureaucracy. Locally, they mostly had to share their power with various other princes and the Church. However, they had some advantages that might be developed further. The leading men in the kingdom were linked to them with ties of loyalty. There was a doctrine of monarchy, including rules of dynastic succession, and based on Christianity, Roman law and ancient philosophy, and there was the Church, whose organization was more bureaucratic than that of the king and which had a developed doctrine of public power delegated from God. Both the doctrine and the organization might serve as models for the king, in addition to the fact that the ecclesiastical organization, in particular, the division into parishes, might be used directly by the royal administration. On the other hand, the Church might be a competitor, limiting the king's power.

The basic features of European society

European society in the Middle Ages and the early modern period was characterized by social inequality. There were great differences of wealth and status between the inhabitants and most countries were ruled by small elites. The following account of government and state formation will therefore mainly focus on these elites. It will nevertheless be useful to begin with a sketch of the main features of European society.

Throughout our period, European society was basically agrarian, although trade and manufacture eventually became increasingly important. The central zone of Europe, between the North and Baltic Seas to the north and the Alps and the Pyrenees to the south, has a mild, temperate climate, a sufficient amount of rain and large, relatively flat areas of deep, fertile soil. It is also little exposed to natural disasters such as earthquakes, volcanoes, tornadoes and periods of draught. During the Middle Ages, the agricultural resources of this zone were fully exploited for the first time in history. Over large areas, forest was cut down and replaced by cultivated fields and the population increased nearly threefold between 1000 and 1350. The same happened in the northern zone, whereas the population south of the Alps also increased, but only doubled. Although the central zone was potentially very fertile, the soil was heavy and labour-intensive. Whereas in the Mediterranean, the plots were usually small and the soil light and easy to turn with the light ploughs that were usual in this area, the soil north of Alps needed deep ploughing, which was achieved by the introduction of the heavy plough, drawn by horses or a large number of oxen. Together with other changes, such as the three-year rotation, according to which one-third of the field lay fallow at any time, this seems to have led to a slight increase in the yield, from 3 to 4 or 4.5 to 1, and some places, such as in Flanders around 1300, as much as 15 to 1. This is far less than in modern agriculture, with 30 to 1, but may nevertheless have led to a reduction of periods of famine.[4]

Socially, by far the largest part of the population consisted of peasants. There had been a tendency already in late antiquity in the direction of large estates owned by members of the elite and cultivated by unfree peasants; these had replaced slaves as the main working force. The continuity between the kinds of labour force is expressed in the English term *serf* for the agricultural labourers in the Middle Ages, a word derived from Latin *servus* = slave. Although there were various kinds of agricultural labourers in the early Middle Ages, including free men who worked on their own land, the main trend in the central agricultural areas was in the direction of large estates, cultivated by unfree peasants and owned by lay or ecclesiastical lords. However, there was no sharp distinction between free and unfree; the latter status included a great variety of conditions. English lawyers defined the right to marry off one's daughter without permission from the lord as the essential criterion of freedom, but such criteria varied from place to place. Over most of this zone, peasants lived in villages, with up to 1,000 inhabitants. The cultivated land was divided between the inhabitants, normally not in the form of solid blocks but in plots interspersed with each other, this in order to secure an equal division of better and worse soil. This land could be transferred to heirs. Outside the cultivated land were the commons, available to the whole village community. Although normally under the rule of a lord, a village community governed itself in many respects, elected its own leaders, employed artisans of various kinds, issued by-laws for its members and with greater or lesser success sought to defend its interests against the lord or other forces. Socially and economically, the peasantry was by no means a homogeneous class. There were considerable differences from small, wealthy elites to cottars (living in a cot) without permanent plots or with plots too small to make a living, so that they had to work for others to survive.

There was a significant difference between the central agricultural areas, with large farms on relative flat and fertile land and the outskirt areas in or near the Alps, Pyrenees and Carpathians and in the Scots or Scandinavian mountains, as well as areas along the coast or on small islands on the coasts towards the North and Baltic Seas, to which access was difficult. In the latter areas, the peasants often had a freer status and to a greater extent governed themselves.[5] As we shall see, this in some cases resulted in independent peasant communities able to defend themselves against neighbouring areas or attempts by the elites to suppress them. Nor were the village communities in the central areas purely passive receivers of the commands and demands of kings and nobles. They were well organized and reacted against what they regarded as injustice and even if their rebellions were always put down, they might often achieve some of their aims. The peasants were in a sense a political class but their main influence was on the local level, which is why they will not be dealt with very much in the following.

The population growth came to a dramatic end in the years 1347–50, mainly because of the Black Death which raged throughout the Continent during these years. Between one-third and half the population is supposed to have died. Moreover, the disease came back repeatedly in the following centuries; the last outbreak, which only affected part of the continent, took place in 1711–12, but there were outbreaks in Russia and in the Ottoman Empire later in the eighteenth century. The mortality caused a drop in land-rents and agricultural production but led to higher salaries and better conditions for peasants and workers. The nobility was hit particularly hard, although this is not obvious from the political history of the period, in which the nobles had a strong influence. Here, however, we have to distinguish between the class and its individual members. High mortality and low rents may have eliminated many nobles whereas a number of wealthy landowners who survived may have profited from buying the lands of their less fortunate colleagues at low prices. When the population began to recover from the mid-fifteenth century onwards, however, it would seem that the profit to a greater extent went to kings and princes; instead of the land-rent rising to its old level, a greater part of the payments from the peasants took the form of taxes, from which, however, the nobles profited, in the form of gifts and offices in the king's service.[6]

Concerning the elite, we can take our point of departure in the well-known contemporary description of society as consisting of 'those who fight, those who pray and those who work'.[7] This is one of several divisions of medieval society, formulated for the first time in England in the tenth century and then the subject of more detailed treatment by two French bishops around 1030. Somewhat later, a division into four is to be found, with the merchants as the fourth category. This corresponds to the increasing importance of towns and trade from the eleventh and twelfth century onwards. A larger population, more surplus from agriculture and more wealthy landowners led to increased demand for luxury goods which stimulated long-distance trade. However, the most important part of the urbanization was the emergence of smaller towns which catered for local markets. For the first time in history, Europe north of the Alps had a substantial urban population, although this is not always reflected in the official ideology.

The statements about the orders clearly reflect the point of view of the elite – the common people rarely give the definitions of social structure. More interesting is what is tells about the character of the elite, which is either military or religious. Both elite classes are landowners and in this capacity rule the third one. There is no professional governing class and the one who is in principle the leader of society, the king, is just one of several members of the warrior class, although, at least in some versions of the description, it may be implied that he is actually its head. By contrast, both in Byzantium and the Muslim world, the ruler (emperor, caliph or sultan) had a far more central position. The state owned more of the land, there were permanent taxes and landholding was more often a temporary grant from the ruler. The division thus points to a characteristic feature of Western society in the early Middle Ages and to some extent later, the absence of a civilian governing class and the relatively subordinated position of the king. In Europe, the king was one of more landowners who only gradually managed to assume the position as an authority qualitatively different from the nobles and the churchmen. Thus, the king is the logical starting-point for discussing the formation of the European state.

The king and the aristocracy

In his account of the deeds of Frederick Barbarossa, Otto of Freising includes a description of Hungary in connection with Frederick's planned expedition against this country.[8] The Hungarians are barbarians, not because they lack a king or an organized government, but because their country differs from Germany and other 'civilized' feudal countries by the unlimited power of the king. The king has full command over the army; he has full jurisdiction over the whole country, including the right to torture and execute counts or local leaders, even for small offences. Such men are arrested by the king's subordinate servants, even when they are surrounded by their own retainers. No judgement by equals exists; the king's will is law. There is no private jurisdiction and no privileges of mint or tolls, and the king's local representatives are only entitled to one-third of the royal revenues. Otto's description must be interpreted in light of his understanding of what constitutes the right way of organizing society and is therefore not an objective account of Hungarian society.[9]

However, it does illustrate the strongly aristocratic German society at the time and the difference between what we may call the central zone of feudal Europe and the new kingdoms in the periphery, with a less well-defined aristocracy, fewer towns and castles and, in some respects, a stronger monarchy. Eventually, the new kingdoms developed in the same direction as the old ones. They adapted the military technology of heavy cavalry and castles and developed a more exclusive aristocracy, which limited the king's power.

As depicted by Otto, Hungary thus illustrates what had happened in Western Europe in the previous period. In principle, the Merovingians and the Carolingians had a stronger position compared to the aristocracy than their successors in the twelfth and thirteenth centuries, although, in practice, they were far from the dictatorship Otto depicts. In Germany, the great wealth of the Ottonians in the form of landed estates was greatly reduced under the later Staufen; under Frederick II, it may have been less than those of the king of Denmark.[10] In the later Middle Ages, there was a reduction of the emperor's revenues from 100,000 guilders per annum in the early fourteenth century to around 13,000 in the early fifteenth.[11] Similar calculations have been made for many other countries, for instance, in Scandinavia and East Central Europe. The problem here, however, is that we know very little about royal revenues in the earliest period and that attempts to reconstruct them on the basis of later ones may easily lead to exaggeration. It seems that in many cases the king owned more land in the early Middle Ages than later, but the loss of this may often have been compensated by other kinds of income, such as taxes.[12]

The following strengthening of royal power did not mean a return to earlier conditions but the development of a stronger state based on a more or less successful cooperation between the king and the aristocracy. Neither the change in military organization and technology nor the development of royal courts of law meant a defeat for the latter. On the contrary, state formation under the king's leadership meant that the aristocracy, i.e., a *de facto* social elite, was transformed into a formally defined nobility, distinct from the rest of the population by hereditary privileges, coats of arms and various other symbols. What characterized European state formation in contrast to other parts of the world, at least until the age of the French Revolution, was the cooperation between the king and this nobility.[13] In the nineteenth and twentieth centuries there were noble families in England able to trace their ancestry back to the Norman Conquest – French names are still a sign of distinction – and similar examples occur in other countries, although for demographic as well as social reasons, the likelihood of such a long ancestry is not very great. The class itself, however, shows great continuity. Even at the time of the First World War, nobles dominated the diplomatic service and higher military ranks in many countries. The nobles adapted to new circumstances. They changed their horses and heavy armour for uniforms with epaulettes and distinctions and commanded large armies instead of fighting in person. Their castles were replaced by elegant country houses and their manners became more peaceful and refined.

The importance of the nobility is a permanent feature of the European state until the period of the French Revolution and to a considerable extent even later. Turning to the early Middle Ages, we find a sliding transition between kingdoms and smaller units, governed by local lords. As we have seen, the latter developed into around 400 largely independent principalities in Germany, while they had to submit to the king in countries like France and Spain.

The concept of feudalism forms a natural point of departure for a discussion of this development. Traditionally, this concept was used to define the society of Europe north of the Alps and west of the Rhine,[14] whereas the rest of the Continent, with some exceptions, was not or only to a limited extent dominated by feudal institutions. The essential feature of feudalism was that the distinction between private property and political power was blurred. The king gave land to his subordinates in the form of fiefs,[15] not as permanent gifts, but to hold them from him in return for various services, notably military service. In addition, such a grant might also include the rights of jurisdiction, taxation and other privileges. In a completely feudalized society, governmental power and private ownership would therefore coincide, although both would in principle be limited by the duties to the king or superior lord of the area and his right to reclaim the territory if he found his vassal's behaviour unsatisfactory. Although fiefs were originally given for a limited period of time, maximum the lifetime of the recipient, they eventually became hereditary; which meant that they could normally only be reclaimed in the absence of legitimate heirs. In practice, this meant that the vassal was in a stronger position than the lord, a development favoured by the contemporary military technology: the vassal would rule his fief from a castle, which was difficult to conquer. In addition to the changes in military technology, the decline of the Carolingian Empire has been regarded as an important factor in the development of feudalism: the competing kings had to give away large parts of their lands in order to gain support in their internal wars.

Since the 1970s, this picture of feudalism has been subject to a series of attacks. The chronology of the process has been revised, notably by French scholars who point to the eleventh century as the crucial period, while attaching little importance to the legal aspect.[16] In England, Susan Reynolds has rejected the idea that government and private property became blurred in the early Middle Ages and that vassals owed services to their lords in return for receiving land.[17] By contrast, all inhabitants in the country owed obedience to the king as the ruler of the country, although in periods these duties might have little importance in practice. The legal concepts of the fief and vassalage were developed by lawyers in the thirteenth century.

These attacks on the traditional concept have led to more nuances and have somewhat reduced the sharp distinction between a feudal and a non-feudal zone of Europe but have not led to general rejection of the idea of feudalism.[18] A number of feudal contracts have been preserved from Southern France in which a castellan takes his land or castles as a fief from his lord and declares his loyalty to him in return. In most cases, the land is not a gift from the lord but more often the vassal's own property (*allod*) which is converted to a fief. Although this would seem to favour the lord, the area, which was completely outside royal control until the early thirteenth century, was in practice dominated by the castellans, whereas the greater lords, such as the Count of Toulouse, had their power reduced in the eleventh and twelfth centuries.[19] There is also plenty of evidence of fiefs and vassals in Germany, although not all the land consisted of fiefs.[20] In England, the lawyers' idea of all land in the country originally having belonged to the king may have some basis in William the Conqueror's grants to his followers, but is essentially a legal fiction. In the twelfth and thirteenth centuries, it served to legitimate the king's rights to aid from his tenants-in-chief, to act as guardian for the heir during his minority and to decide over the marriage of female heirs, but otherwise, land was privately owned and there was a clear distinction between ownership of land and governmental functions.

The following discussion will deal with the main internal changes that took place in the European kingdoms from the early Middle Ages until the eighteenth century, changes which may be characterized by the term 'state formation'. The obvious starting-point for this discussion is the king. State formation largely means extended power of the king, either in person or as an institution. On the other hand, we should not imagine the process as the result of a deliberate attempt by kings over the centuries to create the organization we find in the eighteenth century. Kings and other actors at the time acted to achieve immediate aims but the result of these actions were often unforeseen and might lead to major changes. In hindsight, we can characterize state formation as the building of institutions enabling the king to control his country and the forging of alliances with its leading inhabitants, assuring their loyalty to this project. As we have seen, European states were not created through a continuous struggle between smaller power-holders in which the strongest won but by a combination of pressure from the centre and alliances with local authorities. The king was both part of the feudal aristocracy and its superior. He had similar rights over his vassals as other lords, such as the right to financial aid when marrying his daughter, but he was also qualitatively different from them, for instance, in being anointed, having judicial power over all his subjects and the right to issue coinage.[21] He had to show his utility by solving conflicts between his subjects, make them his servants and allies and defend the realm against external enemies. In practice, most kings in the twelfth and thirteenth centuries had direct control of only a part of their countries; large parts were in most respects governed by nobles. As we have seen, the king of France in the thirteenth century managed to extend the territory under his direct control greatly, which then also had consequences for the rest, whose rulers to a greater extent had to respect the king. However, European state formation did not consist in the king expanding his power until the whole country was under his direct control. On the contrary, it largely consisted in engaging the local rulers, the nobles, in the government of the realm.

Returning to Otto's barbarians, let us address the question of the new kingdoms of Europe, formed in the tenth and eleventh centuries. In most of them, the formation of the kingdom seems to have coincided with the introduction of Christianity.[22] This clearly applies to the three kingdoms in East Central Europe, probably also the Scandinavian ones, although there are some indications that the monarchy may be older in Denmark and Norway. In all of them, however, there is little evidence from the early period. The connection between Christianization and political unification may be due to the fact that the sources become somewhat better from this time on, but the reason is more probably that the Church was an essential factor in state formation. It gave the king both religious legitimacy and an administrative apparatus.

Otto's observation about the relationship between the king and the aristocracy is clearly correct in the sense that there was no consolidated aristocracy with specific rights and privileges; nor were there any heavy cavalry and castles. There is also evidence of powerful warrior kings, such as Boleslaw I of Poland (995–1025), who fought successfully against the German emperor, and Cnut the Great of Denmark (1016–35), who conquered England and Norway. Immediately before the formation of the kingdoms, both the Scandinavians and the people of East Central Europe had posed a threat to the Christian kingdoms in the west. Some scholars have also concluded that the early monarchy in these countries was strong and then gradually declined with the development of castles and heavy cavalry, which in turn led to the consolidation of the aristocracy. Recent scholarship has been more sceptical of this interpretation. It would immediately seem difficult to imagine a sudden rise of a strong monarchy with full control of the country. At least, it is difficult to believe that one successful conquest would have resulted in permanent control over several generations.

If Otto had written 100–150 years later, he would probably have found Hungarian society more familiar. With some exception for Norway, the new kingdoms had become more similar to the rest of Europe. Whether this meant that they had become feudalized, is disputed, but they had certainly developed a stronger aristocracy and taken over the military technology of the centre. At the same time, they had also been influenced by the new development of European monarchy regarding administration, legislation, public justice, the courtly culture, and so forth. Thus, this chapter will mostly deal with the common features of the two categories of European kingdoms.

The formation of dynasties

The first major step towards the impersonal state was, paradoxically enough, the introduction of dynasties. The dynasty is of course no institution, but rather the opposite, a family. The practical importance of its introduction was that it represented a major step towards the solution of the problem of royal succession. Theoretically, it contributed to the institutionalization of the office by removing it from general competition and by underlining the continuity of royal government; the office was permanent, despite the mortality of individual kings.

Medieval and early modern Europe differs from its predecessor, the Roman Empire, as well as from its neighbouring civilization, Byzantium, in practising dynastic succession to the throne; which suggests that the origins of this practice should be sought in the Germanic tribes. However, there is no evidence of strict dynastic succession among them in the early period, apart from what may be regarded as a natural tendency in humankind to leave one's power and possessions to one's offspring. No ruler in the early period would be able to do this without support from his followers. Dynastic succession would thus seem to be the result of a gradual development of more stable political units after the Roman Empire had been replaced by Germanic kingdoms.

Both the Spanish Visigoths and the Frankish Merovingians developed hereditary succession, but in both, all the king's descendants had an equal right to the throne, whether they were born in marriage or not – to the extent that this distinction made sense at all in contemporary society. In both kingdoms, the kings were promiscuous and there was no clear distinction between mistresses and lawful wives. There was fierce competition between the kings' sons and between their mothers on their behalf, both of which resulted in frequent murders and internal conflicts, in which allies within the aristocracy often proved decisive.[23] The Visigoths were defeated by Arab invaders in 711–20, whereas the Frankish kingdom continued to exist. Here power was gradually transferred from the king to his most prominent deputy, the *majordomus* (chief of the household) who replaced him as king in 751. The new dynasty, the Carolingians, eventually introduced new rules of succession: legitimacy, primogeniture and individual succession. As we have seen, these rules did not prevent the division of Louis the Pious' empire but they did prevent further division between the sons of the French and German kings.

Even if the advantages of primogeniture and legitimate birth might seem obvious in hindsight, it is not easy to identify any groups that had a particular incentive to support its introduction. The ruling king wanted to be succeeded by his offspring, but might find it difficult to favour one son over another. It would seem that the impetus for primogeniture therefore came from the aristocracy. The Merovingian kings had maintained a distance from the aristocracy. They married foreign princesses, in addition to having various mistresses, but they did not use marriage or sexual connections as a way of forging links with leading aristocrats. This policy changed with the Carolingians, who frequently married aristocratic women and who also involved the aristocracy to a greater degree in the government.[24] It is thus with the Carolingians that we can identify the beginnings of a strong connection between the royal government and the local aristocracy that characterized the West at least up to the period of the French Revolution. The king now ruled through a tight aristocratic network that risked being dissolved or disturbed by a divided succession.[25] In addition, the size of political units was reduced through the division of the Carolingian Empire; there was simply less land to divide. Ideologically, the development of primogeniture found support in ecclesiastical doctrine: the Church demanded legitimate birth from the king and was normally in favour of individual succession. In addition, bishops and other churchmen formed an important part of the aristocracy. Favouring one son over his siblings would seem to be a recipe for struggles over the throne. There are also some examples of this in the beginning, but in the long run, individual succession led to greater stability and less competition. Even if a younger son might be jealous of his luckier brother and want to challenge him, it became increasingly difficult to get aristocratic support for such an enterprise.

As in most other places, European rulers were normally men. Because of the importance of hereditary monarchy, monogamy and the nuclear family, the chances were nevertheless fairly high that a woman might succeed to the throne. In some countries, however, female succession was rejected, notably, as we have seen, in the Holy Roman Empire, where it could easily be avoided because the monarchy was elective. More surprisingly, it was also rejected in France, where monarchy was hereditary, with reference to the so-called Salic Law which was actually an invention by the lawyers in the mid-fourteenth century. In practice, this was a means for Philip V to succeed his brother Louis X in 1316 instead of Louis' daughter Jeanne, aged 7, as well as a weapon against King Edward III of England, who claimed the throne of France through his mother, the daughter of King Philip IV.[26]

As we have seen, the French dynasty was the most successful in producing heirs, with son succeeding father for more than 300 years. Although most others were less successful, peaceful succession gradually became the norm, determined either by hereditary rules or election by assemblies with the authority to decide the matter. Whereas approximately 94 of 431 or 22 per cent of the kings in Western Christendom were killed by their subjects in the period 600–1200, this applies to only 25 of 333 or 7.5 per cent in the period 1200–1800.[27] We can also date this reduction fairly precisely. In the central parts of Europe — essentially the Carolingian Empire — it had already taken place by the ninth century. There are no examples of royal murders in France between the Merovingian period (i.e., after 751) and the sixteenth century. Similarly, none took place in Germany (i.e., the eastern part of the Empire) between the division in 843 and the thirteenth century. The reduction in regicides continued in England from the reign of Alfred (870–99) onwards, with the last two murders occurring in the tenth century, while in Scandinavia and East Central Europe, it took place from the thirteenth century onwards. When kings were nevertheless killed, the reason was more often discontent with their way of governing than rivalry over the succession. The main explanation of this change must be the rules of succession, which had the advantage that they removed the most important incentive to murder a king, namely, to replace him on the throne. Only the nearest heir would have this incentive and he knew that would eventually succeed in any case. An additional, equally important factor, was the link between the king and the aristocracy; it became increasingly difficult to get aristocratic support to challenge the ruling king or his legitimate heir.[28] Nonetheless, the development of clear rules of succession was a gradual process; in most countries, there was a combination of elective and hereditary kingship up to the twelfth and thirteenth centuries, although the eldest son of the previous king was normally elected if there was one.

The victory of dynasties in the old kingdoms in the post-Carolingian period forms the logical conclusion to a gradual consolidation. It seems more surprising in the new kingdoms in the north and east that were created during the expansion of Christianity from the ninth and tenth centuries onwards. As far as we can see, dynasties were established relatively quickly in all of these and remained in power for several centuries until they became extinct, mostly from the fourteenth century onwards. Although little is known about the exact circumstances, it would seem that Christianity was an important factor in this, giving the king and his descendants a sacred status. Characteristically, all these kingdoms, with the exception of Poland, got their royal saints shortly after the introduction of Christianity. This did not eliminate struggles over the succession, which happened frequently for several centuries, but the competition seems normally to have been limited to real or alleged members of the dynasty. These struggles may largely have had an integrating function, mobilizing magnates from various parts of the country as candidates aiming at control of the whole realm. There were also other kinds of rebellions and civil wars, in which neighbouring countries might interfere. Thus, borders were approximate and changed frequently, particularly in East Central Europe, somewhat less in Scandinavia, where the risk of interference by neighbours was less.

The introduction of rules of individual succession, primogeniture and legitimate birth largely seems to have solved the problem of rivalry over the throne between the king's sons, but it created a new one, namely, the risk that there would be no heir at all. With medieval and early modern child mortality, it might often happen that a king died without leaving a son. The risk increased with the European rules of monogamy and ban against divorce. Admittedly, the latter could in most cases be avoided by having the Church annul the marriage, usually because the partners were or claimed to be too closely related,[29] but there was no remedy for the former. Although monogamy in practice did not prevent the king from having children with mistresses, these children had no right to the throne. This differs markedly from many other civilizations, such as China and the Muslim kingdoms and empires, where the rulers had harems. In the early Middle Ages, the kings' success or lack of it in this respect largely determined the degree of stability of royal succession. Lack of royal offspring might lead to internal conflict, as well as dynastic unions, which became frequent, particularly from the later Middle Ages onwards. Kings and princes normally married members of other royal families, which often resulted in a ruler or heir of one country becoming king of another as well. This changed the political map of Europe far more than the wars, as can be illustrated particularly by the success of the Habsburgs.

Thanks to the Capetians' luck in having male successors, France was the most stable. England, with less dynastic stability, eventually solved the problem by leaving the decision to Parliament, if there was doubt. Other countries developed various compromises between hereditary and elective succession.[30] Not surprisingly, Germany developed elective monarchy. From the late thirteenth century, the election was left to seven of the most important princes of the realm: the Archbishops of Cologne, Mainz and Trier, the King of Bohemia, the Count Palatine of Rhineland, the Duke of Saxony and the Margrave of Brandenburg. Whether monarchy was officially regarded as hereditary or elective, the king's eldest son, if there was one, would in most cases succeed his father. From the point of view of the aristocracy, the advantage of elective monarchy was in most cases not the possibility of electing anyone else than the nearest heir, but the ability to pose conditions for the election.

Depending on the kings' greater or lesser luck in having offspring, election might either be eliminated or strengthened. In both cases, however, there was a significant amount of dynastic continuity and at least a reduction of crises compared to the early Middle Ages. In both cases, although to different degrees, the king's authority increased and special rules were introduced to protect him against murder and rebellion. In another way, the distance was reduced. There is an obvious similarity between the royal dynasty, 'owning' a particular territory, and every other landowner, down to the peasant owning or even leasing his little plot. The similarity in the positions held by the king and the aristocracy is also expressed in the fact that primogeniture was introduced within the European aristocracy at about the same time as it was applied to royal succession, although without becoming a universal rule to the same extent.

There is not only a similarity between the king and other landowners or even tenants but also some common interest. The people – notably the aristocracy –

needed the king to organize the defence against common enemies and to mediate or judge in internal conflicts. No doubt, there were numerous rebellions by peasants and aristocrats or groups of them, but rather than aiming at eliminating royal government, they aimed at reforming it or in gaining specific rights for the rebels. Although the importance of such events should not be neglected, the history of Europe from 1200 to 1648 is not the history of a continuous struggle between petty principalities eventually resulting in the victory of some ancestor of the national state. Rather, it is the history of a limited number of dynasties, partly competing with each other and partly consolidating their rule over specific territories through a combination of alliances and struggles with subordinates within them. The success of these dynasties varied greatly. As we have seen, the most striking contrast was between French success and German failure.

War and the state

Widely different accounts have been given of state formation in medieval Europe and early modern Europe, on the one hand, the gradual growth of orderly government from the twelfth and particularly thirteenth century onwards, as depicted by earlier scholars like Southern or Strayer, on the other, a chaos of fighting lords under the king's formal superiority in Elias, Tilly and most recently Morris.[31]

We have seen that the division of Europe into independent kingdoms was not primarily the result of war. European kings did not increase their power by systematic wars of conquest against independent or semi-independent nobles within the borders of their countries. The king needed to be constantly present, gain the respect and loyalty of his vassals, mediate and solve conflicts between them and involve them in his projects. Internal struggles would normally weaken a kingdom in the short run but might eventually strengthen it by linking the aristocracy more closely to the victorious king and forcing the king to develop his administration to keep control of recently conquered areas. The newly established kingdoms in Scandinavia and East Central Europe all underwent rebellion and struggles over the succession but these often strengthened the monarchy in this way. The baronial rebellion, the depositions of kings and the Wars of the Roses in England as well as the religious wars and the Fronde in France may have had similar effects.

This also applies to external wars, whether or not they achieved their aims. The Hundred Years War was a common project of the king, the aristocracy and even to some extent the people of England and led to more regular taxation and an administration connected with this as well as increasing the importance of Parliament. It had a similar effect in France, mobilizing the nobility and the people against the invaders and increasing the power and prestige of the monarchy. Many of the actual wars discussed in Chapter 1 also combined conflict against external and internal enemies and indicate a relatively vague distinction between the two.

During the first three phases of the military development, covering the period until the mid-fifteenth century, warfare was costly but did not necessitate a large administration. Armies consisted of the king's vassals, mercenaries or people who either voluntarily joined the armies or were forced to do so, such as criminals who might escape punishment by volunteering as soldiers. The forces were relatively small and the soldiers or their commanders got hold of the necessary arms and equipment. To the extent that soldiers had to be recruited locally, this was the duty of the normal local administrator. By contrast, the fourth phase led to a drastic increase in the size of armies, as expressed in the following numbers.

- Spain: 20,000 in 1500, 200,000 in 1600 and 50,000 in 1700.
- France: 18,000 in 1500, 80,000 in 1600 and 400,000 in 1700.
- In the Netherlands, the number increased five-fold between 1600 and 1700, from 20,000 to 100,000.
- The increase in Sweden in the same period was even greater, from 15,000 to 100,000.[32]

It must be admitted, however, that the numbers are approximate and above all that there are great changes over time. In addition, the new fortifications were many times more expensive than the old ones. War was also by far the greatest burden on the budget of the state, 50 per cent or more in most countries.[33] With the development of standing armies from the late seventeenth century onwards, the difference between periods of war and peace in this respect was reduced; military expenditure was high even in peacetime. In addition, the increase in armies and military expenses necessitated an extensive civilian bureaucracy.

This increase is largely the explanation for the increased size and complexity of the bureaucracies during this period. Here there is a quantitative as well as qualitative change from the Middle Ages to the early modern period. Let us begin with the bureaucratization of the armies themselves. The basic unit of the medieval army was the company, commanded by an officer with the title of captain (Latin *capitaneus* = chief). In the late medieval armies, captains were appointed by royal commission which was the origin of the term commissioned officer. The captain's subordinate was the lieutenant (from French *lieu tenant* = holding a position,): deputy, and the ensign, later second lieutenant, who carried the company's flag. With increasing size and specialization, larger units above the company emerged together with new ranks for the officers who commanded them. A group of companies was joined in a column = regiment (from Italian *colonna*) in the later Middle Ages, from which the name of its commander, colonel, is derived. The corresponding term *coronel* (which is supposed to be the origin of the English pronunciation of colonel) was used for the commander of the Spanish *tercio*. The term general (originally captain general) was first used for the commander of a whole army but was then linked to the units established over that of regiment/*tercio*, namely, brigade and division. The former was introduced by Gustaf II Adolf in the early seventeenth century; the latter made its first appearance in France during the War of the Austrian Succession (1740–48) and became standard in the administration in 1787–88 and in the field in 1796. Increasing size of armies led to even larger units in the nineteenth and twentieth centuries with corresponding divisions of ranks.

The ranks in the navy differ considerably from those of the army, originally with fewer distinctions between the commissioned officers, basically only lieutenant, captain and admiral, combined with non-commissioned but high-ranking specialists employed in the navigation and administration of the ship, such as master and purser. This simplicity, combined with the greater prestige and responsibility involved in commanding a ship compared to a company, explains why a captain in the navy outranks one in the army, being equal to a lieutenant colonel.

The different ranks were expressed in uniforms and distinctions and clear rules about command. In addition, the increasing size of armies necessitated an increasingly complex organization, partly military, partly civilian, as did also standardized uniforms[34] and arms, larger and more complex fortifications and the transition from armies living off the land to armies provisioned by the government. Moreover, leading large armies, composed of various kinds of forces, various categories of infantry and cavalry in addition to field artillery, scouts and irregular troops, increased the problem of command. Moving an army was relatively simple as long as it consisted of a few divisions, but became extremely complicated when it increased manifold. In the following period, warfare became increasingly scientific.[35] The main force behind this development was France. Admittedly, the French officers, who were all nobles, mostly believed that their birth gave them the necessary skills and resisted formal education.[36] However, the defeats in the Seven Years War were a stimulus to renewal.

The military reforms during the *ancien régime*, including the improvement of the artillery, were essential factors behind the later victories of the French army during the Revolutionary and Napoleonic Wars. Institutionally, the reforms resulted in the development of military academies and in the formation of a General Staff, a permanent high command responsible for all the military forces and for planning and directing the campaigns. The former grew up in most countries during the eighteenth century; the latter was introduced for the first time in Prussia between 1803 and 1809. It played a central part in Prussian and later German military organization, and was an important factor in the triumphs during the unification of Germany, 1863–70. Karl von Clausewitz, who wrote a famous book about war, was an officer in the Prussian General Staff. In contrast to Prussia, however, there was a strong anti-intellectualism in the British, Austrian and Russian armies,[37] and the French during the Revolution and under Napoleon found the demand for higher education from officers to be against the egalitarian ideas of the Revolution.

Parallel to this was a significant increase in and specialization of the civilian bureaucracy. Whereas the main reason for the formation and growth of bureaucracy in the Middle Ages had been internal administration, notably of justice, its greater growth in the early modern period was largely determined by military needs, equipping and provisioning armies and navies and collecting taxes and other levies to finance them. The increasing complexity of the bureaucracy is expressed both in an increasing number of ranks and in division into branches. Whereas the typical division between the king's local representatives in the Middle Ages was geographical, a royal representative who ruled a particular part of the country on the king's behalf: the sheriff in England, the *bailli* in France, the *Vogt* in Germany, now parallel officers with different duties were introduced. In particular, there was a division between military and civilian officers and separate courts of law manned by legal specialists, in some cases also, a separate police force. When the bureaucracy increased, however, the reason was not only the need for more personnel but also, in some countries, the sale of offices which also largely served to finance wars and military expenses.

Regarding war as the driving force of European state formation, Tilly observes that it worked in different ways. In mainly agrarian countries, taxation of a large population led to absolutism ('coercion'), whereas in urbanized and commercial ones, easy credit and contributions from wealthy merchants led to constitutional government ('capital'). The general importance of coercion is developed in Samuel Finer's theory of extraction and coercion. The ruler had to persuade his estates that it was necessary to vote for taxes to finance a permanent army. Once he had succeeded in this, he could use the army in an 'extraction-coercion cycle': the army could force the population to pay more taxes, which in turn resulted in an even larger army.[38] However, as several scholars have pointed out, Finer's 'extraction-coercion cycle' rarely worked in practice. There are very few examples of the army forcing the population to pay taxes.[39] It might possibly be used against the peasants but certainly not to force the nobles to pay, as its officers were mostly recruited from this class. In France and Prussia, the nobility had an exclusive right – in Prussia also duty – to commissions as officers and in most other countries the majority of them were recruited from this class. Thus, the political consequence of the expansion of armies was not to make the king independent of the nobility but on the contrary to integrate this class into the government of the realm. Admittedly, the way in which this was done marks an important difference between various regimes. In constitutional countries like England, the nobility and other wealthy people were represented in Parliament and could formally limit the king's power, whereas no such body existed in absolutist ones. Here the king at least in theory was free to decide without formal consensus from his subjects, but the importance of the nobles and other elites in practice made it difficult to act against their interests to any great extent. His problems with covering his military and other expenses were also significantly greater than Finer's theory would suggest.

Thus, the importance of war was neither that the state system was created in this way nor that the king gained a power monopoly by defeating his internal rivals. Warfare contributed to state formation primarily by mobilizing the aristocracy in the king's service and by necessitating drastically increased taxation and bureaucratization. This development can be traced back to the twelfth and thirteenth centuries but reached a climax during the fourth phase of the military transformation from the fifteenth to the eighteenth century.

The finances

In contrast to the Roman Empire and many contemporary ones, including the Arab and later Ottoman Empires, European kings had originally no right to tax their subjects; on the contrary, having to pay taxes was considered to be an expression of unfree status. The king was supposed to 'live from his own', meaning his landed estates, fees for various services, rights to various kinds of rent and payment for services he provided, for instance, jurisdiction. To this were added incomes from rights he had in his capacity as a feudal lord, such as to act as a guardian during the minority of a vassal or to decide about the marriage of a female heir. In other words, the king's incomes were largely of the same kind as those of other great landowners. With the development of a stronger monarchy from the twelfth and thirteenth centuries onwards, these incomes clearly became insufficient and had to be supplemented. This was the origin of taxation. The typical argument for the introduction of this was necessity: the country was threatened by external enemies; it was the king's duty to defend it; consequently, it was in everybody's interest to pay the necessary taxes. The Crusades were an important factor in developing this ideology. When a king promised to go on the Crusades, he got the pope's permission to tax the Church and of course also had a strong argument for demanding taxes from his other subjects. In practice, however, the money did not always go to the Holy Land, and beside, the king might argue that not only the Holy Land was in need of defence but also his own. Was not the king the Lord's anointed and did not the good Christian kingdoms of England or France also belong to God?[40]

The king of England repeatedly succeeded in convincing his subjects of this from the thirteenth and fourteenth century onwards. This led to the development of Parliament, which normally granted the king at least a part of the sum he asked for, but often in return for various concessions. In addition, the increasing importance of trade opened new possibilities. The king might levy sales tax or tolls on the import or export of various commodities or he might profit from his minting monopoly. As we have seen, Otto of Freising regarded the royal monopoly on minting as an expression of tyranny, but most kings managed to achieve such a monopoly from the thirteenth century onwards. In most cases, they restored the monopoly that had existed in Carolingian times, either abolishing the right of nobles and prelates to strike coins or forcing them to issue them in accordance with the king's own practice.

The practical problems in gaining these incomes were considerable.[41] Even today, with extensive and professional bureaucracies, computers, telecommunication, fast transport and masses of information about salaries, revenues, sales and profits, large sums escape taxation in the most advanced democracies, not to speak of the many countries without these benefits. Under medieval and early modern conditions, the problems were formidable. The simplest form of direct taxation was the hearth tax: every household had to pay a fixed sum. This was of course manifestly unjust, as a poor peasant would pay the same as a great lord. It also had the disadvantage from the king's point of view that the sum in question had to be very low. Nevertheless, in a country with a large population, such as France, it might yield a substantial sum. Another practice was to demand a percentage of the movable fortune, a tenth or a fifteenth, as was done in England. This in principle meant that wealthy people would pay more than poor ones, but, in practice, it was difficult to assess the individual fortune, and wealthy people of course had greater possibilities to cheat or bribe the tax officials.

Indirect taxes had some practical advantages over direct ones. The Republic of Genoa introduced a tax on import and export in 1274, which turned out to be very profitable. However, the republic of Genoa had only one port and a very small coastline, so import and export could easily be controlled. By contrast, the tax King Edward I introduced on the export of wool at about the same time created greater problems. England had a long coastline which was difficult to control. In the beginning, the tax yielded a very small profit, which eventually forced the government to limit export to a few ports and from 1363 only one for most of it, namely, Calais, conquered in 1347. In the following period, this tax was very profitable; without it, England would not have been able to fight the Hundred Years War. From the late fifteenth century, however, the export of wool declined, because of the development of the textile industry. Still, however, the speaker in the House of Lords is seated on a sack of wool, in memory of the importance of this commodity.

A tax on export sounds strange to modern ears; we are used to taxes on import, which serve to protect trade and production within the country. However, at this time, there was no concern for protection of trade and manufacture in the European kingdoms; only city states, governed by the merchants themselves, would conduct such a policy. For the king, the main purpose of the tax was financial, to get money for his own purposes, not economical. To the extent that the king interfered in the economy, his purpose was to secure sufficient provisions at favourable prices for the inhabitants of his country. Export of local products might endanger this, as it was likely to lead to higher prices. Therefore, the king of France forbade a number of exports between 1274 and 1305.

An important source of income for the states of southern Europe, France, the Spanish kingdoms and the Italian urban communes, was the tax on salt. Salt is a necessary addition to the diet for people living from cereals, which, although not rare, cannot be produced everywhere. Moreover, its production is capital-intensive. It is heavy and thus difficult to transport over land and it needs to be stored for three or four years before it is ready for consumption. Salt therefore became a monopoly of the Italian city communes and formed a cornerstone of their economy. Somewhat later, in 1259, Charles of Anjou introduced such a monopoly in his kingdom of Sicily and Southern Italy, after which it was introduced in Castile and in France in the fourteenth century.

Finally, kings could exploit their control of minting. The use of coinage was based on the idea that a coin contained a certain amount of gold or silver – mostly the latter – and thus could be used to buy some amount of merchandise. However, a coin differed from the same amount of metal in raw form; the king's stamp gave it an extra value. This, of course, meant some profit for the king, although relatively small. Far greater profit could be obtained by striking coins with metal of lower value than the official rate, which kings often did, particularly in periods of crisis. This led to inflation and of course to complaints from the people. Some kings, including Philip IV of France who practised this, nevertheless found that the problems caused by such complaints were less than those caused by direct taxation.

The various methods medieval kings used to finance their government are relatively well known to the historians. It is more difficult to detect their actual incomes. The annual English royal revenues in 1377–89 are estimated at 770,000 florins (one florin = 6,99 gram gold), the French in 1418 at 2.6 million, those of Burgundy under Philip the Bold (1363–1404) at 365,000 and those of Hungary in the second half of the fifteenth century at around 1 million. The high revenues of Hungary may be explained partly by the gold mines in this country and partly by its expansion during the reign of Mathias Corvinus (1458–90). The relative financial strength of some polities at the end of the fourteenth century is estimated in the following way: Papacy = 1, France = 15, England = 4.5, Burgundy 2, Sicily = little more than 1, Pisa = little less than 1. Most striking here are the low incomes of the papacy, which will be discussed later, combined with the high ones of small units like Sicily and Pisa. The wealthiest Italian city states, like Venice, Genoa, Florence and Milan, no doubt must have had considerably more than Pisa. Actually, the revenues of Venice are estimated to have been 60 per cent higher than those of France in the mid-fifteenth century.[42] The proportion between France and England corresponds approximately to the size of the population of the two countries; that of France may have been up to four times that of England. Later, as we shall see, the size of the incomes changed drastically in favour of England.

Absolute numbers give only a limited picture of the kings' finances; we also need to know their expenses, how easily the money became available and the possibility of credit. As we have seen, the general impression of late medieval and early modern kings is that they were permanently short of money, as illustrated by the numerous bankruptcies, mutinous armies and wars and expeditions that had to be broken off because of lack of money. On the other hand, some of these features also illustrate the strength of the kings. Charles V, Francis I and Philip II could continue borrowing money despite their bankruptcies; they had numerous ways of rewarding or harming their creditors. For a long time, they could continue to spend large sums on warfare as well as festivities and building projects. In the long run, however, from the seventeenth century onwards, even the mightiest princes, the emperor and the kings of France and Spain, came to face serious problems. Historians have for a long time discussed the Crisis of the Seventeenth Century, which for a period marked a reversal of the recovery after the plagues from the mid-fourteenth century onwards. A likely explanation is the expansion of the state, mainly the costs of warfare but also the building projects, lavish courts and the growth of the bureaucracy.[43]

Towards a monopoly of violence: the royal courts of law

At about the same time as King Charles VII chased the English out of France, on 17 April 1453, Georg von Puchheim declared a feud against the Holy Roman Emperor Frederick III.[44] Georg had for twelve years served as a councillor in the regency government of Austria, fought in many wars as a mercenary captain, had spent large sums on fortifications and suffered much harm from the emperor's enemies. Altogether, the emperor owed him £24,000 for his services and as compensation for his losses. Having in vain claimed this sum, he finally resorted to open feud, issuing a formal letter to the emperor to this effect and informing a number of prominent princes of his intentions. The emperor's reaction to this was not to condemn Georg as a rebel and traitor, but to accept the challenge and prepare to defend himself. Contrary to modern ideas of the matter, Georg's action was not rebellion. He had no intention of replacing the emperor as ruler, nor of changing the government in any other way. He simply wanted his money back and saw no other option than open feud to achieve this.

In most countries, feuds were lawful and acceptable means for nobles to achieve their rights. They were not banned in France until the first half of the fourteenth century and then as a temporary measure to unite the country against attacks from England during the Hundred Years War. England forms an exception in this respect, for here a system of public justice and strict rules against feuds and revenge developed from the twelfth century onwards, which reduced the feuds, although it did not eliminate them.[45] The same applies to Norway, where feuds were banned from the thirteenth century, whereas they were allowed in Denmark until 1683. Nevertheless, it was no longer acceptable in most countries to use such means against the king in the fifteenth century. In France, the king's vassals normally avoided direct confrontation with the king even in the eleventh and twelfth centuries.[46] Generally, rebellions did occur in most countries but then took the form of leagues of nobles claiming to reform the government and abolish abuse and tyranny. Georg's challenge to the emperor is therefore a specifically German phenomenon, reflecting the fact that this country actually consisted of a number of petty principalities under the formal authority of the emperor.

A little more than hundred years earlier, in 1322, a number of English nobles, led by Thomas, Earl of Lancaster, rebelled against the very unpopular King Edward II.[47] The rebellion was quickly put down and the leaders taken captive. Based on earlier precedent, they probably expected to be heavily fined, but the punishment was far worse. They were executed by being hanged, drawn and quartered and having all their estates confiscated. This form of execution was painful as well as humiliating. The victim was first hanged, then cut down before he died, disembowelled and finally cut into four parts. Then his body was burned and the ashes spread. Thus, the punishment symbolized the utter destruction of the king's enemies. Only Thomas of Lancaster received the privilege of death by beheading due to his high rank.[48] According to recent scholarship on this subject, the rules underlying the new treason laws were not new: rebels and assassins had always

been at the king's mercy.[49] However, before this period, leniency had been practised, at least towards noble criminals, according to the rules of chivalry that had
developed in the post-Carolingian period.

Whereas the Carolingians normally punished rebellious nobles by execution or
blinding,[50] this changed in the post-Carolingian period, under the Ottonians in
Germany from 919 onwards (after the interlude with Conrad I, 911–19) and the
Capetians in France from 987.[51] Aristocratic prisoners were normally released after
payment of a ransom, while public humiliation (*deditio*) replaced execution as the
punishment for the kings' enemies. The introduction of this kind of chivalry has
been explained partly by the weakening of the monarchy after the Carolingian
period and partly by the changes in military technology. The aristocracy had
become stronger and the distance between the king and his leading vassals was
reduced. Fear of revenge therefore prevented the king from executing noble rebels,
while the introduction of heavy armour made it less likely that a noble would be
killed immediately in battle, and instead made it more profitable to capture and
ransom him than to kill him. However, despite the fact that the military technology was the same in Italy, captured enemies were treated much more harshly there,
notably in Norman Sicily, but also in the rest of the country,[52] probably because
the aristocracy was a less exclusive class in the south than in the north.

The new practice was clearly inspired by the Roman Laws of Treason, the
Lex Iulia maiestatis and the *Lex quisquis*, which had both a theoretical and a
practical influence on the law in England, France and other countries. The direct
initiative to applying these laws most probably came from the professional lawyers in the king's service. Their introduction led to strong reactions from the
aristocracy and the practice of them may have been one of the causes of the
internal conflicts and the depositions of Edward II and Richard II.[53] The Law of
Treason was passed by Parliament in 1352, which was a compromise between
the king and the aristocracy.[54] The Wars of the Roses in England, fought
intermittently between 1455 and 1485, illustrate the rules applied to internal
conflicts. In contrast to the war in France, there was no wasting of the land and
ordinary soldiers were normally released when taken captive. By contrast, captive
aristocratic leaders were executed, instead of being released against ransom. They
were traitors to the king their captors regarded as the lawful ruler of the country.[55] The Law of Treason was also introduced in France at about the same time
as in England but was practised more leniently because the king could not afford
to alienate influential nobles.[56] The stricter practice of the Law of Treason thus
has a counterpart in the rules of chivalry towards external enemies who owed
loyalty to another king, as mentioned in Chapter 1.

The introduction of the Law of Treason and the stricter practice of it form one
aspect of the increasing involvement of the king in the administration of justice.
While this was in principle delegated from the king under Charlemagne, the
decline of the monarchy in the following period gradually divided the power in
this and other fields between a number of lords of various rank. Cases between
nobles were normally solved by arbitration, often preceded by or combined with

open feud, whereas those between commoners might be adjudicated by their superiors. Early medieval justice, dealing with matters that could not be solved by arbitration, was mainly formal. First, the system was based on formal rules and procedures and relied on the testimony of formally appointed witnesses or oath-helpers. Laws mainly dealt with procedure; they did not lay down rules for what was right or wrong. There was no distinction between fact and law. The process was accusatorial; it was a conflict between two parties, where the defendant had to refute the claim of the plaintiff, not vice versa, as in modern law. The means of such a refutation was normally compurgation; the defendant had to swear either alone or aided by a number of co-jurors, the more jurors, the more serious the accusation. In some particularly serious cases, he or she might also have to undergo an ordeal, by carrying or walking on hot iron or by fishing an object out of a boiling kettle. In addition, trial by battle was used, particularly in conflicts between prominent men. In principle, all cases were between private parties. There was no distinction between civil and public law. Thus, a murder case would be dealt with in the same way as a dispute over property and would be settled by the killer or his kinsmen paying compensation to an injured party. There was also a thin line between legal and extra-legal disputes. Powerful men were not necessarily bound to bring their cases before the court, they might prefer to let arms decide.

The changes that took place from the twelfth century onwards were caused by three factors: (1) the reception of Roman Law; (2) the development of canon law; and (3) the increasing power of the central government of the kingdoms and the Church.

The Romans had a long tradition of law going back to early republican times, which continued in the late republic and during the empire. In addition, the emperors issued edicts that were legally binding. In the mid-sixth century, the Emperor Justinian decided to create a law code based on all previous legal material. The result was a collection in three parts, the *Institutes*, the *Codex* and the *Digest*, which was officially promulgated in 534. A fourth part, the *Novellae*, consisting of Justinian's own legislation, was added later. The *Institutes* were intended as an introduction for law students, containing the most important laws and principles. The *Codex* contained the laws of the emperor, while the *Digest* contained excerpts from leading jurists. This was by far the largest part and the most important one for the later legal development. The whole collection was given the force of law by Justinian. As the king of Germany was also Roman Emperor and other kings also in some respects claimed to be Justinian's successors, Justinian's Laws came in various ways to influence European legislation and legal practice in the Middle Ages and the early modern period.

Apart from its concrete rules, Roman law was important for the general development of legal method. Most of the texts represented in the *Digest* were not general or philosophical treatises but decisions of concrete issues. However, the numerous comments in schools and universities resulted in more explicit rules, while at the same time, they laid the foundation for a new juridical method. The clearest expression of this is Gratian's *Decretum*, a systematic collection of canon law from the mid-twelfth century. Whereas similar collections earlier had mostly consisted of excerpts from various authorities in a chronological sequence, Gratian begins with posing a problem and then adduces statements by various authorities which had dealt with it previously and which seemingly had come to different conclusions. Through comparison and interpretation of these sources, he then ends up with a solution that dissolves the apparent contradiction and lays down the principles that are to be followed. Gratian's *Decretum* in practice came to be regarded as valid law in the following period, although it was never formally authorized by the pope. It also formed the model for later papal legislation, listed below, which also had a close connection to decisions in individual cases.

Both Roman and canon law in various ways served as sources of inspiration for royal legislation. The first example of this is the Emperor Frederick II's *Liber Augustalis* or Constitutions of Melfi from 1231 for the Kingdom of Sicily. This was followed by *Las Siete Partidas* (The Seven Parts), issued by King Alfonso X of Castile (c. 1265) and the *Code of the Realm* for Norway (1274–76), issued by King Magnus VI, nick-named the Law-mender. Sweden had its Code of the Realm in 1350, while Denmark only got a law for the whole country in 1683. By contrast, neither England nor France had a code of law in the Middle Ages; France only got it in 1805 and England still has not got one. Instead, the English and French kings issued statutes regarding concrete issues. Such statutes, together with the precedent from previous legal decisions formed the English Common Law. The reign of Edward I (1272–1307) was particularly important in this respect. More laws were issued during the first thirteen years of his reign than in any period before the reign of William IV (1830–37).[57] Edward is also often referred to as the English Justinian. By contrast, the weakening of the imperial power in Germany prevented the emergence of a common law for this country; instead, Roman Law increasingly formed the basis for legislation and jurisdiction.

The practical result of this development was the introduction of royal courts of law and legal experts educated at the universities, which also changed legal procedure. The crucial period in this in England was the reign of Henry II (1154–89). He developed the practice of *writs*, known already in the Anglo-Saxon period. A writ was a short, formulaic message from the king to a local official ordering him to deal with a particular legal case according to a standard procedure. If not, the king himself would settle the case. Originally, English tenants – who formed the majority of the population – were to be judged or have their conflicts adjudicated in manorial courts. Some of them also had the possibility of appealing to the king. Eventually, the king's courts largely replaced local ones. In addition to the various courts of law, the king and his council as well as Parliament served as courts of appeal. A considerable part of the business of Parliament was to deal with such matters. Finally, special rules applied for cases involving the king or the royal government: impeachment and attainder, in which the amount of evidence needed for a conviction was less than in normal cases and the defendant's possibility to refute the accusations was reduced or abolished. Impeachment was used by the royal government against Members of Parliament or other subjects, whereas attainder was used by Parliament against the king's councillors.

An important step towards a new administration of justice was the abolition of the ordeal by the decree of the Fourth Lateran Council in 1215 which forbade clerics to consecrate the iron or other instruments used to perform the ritual. As soon as this was respected, ordeals were impossible to carry out and they gradually disappeared. Intellectually, the ban against ordeals might seem to be the result of more secular thinking, but a more important reason for its disappearance was probably the idea that it is not lawful for humans to try to force God to answer their questions.[58]

The abolition of ordeals created a gap, in England as well as in other countries. The English solution to this was trial by jury (from Latin *jurati* – who have sworn), consisting of local men. The background for this was the common practice in England as well as in other countries to examine local people as witnesses. Gradually, this changed into the modern jury. There was – and still is – a distinction between the grand or presenting jury, which was necessary to start a process, and the trial jury, which gave the verdict. The grand jury has its counterpart in the summons of local people in canon law who were asked if they knew of a crime and whose affirmation or at least partial affirmation was necessary for a process to begin. The trial jury was originally supposed to base its verdict on previous knowledge of what had happened, but gradually developed into a court to which witnesses were presented and which gave the final verdict, which had to be unanimous. Thus, no confession by the accused was necessary for conviction. He or she had been found guilty by equals and had to suffer the appropriate punishment. Greater trust was thus placed in a committee of ordinary people, equal or approximately equal in status to the accused, in England than in a professional magistrate on the Continent.

A similar practice developed in Scandinavia, the Low Countries and parts of Germany. In France and southern Europe, however, the solution was a stronger influence of professionals in jurisdiction. Parallel to this, a clearer distinction between civil and criminal justice began to emerge. In the twelfth and thirteenth centuries, the Church introduced public justice, based on the idea that certain acts were offences against God, society, and the social order and had to be punished. It was not only damage done to an individual or kindred that had to be repaired or compensated. Thus, a concept of crime evolved and, beyond that, the idea of subjective guilt, which meant that not only the act itself but its background and the criminal's intentions had to be taken into account. Crimes committed as the result of weakness, without knowledge of the seriousness of the act or under duress, should be punished mildly, whereas those done out of haughtiness or malice should be punished severely. This is not to suggest that the distinction between intentional and unintentional acts was unknown in the previous period, but such a distinction was more difficult to apply when there was no judge above the parties.

These changes in the understanding of crime and legal evidence necessitated changes in the administration of justice. Skill and education were needed both to evaluate the evidence presented in court when it was no longer formal, and to mete out punishment in accordance with motives and circumstances in criminal cases. A court of law also needed authority to intervene against powerful men in local society. Consequently, the administration of justice was professionalized. This applied above all to the ecclesiastical courts of law, where the bishop was the highest judge. He often had a university education in law and in addition often delegated his judicial powers to officers with a similar education, to his deputy (Latin *officialis*) or to provosts or archdeacons. However, ecclesiastical courts continued to use local people, mostly as witnesses but to some extent also as judges.

Even after the thirteenth century, large parts of France were governed by local princes and lords who also controlled the courts, although appeals to the king and the Parliament in Paris eventually became a possibility.[59] French jurisdiction was based on a combination of local custom and learned law. Thus, institutions similar to the jury were not unknown in France. Eventually, however, increasing influence from canon law reduced the role of such institutions and replaced them with learned specialists. French and continental law in general also developed a clear distinction between civil cases, where two parties disagreed about an issue, and criminal ones, which were prosecuted on behalf of the Church or society. Concerning the latter, the inquisitional process was developed in this twelfth and thirteenth centuries, particularly in order to trace and condemn heretics.

Although a clearer distinction between criminal and civil jurisdiction did develop from the twelfth century onwards, systematic persecution of crime was not common in the Middle Ages; nor was there any police in the modern sense. In many places, even the adjudication of murder necessitated an individual plaintiff. Thus, in England public prosecution was instituted as late as in 1487 through the Star Chamber Act. Before that, legal process always had to be initiated by individual complaint, even if public peace had been broken.[60] For a long time, ecclesiastical courts were also reluctant to open a case unless there was a complaint by an individual. Originally, canon law also had very strict demands of evidence to declare a verdict of guilty. Either the accused had to confess or two eye witnesses, independent of each other, were needed.

To fight heresy, the Church established a separate court of law, the Inquisition, which developed an entirely new form of process. Here a professional magistrate, educated in law, both led the examination and passed the sentence. He examined the accused as well as the witnesses separately to arrive at the truth. In order to guarantee that those who were examined, the accused as well as the witnesses, should tell the truth exactly as they knew it, neither of them was informed about the content of the accusation. The only concession to the accused in this respect was the permission to name enemies, so that the judge himself might eliminate their testimony. The judge reached his verdict on the basis of this evidence, but his discretion was nevertheless insufficient for full conviction. For this, a confession was necessary. If the judge found that there was strong evidence against the accused, he was allowed to use torture to force a confession. The inquisitional process was gradually taken over by a number of secular courts. It was introduced in the Holy Roman Empire by Charles V in 1532, in the Netherlands by Philip II in 1570 and in France by Francis I in 1539 and further developed by Louis XIV in 1670.[61]

The great transition to public justice took place in the sixteenth century. Now governments actively sought to trace and punish crime and made use of the inquisitional process for this purpose. At the same time, punishments generally became stricter. Punishments were intended to prevent crime; public executions, often with extreme cruelty, aimed at warning others against committing the same crime. Louis XIV's edict of 1670 lists a whole series of death penalties whose severity corresponds strictly to the seriousness of the crime committed, from hanging or decapitation to being burnt alive, broken on the wheel or tied to horses and torn apart. To each of these, separate punishments might be added before the execution, such as having the hand or tongue pierced or cut off. The execution of Damiens, who had attacked Louis XV with a knife, shows the maximum severity: he was burnt with sulphur and pierced by red-hot tongs on his way to the place of execution, where he was tied to horses and torn apart.[62] Of course, an attack on the Royal Majesty was the worst crime that could be imagined at the time. At the same time, there was some room for mercy in practice. The law was not always applied in its full severity; the judge might use his discretion and mete out a milder punishment if he found some attenuating circumstances or detected strong repentance in the accused. Thus, there were around thirty capital offences in England around 1640 which had increased to at least 200 around 1790, but during the same period, there was also a significant decline in the number of people who were executed.[63] At the Châtelet in Paris, 9–10 per cent of those convicted were sentenced to death between 1755 and 1785, but as many as 15 per cent in Flanders in 1721–30, which was reduced to 5 per cent in 1781–90.

The crimes punished most severely in the sixteenth and seventeenth centuries were heresy, witchcraft and sexual crimes, in addition to crimes typically committed by people outside established society, notably armed robbery. In addition, vagrants and the homeless were subject to suspicion and easily arrested. By contrast, violent crime as the result of conflicts between ordinary, respectable people was punished more leniently and more easily pardoned.[64] Women were also mostly punished less severely than men. They also were more rarely convicted; only around 20 per cent of the criminals were women.[65] Paradoxically, from a modern point of view, the increased severity was combined with care for the criminal who should be made to atone for his sin and thus avoid eternal damnation.[66] The logic is expressed in numerous sources, for instance, in *The King's Mirror*, composed in Norway in the thirteenth century. Here the Father, who is the author's voice in this work, explains to his son, who asks the questions, that the death penalty is actually a benefit for the condemned because God does not punish the same crime twice; thus, suffering in this world protects against eternal damnation.[67] However, the criminal must also be made to repent. Consequently, it was important for him to confess his crime. This may form part of the explanation for the use of torture, in addition to the need for being absolutely sure of the guilt of the accused before he is executed. It was believed that a guilty person would be more likely to confess under torture than an innocent one. The importance of the confession is further illustrated by the fact that the accused had to read his confession aloud before the execution and of course, that a priest was present at the scaffold to console him. In the reports from the execution of Damiens, it is mentioned that Damiens, who was known to have been a great swearer, never swore during his suffering but that he prayed to God for help and that he was all the time consoled by a priest. His suffering would thus seem to have prepared him for eternal salvation.

Thus, torture became a relatively normal practice in criminal cases on the Continent, while it was not used in ordinary jurisdiction in England, only in cases of treason or conspiracy against the government. In addition, torture might be used to force the defendant to accept trial by jury, which was in principle voluntary. However, despite cruel punishments and judicial procedures that seem to have offered the accused little protection, the system was not arbitrary; there were general laws that were applied in criminal as well as civilian cases. From the point of view of the upper and middle classes, the severity of the system and the lack of protection for the accused might seem less menacing that it would do for us. They would hardly risk torture and severe punishments but might regard the severity as protection against brigands and dangerous people. Parallel to the changes in judicial procedure in the early modern period was the introduction of an organized police which took place in France in the seventeenth century. In this and the following period, French cities, notably Paris, were safer and better organized than English ones; eighteenth-century London was notorious for crime and violence. During an anti-Catholic riot in 1780, ten times more property was destroyed in London than in Paris during the whole French Revolution.[68] Only in the first half of the nineteenth century was a proper police force introduced in Britain. The name 'bobby' for the British police officer alludes to Sir Robert Peel who introduced the reform as Home Secretary, 1822–27.[69]

An apparent exception to the rule of law are the *lettres de cachet* (sealed letters) in France, issued by the king and ordering the imprisonment, confinement to a monastery or exile of a named person, without trial and the possibility of appeal. Such letters could be issued at the initiative of the king or the royal government, but were usually the result of private initiatives, normally from the victim's parents or relatives. They might be used against sons or daughters who wanted to marry against the wish of the family or against relatives who in some way or another might shame their families. Count Mirabeau, who had himself been a victim of the practice at the initiative of his father, condemned it with great eloquence at the beginning of the Revolution. The reason for Mirabeau's imprisonment was his love affair as a young officer with a woman to whom his colonel was attached, which led to a great scandal. Although the *lettres de cachet* were rarely used for political purposes, the practice is hardly compatible with the rule of law. However, a detailed study from the district of Caen nevertheless concludes that it was less arbitrary than it would immediately seem.[70] The main aim of the practice was to avoid scandal; in some cases, it was applied to people who would normally have been sentenced by a court of law, as in the case of a family member who had forged coins, a crime punishable by death, which in this way was changed to life imprisonment. The royal government demanded extensive documentation and consent from the whole family and, in the cases of marriage, there were strict criteria for preventing it in this way.

Most countries on the Continent developed in the same way as France, with mainly professional judges, whereas Scandinavia in the Middle Ages shows greater similarity to England. Both in Denmark and Norway, the judges were normally committees of local men, similar to English juries, in Denmark either permanent committees or committees appointed by the plaintiff. Norwegian juries were selected from the local assemblies. In both countries, royal officials, in some cases with professional legal education, increased their importance from the thirteenth century onwards.

Until recently, the development described above was described as a transition from chaos to order. Thus, to Strayer, the introduction of royal justice from the twelfth and thirteenth centuries onwards represents a major step in the direction of an ordered society in Europe.[71] The decline of royal power and the rise of a large number of nobles who controlled the surrounding countryside from their castles in the post-Carolingian period have been regarded as the breakdown of social order and widespread anarchy, with dire consequences for the weak and unarmed: clerics, merchants and peasants. More recent research, often based on analogies from fieldwork by social anthropologists in Third World countries, has modified this picture, claiming that the conflicts were after all limited and often ended in a compromise and that the descriptions of violence in the sources mostly stem from clerical writers hostile to the secular aristocracy who exaggerated the chaos.[72] Seemingly arbitrary acts of violence were mostly carefully calculated steps towards making the adversary come to terms. Moreover, learned law was not the only means to solve conflicts; early medieval law, based on arbitration, was also able to do so. Here the main question was not which of the parties had the better claim but how to reach a solution that satisfied both parties. A conflict in the early Middle Ages was first and foremost about honour; it was shameful for nobles to have to give up a claim, in the same way as for the king himself when fighting another king. Moreover, honour was an incentive for nobles to fight feuds in the same way as for kings to fight wars. Much diplomacy was therefore needed from the arbitrators to find a solution that would save the honour of both parties. It must be added that this consideration was still important when powerful men were involved, also after the rise of royal courts of law.

There is no doubt some justice in these arguments. On the other hand, they are no longer supported by analogies from contemporary Third World countries, which have recently been shown to be extremely violent.[73] It must also be added that European society in the early Middle Ages was significantly more stratified than the Third World societies often used for comparison; only small-scale societies like Iceland – which has often been used in discussions about feuds – conform to the non-European pattern. Feuds therefore did not primarily take place between individuals who fought one another, but between armies led by nobles, which killed or plundered the enemy's peasants.[74] Casual references to such plundering occur frequently in contemporary historical writings.

The case of Acharias of Marmande in the Noyers region of France around 1074 may serve as an example. Acharias had been at war against a union of powerful lords who had destroyed his castle and taken his land away from him. Acharias sought an alliance with another lord and conducted a kind of guerrilla warfare against his enemies. One night, he raided the hills of Grisay and attacked a house where some men were assembled. When they took refuge in a cave under the house, Acharias set fire to the house which burnt down and killed the people underneath, men, women and children. Shortly afterwards, Acharias was taken captive and confronted with his sin. He then appealed to the Abbot and monks of Saint Mary of Noyers to seek peace for him and donated land to the monastery to achieve this. Killing by burning was considered aggravating in the Middle Ages, as was also killing women and children, but Acharias' main problem was that it turned out that some of his victims were nobles. Had they been ordinary peasants, he would hardly have had any problem.[75]

Nor is it likely that a military aristocracy would regard war or feud as a necessary evil but rather as a good sport and a means to gain honour and renown – in a similar way as kings did in this and the following period. Further evidence of the problems caused by the conflicts include protest movements from the people, supported by the clergy, demanding cession or at least limitation of the fighting. Rules about this were also introduced in the form of the Peace or the Truce of God which was introduced in various countries in the eleventh and twelfth centuries. Clergy, women, peasants and merchants should be protected from warfare and feuds were to be forbidden on certain days, notably Sundays and religious holidays. This was gradually extended in some areas to include all weeks from Thursday to Sunday.[76] As we shall see, the available statistical evidence about homicide also indicates that the early Middle Ages must have been a very violent period.

This does not mean that the references to conflict solution by arbitration and negotiation are wrong or irrelevant; such institutions clearly existed, but their ability to reach peaceful solutions depended on the willingness of the warring parties. To take the example from the Icelandic sagas: the conflicts always reached a solution but not until some people had been killed – normally the same number on both sides. Admittedly, there would not have been a saga unless some people had been killed but the general point nevertheless remains: peace is more likely to occur when it is compulsory than when it is optional.

The expansion of royal justice was clearly in the king's interest as it increased both his power and his incomes. However, it is unlikely that he would have succeeded if the rest of society were opposed to it. He received support from the Church and the popular peace movements. Merchants became increasingly important from the twelfth century onwards and were clearly interested in a central power to keep law and order, as they were travelling over long distances and could hardly rely on local power. The clerics had their own, ecclesiastical courts, although they often made use of royal courts as well, while the merchants were in a weak position towards the aristocracy and were likely to seek aid from the king.

In countries where the king increased his power during the high Middle Ages, such as England and France, there was a tendency for royal courts to increase their business at the cost of local ones. This was a logical development as soon as the royal courts became strong enough to overrule verdicts from local ones.

Concerning the general need for royal justice, Frederick Cheyette comments that 'there is no reason to believe that individuals (any more than collectives called "nations") prefer objective neutrality to partiality in their own favour'. Cheyette's point here is not that the introduction of the ideal of objective justice was the result of force but the importance of arbitration in the early period: both parties had to be satisfied before the case could be solved. When formal public justice and royal courts of law were introduced in the southern regions of France in the mid-thirteenth century that he has examined, he explains it by social changes. New landowners had established themselves in the region, partly as a consequence of the war against the Albigensians, and, as newcomers, were less inclined to accept local arbitration. Moreover, there is hardly a total change from the old to the new practice. On the top of society, the king's arbitration was still for a long time an important factor. The concern with honour in aristocratic circles included the duty to take revenge for insults and killings of relatives, which means that members of the class might easily regard it as a humiliation to be forced to submit to the judgment of a royal court. Eventually, however, the king's increasing authority made it more difficult to oppose his decisions.[77] Concerning the general point about the choice between objective justice and partially in one's own favour, most of us would probably still prefer the latter, but the point is that we cannot have it and then objective justice is preferable to partiality in the other party's favour.

It is also clear that the growth of royal jurisdiction was the result of initiatives from below rather than above; an increasing number of litigants brought their cases before the royal courts of law.[78] In addition, it must be pointed out that an even stricter public justice was introduced in the city republics, for instance, in Florence, where Giano della Bella's reforms in the 1290s were intended to curb the violence of the aristocracy. This need for public justice was largely caused by the social and economic development during the high Middle Ages: a larger population, clearing of new land, increased agricultural production, greater economic surplus, urbanization and increased communication between various parts of the realm created new conflicts that were less likely to be solved through local arbitration.

This also affected the aristocracy. The right to conduct feuds remained a noble privilege for a long time after the introduction of public justice but was eventually abolished and replaced by litigation.[79] Nevertheless, duels were practised until the nineteenth or early twentieth century, particularly among the nobility but also to some extent by others. On the one hand, this was forbidden by the government, on the other, it was considered a duty among gentlemen to the extent that a man who refused a challenge was excluded from polite society. Although the members of the aristocracy would normally try to preserve their rights regarding local jurisdiction, it was in practice difficult for local courts to compete with the central ones when the litigants had the opportunity to appeal to a higher court. The loser at the local courts would then be likely to bring his case before the royal one and eventually, there would be a tendency to bring it there in the first place. This was of course in the king's interest, as settling cases in the Middle Ages was normally profitable, in addition to strengthening the king's power. However, it was also in the interest of the litigants, as demonstrated by the enormous increase in cases brought before the royal courts of law from the thirteenth century onwards. Thus, in England and to a lesser extent in other countries, the royal courts had largely replaced local ones by the end of the Middle Ages. The king had increased his power within his realm, not primarily by defeating rebellious nobles but by settling issues between an increasing number of litigants.

Since the 1970s, a series of studies have shown a decline in homicide in Western Europe from between 20 and 100 per 100,000 in the thirteenth century to 19 in the sixteenth, 11 in the seventeenth and 3.2 in the eighteenth century, with a further decline to around 1 in 1950.[80] The numbers are of course uncertain, particularly for the earliest period, but the general trend is likely to be correct. No statistics are available from before the thirteenth century but there is little to suggest that the rate then was lower; in all likelihood, it was higher. Although the sources, particularly from the early period, are often scanty, they all point in the same direction. It also seems clear that the decline must be related to the growth of royal government and justice, including stricter punishment and more thorough prosecution of crimes.[81] However, there is no exact correlation between the severity of punishment and the increase of the judicial administration, on the one hand, and suppression of homicide, on the other. The lowest rates are to be found in England and the Netherlands, both of which had less developed prosecution of crime than France, Spain and Italy. As we have seen, England even lacked a proper police force until the 1820s. However, in both these countries, there was a close relationship between the authorities and the local population, combined with relatively effective courts of law, which may have served to prevent crime and replace violence; the concern for honour might have been expressed in the numerous cases of libel brought before the courts rather than in violence. Generally, the existence of courts of law to solve disputes and the gradual recognition of them as an alternative to the use of arms may have been as equally important as prosecution and punishment.

Religious and cultural changes may also have played a part. The typical medieval and early modern homicide took place in or near a tavern or at a drinking party and was the result of a quarrel between two, usually younger, men. What was at stake was honour; an insult would diminish a man in the eyes of his equals and could only be atoned by violence; not necessarily killing, but this was often the result when both parties used knives. It has been suggested that the Reformation may have had some importance in limiting this kind of violence by focusing on internal values rather than honour and esteem from others. In particular, as we shall see, the close communities created by Calvinism may have worked in this direction. However, as the decline of violence is approximately the same in the Southern as in the Northern Netherlands in the sixteenth century, the Counter-

Reformation may have had the same effect, at least in some places. There is also a long-term decline of violence in the upper classes, which were the most violent part of the population in the Middle Ages, while they had been replaced by the lower classes in this respect in the nineteenth and twentieth centuries. In addition to religion, the development of bourgeois values in the seventeenth and eighteenth century may have been a factor. The development of trade and business, particularly in the eighteenth century, led to new ideals of behaviour, self-control and rational calculation replacing passions and honour.[82]

Whatever the exact idea of the relationship between the king and the law, there is no doubt about the fundamental importance of law in European culture and state formation. Law and justice were main tasks for the state. By controlling justice and punishment and becoming the source of law, the monarchy took a great step towards institutionalization. In accordance with Roman law as well as ecclesiastical doctrine, the king holds an office which makes him a different man and makes assault on him a far more serious crime than the same act against anyone else.

In addition to its practical consequences for solving conflicts and convicting and punishing criminals, the development of law in the twelfth and thirteenth centuries has been regarded as a major intellectual revolution. Law was understood as a coherent body, an integrated system but developing over time. This development was believed to have an internal logic; changes were not only adaptations of old to new, but formed a pattern. The historicity of law was linked to a concept of its supremacy over the political authorities. Although the monarch might make law, he might not do so arbitrarily; he was bound by the existing law until he had changed it and he was bound by the main principles of the legal tradition. Finally, Western law was characterized by coexistence and competition between various legal systems.[83] Moreover, it was to be practised by a community of experts who had to apply its paragraphs to particular cases in accordance with legal precedence and other relevant paragraphs. The law of corporations thus became an important factor in the development of business; the modern limited company has its background in medieval doctrine, although it took some time to develop. Parallel to this, merchant law developed and, as we shall see, became one of the comparative advantages of Europeans during the Great Discoveries.

The statistics about the decline of homicide gives a similar picture as that of warfare: the greatest change seems to have taken place in the seventeenth and particularly eighteenth century. Thus, Morris may be right that there is a connection between external war and internal peace; the state became more eager to interfere in internal conflicts when fighting external enemies. On the other hand, there is more evidence of state formation in the early period in the legal than in the military field. Significant changes took place in legislation, new legal methods and public justice and courts of law were introduced and there was an enormous increase in issues brought before them. Europe was far from peaceful in the thirteenth century but there is nevertheless a considerable distance from the chaos depicted by Elias, Tilly and Morris.

The central administration

A miniature painting in a register of gifts to the diocese of Oviedo in the kingdom of Asturias in northern Spain from the 1120s gives a glimpse of an early medieval court. The king is surrounded by the queen with two servant women, a bishop, two clerical scribes and three knights. The court at this time was an undifferentiated group of the king's friends and relatives who served both as a court in the later sense of a ceremonial and representative assembly and as a council and central administration. The presence of the queen may seem an indication of this. Whereas in the Merovingian period, the distinction between the queen and the king's mistresses had been vague, it became more clearly defined in the following period. Only the queen's offspring could claim the throne. Her higher status was also expressed in that she was crowned in the same way as the king.

On the other hand, she was also often in an exposed position. With the sharper distinction between the king and the aristocracy from the twelfth and thirteenth century onwards, the king usually married the daughter of another king, which meant that the queen was always a foreigner, arriving very young, normally in her teens, without knowing the language and culture of her new country. In some cases, her marriage might be a means to end a war against this country, which meant that she might easily be suspected of disloyalty to her new homeland. Her main duty was to produce an heir, not to participate in the government of the realm, but depending on her personal qualities, she might also play a part in politics. At least, if she had her husband's confidence, she might be an important link between him and the many people who sought access to him, or she might intercede for people in trouble, as Queen Philippa is said to have done on behalf of the burghers of Calais in 1347. In practice, however, she might have considerable political influence; there was no sharp distinction between the court and the bureaucracy. In many cases, the queen's court – she usually had her own – became a cultural centre.[84]

It has been pointed out that women were consistently barred from all positions of authority in medieval and early modern Europe; all employed or elected officers, from army commanders and royal councillors to jury members and local administrators, were men.[85] However, access to many of the most important positions in society at the time was based hereditary claims or personal links. Women might inherit the throne or great estates or get access to them by marriage. Although the husband mostly governed the common property during his lifetime, his widow might take over after his death.

The success or failure of these queens of course depended on their personal qualities, but some of them rank as among the most important European rulers, such as Isabella of Castile, Elisabeth of England and Maria Theresa of Austria. Margareta of Denmark, who founded the union between the three Scandinavian countries in the late fourteenth century, also belongs in this category, although strictly speaking, she never held royal office herself. She acted first on behalf of her son and then, after his death, her nephew, who was also a minor, but continued to do so until her death, long after he had reached majority. Margareta illustrates an important phenomenon; the dowager queen ruling during her son's minority. This was not the general rule, an alternative might be another member of the dynasty or one or more prominent nobles, but there are several examples of queens acting in this capacity. Queen Agnes ruled Germany on behalf of her son Henry IV but was later deposed and replaced by two archbishops. Blanche of Castille ruled France in a critical phase during her son Louis IX's minority and suppressed several aristocratic rebellions.[86]

The titles of the five leading officials around the king give a further impression of the combination of household and administration. The steward combined various services in the household. The butler originally filled the king's cup and then became responsible for providing wine and eventually food and drink in general. The chamberlain was concerned with the king's clothes and moveable goods and the constable, assisted by the marshal, was responsible for the stable and horses. Finally, the chancellor, almost always a cleric, was responsible for the king's correspondence and kept the seal by which he authenticated the king's letters and charters. Later, this office became the most important and its holder often became the actual leader of the central administration. The other offices developed somewhat differently in the various countries. They might be purely honorary titles that served to distinguish important people in the king's surroundings or they might be combined with military leadership or important administrative functions.

The word court (Latin *curia*) had a wide range of meanings in classical antiquity and the medieval and early modern period, some of which are retained in modern English and French, notably its use in the sense of both court of law and the king's household. Originally, the term implied no distinction between the household and the central administration, as indicated by the titles of the leading household officers. Although such a distinction gradually emerged, this fact points to important differences from the conditions usual in modern democracies. While kings and queens and to some extent even presidents have courts, these institutions have no formal political importance but deal with ceremonials and various practical matters to cater for the needs of the head of state and his or her family and guests. Concerning the government, led by a prime minister or a president, there is a clear distinction between the political and the administrative sector. The former consists of representatives elected by the people, who legislate, govern the country and are responsible for its welfare, while the latter are professionals in permanent positions, appointed according to merit and with the possibility of promotion through long service or distinction. Various demands of education are directed to these people, according to rank in the service. Their duty is to prepare cases for political decision and carry them out afterwards. In practice, governments may look to political colour when appointing higher officials, but in principle, such offices are non-political. As we know, the distinction between politics and administration is less clear in practice than in theory, but it is nevertheless difficult to imagine a modern democratic government without such a distinction.

This system hardly goes further back in European history than to the nineteenth century. In the period we are dealing with here, there was no clear difference between political and administrative offices and only a vague distinction between the court in the sense of the administration and that of the household. On the other hand, there was an enormous quantitative change from twelfth-century Oviedo to the seventeenth and eighteenth centuries. The most obvious expression of this is the expansion of the chancery, determined by the increasing importance of writing. Based on what is extant, the king of England issued 115 letters per year under Henry II (1154–89) but the actual number is probably much higher. A great increase took place in England from the thirteenth century. Already Henry III (1216–72) issued around 5,000 letters per year, which had increased to 30,000–40,000 by the mid-fourteenth century.[87] Philip IV (1285–1314) of France issued 15,000 per year, while estimates from the French chancery in the 1330s suggest 20,000 letters issued annually under the great seal and 15,000 under the secret. Another change took place at around the same time in the thirteenth or fourteenth centuries in most countries: the language of the letters changed from Latin to the vernacular, indicating both the greater importance of the national language and an increase in the number of people to whom the royal letters were addressed.

The output from the chanceries continued to increase manifold during the following centuries, corresponding to the increase in the bureaucracy and the interference by the central governments in the life of their subjects: legislation, judicial decisions, taxation, and so forth. It also meant a more impersonal government, a change from king to state in the elementary sense that it was simply impossible for the king to deal with all the matters that had to be decided.

As all letters had to be written by hand, this evidently led to an increase in the number of scribes. It also led to routinization. From the early Middle Ages, letters were issued according to standard formulas and a number of cases were decided according to precedent and routine. Although most of the men recruited to the royal service for these purposes had little political influence and little hope of advancing to important offices, the necessity of delegation did not stop at purely routine matters. Eventually, the king was confronted with so many decisions that he had to delegate even important ones to others. The use of seals in the English chancery gives a glimpse of this development. Seals rather than signatures were used to authenticate documents in the Middle Ages. Originally, the seal was supposed to be attached to the document by the king himself or in his presence. The great seal was kept by the chancellor who became the leading royal minister in the later Middle Ages. The growth of business and the distance between the king and the chancery in England meant that the king could no longer supervise what was sealed by the great seal. Instead, he used the smaller privy seal to give direction to the chancellor and for matters directly relating to the king. Eventually, a special keeper of this seal was also appointed, the keeper of the privy seal, and the same happened with this as with the great seal; it became divorced from the king in person. In the sixteenth century, the king had one or two private secretaries who kept his signet. Documents issued by the king in person were signed by the king's own hand, countersigned by the secretary with the signet and passed on for further sealing with the privy seal or great seal or both. Only documents signed in this way were recognized as authentic royal documents.

This of course placed a heavy responsibility on the royal ministers and gave rise to the doctrine of ministerial responsibility, which assumed great importance under later parliamentary rule. In contemporary monarchies, of course, it is obvious that what is issued in the king's name is actually the work of his ministers. At the time when the king in person still had governing power, it was normal practice that he could not directly be made to answer for his decisions, but that his ministers were responsible. Thus, the minister would have to resign to avoid punishment for a decision with which he disagreed or feared would lead to accusations from Parliament. No formal system like this existed in the sixteenth and seventeenth centuries, but attacks against royal ministers were an important instrument for oppositional Parliaments, notably under Charles I. It is also easy to see that the idea of monarchy as an institution was not only developed by lawyers and philosophers but is the result of the practical experience of the royal bureaucracy and government.

The actual influence of kings on government varied greatly, depending on the country as well as the skills, interest and character of individual kings. Some kings might decide on a remarkable number of cases as late as in the eighteenth century, whereas others left most decisions to their ministers. According to contemporary opinion, the king was not supposed to be a specialist; he should rely on expert opinion on law and finance, eventually also on military matters, although he was usually more involved in the latter; kings might lead their armies in the field as late as in the early nineteenth century. Nevertheless, the growth of bureaucracy did not generally reduce the importance of the king in person. He was still responsible for the main decisions, on war and peace, alliances and the main lines in internal policy. As we shall see, there is much to indicate that the king's skill was crucial for the success or failure of a country. Admittedly, an excellent first minister might have the same effect but the problem was that he could only rule as long as he had the king's confidence, which meant that he might easily be replaced by someone less competent.

The pressure of business, illustrated by the increasing number of letters and charters emanating from the royal chancery, evidently increased the number of people in the king's administration. In recruiting these people, various considerations had to be taken into account. On the lower level, the most important was to recruit qualified people who could write quickly and correctly, knew Latin or other useful languages and had some knowledge of law and administration. On the higher level, political considerations became more prominent. *The King's Mirror* puts it in this way: people who have no wealth and position in society will be more loyal to the king, because they only depend on his favour.[88] On the other hand – as the author is also aware of – such people may easily cause resentment, while in addition, a good relationship with the leading men in the country is necessary and the king can hardly rule without their advice. The balance between these considerations varied from country to country and from king to king. In some cases, as under Philip IV of France, the inner circle consisted of men of low rank, whereas the members of the top aristocracy were also consulted but more rarely.[89] A frequent solution was to use clerics, often high-ranking ones who might nevertheless come from a fairly humble background. This had the further advantage that their ecclesiastical benefices could serve as salaries. In addition, kings sought advice from the leading men in the country, formally or informally. Although the rules about consent were mostly vague, the king would be subject to criticism and risk rebellion if he consistently acted without consulting important people.[90]

There are many examples of prominent first ministers, many of them clerics, who often seem to have been the real rulers of a country, such as Cardinal Wolsey under Henry VIII of England and Cardinal Richelieu under Louis XIII of France. An alternative practice was to use a number of high officials with responsibility for particular fields, either the five traditional offices or some other kind of division. This was practised by Elizabeth of England and Louis XIV of France, in Denmark and Sweden and later in Prussia and eventually developed into the modern cabinet.

From ugly toes to the King's napkin

The royal palace at Versailles, built by Louis XIV in the second half of the seventeenth century, stands as the main monument of the monarchy of the old regime. Its oldest part, the façade facing the town, still dominates its surroundings and must have been even more impressive in the seventeenth century, when the rest of the area was uninhabited. On the other side, it faces a landscape created for the sake of the king's glory, an enormous park, with paths, statues, fountains, trees and flowers, all carefully and symmetrically arranged, forming a world to itself; even today, no other building is to be seen. This world is created by the king; here his will is law and everybody bows to him.

This impression is further confirmed by the building itself and the courtly ceremonials taking place there. The ground plan of the palace essentially corresponds to that of a noble house in town (*hôtel*), with two main wings, one for the husband and one for the wife, and a court in the middle, only enormously extended.[91] Life at court was minutely regulated by ceremonies, starting when the king got up in the morning (*lever*) and the greatest nobles in the country stood at attention in order to dress him, one after the other solemnly helping him with the various garments, and ended at night with a similar ceremony of undressing (*coucher*). The king's meals were ritualized in the same way. It was an honour to be invited to watch the king eat, a greater one to be spoken to by the king during the meal and an even greater to be allowed to serve him food or eat with him. In addition, the king's afternoon trip in the garden, audiences, entertainment and other events were solemnly regulated. Strict rules about rank determined the relationship between the members of the court, although the king might all the time show his favour or lack of it to individuals depending on their merit. Not only the king in person was subject to special reverence but also his portrait or objects used by him. The king's portrait should be treated like the king himself; it was an offence to turn one's back on it. The same respect was due to his coat of arms, his personal device, his bed or the table laid for his meal.[92] Louis explains the system in his memoirs:

> These people are gravely mistaken who imagine that all this is mere ceremony. The people over whom we rule, unable to see the bottom of things, usually judge by what they see from the outside, and most often it is by precedence and rank that they measure their respect and obedience. As it is important to the public to be governed only by a single one, it also matters to it that the person performing this function should be so elevated above the others, that no-one can be confused or compared with him; and one cannot, without doing harm to the whole body of the state, deprive its head of the least mark of superiority distinguishing him from the limbs.[93]

In his history of the kings of Norway, the Icelandic saga writer Snorri Sturluson (1179–1241) includes an anecdote about the national saint of the country, King Olav Haraldsson or St. Olav (king 1015–30). One morning the king is lying awake in his bed, while his men are asleep around him. The sun has just risen and the room is in full daylight. The king notices that one of the men, called Thorarin, has stuck one of his feet outside the bed. Then the other men in the room wake up:

> The king said to Thorarin, 'I have been awake for a while, and I have seen a sight which seems to me worth seeing, and that is, a man's foot so ugly that I don't think there is an uglier one here in this town.' And he called on the others to look at it and see whether they thought so too. And all who looked at it agreed that this was the case.

Thorarin understood what it was they talked about and said, 'There are few things so unusual that their likes cannot be found, and that is most likely to be true here too.'

This discussion then leads to a bet between the king and Thorarin as to whether or not there can be found an equally ugly foot, the winner having the right to demand a favour from the loser. Thorarin then produces his other foot, saying:

> 'Look here, sire, at my other foot. That is so much uglier for lacking a toe. I have won.'
>
> The king replied, 'The first foot is the uglier because there are five hideous toes on it, whilst this one has only four. So it is I who has the right to ask a favour of you.'[94]

It is hard to imagine a greater difference from Louis XIV's court at Versailles than this episode. Here we find a very small distance between the king and his men. They are sleeping in the same room and there is a playful tone between them. At the same time, there is an element of competition, in which the king has to show that he is not only their lord by birth but is able to gain their respect through his personal qualities, in this case, humour and argumentative skills. The king is also only to a limited extent able to command these men. He has to reward and respect them; if not, they may leave him for another lord. Early thirteenth-century Norway was a relatively new kingdom, and besides, other sources show that the relationship between the king and his men was less democratic than this episode implies. Nevertheless, the story can be regarded as a kind of starting-point for a development that led to the court of Versailles, from simplicity to complexity and from the king as the leader in virtue of his personal qualities to the celebration of the royal office rather than the king in person.

In tracing this development, we first have to consider geography: from the travelling king to the stationary king. Personal contact with the aristocracy was essential in the seventeenth century as well as before but in the earlier period, this contact mostly meant that the king had to travel. The kings' travel pattern has been extensively studied in Germany, where royal government largely consisted in combined meetings and festivities in its various parts, often according to established patterns, celebrating particular holidays in particular places.[95]

On their travels, Louis' predecessors might stay in the palaces of their noble subjects or in monasteries or at episcopal sees, but they also had various palaces in different parts of the country. The leading aristocrats only occasionally visited the royal court; they had their own courts, where from time to time they entertained their subordinates in the same way as the king entertained them. With the increasing importance of towns, kings also visited them and were received with processions and various festivities, eventually, from the later Middle Ages onwards, very elaborate ones.[96] In most countries, contact between the king and the leading men in the country increased over time, partly through entertainment and festivities and partly through formal political meetings, which became particularly frequent in the later Middle Ages. Such meetings partly served as a means for the king to engage the aristocracy and the people in his purposes, notably wars, partly as fora for discussion or even opposition against the king. In both cases, we are dealing with centralization.

Not only the aristocracy but also ordinary people must at least have seen the king fairly often during his many travels, at least people in towns. In addition, his portrait was on coins and seals and his letters to particular communities were read in the churches and meeting-places. In times of crisis, kings might appeal directly to his subjects. In 1302, when a defeat against Flanders came in addition to Philip IV's conflict with the pope, he stimulated propaganda directed at the common people, prayers throughout the country and a general appeal to his subjects' love of their country and for their financial aid to its salvation. An anonymous sermon from this period celebrates the sacred character of the kingdom of France, its noble and saintly king, and urges the people to fight and die for their fatherland.[97]

The gradual development of capitals from the thirteenth century did not put an end to the king's travels. Capitals were mainly the residences of the royal administration, rather than the king in person. England is the main example. Already in the eleventh century, under William the Conqueror, royal revenues were larger than in most other countries and were subject to close supervision, as can be seen from the famous Domesday Book, listing the king's resources all over the country: the number of households and the taxes and rents due from them. The administration increased with the expansion of justice during the following century, particularly during the reign of Henry II (1154–89). The decisive separation between the two parts of the court took place in the early thirteenth century, when the chancery and the central administration became permanently located at Westminster, while the king continued to move around in the country. This, of course, is also evidence of the size of the royal administration; it had become too large to continue to move. Paris assumed a similar importance in France when Philip IV greatly extended the royal palace on the Île de la Cité in Paris, part of which still remains. It was later turned into a prison, famous as the place where Queen Marie-Antoinette was kept during the Revolution. In the large hall, where the poor prisoners (*les pailleux* = those who slept on straw) were kept, beautiful Gothic arches are still to be seen – a meagre consolation for the prisoners who lived in squalor and stench. Typically, medieval residences were combinations of fortifications and living quarters. They were therefore often converted into prisons or fortifications in the following centuries and replaced as residences by more comfortable and representative buildings, partly in the city and partly outside, such as the Louvre, Fontainebleau and finally Versailles in France, in addition to a number of smaller residences, often intended for hunting.

Although Louis XIV occasionally still travelled, he did so far less than his predecessors, so by this time, the royal residence in or near the capital had become the main centre of the court. The same happened in most other countries. The reason is clearly increased political centralization, at least partly resulting from increased royal power, although not necessarily at the cost of the nobility. This development is also expressed in the change of rituals and ceremonials.

With the introduction of dynastic succession, the king was distinguished from his people by his birth. Even before this, he was distinguished by a specific ritual: the unction and coronation. The ceremony was introduced by the Spanish Visigoths in the seventh century and later taken over by the Carolingians and eventually most other dynasties. The direct source of influence was the royal unction in the Old Testament. In addition, the crown, the most important material symbol of royalty, was derived from the Roman diadem, as were also elements of the ritual, such as acclamation. The liturgy on the occasion was full of allusions to the kings of Israel in the Old Testament and to the ecclesiastical doctrine of monarchy, the just king (*rex iustus*) whose duty it was to protect the poor and needy, widows and orphans, to judge justly between his subjects and to protect the Church and the country against all enemies. Accompanied by a series of prayers, the king was solemnly anointed and dressed in liturgical clothes, resembling those of a deacon, and received the symbols of his power: crown, sword, staff or globe, symbolizing that he had become 'a different man', as expressly stated in the liturgy.

The unction and coronation were regarded as a sacrament in the early Middle Ages. From the Investiture Contest onwards, its status was somewhat reduced; it was no longer a sacrament, and the Church insisted on a clearer difference between the royal and the priestly office. Nevertheless, this did not really change the sacred status of the king.[98] The allusions to the kings of the Old Testament remained in the liturgy and were also emphasized in the mirrors for princes and other texts dealing with monarchy, as well as in the churches. The Sainte Chapelle in Paris, built by Louis IX to house a costly relic, Christ's crown of thorns, and officially consecrated in 1248, is almost wholly in glass, decorated with paintings from the Old and the New Testament, in which the kings have a central place.[99] The Old Testament kings also figure prominently in the Cathedral of Reims, the coronation church. The kings of the Old Testament were the rulers of the people of God and were clearly superior to the priests, which led the popes to emphasize the difference between the Old and the New Testament, while kings tended to point to the continuity between the two epochs. The king was the most Christian king, the protector of the Church, the clerics and the people of his realm which he ruled on God's behalf.

A royal coronation was normally celebrated in a great cathedral and performed by the leading prelate of the country. There were processions and festivities, leading prelates and nobles arrived with numerous followers and all inhabitants of the town participated and were entertained in various ways. At the coronation of the Emperor Matthias in Frankfurt in 1612, the coronator, the Archbishop of Mainz, arrived with 257 followers; at the coronation of Joseph II in 1764, the number had increased to over 900.[100] All the electors were of course present at the coronation of a German emperor, together with a large number of followers, in addition to many other distinguished people.

Compared to Louis XIV's courtly rituals, however, the coronation had the disadvantage that it only happened once in a king's reign, although he occasionally wore the crown also after the coronation. Nevertheless, he was distinguished in several other ways. He was met in solemn procession when he entered a town, and as kings travelled frequently, this happened often. 'Joyeuse entrée' (joyful entrance) became a usual term for such occasions; an important privilege for the Duchy of Brabant (1356) is referred to by this term. The ceremonials and rituals used to receive the king when he arrived in a town became increasingly more complex during the later Middle Ages, thus anticipating much of the ceremonials at Versailles. Royal weddings and funerals were great occasions, performed with elaborate ceremonial and festivities.[101] These ceremonies, as well as king's visits, also became more exclusive; the common people were increasingly kept at a distance from the king and the courtiers surrounding him.

Most importantly, the English and French kings had healing powers. On regular occasions, the king performed a healing ceremony by laying his hands on people who suffered from scrofula, a disease related to tuberculosis, which, however, often heals spontaneously. Such healing ceremonies are mentioned for the first time in the eleventh century but they seem to have become a permanent institution only from the mid-thirteenth century, the reigns respectively of St Louis of France and Henry III of England. They continued until the 1820s in France.[102] In the eighteenth century, however, there were sceptical voices, including, of course, Voltaire. Pointing out that one of Louis XIV's mistresses, Madame de Soubise, had died from scrofula, Voltaire wrote to Frederick II that he had lost confidence in the king's healing power, as the woman in question 'must have been very well touched' by the king.[103] In contrast to France, the healing ceremonies ceased in England in the late seventeenth century, when the Calvinist William III abolished them. Apart from some attempts by Queen Anne, they were not taken up again.[104] On the contrary, the Hannoverians deliberately proclaimed their belief in modern science in opposition to the Stuart's superstitious adherence to the power of healing. At the initiative of Queen Caroline (1683–1737), married to George II, the princesses were vaccinated against smallpox, which introduced this procedure in Britain.[105]

Thus, from early on, the king was regarded as different from other humans and treated with particular respect. Rituals of different kinds were also frequent, but they did not to the same extent as the later ones emphasize the distance between the king and his surroundings. They were also less prominent in daily life at court. Before around 1300, oriental visitors to European courts would be struck by the simplicity there. Thietmar of Merseburg comments that the German nobles resented Otto III's practice of eating at a table elevated from that of the rest of his guests, a practice he had imitated from Roman palaces.[106]

The changes from around 1300 onwards show some of the features that were further developed by Louis XIV. The number of courtiers as well as the expenses at court increased, as did the luxury and ceremonials.[107] The seating order at meals, the composition of menus and the price of fabric the various members of the court were allowed to use were regulated. The influence probably came from Byzantine and Muslim courts, first apparently to Sicily and later to other European courts. In the early fifteenth century, the Burgundian court was the most lavish as well as the most strictly regulated, partly because this was a very wealthy area with easy access to fine cloth and other luxuries, partly because of the need for the duke to gather the nobles around him to keep together his divided lands. Burgundian impulses came to Spain through Charles V's succession to the Spanish throne in 1516, although Charles in the beginning preferred a simpler court etiquette, in accordance with Castilian traditions. However, he later changed his attitude and formally introduced the Burgundian etiquette. Prince Philip of Spain, the later Philip II, dined in public for the first time according to the ceremonials laid down by the Dukes of Burgundy on Assumption Day, 15 August 1548.[108] This led to a doubling of the number of higher court officials to 200. Although the new ceremonials met with a series of protests in Spain, they remained in force as long as the Habsburgs ruled the country. With the political importance of Spain and the Habsburg Empire in the following period, Spanish etiquette influenced other countries as well, including France under Louis XIV.

The ceremonial novelties introduced by Louis XIV were, first, the minute regulation of daily life; all the activities the king had in common with other human beings were ritualized in a way that all the time made him unique. Thus, the royal majesty was present in full, not only when the king received his crown, led his army in the field or presided over assemblies and government meetings but all the time from when he woke up in the morning until he went to bed at night. The court at Versailles forms the climax of the increasing pomp and ceremonials of the royal courts since the fourteenth century. As the same time, the religious character of the court was continued and developed. Ecclesiastical holidays largely regulated life at court, particularly in Catholic countries. The cult of the king's person assumed religious overtones. His meals were celebrated in a way associated with the Eucharist. It was a great privilege to hand the king his napkin at the meal, which, after he had touched it, was treated as a relic. Despite the greater simplicity of religious rituals, courtly ceremonials developed in a similar way in Protestant countries. The festivities, performances of music and poetry and hunting expeditions, and the ceremonies they involved, also combined social events with occasions of political importance. Not least, they gave the king an impression of the people he might use for important offices.

This development seems to manifest the total victory of the king over any form of opposition, as expressed most clearly by Norbert Elias, who regards the courtly culture as a decisive step towards the civilization of European society, by suppressing the spontaneous passions of medieval people through strict discipline.[109] The violent and quarrelsome nobles changed into polite courtiers and loyal servants of the absolute king. Versailles became a golden cage where the French nobility competed for royal favour, expressed in pensions and empty titles, while the real government was run by non-nobles. There is some truth in this description. Never before had the personal contact between the king and the high nobility been so close, and the king's intention in this was clearly to prevent opposition from this class and avoid internal struggles within in it, as had recently taken place during his own minority. However, such pacification would not have succeeded unless the nobility also retained its privileges and political power. Although Louis excluded the old nobility from ministerial posts – these were held by members of the 'new' nobility, ennobled by the king ('*noblesse de robe*') – the old nobility monopolized positions in the army and the diplomacy. Under Louis' successors, some of them also held important ministerial posts. The price the king paid for abolishing the formal assemblies that had earlier limited his power was to share it with individual nobles, admittedly with a certain freedom in deciding whom to favour. Louis did succeed in centralizing France and above all in preventing the internal conflicts that had often occurred in the previous period but he never developed the kind of absolute rule to be found in, for instance, China or the Ottoman Empire.

In addition to making Versailles his permanent or almost permanent residence, Louis also made it the main residence of the French nobility. Earlier, the members of the nobility had mostly lived in their own palaces, which, of course, still existed, but were less in use. Now, they had to spend much of their time at Versailles if they wanted positions or favours. About those who tried to make a career without doing so, the king would just say: 'I don't know him.' When the court was fully established at Versailles, it numbered around 20,000 people, with 1,000 nobles and 4,000 servants living in the palace itself and another 4,000 nobles and their servants living in the town. Living at Versailles also made the nobility financially dependent on the king. Madame de Maintenon, Louis' mistress, estimated the cost of living there at 12,000 livres per year, a sum only a small minority of the nobles could afford. However, Louis paid great sums in pensions and sinecures; in 1683, the expenses for this purpose amounted to 1.4 million livres or 1.2 per cent of total government expenditure.[110]

King Philip II had practised similar principles as Louis XIV in Spain in the previous century, where the etiquette was also very strict and partly a source of inspiration for Louis. However, Versailles is far from being a direct copy of Escorial. Escorial is a combination of monastery and palace, where the monastery forms the centre of the building. Although Versailles also had a chapel and religious ceremonies played an important part, the royal bed-chamber forms the centre of the building, thus emphasizing its exclusively royal character. Nor did Escorial become the Spanish kings' main residence in the same way as Versailles. In addition, the Spanish kings seem to have formed the centre of their kingdoms through their absence rather than their presence. The royal apartments at Escorial were isolated from the rest of the palace and too small for any great gathering of people. The Spanish king also appeared more rarely in public. In particular, Philip II is often depicted as ruling through papers rather than direct contact with his subjects,[111] although he travelled quite a lot, perhaps as much as ten out of the forty-two years of his reign.[112] Although Louis XIV was also seen more rarely by his ordinary subjects than his predecessors had been, he still appeared in public and it was also possible for ordinary, well-dressed people to visit the palace of Versailles. Moreover, the whole point in the elaborate ceremonial of Versailles was the royal presence, which was able to reward as well as to punish the courtiers with simple gestures. The French court ceremonial was both more elaborate and psychologically more skilful than its Spanish counterpart.

Fortunately for Louis' courtiers, the atmosphere at Versailles was also more cheerful than at Escorial, with music, dance, balls, fireworks, theatre performances and love affairs, in which the king himself in his younger days was also engaged. This was the golden age of French drama and literature in general and the king was an eager audience. He enjoyed Molière's comedies, defending him against the accusations of blasphemy that were directed against him after *Tartuffe* and laughing at *Le Malade Imaginaire*, despite suspicions that he might himself be a target. He rewarded artists of various kind and deliberately worked to make France a centre of artistic creativity. Later in his reign, when his health deteriorated and he became more religious as well as affected by the many defeats and the financial crisis during the War of the Spanish Succession, the atmosphere became more sombre.

The month of April in the Duke of Berry's Book of Hours (*Les très riches heures du Duc de Berry*) from around 1400 shows a hunting-party of young men and women.[113] It is a hot day, as is evident from the people swimming in the river nearby, but the hunters are fully dressed in elegant, colourful clothes. They are five all together; one man and one woman on each horse, while a third horse only carries one woman. The hunters as well as a servant on foot, guiding them, carry falcons; otherwise, they have no arms. The painting shows hunting as the typical aristocratic entertainment. The use of falcons was also a fine art, cultivated by aristocratic connoisseurs; the falcons needed much training as did also their users, as described in great detail in the classical work on the topic ascribed to the Emperor Frederick II of Hohenstaufen (1212–50), *On the Art of Hunting with Falcons*. [114] In the Middle Ages, the use of falcons or hawks for hunting birds and smaller animals was very popular and these birds were bought at high prices or were costly gifts for kings or nobles; thus the king of Norway often sent falcons as gifts to the kings of England or France. Hunting had of course been a royal and aristocratic sport from far back in history. In the Middle Ages, the king's travels were often determined by attractive areas for hunting rather than by political reasons. In England, one-fifth of the country was the king's hunting-ground where special laws applied and poachers were severely punished. Surprisingly much forest still remains around Paris because it was the king's hunting-ground; nowadays, the president enjoys some of the same privileges. In intensely cultivated and densely populated parts of Europe, including most of France, hunting was strictly reserved for the nobility, whereas in mountainous or thinly populated areas, it was still allowed for peasants and ordinary people. As indicated by the painting, hunting was not only about killing animals but also about entertainment and display in the countryside and formed a good occasion for young men and women to meet – women were usually present at hunting-parties. Hunting was also a means for the king to meet the members of the nobility.

The splendour of the Duke of Berry's hunting-parties was not necessarily surpassed by those of Louis XIV 250 years later, but their size and formality certainly were. One of Louis' reasons for building his main residence outside Paris in an area surrounded by forest was the opportunity to practise this royal entertainment *par excellence*. Louis XIV and his successors hunted between one-third and half the days of the year.[115] With the advent of firearms, birds became less popular and eventually, Louis XVI closed down the hawking establishment. Anyway, the most important game during all three reigns was the stag. Like anything else at Versailles, this chase was highly ritualized. A number of professional hunters and their dogs localized and pursued the stag and brought it within sight of the hunting-party who were able to follow from horseback or even in carriages on hunting roads cut in the forest. Hunting was thus an important part of life at the court of Versailles and evidently, it was a great privilege for the courtiers to be invited to a hunting-party with the king.

In addition to making the court into a kind of theatre where everything circled around the king, Louis also celebrated his own glory and that of France through paintings, coins, medals, statues and various kinds of panegyrics to his subjects as well as to other countries. The famous portrait by Rigaud shows how he wanted to appear to his surroundings and the general public. It was painted around 1700, when Louis was in his early sixties – he was born in 1638. The face is that of an elderly man; in contrast to the Emperor Augustus, he is not eternally youthful. The expression is blank, as usual in royal portraits in this and the previous period; such as Titian's of Charles V and Philip II. However, the legs are elegant and youthful, an allusion to the young Louis' skill at dancing. The royal insignia have no prominent position. There is no crown, the sword is just to be seen, half covered by the large coronation robe, and he uses the sceptre like an ordinary cane, possibly alluding to Van Dyke's informal portrait of Charles I. These features depict Louis as the first gentleman of the kingdom rather than the Lord's anointed wearing the traditional insignia. However, the great robe with the French lilies and the Roman column in the background suggests the French state, whose first servant Louis is.[116]

As Louis' own comment indicates, the pomp and ceremonials were not simply vanity but an instrument in the government of the kingdom. To what extent Louis himself enjoyed the respect paid to him and to what extent he regarded the rituals as purely instrumental are difficult to know, but there is no doubt that he was a clever psychologist and in addition a hard-working ruler, despite all the time he spent on ceremonies. He had regular meetings with his leading ministers who formed a permanent group around the king, similar to a modern cabinet, for which it was also a model. According to the Duke of Saint-Simon, Louis only went against the advice of the majority of his ministers six times in the course of forty-five years. As no minutes from government meetings were kept, we do not know if this is true, but at least it indicates that despite the quasi-divine atmosphere surrounding the king, there was open discussion in the council and that the king might be contradicted.

In dealing with his ministers, Louis seems to have adhered to Richelieu's advice to his father:

> I will dwell a bit on the bad effects which result from the remarks of those who speak too loosely about their subjects. The blows from a sword are easily healed. But it is not the same with blows of the tongue, especially if they be from the tongue of the king, whose authority renders the pain almost without remedy unless it be provided by the king himself ... a great king should never insult his subordinates since they too are relatively weak.[117]

As illustrated by the subtle ways of showing royal approval or discontent, Louis had no need of harsh words to convey his opinion of subordinates. When the Duke of Saint-Simon resigned from the army, Louis first went out of his way to distinguish him during the *coucher* and then ignored him completely for three years.[118] 'If Hell is to be the denial of the face of God, Heaven in Louis XIV's France was proximity to the king.'[119] It must also be added that Louis not only impressed through his ceremonials; he was actually an impressive personality. Even one of his greatest critics, the Duke of Saint-Simon, had to admit:

> Louis XIV was made for a brilliant court. In the midst of other men, his figure, his courage, his grace, his beauty, his grand mien, even the tone of his voice and the majestic and natural charm of his person, distinguished him till his death.[120]

Mostly, however, he seems to have treated his ministers and generals with great consideration. When intendants, ministers or officers fell in disgrace, they were almost never punished in any other way than by being dismissed from their office. Even dismissal was rare, largely because courtiers tended to belong to prominent families whom the king did not want to offend. As usual, it was not particularly dangerous to hold high office in Europe during the old regime, in contrast to other parts of the world. In this respect, Louis XIV's court forms the rule and, as we shall see, that of Henry VIII of England forms the exception. By contrast, various additions to the death penalty in the list from 1670 were applied to leaders of peasant rebellions.

Another means for kings to link the nobility more closely to themselves was the introduction of the chivalric orders. The earliest is the Order of the Sash, instituted by King Alfonso XI of Castile in 1330. The English Order of the Garter was instituted by Edward III, probably in 1348, while King John of France instituted the Order of the Star in 1351–52. The Order of the Golden Fleece, instituted by Duke Philip of Burgundy in 1430, became one of the most prestigious, as it was led by the Habsburgs, who are shown on portraits with its symbol around their necks. Originally, the orders were corporations with a largely military purpose, similar to the real military orders, like the Templars, the Teutonic Order and the Spanish Order of Calatrava. They aimed at linking the aristocracy more closely to the king and serving him in war. Some of these orders still exist, but mainly serve as medals for high-ranking persons or people who have distinguished themselves in some way. However, the members of the Order of the Garter still have their stalls in the chapel of Windsor where they gather on 15 June every year for religious service, lunch and the inauguration of new members.

The increasing size of the courts and the elaborate ceremonials are to be found in most European monarchies of the period. Thus, we find a significant increase in the imperial court in Vienna from the late seventeenth century onwards.[121] In the seventeenth century, Louis XIV's Versailles also became a model for other rulers, such as Schönbrunn outside Vienna, Caserta outside Naples and a number of palaces in the German principalities. What these rulers imitated was the idea of a palace outside the capital and the luxury and ceremonials of Versailles, not the style, which was rather influenced by Italian palaces. By contrast, Louis XIV was more successful in exporting French language and literature than architecture.[122] While French had earlier competed with Latin, Italian and Spanish, it became established as the main international language during Louis' reign.[123]

From the early eighteenth century, England became a great power and the most important rival of France. Although the ceremonial at the English court followed the common European pattern, there was no equivalent to Versailles in England.[124] In 1698, the Duke of Saint-Simon described the main residence, Whitehall, as the largest and ugliest building in Europe. Actually, very little had been built by the monarchy since the reign of Henry VIII. In 1698, Whitehall was destroyed by fire and in the following period, the king's main residence was usually Kensington Palace – a tiny building compared to Versailles – in addition to

Hampton Court, which was also extended in the Baroque style. The present main residence, Buckingham Palace, was bought by King George III in 1761 and later restored several times.

The lack of great building projects is a consequence of the reduced importance of the court as the main political centre of the realm, which in turn was connected to the first two Hanoverian kings' lack of interest in their English realm. Both George I (1714–27) and George II (1727–60) preferred Hanover to England and stayed there as often as they could. By contrast, Queen Caroline (1683–1727), married to George II, was beautiful as well as cultured and intelligent. She became very popular and played an important part in English cultural life. Neither of the two kings mastered the English language very well and neither was a particularly impressive personality. The third Hanoverian, George III (1760–1820), George II's grandson, was different, familiar with English language and culture and identifying thoroughly with his English realm. Although his attempts to control English politics were not very successful, he adopted an English-style monarchy and kept little distance from his subjects. However, the relative decline of the court also has to do with the general development of English politics. Parliament became increasingly important during the seventeenth century and the organization of the government led by the prime minister from the early eighteenth century resulted in a further development in the same direction.

The difference between the English and the French monarchy is also expressed in the two central fields of hunting and gardening. Hunting for stags was practised only a few places in England; the landscape was used so intensively for agriculture or pasture that in most places there were no deer left; to hunt for them, one had to go to Scotland. Instead, fox hunting became very popular. Although this game could not be used for food – 'the unspeakable in pursuit of the uneatable', as Oscar Wilde expressed it – a good excuse was that the fox ate chickens and other useful animals. Whereas fox-hunting was recently, until it was abolished, considered specifically aristocratic, it had a more popular character in the eighteenth century and was very different from the strictly formalized hunting at the French court. In a similar way, the English garden that developed from the early eighteenth century onwards is very different from a French one. Although an English garden may well be equally artificial, it is arranged so as to look natural, without symmetry, with flowers growing in various places apparently without any strict plan and, above all, with enormous oaks, beeches and other trees stretching their branches over the lawns. To eighteenth-century Englishmen, their gardens formed a symbol of their liberty in contrast to French symmetry and centralization.[125]

In tracing the development of the medieval and early modern state, the main focus among social scientists and until recently also among historians, has been on the purely administrative development which seems most relevant from a modern point of view. Including the court and ceremonials increases the difference from modern conditions. The development of the state is not only an expression of the need to regulate society and carry out functions that are necessary for the population but also aims at linking local elites to the central government around the king.

Nor were the pomp and ceremonials at court purely instrumental; they were also an expression of the wish of the king and his surroundings for pleasure and entertainment and to show off their wealth and glory. Together with more frequent and costly warfare, however, it also became an increasing problem for the state finances and for the relationship between the elite and the common people, as will be discussed later.

Common to all European courts, from early medieval Norway to Louis XIV's Versailles, is their close links to the elites of the country. The nobles were supposed to spend some time at court, at least to have a personal relationship to the king. Younger members of noble families usually spent some years at court as pages and ladies-in-waiting and members of the lower aristocracy might seek the royal court in the hope of patronage and social advancement. Louis XIV linked the high nobility more closely to the king than before but the personal connection between the king and the nobility had been there all the time.

This composition of the court seems so obvious to students of European history that we forget how rare it is in a global context. A typical oriental court had no close connection to local elites. It consisted of eunuchs, slaves or people who for some reason or other had received the ruler's favour and been promoted. In short, a proper oriental court was supposed to consist of people whom the ruler could 'promote without jealousy and destroy without fear of revenge'. Although this was not always the case in practice, the distance between the ruler and the local elites was significantly greater in China or the Ottoman Empire than in Europe. China had a competent bureaucracy, recruited through strict examinations but the top bureaucrats did not belong to the inner circle around the emperor; only eunuchs and the imperial family had access to the inner palace where the emperor resided. The Ottoman court was supposed to consist of slaves and foreigners, while Turks were in principle excluded. Although exceptions were made in practice, there was no close connection with the local elites. By contrast, the European court is the expression of the ruler's need to establish relationships to the leading members of society, which is also expressed in the development of the administration and political institutions.[126] Admittedly, some rulers managed with very simple courts, such as Charles XII of Sweden and Frederick William I of Prussia, to some extent also his successors. Prussia became a great military power largely because of the kings' austerity. Apparently, the Prussian kings also managed to integrate the nobility in the state without a lavish court. However, Prussia was a small and poor country surrounded by enemies, which may have made it easier for the king to mobilize its nobility. In a large and composite country like France, the court seems to have been an important instrument for the king's power.

The emergence of a courtly culture and a permanent or almost permanent royal residence linked the nobility more closely to the king but removed him from the common people. This was partly compensated for by other means. The royal bureaucracy had increased its control of local society. The king's portrait was still on coins and seals, in addition to the fact that his statue might be present in some towns, notably the capital. Still, the Church had a tighter local network but after the Reformation, this network was controlled by the king in Protestant countries and was under a stronger influence from him in Catholic ones as well. New media could be exploited by the king to influence his subjects, such as the printing-press with newspapers and pamphlets and the woodcuts and prints which allowed pictures to be reproduced easily in many copies. Louis XIV was very skilful in the use of these media, directed to his subjects as well as to foreign audiences.[127]

The formation of the sovereign state

In his life of the Emperor Conrad II from around 1040, the German chronicler Wipo refers the story of the emperor's visit to Pavia in Italy on his way to receive the imperial crown in Rome (1027). On his arrival, Conrad discovers that the Pavians have destroyed the imperial palace, defending their behaviour by stating that the palace belonged to no one, since the imperial throne was vacant. Conrad answers in the following way:

> If the king is dead, the kingdom remains, as a ship remains whose captain dies. The buildings were public, not private; they belonged by right to another, not to you. Those who usurp what belongs to others, are guilty before the king. Therefore, you have become usurpers of the property of others and consequently, you are guilty before the king.[128]

Although the Pavians are probably more representative of contemporary attitudes than Conrad, Wipo's story is an important expression of the idea of the monarchy as an institution, existing independently of the individual rulers. According to the New Testament, monarchy was instituted by God and consequently, rulers had to be obeyed whether they were pagan or Christian. However, this did not necessarily imply an idea of the state. In Carolingian ideology, there was no sharp distinction between state and Church; the king ruled *ecclesia* together with the bishops. Characteristically, the popular allegory of the human body represented *ecclesia*, usually headed by the king and with various ecclesiastical and secular dignitaries as its various limbs.[129] Later, however, the body is identified with *res publica* in John of Salisbury's *Policraticus* (1159).[130] By this time, the Gregorian Reform had led to a clearer distinction between the sacred and the secular sphere and the division of the *ecclesia* into two organizations. Although the idea of the king as God's representative on Earth lived on until the period of the French Revolution, secular theories of monarchy became more prominent from the late eleventh century onwards. Roman law was used already in the polemics of the Investiture Contest and increased its importance in the following period. It served to bolster the king's authority over the people as well as his independence from the Church.[131]

Roman law could of course easily be applied to the king of Germany, who held the title of Roman emperor and regarded himself as the successor of the ancient Roman emperors, including Justinian, who had issued the law. However, other kings made the same claim. Already the canonist Étienne de Tournai in the mid-twelfth century identified the king of France with the emperor in the *Codex*. [132] This idea later received support from Pope Innocent III, who, in 1202, stated that the king of France recognized no temporal superior. The idea of monarchy as an institution was expressed in the term *corona* = the crown. The king's lands did not belong to him but to the crown; therefore, the individual king was not allowed to alienate them. The same idea was eventually expressed in the doctrine of the king's two bodies, one mortal and one immortal, representing respectively the individual king and the institution. The doctrine was not formulated explicitly until the sixteenth century but was anticipated in various ways in the Middle Ages.[133]

The reception of Aristotle's political thought formed a particularly important step in the development of a secular theory of the monarchy and the state. Aristotle's *Politics* was translated into Latin in the 1260s and was shortly afterwards used by Albertus Magnus and Thomas Aquinas. The latter's *De regno* (*On Kingship*, 1271–73) marks a new epoch in the history of political thought. Whereas earlier mirrors for princes, the most important genre dealing with royal power in the twelfth and early thirteenth century, took monarchy for granted and essentially consisted of advice to the king about how to govern, Thomas began with Aristotle's arguments for the necessity of the state. Human beings need a community to live a good life, therefore, government is based on human nature. Thomas further follows Aristotle in discussing various ways of organizing this community. Although, in contrast to Aristotle, he arrives fairly easily at the conclusion that monarchy is the best form of government, it is significant that he does not take it for granted. Thus, he introduces a prolonged debate about various constitutions, a debate that continued, largely on the basis of Aristotle's categories, until Montesquieu in the eighteenth century.

The Aristotelian idea of the state (Greek *polis*) as based on the social nature of humans was shared by most medieval thinkers in the following period. The state was necessary for a good life, while at the same time its inhabitants had natural rights to freedom, earning a living and right to property. The right to the latter was somewhat more limited by social concerns than it became later but was not fundamentally different.[134] Some scholars even claimed that serfdom – a common condition in the Middle Ages and to some extent later – was against natural law, meaning than men's natural right had been taken away.[135]

Aristotle's theory also laid the foundation for an idea of popular sovereignty more explicit than the one that might be derived from Roman law. When the state was based on human nature and monarchy existed because it was the most practical form of government, it followed logically that the people must have the right to depose a king who ruled unjustly. Consequently, Thomas Aquinas discussed in detail the conditions that might necessitate such a step. The ruler must have committed serious injustice, to the extent that regicide was a minor evil in comparison, and it could only be undertaken as the result of a united action by society. Thomas was thus clearly aware of the threat to the social order resulting from a too liberal interpretation of the right of resistance; it has also been pointed out that the conditions demanded by Thomas would not often occur in practice.[136] Nevertheless, as we shall see, the baronial rebellion in England might be an example of what Thomas had in mind, although there is no evidence of a direct connection with his ideas. A comparison with a previous version of the idea, by John of Salisbury in his *Policraticus* (1159) shows the greater awareness of the political community after the reception of Aristotle. John seems inconsistent, allowing regicide while at the same time referring to the traditional doctrine that a Christian has to suffer in patience in this world. He regards resistance as an individual right; characteristically, his restriction of it concerns the oath of fealty, which prevents resistance.[137]

Thus, there was clearly an idea of the state in the Middle Ages in the sense of a political community represented by the king but which existed independently of him. More doubtful, however, is the question of the consequences of this idea, in particular, the question of sovereignty. The modern idea of law is formal, a result of what is decided by the supreme legislative authority, in democratic states a legislative assembly elected by the people, in absolutist states the king. The king was usually recognized as the supreme legislator in the Middle Ages, in accordance with the doctrine of Roman law '*Quod principi placuit legis habet vigorem*' ('What the king decides has the force of law') and '*Princeps legibus solutus est*'. [138] The king was therefore above the law he had himself given and could not be accused by his subjects of having broken it (the Prince is not bound by the laws), but he was nevertheless morally obliged to obey it and would be punished by God if he did not. In addition, the positive law must not contradict natural law and divine law as laid down by God in the Bible. Concerning what the subjects might do if the king acted against divine and natural law, the lawyers in the king's service saw a close connection between the king and social order and were more reluctant than Thomas Aquinas to allow the subjects to rebel against or depose a king whom they found unjust. Consequently, the various attempts to influence the king, which will be discussed later, took the form of charters where the king promised to respect various specific rights or rule in the interest of his subjects and with their consent, but the political bodies giving this consent were rarely involved in the daily running of government. The reason for this moderation from the subjects, however, should be sought less in the king's overwhelming power than in a general understanding that disorder was a greater danger than tyranny. Moreover, the same considerations applied to the king's relationship to the law as that of the pope. There was a body of law that could not be changed radically by the intervention of one ruler and the law had to be applied by a number of professional experts whom the king had limited possibilities to control.

As already mentioned, there are various opinions among scholars concerning the development of the European state. One issue in this discussion is the term itself, Latin *status* = state or condition (derived from the verb *stare* = to stand) which is mostly believed to have been developed from the sixteenth century onwards. However, the word was also current in the Middle Ages in the combination *status rei publicae* = the condition of the realm. Strictly speaking, we are here dealing with a new term for an old reality, *res publica* or *regnum* being replaced by *status* in the sense of the political community. Although these terms did not always refer to what we would consider the state but might also simply be synonyms for the king, there is considerable evidence of the distinction between the ruler as a person and the realm as an institution already in the Middle Ages. However, there is clearly a more technical use of the term 'state' from the early sixteenth century. In *The Prince* (1513), Machiavelli refers to the people's duty to aid the prince in times of adversity; because in such circumstances 'the state has need of its citizens' (*'lo stato ha bisogno de' cittadini'*). Later, he refers to 'the majesty of the state' (*'la maestà dello stato'*). However, his most frequent use of the term is in the traditional sense of the position and range of powers of the prince. The full development occurs later in the sixteenth century, first, in France, with authors like Guillaume Budé and Jean Bodin and then in England from the period of Cromwell's regime in the 1530s. Here the state is clearly distinguished from the prince as well as from the citizens, referring to the organized political community.[139]

In practice, one of the clearest expressions of the idea of royal sovereignty was the result of the conflict over Henry VIII's divorce of Catherine of Aragon in order to marry Anne Boleyn. Having applied for many years for a papal annulment of his marriage, Henry was persuaded by the Cambridge scholar Thomas Cranmer whom he shortly afterwards appointed Archbishop of Canterbury, that he did not need a papal annulment, as he was himself the head of the Church of England. The doctrine of royal sovereignty over the Church was then formally stated by the king's new head minister, Thomas Cromwell, and accepted by Parliament.[140] As a sovereign ruler, the king could not be subordinated to any external power, including the pope. Similar proclamations were made in other Protestant countries. Catholic kings continued to recognize the pope's spiritual authority after the Reformation but interpreted it in a more restrictive way than previously.

In principle, the state is an abstract entity, not identified with any individual person. The servants of the state vary over time and they only represent the state in their official capacity. In the monarchies that still exist, the king serves as a symbol of the state without any power to represent it in practice. By contrast, both in the Middle Ages and in the early modern period, the state was largely identified with the king. The development of central political institutions, the council of the realm, the supreme courts of law and the increasingly more extensive royal bureaucracy, did not reduce the importance of the king as the expression of the state. Although Louis XIV neither said nor meant that he was the state (*'l'État c'est moi'*),[141] to the extent that there was a sovereign ruler, it was the king. Whether he had his power from God or from the people – both theories existed – he had received a decisive power that he could not give up or be deprived of.

At least in some respects, Louis XIV distinguished clearly between himself and the state, as when he said on his deathbed that he would die but the state would continue to exist. His introduction of the courtly ceremonial with its cult of the monarchy may be interpreted as evidence of a strong idea of the state but also as an expression of the link between the state and Louis himself and the dynasty. Frederick William I of Prussia (1713–40) is depicted as a great landowner, regarding the country as his own property which he tried to leave in the best possible condition to the next generation. However, his son, Frederick II (1740–86) made a sharp distinction between himself and the state, for instance, in tolerating criticism of himself but not of the state and distinguishing between his own interests and those of the state, whereas French kings were less explicit in this respect.[142] Regarding foreign policy, there is also a difference between Francis I's honour, chivalry and attachment to family possessions and the focus on territorial interests and the balance of power in eighteenth-century diplomacy. On the other hand, the distinction between the state and the king's person did not imply an idea of the state being identical with all its inhabitants. Unlike modern democracy, the medieval and early modern state did not exist for the sake of its inhabitants but as an institution that had to perform in competition with other, similar ones and whose success was the king's responsibility.

Turning to political practice, the most important criterion is the monopoly of violence. Only the state may wage war and prosecute and punish crimes. All inhabitants of the country are subject to the authority of the state but may also appeal to it, regardless of their social status. In thirteenth-century Norway, the author of *The King's Mirror* expresses this doctrine somewhat crudely in the statement that the king is so powerful that he controls the life of his subjects; he may kill without punishment or revenge. This gives occasion for a long discussion of the death penalty and the king's heavy responsibility for judging justly. Although no human can judge him, God can, and the king must therefore always act in the awareness of this.[143]

Whereas the idea of the office in modern society is so familiar that elaborate formalities are mostly unnecessary when high officials are appointed or a new government or president replaces the old one, the royal office was, as we have seen, subject to increasingly elaborate ceremonials in the medieval and early modern periods. Although the king in person eventually became more distant from his subjects, his symbols were everywhere, in the form of coins, seals, charters and public buildings and of course his officials, whose authority depended on their relationship to him. These became more numerous as well as more professional, held office in different districts and formed an organized hierarchy. In this sense, the state had made great advances from the Middle Ages until the eighteenth century, although traces of the old order remained, in the form of some right to government and jurisdiction for the landowners over their peasants. Ecclesiastical courts of law continued to exist in Catholic countries after the Reformation, although they could not inflict the death penalty and eventually also came under increased royal control. Finally, there were still composite states where more than one ruler had state-like authority over his subjects.

We may also ask to what extent officers in the royal bureaucracies regarded themselves as servants of the state in a similar way as modern bureaucrats. Here an anecdote about the Norwegian government minister Niels Vogt (1817–94) may serve as an illustration. Vogt had two inkpots on his desk, one owned by the government for official letters and one by himself for private ones. When asked whether he actually wrote private letters when working in his office, he answered that of course, he did not, but it happened that he stayed in his office after working hours to write some private letters. Vogt was known to be pedantic and the two inkpots are of course an extreme case, which appears ridiculous to us, but would probably have been comprehensible in the seventeenth or eighteenth century.

The relationship between rulers and their officials is probably better illustrated by the following story from the reign of Queen Elizabeth I of England. Sir Robert Carey, a local governor near the Scots border, had for a long time dealt with various difficult problems in the area without receiving any letters or money from the queen. He became more and more irritated and finally decided to approach her directly and complain about the way he was treated. On his way south, he was intercepted by friends, who warned him against what he was planning. He must under no circumstances come unbidden to the queen, nor demand payment of money. Carey returned and finally found the solution. He got in touch with a member of the queen's privy chamber who told her about Sir Robert's love for her, which was so great that, having not seen her for over a year, he could no longer endure the pain of absence that had deprived him of all happiness; he requested only to kiss the queen's hand once. The invitation arrived in due time, the queen received him very graciously and gave him £500 from the exchequer along with other favours.[144]

A distinction between private and public is essential in a modern bureaucracy and rules against corruption are extremely strict, based on a distinction between the state as an entity which the official serves in his public capacity and private matters concerning which he is in the same category as anybody else. It is difficult to imagine this distinction to have been fully developed in countries like France and Spain, where officials bought their offices or in England where they largely consisted of local gentry who served the government in addition to their own business. Richelieu and Colbert were both brilliant politicians and administrators who increased the power and prestige of France and its kings, but in serving their own ends, they did not stop at the inkpots. Both became incredibly wealthy and both favoured their family and friends, building up large networks of clients, linked to themselves rather than to the state. There is little evidence of bureaucracies in the modern sense before the eighteenth century, when they begin to appear in Germany, notably Prussia, and Scandinavia.

The state did become an institution in the early modern period, but not in the sense that the king was replaced by an impersonal bureaucracy, nor in the sense that this bureaucracy corresponded to the Weberian ideal, but in the sense that the king became an institution.

King, nobility and people, and the idea of the nation

For as much as all other nations are wont to vaunt the glory of their achievements, and reap joy from the remembrance of their forefathers: Absalon, Chief Pontiff of the Danes, whose zeal ever burned high for the glorification of our land, and who would not suffer it to be defrauded of like renown and record, cast upon me, the least of his followers—since all the rest refused the task—the work of compiling into a chronicle the history of Denmark, and by the authority of his constant admonition spurred my weak faculty to enter on a labour too heavy for its strength.[145]

In this way, Saxo Grammaticus opens his work on the history of the Danes, composed in the early thirteenth century, expressing his pride in the history of his nation and explaining to his readers why such a work is so necessary that he has taken it upon him, despite his incompetence. The latter statement is denied by the form of the preface; even in English translation the complex syntax and the refined rhetoric of the original Latin come through. In the Middle Ages and the Renaissance, Saxo was highly admired for his language, modelled on Silver-Age Latin, i.e. from the first century AD. Saxo's preface corresponds to numerous others all over Europe, celebrating their nations in similar ways. In particular, such historical works were important in the new kingdoms in Northern and Eastern Europe, formed in the ninth and tenth centuries.[146]

The recent upsurge of partly violent nationalism in the new countries in the Third World and in Eastern Europe after the fall of communism has stimulated research in nationalism, mostly emphasizing its contingent character. Nations are 'imagined communities'; contrary to the ideas of their most eager adherents who claim a fundamental unity in virtue of race, religion, language or other characteristics. Nations are also regarded as flexible; the features a particular group regards as characteristic of themselves are adapted in a way that serves to distinguish them from another group.[147] A widespread attitude has further been to regard nationalism as essentially a modern invention.[148] One of the most articulate and influential spokesmen of this theory is Ernest Gellner.[149]

Gellner distinguishes between group identity and nationalism in the strict sense. The former is to be found in any period, whereas the latter is exclusively modern, consisting in the idea that a state should be a national community and that a nation is entitled to have its own state. Although not particularly attracted to national ideas from an intellectual point of view, Gellner regards them as essential for the existence of a modern state. The strong modern state interferes so much in the lives of its inhabitants that it needs a feeling of community and a common loyalty to exist. By contrast, the pre-modern state was governed by a small and exclusive elite who did not want any patriotic engagement from the people but rather that they should be kept in their place and interfere in the matters of the state as little as possible. Nor were the members of the elite particularly nationalistic, but identified themselves as members of a pan-European community, often with a common international language, Latin or French.

Gellner's theory points to important differences between modern and pre-modern attitudes. The common people were clearly less affected by the state, at least in the positive sense, and the elite often behaved in ways that today would have been considered unpatriotic. What seems the most specifically modern aspect of nationalism is the struggle by ethnic groups to create a nation state, which had not existed before or to restore one that had been destroyed. Thus, in the nineteenth century, there was a German and an Italian movement for unification as

well as movements for the creation of independent states among groups that regarded themselves as a particular people ruled by foreigners: the Irish and later the Scots
under English rule, the Slavs in the Austro-Hungarian Empire or the Basques and
Catalans in Spain. The late nineteenth-century Zionistic movement for the Jews to
return to Israel to form their own state belongs in the same category. Some of these
peoples had previously had their independent states, such as the Poles, Czechs and
Catalans; other based their claims more on language and culture, as some of the new
nations that emerged after the First World War and then after the fall of the Soviet
Union: the Baltic countries and Ukraine. Finally, there are also examples of peoples
in border regions wanting to join another state than the one to which they belong,
such as the Germans and Danes in Schleswig-Holstein, the Austrians and Italians in
South Tyrol and the French and Germans in Alsace-Lorraine.

The propaganda of these national movements suggests that they are essentially
the products of strong emotions and dominated by poets and freedom fighters
willing to die for their country. There has also been a tendency to regard nationalism as irrational: 'Why and how could a concept so remote from the real
experience of most human beings become such a powerful political source so
suddenly?' asked Eric Hobsbawm, who, as a Marxist, regarded class as the social
category that expressed people's real interests.[150] The answer is that the concept is
not remote from the real interests of most human beings. Nationalism is not only
the willingness of some idealists to sacrifice everything for an imagined community,
but an expression of the fact that every organized government involves a number
of people who are interested in its continued existence. The increasing importance
of the national community in the nineteenth century was a result of the fact that
the state became more important to a larger part of its population. The building or
location of infrastructure like railways, harbours and steamships, the competition
for jobs in the expanding national administration and not least the institution of
compulsory schools and military service were likely to engage a large part of the
population in the government and affairs of the state.[151]

Turning to the Middle Ages and the early modern period, the state was of
course less important in the lives of most people than in the nineteenth and
twentieth centuries. However, in his history of the Norwegian kings, the Icelandic
chronicler Snorri Sturluson repeatedly points to the difficulties kings had in being
accepted in other countries, clearly because they lacked networks.[152] There was a
national elite in each country who resented attempts from foreigners to gain
influence there, whose own position was limited to that particular country and
who could expect prominent and advantageous positions in the royal government.
An example of this is the promise demanded from the newly elected John of
Luxembourg as king of Bohemia in 1310 not to give foreigners offices in the
country. Similar demands were directed to other union kings. One of the main
objections against Henry III of England during the conflict 1258–67 was his reli-
ance on foreign favourites. Moreover, wealth at the time was largely based on
landownership, which meant that loss of territory or increased foreign influence
might threaten the landowners' interests. Finally, increasing bureaucratization in

the early modern period also increased the number of people with a vested interest in the state. There is also clear evidence of national attitudes in the literature of the period, for instance, the celebration of English freedom, cultural values and national heroes, in Shakespeare's plays.[153]

These considerations apply not only to the lay nobility but also to the Church. Although the Church was a universal organization, it was, in practice, largely local and territorial, having its main income from land, which in most cases was located within one particular country. The churchmen had the same interests as the lay aristocrats in protecting their property and, in addition, needed organized government and peaceful conditions to carry out their work. Their long-term interests therefore largely coincided with those of the king, although there might in periods be conflicts between the two. According to ecclesiastical ideology, the king who held his power from God was a territorial king, whose power was confined to one country and who had to respect the rights of his counterparts in other countries. Moreover, religion was a strong force of social identification. Philip IV of France quite successfully depicted himself as the most Christian king in his conflict with the papacy. Such proclamations were of course particularly effective in wars against non-Christian peoples. With the religious division during the Reformation, similar appeals could be used in wars against confessional enemies.[154]

There are also examples of major popular movements with aims of a national character. In 1434, the people of Dalarna in Sweden rebelled against their bailiff, the Dane Jøsse Eriksen, under the leadership of Engelbrekt Engelbrektsson, a man of the lower nobility, after several complaints about him to the Danish King Erik, who had ruled the three Scandinavian countries since 1397.[155] A contemporary vernacular chronicle gives a vivid picture of the dramatic course of events, presenting Engelbrekt as a great hero and celebrating his and his followers' triumph over the tyrannical bailiffs and his success in forcing the reluctant Swedish nobility to join the rebellion. We see Engelbrekt entering Vadstena, where a number of councillors and leading men are assembled, proclaiming, 'All of you should now join the kingdom if you want to live longer. I now intend to win the freedom of the realm.' When they refuse, Engelbrekt grasps one of the bishops around the throat and threatens to throw him and his colleagues to the rebel army outside, after which he dictates a letter of deposition to the king, which he forces the assembled lords to seal.

The rebellion proved very successful and led to the deposition of Erik in all three countries in 1439–42. Peasant rebellions were frequent in Europe in the Middle Ages but rarely led to great changes, particularly not the deposition of kings. Nor was the deposition of Erik in Sweden the exclusive result of the peasants' action; it also necessitated the cooperation of the nobility. Erik had conducted an expensive foreign policy, including twenty years of war to join the county of Schleswig to Denmark and he had mostly governed without involving the council of the realm in the government. His regime illustrates that dynastic unions often led to discontent in the country that was not the king's main residence and demonstrates the general problem of the relationship between the king, the nobility and the common people.

During most of the period 1470–1520, Sweden was without a king and ruled by members of the aristocratic Sture kindred, who used the title 'protector of the realm'. The Sture held their faction together by skilful propaganda in the form of letters, speeches and a number of verse chronicles, clearly intended for oral performance, which celebrated the Swedish nation, blackened the Danes and stamped the opponents of the faction as traitors. Many modern scholars have dismissed this propaganda as a cynical attempts to serve the Sture's own interests, but what was the use of propaganda if it had no correspondence in the sentiments of the people to whom it was directed? Nor is such propaganda unique to fifteenth-century Sweden.

Many tourists in Prague notice the statue of St John Nepomuk on the Charles Bridge, one of the most popular saints in East Central Europe. The statue was erected in 1683, on the 300th anniversary of his martyrdom. According to the legend, John Nepomuk was killed and his body thrown into the river by the evil King Wenceslas because he had refused to reveal what the queen had said in her confession. Actually, Wenceslas did execute John, but the reason was a conflict over the election of an abbot and thus had nothing to do with the queen's confession. The story is found for the first time in 1459 but became really widespread during the Counter-Reformation, leading to John Nepomuk's canonization in 1721. There was a great need for a national saint in the 1620s, when the Czech Protestants had been defeated and the country was forced back to the Catholic faith. In addition, the story celebrated one of the most important sacraments by underlining the priest's absolute duty to hide what the penitent had told, even at the cost of his own life. It is also possible that St John Nepomuk was deliberately used to replace another martyr from the same period, namely, the reformer John Hus.

Since 1310, Bohemia had been ruled by the Luxembourg Dynasty after the national one, the Přemyslids, had become extinct in 1306.[156] Although the new king, John (1310–46), had promised to make Bohemia his main residence and rule in cooperation with the Czechs, he did not keep his promise but spent most of his reign promoting the interests of his dynasty in various parts of Europe. As the son of the Holy Roman Emperor Henry VII (1309–13), he aspired to the imperial throne. He was succeeded by his son, Charles IV, who became Holy Roman Emperor in 1347. Despite the extensive political interests resulting from this position, Charles' engagement and interest in Bohemia were far greater than that of his father. In his autobiography, he describes his upbringing in France, where he forgot his Czech mother-tongue, so that he had to learn it again when he returned.[157] But he did learn it and he made Prague the most important city in the Holy Roman Empire, founded the New Town on the undeveloped land between the Old Town and the ancient Přemyslid settlement on Vyšehrad, built the Charles' Bridge and restored and extended the cathedral.[158] He also showed great interest in the Czech language, which is probably the main motive for his foundation of a monastery in Prague, using the Old Church Slavonic liturgy.[159] Finally, he founded the first university east of the Rhine in Prague (1348). He also seems to have solved a number of internal conflicts and restored the government after the lack of firm rule during his father's reign. His eldest son and successor Wenceslas was less successful and was deposed as Roman emperor in 1400. His reign also saw an outburst of national and religious conflict.

There had been a considerable immigration of Germans to Bohemia, partly as merchants, artisans or craftsmen and partly as followers of the Luxembourg. Some of the wealthiest burghers were German and some of the towns, including the Old Town of Prague, were dominated by Germans. John Hus (1369–1415) was professor and for a period (1402–3) also rector of the University of Prague as well as a preacher in the Church of Bethlehem. He worked for reform of the Church, morally as well as doctrinally, was influenced by John Wycliffe, who had opposed the Church in England, and, like him, rejected all other sources than the Bible as authoritative. He was a strong adherent of the Czech language, both in general and for use in religious contexts, and published a translation of the New Testament, the Psalms and the Wisdom literature in 1406, which replaced some previous translations from the 1380s onwards. For a long time, the king supported Hus and his adherents. In 1409, a conflict at the university made the German professors and students leave and found their own university in Leipzig. Later, in 1412, when Hus had been excommunicated, the king changed sides and supported the Church. In 1414, Hus was summoned to the Council of Konstanz where he went under promises of safe conduct, but the prelates persuaded the Emperor Sigismund, Wenceslas' brother, that it was not necessary to keep promises to a heretic. Hus was then arrested, condemned and burnt at the stake on 6 July 1415.

The result was rebellion in Bohemia. Large parts of the population supported Hus, the nobles, gentry and peasants, most of whom were Czechs, whereas the Germans largely supported the Church and the clergy. The opposition, Hussites as they were called, combined religious zeal with Czech patriotism and fought the emperor, Wenceslas' successor Sigismund, with considerable success.[160] However, they were divided into a moderate and a radical branch, largely corresponding to the social difference between the elite and the people. The conflict resulted in a large part of the ecclesiastical lands being taken over by the laity, mainly the nobility. Sigismund fought for twenty years to suppress the rebellion but finally agreed to a compromise with the moderate party in 1436. The Bohemian estates, towns, gentry and nobles were confirmed in their privileges, the rights of the Germans were restricted, communion was to be given to the laity in both species – one of the central demands of the Hussites – and the cities received the right of resistance against attempts to prevent them from practising their faith. Several conflicts occurred in the following period but the Hussites remained in power until they merged with the new Reformation movement in the early sixteenth century. By contrast, the Church was reduced to a minor property owner. However, the great winners from this were a small number of noble families, which turned out to be a weakness the next time the religious freedom of the country was challenged, at the outbreak of the Thirty Years War.

Sweden and Bohemia had in common that they were in a union with another country, Sweden with Denmark, whereas Bohemia was a part of the large and composite Holy Roman Empire. Generally, dynastic unions often seem to have resulted in conflicts or rebellions. Other examples are Scotland and England in the seventeenth and partly the eighteenth century, Aragon and Castile in 1640–60 and again during the War of the Spanish Succession (1702–13), the Dutch War of Independence against Spain in 1572–1609 and the rebellions against Spain in Sicily and Southern Italy. A common feature was the need for the continuous presence of the king. This might of course also be a burden – entertaining a king is not cheap – but had the advantage that it was possible to negotiate with him in person and solve problems in this way. In addition, kings tended to favour people they knew and would therefore appoint men from their main country of residence to most positions. Political or cultural differences might then easily lead to reactions against officials from another country.

Admittedly, such reactions may also be found within one country, notably such a large and composite country as France, but the more well-developed and advanced the institutions in a country entering a union with another one, the more likely are such problems to occur. In short, without assuming the strong identification with the nation to be found in nineteenth- and twentieth-century national states, sentiments of this kind were strong enough to have political importance and to cause tension within dynastic unions. One condition for this to happen, however, is that group identification extends to national borders, not only to localities within the country. This does not mean that the latter identity is abolished; it continues to exist even in modern national states. It is reasonable to assume that the regional identity was relatively more important in the Middle Ages and the early modern period than today, considering the means of communications at the time, which meant that most people had not travelled far from the place they lived. The most likely category of people to have felt a national identity would therefore have been the elites, nobility, the higher clergy and the higher bourgeoisie, above all the people who held or wanted to hold office in the service of the state. Finally, we must also point to the importance of the king as an object of identification.

There are also numerous examples, mostly from the later Middle Ages, of resentment against people of a different race, language or religion. The many persecutions of the Jews is an obvious example, but there were also other conflicts, such as the one between the English and the Irish in Ireland and Germans and Slavs in various parts of Eastern Europe.[161] Although most known examples of this are from the later Middle Ages, it seems more doubtful whether it was a new phenomenon at the time; there is evidence of such resentment at various times in many parts of the world; it is enough to refer to the Jews and the gentiles in the Old Testament. In some cases, such sentiments may have contributed to national identification, as the persecution and expulsion of Jews and Muslims in Spain, but they might also have the opposite effect, as in Bohemia and other places in East Central Europe, where resentment between ethnic groups made it more difficult to hold the country together.

As we have seen, the 193 states existing today are very different, many of them lacking most of the criteria people in the western world associate with a state. Not surprisingly, civil wars are more frequent today than wars between states. Here we may see a certain parallel to medieval Europe. All medieval states underwent periods of internal conflicts, struggles over the succession or between nobles with bases in different parts of the country. There might also be a sliding transition between external and internal wars, as illustrated by the Hundred Years War. The intensive period of wars between states in the sixteenth and seventeenth centuries may from this point of view be regarded as evidence that the internal conflicts in each country had been overcome. This in turn indicates some internal cohesion, not necessarily patriotism in the modern sense, but that the elites were attached to the central government and that the common people were used to being ruled in a certain way by the representatives of the state. In parts of Europe, notably along its western coast from Norway to Portugal, the units that developed before the thirteenth century have continued to exist until the present. In other parts, further east, great changes occurred during and after the Napoleonic Wars. Entirely new states have developed through the division or unification of earlier territories: Germany and Italy have become united, while a number of new states were created from the ruins of the Austrian Empire. Without claiming that this development was a logical and inevitable outcome of existing loyalties in the countries in question, it may be pointed out that it was very different from the creation of modern states from the European colonies in Africa and the Middle East. The new states had some basis in political and cultural traditions, language, common history, religion or commercial connections, like Germany and Italy, or they had been partly independent units within the old empires, like Belgium, Bohemia and Hungary. The continuity between the old Europe and the new is greater than it immediately seems. Although the modern democratic state in many respects is a radical novelty, it has some basis in the institutions and ties of loyalty developed in the previous period.

The state and the people: the peasant rebellions

Although social inequality was a characteristic feature of all states at the time, whether absolutist or constitutional, peasants and ordinary people were not passive recipients of the decisions and orders of their superiors. One of the most well-known examples of this is the peasant rebellion in England in 1381, which took place in a period of improved conditions for the peasantry. After the disaster of the Black Death, when between one-third and a half of the population of Europe died, there was plenty of arable land and too few peasants to cultivate it. This would mean that land rents would drop and that peasants would get better conditions. However, the landowners tried to resist this by new legislation; the *Statute of Labourers*, issued by Parliament in 1351, tried to impose the same conditions on the peasants as before the plague.

The direct cause of the rebellion that broke out in 1381 was the third poll tax in four years, imposed by Parliament.[162] The tax was set at a fixed amount, decided in 1334, but now the burden on the individual tax-payer had increased because of the reduction of the population resulting from the Black Death. Moreover, the rebels suspected that the money would be wasted in inefficiency and corruption, in accordance with the severe criticism directed at the authorities, in particular, John of Gaunt, Duke of Lancaster, son of King Edward III who had died in 1377. The new king, Richard II, was still a minor, aged 14. The rebellion began in Essex in May and spread in late May and early June until it included the larger part of southern England. Two peasant armies converged in London on 12 June, where they burned the palace of the bishop of London and the hated John of Gaunt's Savoy palace and sacked the Temple. They also plundered and killed Italian and Flemish merchants in the city. The king and his entourage sought refuge in the Tower of London. The king went out to meet the rebels and accepted a number of their demands. In a new meeting on the next day, the leader, Wat Tyler, made new demands, including the abolition of all lordship except that of the king, the distribution of Church property and the abolition of all bishops except one. Tyler is reported to have behaved arrogantly, drinking beer in the presence of the king, and was finally killed by the mayor of London, after which the king declared that he was the leader of the peasants. The rebels were then dispersed relatively easily.

The young king's courage and determination seem remarkable but his action also illustrates the position of the king in contemporary society. Peasant rebels normally directed their anger at the nobles and the king's officials but respected the king and often believed that he was on their side. According to Harriss, the whole meeting, including the killing of Wat Tyler, had been planned in advance and Tyler's arrogant behaviour was the result of provocation. The leaders of the central government, including the king, wanted severe reprisals afterwards, but the local authorities resisted, not out of sympathy with the rebels but for pragmatic reasons. Too great severity might lead to new unrest. The result was that the leaders were sought out and many of them executed, but otherwise, punishment mostly came in the form of fines rather than executions.

Concerning the aims of the rebels, there were elements of millenarianism, notably in the sermons by the preacher John Ball, who pointed to the Christian doctrine of the equality of all men, expressed in the sentence: 'When Adam delved and Eve span, who was then a gentleman?' There were also some references to Wycliffe. The most important motives seem nevertheless to have been immediate anger over taxes and other burdens and concrete proposals for reform: personal freedom for the peasants, land rent fixed to 4 pence for an acre, free contracts between peasants and lords and free buying and selling. Despite the large number of men assembled, the rebels were relatively disciplined and moderate in their use of violence; the violence was directed at special groups and individuals whom the peasants regarded as oppressors. Most of the leaders were wealthy, middle-aged, responsible men with experience of local administration and were clearly well informed about political matters. Many of them might afterwards be found in the same positions of authority as before.

It has been commented that peasant rebellions were an essential element of agrarian society in the same way as strikes in industrial society. There were always conflicts of interest but on the other hand, the aim of the rebellions was rarely the total abolition of the landowning class. More often, they concerned specific burdens, particularly new ones, or they were sparked off by special circumstances. The great peasant rebellion in France in 1358, which coincided with Etienne Marcel's rebellion in Paris, was the result of the English devastation of the French countryside which the French king and nobles had been unable to prevent.[163] The Hungarian rebellion of 1514 developed from the mobilization of a large peasant army for a Crusade against the Turks. The nobles were against this, as they wanted the peasants for work on the land. Moreover, the provisioning of the army led to plundering, particularly of noble residences. The peasants also refused to pay taxes. When Archbishop Tomas Bakócz who had originally organized the Crusade, was pressured by the nobles to suspend recruitment, a full rebellion broke out.[164]

The great peasant rebellion in Germany, 1524–25. was partly provoked by Luther's Reformation.[165] The attack on the Church, the greatest landowner in the country and Luther's proclamation of the freedom of the Christian might easily be turned into a social revolt. However, the peasants also had a number of concrete grievances about oppression and taxes, extension of labour services, restriction of informal rights to access to wood, water and grazing, imposition of new obligations and the extension of fines and penalties. The early sixteenth century was a period of recovery after the labour shortage caused by the Black Death, which may have led the landowners to increase the burdens on the peasants. The peasants began by demanding negotiations over their grievances, which the lords refused. However, the latter largely lacked military means, as the result of the war in Italy – this was the period of the siege of Pavia and Charles V's victory over Francis I. During a few months, the rebellion spread over Upper Swabia, the Black Forest, Alsace, Tyrol, Franconia and towards the Thuringian Forest and Saxony. Appeal to the Bible and religious ideas had already occurred in July 1524 but became particularly prominent in February–March 1525, when 'the Christian Union of the Peasants of Upper Swabia' was formed. The peasants referred directly to Luther's idea of the freedom of the Christian and appealed to the authority of the Bible regarding social and economic laws. However, Luther rejected their appeal. After some attempt at mediation in the beginning, he turned to outright condemnation of the peasants, urging the authorities to take a savage revenge on them, which they of course did. Generally, the cruelty of the authorities in suppressing the rebellions exceeded the violence of the peasants themselves. Of course, the cruelty was particularly directed at the leaders. Thus, the leader of the Hungarian rebellion was fried on a throne of glowing iron, while some of his subordinates were forced to eat pieces of his flesh before they were executed. On the other hand, those who escaped the immediate suppression were left alone; there was rarely any long-term revenge. Rebellion might also in some cases lead to some improvement in the peasants' conditions.

There have been widely different interpretations of the peasant rebellions. To the Marxists, they were the expression of a deep conflict of interest between the peasants and the landowning classes, as expressed by Marx and Engels themselves, and modern historians, such as Rodney Hilton in his interpretation of the English peasant rebellion.[166] An opposite point of view is represented by French scholars, such as Roland Mousnier and Guy Fourquin, who point to religious ideas and particular grievances as their causes and to the fact that most leaders of the rebellion were well-to-do people, often belonging to the aristocracy. It may be adduced in favour of the Marxist interpretation that there was in fact a conflict of interest between peasants and landowners; the latter largely lived off the surplus of the production of the former. On the other hand, the peasants rarely wanted a social revolution; they accepted the position of the king and the landowners but reacted at specific deterioration of their conditions, such as the new taxes imposed on them in England in 1381 or the landowners' failure to protect them in France in 1358. As we have seen, religious and millenarian ideas might also be a factor.

Concerning the relationship between the peasants and the elite, there is a clear contrast between the centre and the periphery of Europe, the flat, densely populated areas in the central zone versus the forested and mountainous areas to the north and south. The great peasant rebellions and the conflicts between the peasants and the authorities are characteristic of the former region, while the peasants had greater liberty and to a greater extent governed themselves in the latter. In these regions, the king or the prince might often conduct much of the local government through the peasant communities or peasant representatives might themselves form the government, as in parts of Scandinavia and the Swiss Confederacy.[167]

Ordinary people were less likely to have interests in matters of state, but as the example of the Engelbrekt and Hussite rebellions show, they might resent being governed by foreigners. In addition, even peasants were organized at the local level and might try to address the king and the governing elite with petitions or, if these failed, resort to open rebellion. The English rebellions in the thirteenth and seventeenth centuries which will be discussed in Chapter 5 were not confined to the nobility, but also included a considerable number of people from the lower ranks of society, although gentry and yeomen rather than ordinary peasants. These latter layers of society were also represented in the House of Commons in Parliament which became an important and influential part of the assembly during the later Middle Ages.

The king usually had little direct influence on the peasants in the beginning. This gradually changed from the thirteenth century onwards and particularly in the early modern period, with increasing taxation and the development of royal jurisdiction. The peasants might appeal to the king against their lord or they might seek protection from the lord against taxes and other demands from the king. It seems that the latter was the more common. In France, between 1360 and 1775, peasant revolts were almost exclusively directed at royal taxation or other financial demands.[168] The military mobilization under Richelieu was a particularly violent period.[169] At this time, however, the peasants often had support from other groups, even members of the elite; the rebellions were not confined to the peasants but were often the expression of reactions against interference in local affairs by the central authorities. A number of issues led to protest: new regulations, the billeting of soldiers – who often oppressed their hosts or raped their wives or daughters – various indirect taxes or regulations of the economy. In some areas, like Burgundy, where the lords had extensive control over the peasants, they might also protect them against demands from the central authorities. In principle, lordship not only involved authority but also protection; traditionally, lords were supposed to aid their peasants against famine and other disasters.[170] The number of rebellions decreased during the reign of Louis XIV, hardly because the demands from the state became less but because the government had increased its control of the elites.

Thus, the increasing power of the state did not generally improve the condition of the peasants. Nevertheless, the rivalry between their lord and the king gave them some opportunities to ally with one of them against the other; they might sue their lords at the royal courts and might even in some cases win their suits. As appears from the example of the English rebellion of 1381, the peasants often appealed to the king and regarded him as their protector, while blaming his officers and the nobility for injustice and oppression. Although kings rarely had any particular sympathy with the peasants, this belief was certainly an important factor in the development of monarchy. It would seem that the financial burden on the peasants increased with the development of the state, although to some extent, the increasing taxes were compensated for by reduced dues to the lord in the period after the Black Death.

Finally, even if the state was a burden more than an aid for the peasants and their belief that the king was their friend was often an illusion, one condition was even worse than the presence of the state, namely, its break-down. Whereas a country like France after the fifteenth century was mostly strong enough to conduct its external wars in the enemy's country, the civil war of 1562–98 was a terrible disaster.[171] Both parties used mercenaries who fought to gain booty and plundered where they went, in addition to the cruelties resulting from religious fanaticism. The peasants were not passive victims but organized to protect themselves and in some cases managed to defeat the invaders, although they were usually defeated and often massacred in pitched battles.

Conclusion

Did war make the state and did the state make peace or war? European states did make war and war was also important for their development but in a way that conforms neither to Tilly's nor to Morris' picture. Their internal development was not the result of a strong conqueror – 'a stationary bandit' – suppressing an area and forcing its inhabitants to live in peace together. On the contrary, remarkably stable states were created from the ninth and tenth centuries onwards through the introduction of dynastic succession, that is, stable in the sense that the dynasties usually continued to rule until they became extinct, although they had no monopoly of violence and only limited control of their subjects. When they eventually achieved this, war was clearly an important factor, mainly through the mobilization of the leading men in the country for the king's war, first, as his allies, then as officers in organized armies. Warfare and military preparation were by far the largest items on the budget of most states, the main explanation for the increase in taxes and the growth of bureaucracy in the early modern period, of crucial importance for the technological development and for increased professionalization of the armed forces as well as the civilian bureaucracy. There was also a clear trend in the early modern period in the direction of warfare between the states replacing internal conflicts within them. There was even a direct connection between the two; uniting the aristocracy against an external enemy was a means to prevent internal conflicts, as can be illustrated by the Spanish kingdoms which were united against external enemies until the mid-thirteenth century and from the late fifteenth century onwards but suffered from internal unrest in the intervening period. So far, there is much to say in favour of war making the state.

An equally important factor, however, was conflict solution. This can also be traced back to the early Middle Ages. In the beginning, the king was only one of several powers that might be involved in it. It mainly took the form of arbitration, as pointed out by a number of recent scholars, who have also argued for the positive effects of this, often in contrast to the later system of royal justice. It is also easy to sympathize with arbitration when comparing it to the inquisitional process and the brutal punishments in the early modern period. Nevertheless, the statistical evidence clearly supports the view that the state's monopoly or near monopoly of violence led to a dramatic decline in homicide and in general made societies more peaceful. In addition, the growth of public justice may be considered against the background of changing social and economic conditions: increase in trade and urbanization, greater geographic mobility and the need for protection of travellers and for predictable justice in commercial cases.

The state developed first in the judicial field and had reached a fairly advanced level already before the military revolution from the mid-fifteenth century onwards. There was also a sliding transition between the struggle against internal and external enemies, as illustrated by the conflict between England, France and Germany in the early thirteenth century, partly also the Hundred Years War. Moreover, the 'most governed' country of Europe, England, did not participate in the military revolution and was weak militarily until the second half of the seventeenth century. By contrast, this country probably had the most efficient judicial system. Finally, it must be added that the militarization did not lead to military dictatorship, unlike what happened in many other places in the world, such as the Arab and Ottoman Empires. There was no 'extraction-coercion cycle' and the army was under civilian control.

In addition to these two factors of a concrete and institutional character, we must add a third one of a less tangible nature, namely, norms, ideology and culture. The legitimacy of dynasties was a crucial factor in state formation. It largely determined the territorial divisions and whether or not a particular unit would remain separate or be joined with another in a personal union. Internal conflicts in a country were mostly over the succession to the throne. The existence of clear rules for this and whether or not there was a successor in the direct line might determine the question of internal peace. In most cases, hereditary monarchy led to greater stability than rule by elected officers, as will be further developed in the following. A further contribution to this was the ideology celebrating the ruler as

God's representative on Earth, expressed in unction and coronation and courtly rituals, as well as strong links between him and the elites of the country, as expressed most clearly in Louis XIV's Versailles. Although the instrumental character of the courtly culture has sometimes been exaggerated and there are also some examples of successful state formation without it, notably Prussia, it nevertheless remains an important factor in linking the elites to the monarchy.

Finally, these three factors are not just additions to Tilly's and his successors' exclusive focus on warfare but imply a different perspective according to which alliances and cooperation become more important than force. Tilly is right in pointing to the relative independence of the state, in contrast to the Marxist idea of 'the executive committee of the aristocracy'. There is always an advantage in being in the centre; institutions have a power in themselves, in addition to the one delegated from the forces they are supposed to represent. On the other hand, when the 'extraction-coercion cycle' can be shown not to have worked in practice, we have to look for another basis for the king's power; he had to seek support from society. Although state formation involved a considerable amount of oppression, and it can hardly be said to be in the interest of the whole population, it did not consist in a general competition between power-holders in which the strongest won. From early on, there was an idea of the royal office on which only a limited number of people might have a claim. A further expansion of state power could only take place by the ruler creating alliances with and serving the interests of other leading men in the country, through the distribution of justice, feasts, ceremonials and courtly culture and through mobilizing them in war against foreign enemies. The relative importance of these three main factors varied over time and from country to country, as will be discussed more in the following, mostly in Chapter 5.

Notes

1 Morris, *War*, p. 18.
2 Ibid., pp. 29–47.
3 Cf. Reinhard, *Geschichte der Staatsgewalt*, p. 16, who observes that, according to the strictest criteria, there were only sovereign states in Europe during a short period from the late eighteenth to the mid-twentieth century.
4 Verhulst, 'Economic Organization', p. 487; Fossier, 'Rural Economy', p. 59 and Reyerson, 'Commerce', p. 51.
5 Imsen and Vogler, 'Communal Autonomy'; Blickle, 'Conclusions'.
6 Zmora, *Monarchy*, pp. 17–21.
7 Duby, *Les trois ordres*; Oexle, 'Deutungsschemata'; Le Goff, 'Les trois fonctions'.
8 *The Deeds of Frederick*, vol. I.32, pp. 66–7.
9 Bagge, 'Ideas and Narrative'; Berend *et al., Central Europe*, pp. 192–3.
10 Fryde and Postan, 'Public Credit', pp. 507–11.
11 Scales, *The Shaping*, p. 93.
12 Bachrach, *Warfare*, pp. 179–83, on the provisioning of Ottonian armies, which imply extensive royal estates.
13 Zmora, *Monarchy, Aristocracy and the State*, pp. 1–36.
14 The classic account is Ganshof, *Feudalism*.
15 The etymology of the word is disputed. The most common opinion is that it is derived from Old French **fehu-ôd*, in which *fehu* means 'cattle' (cf. German *Vieh*) and *-ôd* means 'goods', in Latin *feudum* which replaced the earlier Latin term *beneficium* (= gift).

16 Poly and Bounazel, *La mutation féodale*, pp. 1–85.
17 Reynolds, *Fiefs and Vassals*.
18 For example, Bisson, *The Crisis*, pp. 24–5; Debax, 'L'aristocracie languedocienne' and Althoff, 'Establishing Bonds'. The opposite point of view is expressed by Reynolds, 'Fiefs and Vassals' and Kasten, 'Economic and Political Aspects'.
19 Debax, 'L'aristocracie' and *La Féodalité langedocienne*.
20 Althoff, 'Establishing Bonds'.
21 Bartlett, *England*, pp. 121–2.
22 For the following, see Helle, *Cambridge History*, pp. 105–234; Berend *et al.*, *Central Europe*, pp. 110–249 and Bagge, *Cross and Scepter*, pp. 9–118.
23 Nelson, 'Queens as Jezebels'; Stafford, 'Sons and Mothers'.
24 Nelson, 'Kingship and Royal Government', pp. 400–1; Airlie, 'The Aristocracy', pp. 431–50, on mothers.
25 Tellenbach, 'Die Unteilbarkeit des Reiches'; Schmid, 'Das Problem der Unteilbarkeit des Reiches'; Becher, *Die mittelalterliche Thronfolge*.
26 Collins, *From Tribes to Nation*, pp. 150–2.
27 Eisner, 'Killing Kings', p. 556; Morrill, 'Conclusion', p. 297.
28 Bagge, 'The Decline of Regicide'.
29 Duby, *Medieval Marriage*.
30 For practice in various countries, see e.g., Lachaud and Penman, *Making and Breaking the Rules*.
31 Morris, *War*, pp. 134–9.
32 Tilly, *Coercion*, p. 79.
33 Contamine, 'Introduction', p. 3.
34 Admittedly, this came late in the British navy. In 1747, some young officers met in a coffeehouse and agreed that uniform would be a good idea for naval officers (Morris, *War*, p. 189).
35 See McNeill, *The Pursuit of Power*, pp. 158–84 for the following.
36 Kroener, 'The Modern State and Military Society', pp. 202–3.
37 The attitude is aptly illustrated in Tolstoy's caricature in *War and Peace* of the Prussian officer Pfuel during the campaign in 1812, who insists on well-planned and scientific campaigns, regardless of their results.
38 Finer, 'State and Nation Building', pp. 90–7.
39 Tallett, *War and Society*, pp. 191–3.
40 Post, *Studies*, pp. 434–53; Kantorowicz, *The King's Two Bodies*, pp. 259–67; Menache, *Vox Dei*, pp. 177–87.
41 For the following, see Guenée, *States and Rulers*, pp. 91–110, and Ormond, 'The West European Monarchies', pp. 133–5.
42 Spruyt, *The Sovereign State*, p. 157.
43 Trevor Roper, 'The Crisis of the Seventeenth Century', pp. 43–81; Steensgaard, 'The Seventeenth Century Crisis' and 'The Seventeenth Century Crisis and the Unity of Eurasian History', the latter arguing that the crisis was specific to Europe.
44 Brunner, *Land und Herrschaft*, pp. 11–17.
45 Fryde, *The Tyranny*, p. 150; Hyams, *Rancor & Reconciliation*, pp. 264–5; Cf. also Carpenter, *Wars of the Roses*, pp. 44–66, on English government in the fifteenth century.
46 Barthélemy, *Nouvelle histoire*, pp. 79, 246–52.
47 Edward has a bad reputation among medieval chroniclers as well as modern historians. The recent biography by Phillips, *Edward II*, offers a rehabilitation on some points.
48 Fryde, *The Tyranny*, pp. 58–68; cf. the comparison with the greater leniency in the 1260s, pp. 78–9.
49 Gillingham, 'Enforcing Old Law'; Strickland, '*In coronam regiam iniuriam*'.
50 Nelson, 'The Frankish Kingdoms', p. 134.
51 Althoff, *Spielregeln*, pp. 36–8.
52 Broekmann, *Rigor iustitiae*.
53 Valente, *The Theory and Practice of Revolt*, p. 205.

54   Bellamy, *The Law of Treason*, and Gillingham, 'Enforcing Old Law'.

55   Harriss, *England 1360–1461*, pp. 644–5.

56   Cuttler, *The Law of Treason*.

57   Maitland, *The Constitutional History*, p. 19.

58   Brown, 'Society and the Supernatural'; Bartlett, *Trial by Fire and Water*; Davies and Fouracre, *The Settlement of Disputes*, pp. 207–40; Hyams, 'Trial by Ordeal'.

59   Berman, *Law and Revolution*, pp. 467–81.

60   Harriss, 'Government in Late Medieval England', p. 53.

61   For this and the following, see Foucault, *Surveiller et punir*, pp. 10–72; Dupont-Bouchat, 'Guilt and Individual Consciousness', pp. 123–38; Berman, *Law and Revolution*, vol. II, pp. 131–55.

62   Foucault, *Surveiller et punir*, pp. 9–11 and 36–7.

63   Berman, *Law and Revolution*, vol. II, pp. 317–19.

64   Dupont-Bouchat, 'Guilt and Individual Consciousness', pp. 128, 136.

65   Castan, 'Criminelle'.

66   Berman, *Law and Revolution*, vol. II, pp. 133–7; Foucault, *Surveiller et punir*, pp. 47–51.

67   *The King's Mirror*, p. 319; Bagge, *The Political Thought*, pp. 63–4. The statement about God not punishing twice ('non iudicat Deus bis in idipsum') stems from Jerome and was often quoted in the Middle Ages, including by Thomas Becket in his dispute with King Henry II about clerics who had committed crimes (Brooke, *The English Church*, p. 205, n.1).

68   Blanning, *The Pursuit of Glory*, p. 326.

69   Bayley, 'The Police', p. 342.

70   Quetel, 'Lettres de cachet'.

71   Strayer, *On the Medieval Origins*, pp. 23–5.

72   For the following, see Cheyette, 'Suum cuique tribuere'; Davies and Fouracre, *The Settlement of Disputes*, pp. 208–40; Esmark *et al.*, *Disputing Strategies*, pp. 1–31. See also the debate about the Feudal Revolution in *Past and Present* 1994 and 1997 between Thomas Bisson, Timothy Reuter and Chris Wickham.

73   Diamond, *The World until Yesterday*, pp. 139–40; cf. also Morris, *War*, pp. 7–19.

74   Miller, *Blood-Taking and Peace-Making*, in particular pp. 221–308; White, 'Feuding', p. 202.

75   White, 'Feuding', pp. 214–21.

76   Bisson, *The Crisis of the Twelfth Century*, pp. 48–9, on the peace movement. Generally, Bisson is a strong spokesman for the traditional view.

77   Reuter, 'The Origins'; cf. Harriss, 'Political Society', pp. 51–3, on arbitration in the later Middle Ages.

78   Harriss, *Shaping the Nation*, p. 81; Spruyt, *The Sovereign State*, pp. 158–67; Watts, *The Making of Polities*, pp. 207–19.

79   See e.g. Wieland, *Studien zur Integration*, on this process in Bavaria in the sixteenth century. An example of increasing royal involvement in justice in local society in France is Firnhaber-Baker, *Violence and the State in Languedoc*.

80   Eisner, 'Long-Term Trends in Violent Crime'; Pinker, *The Better Angels*, pp. 71–102. For a case study, see Sharpe and Dickinson, 'Revisiting the "Violence We Have Lost": Homicide in Seventeenth-Century Cheshire'.

81   By contrast, if the chronology is correct, it is obvious that the explanation cannot be better health care. No significant improvement in this field took place until the twentieth century.

82   Hirschman, *The Passions and the Interests*.

83   Berman, *Law and Revolution*, pp. 9–10.

84   Davis, 'La femme au politique'; Oakley-Brown and Wilkinson, *The Rituals and Rhetoric of Queenship*; Duggan (ed.), *Queens and Queenship in Medieval Europe* and Fössel, 'The Political Tradition of Female Rulership in Europe', pp. 68–83.

85   Davis, 'La femme au politique'.

86   Le Goff, *Saint Louis*, pp. 99–128.

87   Guenée, *States and Rulers*, p. 128; Clanchy, *From Memory*, p. 45; Harriss, 'Government in Late Medieval England', p. 35; Weiler, *Kingship, Rebellion and Political Culture*, p. 35.

88   *The King's Mirror*, p. 169.
89   Strayer, *The Reign of Philip the Fair*, pp. 36–99.
90   Althoff, *Kontrolle der Macht*, pp. 152–87 on Henry IV of Germany's failure to listen to advice.
91   Elias, *The Court Society*, pp. 42–65; Bluche, *Louis XIV*, pp. 179–97, 363–80; Burke, *The Fabrication of Louis XIV*; Chaline, 'The Kingdoms of France and Navarre', pp. 67–93; Collins, *From Tribes to Nation*, pp. 375–88.
92   Burke, *The Fabrication of Louis XIV*, pp. 9, 87–91.
93   Blanning, *The Culture of Power*, p. 32.
94   *Heimskringla*, pp. 327–9.
95   Bernhardt, *Itinerant Kingship*, pp. 45–84; Zotz, 'Carolingian Tradition'.
96   See e.g. Mulryne *et al.*, *Ceremonial Entries in Early Modern Europe*.
97   Kantorowicz, *The King's Two Bodies*, pp. 249–58.
98   Erkens, 'Thronfolge und Herrschersakralität', pp. 361–8. On coronation and sacred monarchy in the Middle Ages, see e.g. Kantorowicz, *The King's Two Bodies*; Schramm, *Der König von Frankreich* and *Geschichte des englischen Königtums*, and Le Goff, 'Le Roi dans l'Occident médiéval'.
99   Le Goff, *Saint Louis*, pp. 574–85 ; Cohen, *The Sainte-Chapelle*.
100 Götzmann, 'Weihen', pp. 22–3.
101 Kolmer, *Der Tod des Mächtigen*; Monod, *The Power of Kings*, pp. 33–42.
102 Bloch, *Les rois taumaturges*, pp. 27–49; for the date, see Le Goff, *Saint Louis*, p. 832.
103 Bloch, *Les rois taumaturges*, p. 398; Blanning, *The Culture of Power*, p. 408. According to Bloch, the story, which stems from Saint-Simon, is probably not true. There is no clear evidence either of the cause of Madame de Soubise's death or of her having been the king's mistress.
104 Adamson, 'The Kingdoms of England and Great Britain', p. 117.
105 Worseley, *Courtiers*, pp. 229–30.
106 Thietmar, *Ottonian Germany*, p. 185.
107 Guenée, *States and Rulers*, pp. 78–9, on numbers and sums.
108 Redworth and Checa, 'The Kingdoms of Spain', p. 47.
109 Elias, *The Court Society*.
110 Blanning, *Culture of Power*, p. 41.
111 Redworth and Checa, 'The Kingdoms of Spain', pp. 54–8.
112 Ruiz, *A King Travels*, p. 18.
113 Pognon, *Les très riches heures*, pp. 30–1.
114 Stürner, *Friedrich II*, vol. 2, pp. 429–47.
115 Blanning, *Pursuit of Glory*, pp. 393–401.
116 Burke, *Fabrication*, pp. 32–5.
117 *The Political Testament of Cardinal Richelieu*, p. 41.
118 Elias, *The Court Society*, p. 89.
119 Blanning, *Culture of Power*, p. 31.
120 Ibid., p. 40.
121 Ibid., pp. 54–5.
122 Blanning, *Pursuit of Glory*, pp. 430–7.
123 Ibid., p. 51.
124 Adamson, 'The Kingdoms of England and Great Britain', pp. 95–117; Blanning, *Culture of Power*, pp. 316–22.
125 Blanning, *Pursuit of Glory*, pp. 440–4.
126 Tullberg, *Beyond Feudalism*; Dabringhaus, 'The Monarch'; Kunt, 'Turks'.
127 Burke, *The Fabrication*.
128 *Gesta Chuonradi*, Chapter 7, p. 130. My translation. Cf. Beumann, 'Zur Entwicklung' and Bagge, *Kings, Politics*, pp. 200–4.
129 Arquillière, *L'augustinisme politique*; Kempf, 'Das Problem der Christianitas im 12. und 13. Jahrhundert', pp. 104–23.
130 *Policraticus*, V.2.
131 Melve, *Inventing the Public Sphere*, pp. 349–74, 35.

132 For this and the following, see Krynen, *L'empire du roi*, pp. 70–84.
133 Kantorowicz, *The King's Two Bodies*, pp. 42–313.
134 Coleman, 'The Individual and the Medieval State', pp. 14–34 and 'Property and Poverty'.
135 Pierre de Belleperche (c. 1250–1308), quoted in Schmale, 'Liberty is an Inestimable Thing', pp. 171–2.
136 Dunbabin, 'Government', p. 494.
137 On John's political thought, see Nederman, *John of Salisbury*, pp. 59–62.
138 *Inst.* I.2.6 = *Dig.* I.4.1. and *Dig.* I.3.31.
139 Skinner, *The Foundations*, vol. II, pp. 353–8.
140 Elton, *England under the Tudors*, pp. 130–7, 160–5.
141 Bluche, *Louis XIV*, p. 615.
142 Blanning, *Culture*, p. 195.
143 *The King's Mirror*, p. 246; Bagge, *The Political Thought*, p. 63.
144 Jaeger, 'Courtesy and Treachery', pp. 202–3.
145 Saxo, *History of the Danes*, 'Preface'.
146 Kersken, *Geschichtsschreibung*, pp. 788–9.
147 Barth, *Ethnic Groups and Boundaries*.
148 Hobsbawm, *Nations*; Breuilly, *Nationalism*. By contrast, Smith, in *Theories* and *National Identity*, points to trends in this direction in earlier ages. See also Guiberneau and Hutchinson, *Understanding Nationalism*, a collection of articles representing different views.
149 Gellner, *Nations and Nationalism*.
150 Hobsbawm, *Nations and Nationalism*, p. 46.
151 Gellner, *Nations and Nationalism*, pp. 20–38.
152 Bagge, *Society and Politics*, pp. 100–5.
153 Ibid, pp. 100–5; Maddicott, *Simon de Montfort*, pp. 145–6; Blanning, *Culture of Power*, pp. 21–5; cf. also 16–20.
154 Whereas many scholars have seen a conflict between religion and nationalism, Smith, *Theories of Nationalism*, p. ix and Blanning, *Culture of Power*, p. 23 point to the connection between the two.
155 For the following, see Bagge, *Cross and Scepter*, pp. 250–68.
156 For the following, see Michaud, 'The Kingdoms of Central Europe', pp. 756–63; Scott, 'Germany and the Empire' and Klassen, 'Hus, the Hussites and Bohemia'.
157 *Karoli IV Vita*, pp. 66–9.
158 Crossley and Opačić, 'Prague as a New Capital'.
159 Opačić, 'Sacred Topography'; Dolezel, 'Die Gründung des Prager Slavenklosters', pp. 112–14.
160 Housley, 'Sanctified Patriotism', pp. 236–41.
161 Bartlett, *The Making of Europe*, pp. 236–42.
162 For the following, see Dyer, *Making a Living*, pp. 286–93. There is a considerable literature on the rebellion, including Hilton and Fage, *The English Rising*; Freedman, 'Rural Society', pp. 98–100 and Harriss, *Shaping the Nation*, pp. 447–9.
163 Fourquin, *The Anatomy*, pp. 134–9.
164 Engel, *The Realm of St Stephen*, pp. 362–4.
165 Scribner, 'The Reformation Movements in Germany', pp. 87–92.
166 Hilton and Fagan, *The English Rising*.
167 Blickle, *Resistance, Representation and Community*, pp. 325–38; Imsen and Vogler, 'Communal Autonomy', pp. 18–27; Blickle *et al.*, 'The Commons and the State', pp. 121–4, 128–32, 147–50.
168 Ladurie, *The French Peasantry*, p. 372.
169 For the following, see Mousnier, *Peasant Uprisings*, pp. 32–149.
170 Tilly, 'Food Supply', p. 411.
171 Collins, *From Tribe to Nation*, pp. 321–6.

3

THE STATE AND ITS COMPETITORS

The Church and the papal monarchy

The little village of Montaillou in the Diocese of Pamiers in southern France, high up in the Pyrenees, was made famous by Emmanuel Le Roy Ladurie, who gave a uniquely vivid and intimate picture of a peasant community in the early fourteenth century.[1] What enabled him to do this was the fact that the bishop suspected the inhabitants of the village of being adherents of the Cathar heresy and had them arrested and interrogated by the Inquisition. The bishop, Jacques Fournier, later became Pope Benedict XII (1334–42), and brought the protocols with him to Avignon where they were preserved in the papal archive, later transferred to the Vatican. The bishop was a zealous guardian of orthodoxy but also a clever psychologist who let the people he interrogated speak freely, telling long stories about local events and reporting various kinds of gossip. This makes the protocol resemble a modern report from ethnographic fieldwork, although of course, when using it, we have to remember that the informants risked torture or death if they revealed dangerous information.

The geographical horizon of the villagers is expressed when one of them compares Paradise to an enormous house, stretching from the Hill of Mérens to the city of Toulouse.[2] The main authorities to whom they related were the Count of Foix, the lord of the area, and of course the Bishop of Pamiers. Despite the impressive state building under Philip IV, the king of France is far away, although occasionally mentioned as a threatening force.[3]

While the state was gradually extending its control of the limited areas ruled by kings, the Church was present in every village across Europe. The bishop could arrest and interrogate the whole population of a village in order to uncover a potential crime, in a period when public authorities rarely instigated a prosecution unless there was an accusation from an individual person. Departure from Christian orthodoxy was thus in practice the most serious crime in medieval Europe. Moreover, the Church did not turn up in local society only in order to prosecute specific crimes; the whole of Europe was divided into parishes where a priest was responsible for upholding the faith and administering the sacraments to the local population. Although these priests were not always loyal and conscientious servants of the Church – they are often criticized for lack of learning, in some cases barely understanding the Latin of the liturgy, and for failing to observe the rule of celibacy, introduced in the late eleventh century – the Church was in possession of a formidable apparatus.

People were supposed to attend mass once a week, go to confession and receive Holy Communion at least once a year and pay a certain percentage of their income to the Church. Moreover, they had to keep track of a large number of holidays when it was forbidden to work, as well as fast days, when it was forbidden to eat meat and have sexual intercourse. The former included on average every four days (Sundays and a number of feasts for God and the saints), the latter all Fridays, days before great feasts as well as four weeks before Christmas and seven weeks before Easter. Finally, the Church banned marrying relatives, first in seven, then, from 1215, in four degrees. Transgressing these rules not only constituted sins that demanded confession and absolution, but also crimes, subject to prosecution by ecclesiastical officers. It took a long time before the king was able to interfere in a similar way and when this did happen, it was largely by taking over the functions of the Church.

Religion is an important factor in all traditional civilizations but it may take very different forms. Christianity is one of several transcendental religions that originated in the period after around 500 BC: Hinduism, Buddhism, Judaism, Christianity, Islam and some others. These religions focused on the life after death rather than the present one; they had religious elites, different from the secular ones; they had a doctrine; and they distinguished clearly between adherents and non-adherents of the faith, all this in contrast to ethnic religions, like the religions of China and of ancient Greece and Rome.[4] Nevertheless, Catholic Christianity differs significantly from the others, if not in kind, at least in degree. Its doctrine is probably the most elaborate and it certainly surpasses all others in the degree of bureaucratization and centralization of its organization. This was particularly the case from the eleventh century onwards, when the reformed papacy claimed full control of the Church and fought secular rulers, notably the German emperor, for this role (The Investiture Contest, 1075–1122).

Monotheistic religions generally make a sharp distinction between orthodoxy and heresy and often persecute the latter. Such persecutions took place both in Western and Eastern Christendom from late antiquity onwards and within Islam as well as to some extent Judaism. However, there are few examples of religious persecution in the West between late antiquity and the twelfth century. In the following period, new religious movements developed in opposition to the Church, the best-known of which are the Cathars or Albigensians and the Waldensians. The former rejected most of the dogmas of the Church while the latter was originally an attempt at reforming the Church through poverty and simplicity. The Church reacted to the new movements by instituting the papal Inquisition, which was not bound by diocesan borders, but was entitled to trace and punish heresy everywhere. It was usually staffed by friars, notably Dominicans. Previously, however, it had been the responsibility of the local bishop to deal with heresy, a practice that still continued, for instance, in Montaillou. The development of the Inquisition has usually been explained as a reaction to new religious movements. An alternative explanation, most recently put forward by R.I. Moore, claims that it was mainly a result of stricter attitudes within the Church and that the doctrines attributed to the heretics were largely invented by the inquisitors. However, although changing attitudes within the Church should not be neglected, it is difficult accept this as full explanation for the persecutions.[5]

What we know of the methods of the inquisitors – information also accepted by Moore – makes it difficult to explain that the inquisitors invented the opinions of their victims. Why would the Inquisition produce documents like the detailed protocol forming the material for Le Roy Ladurie's famous book on Montaillou where we hear the people in the village giving lengthy accounts of conversations, religious speculations and daily life? Would people with this willingness to listen and write down detailed information of what they heard simply attribute to their informants an invented theology? Nor do other records of the thirteenth-century Inquisition suggest the invention of heresy. In contrast to the Crusaders against the Albigensians in the first half of the thirteenth century who often massacred their defeated enemies without examining them about their faith, the Inquisition seems in most cases to have examined their victims thoroughly and only executed very few of them. This is also accepted by Moore. Moreover, if found guilty, the victims had the possibility of recanting. So why would they not do so rather than be burnt if they did not believe in the doctrines the inquisitors attributed to them? And why would the inquisitors invent two distinct forms of heresy if they consistently took their information from ancient books?

Finally, there is also other evidence of a new engagement by the laity in religious issues from the late eleventh century onwards. There was a popular movement in favour of religious reform during the Investiture Contest and the crusading movement not only mobilized the aristocracy but also the common people. Although we know far more about the official Church and its doctrine than about popular religion, there is evidence that the Church at least to some extent had manage to transmit its message to the people, despite numerous examples of ideas and practices that did not conform to orthodoxy.[6] A popular Crusade headed towards Jerusalem before the 'official' one but most of the participants were killed before they reached their goal.[7] There is thus a significant difference between the period from the late eleventh century onwards and the previous one regarding popular religious movements, which at least indirectly forms a further argument in favour of the traditional interpretation of heresy.

In principle, the religious monopoly of the Church was confined to the Christians. It was a crime for them to reject the Christian faith or have another interpretation of it than the Church. After the general conversion of Europe to Christianity, alternative religions were forbidden in most places. However, there were exceptions. Large Muslim populations continued to be tolerated for a long time in countries conquered by Christians, such as Spain and Sicily, probably mainly for pragmatic reasons. In addition, there were Jewish communities in most European countries.[8] The official doctrine of the Church was that the Jews should not be forced to convert. Adherence to the Christian faith should in principle be voluntary but once conversion had occurred, it was a crime to reject the faith. Regarding the Jews, both the Church and secular authorities introduced various restrictions. Most seriously, they were increasingly blamed for various disasters or were subject to popular persecution with outbreaks of religious fervour. In the late eleventh century, the Crusading movement led to massacres of Jews, as did also the Black Death in the mid-fourteenth century, when the Jews were accused of having caused the disease by poisoning the wells. Easter time, when Christ's passion was celebrated, was a particularly dangerous period for them, which often led to pogroms. Joinville tells that the pious St Louis of France approved of a knight who broke off a debate between the monks of Cluny and the Jews by chasing away the Jews with his sword.[9]

However, the latter story does indicate that there were also theological discussions between the two religions. Moreover, the Jews had some influence on Biblical studies at the time. Some Christian theologians learnt Hebrew from them and consulted them on difficult passages in the Old Testament.[10] It is no coincidence that the discussion Joinville mentions took place at Cluny, which was an important centre for attempts to convert members of other religions by intellectual discussion and it was where the Quran was translated into Latin at the initiative of the Abbot, Peter the Venerable, in the twelfth century.[11] The Jews were also under the king's special protection, which, however, did not come cheap. Kings might profit from their wealth and make use of them because they were not bound by the Church's ban on lending money against interest. They therefore had an influential position at some royal courts, notably in Spain, until they were expelled in the sixteenth century. They had earlier been expelled from England (1290) and France (1306). The Jews might easily be resented because of their difference from Christians, not only in religion but also in language, dress and manners, although religion is clearly the main reason for their difficult position. The greater the influence of the Church and its success in teaching its message to the European population, the more persecution of the Jews, despite the fact that pogroms were not usually the result of initiatives from the official Church.

The use of magic and belief in it are widespread in most cultures and of course also existed in Christian and pre-Christian Europe.[12] In the early Middle Ages, the Church in most places condemned magic but did not believe that it had any effect. This gradually changed during the thirteenth and fourteenth centuries. Some trials of witches took place in the fourteenth century. They increased in the fifteenth century, when also a theory of witchcraft was developed, most famously in the *Malleus maleficarum* (the Hammer of Witches) by the German inquisitors Heinrich

Kramer and Jacob Sprenger, both Dominicans. The book was published in 1486, two years after the two inquisitors had obtained a bull from Pope Innocent VIII, authorizing them to proceed against the witches. The witch hunts reached their climax between 1550 and 1650. According to recent calculations, between 40,000 and 60,000 people, the great majority (around 80 per cent) women, were executed as witches, but many more were accused; apparently around half of the accused were acquitted. When women were overrepresented, it is probably because they were considered more emotional and more easily tempted than men. Elderly women were particularly likely to be accused. The typical witch has been depicted as a poor elderly woman accused of having sought revenge over people who had offended her, but another alleged motive may have been the loss of fertility and accompanying status. While the persecution of witches began in the Catholic Church, it was continued in Protestant countries as well. Eventually, the persecution was largely taken over by secular courts in Catholic as well as Protestant countries.

The persecution of heretics and witches is the most drastic example of ecclesiastical jurisdiction. However, ecclesiastical courts dealt with many other matters, such as disputes among clerics, cases about ecclesiastical property, various minor offences against ecclesiastical law and accusations against clerics, which the Church demanded should be dealt with by ecclesiastical courts. Finally, ecclesiastical courts dealt with marriage. In the late 1460s, the Paston family, having recently emerged from obscure origins to become one of the most prominent families in East Anglia, was planning a marriage for their daughter Margery that would increase their status further. At last, an excellent offer came from the wealthy Strange family in Northern Norfolk, which was accepted. However, Margery refused, to the great surprise of her family. Eventually, in 1469, the reason became clear: she was already married to the domain inspector Richard Calle. The family appealed to the Bishop of Norwich to declare the marriage invalid, but he refused; despite his sympathy with the family interest, he would not risk the salvation of his soul for their sake. The bishop declared the marriage to be valid and the family had to resign. Richard and Margery were married until she died, apparently in the late 1470s, while Richard lived until 1520.[13]

The doctrine to which the Bishop of Norwich refers goes back to Pope Alexander III (1159–81). The main issue in the previous discussion was whether marriage was defined by the will of the partners or by their sexual intercourse. Pope Alexander decided in favour of the former. As we have seen, the Church considered marriage less meritorious than celibacy, although it tended to have a more positive evaluation of it from the twelfth century onwards. In any case, it was necessary for the survival of humankind and served as a protection against sin; leading people to a disciplined life with care for family and children rather than seeking lust by promiscuous intermingling. According to Biblical doctrine, marriage should be monogamous and permanent, but such a union could only be entered voluntarily. Consequently, the Church had to insist on consent from both partners.

A further argument in favour of this point of view was the wish of the Church to bring an end to or at least reduce concubinage by increasing a woman's possibility to demand that a man with whom she had a sexual relationship marry her. A case from Bergen in Norway illustrates the point. On 16 March 1325, Bishop Audfinn gave sentence in the case between Domhild and Eirik.[14] Domhild had claimed that Eirik had wanted to go to bed with her, but that she had not been willing to do so unless he promised her marriage. As the bishop renders the conversation in solemn Latin: 'You shall tie yourself to me with promise of marriage if you know me carnally tonight.' There were several witnesses to this, as the surroundings were not the most respectable, an alehouse, perhaps combined with easy access to sexual services. Technically, however, Domhild's case was not watertight. A promise of marriage did not constitute a marriage; if the man said: 'I shall marry you' it was a promise for the future and not binding ('verbum de futuro'), but if he said 'I marry you' ('verbum de presenti') it was. However, if the promise was followed by intercourse, it constituted a marriage.[15] Therefore, the bishop, after some doubt, declared the marriage valid. Generally, from the twelfth century onwards, the Church became less tolerant of concubinage than before, although it was unable to abolish it completely.

Although the Church was not particularly concerned with romantic love between young people, its doctrine might support rebellions against parental authority and thus create problems for established society. From a secular point of view, particularly for the elites, marriage was a way to increase or uphold the power and prestige of the family. The doctrine of the Church in several ways endangered this interest. A daughter might refuse to marry the man her parents had found for her, while the ban against divorce made it impossible to get rid of unwanted partners, either women who did not produce sons or alliances that turned out to be liabilities more than assets. Concerning the latter, the Church had some remedies; although divorce was impossible, a marriage could be declared invalid, notably if it turned out that the partners were too closely related. Clever experts could always be found who proved kinship with a partner – normally a wife – who was no longer wanted.[16] As the Paston example shows, the insistence on voluntary marriage might complicate matters within the elite but most daughters nevertheless accepted the husbands their parents had found for them. Moreover, things changed after the Reformation. The Protestants accepted the secular idea of marriage and insisted on marriages being contracted in public and the parents' right to decide for their daughters. Similar rules were introduced in Catholic countries as well, for instance, in France, where *lettres de cachet* might be used against recalcitrant sons and daughters.

Among ordinary people, however, voluntary marriages seem to have been more widespread, particularly during the early modern period, possibly also in the Middle Ages, when we have fewer sources. The reason for this is not necessarily ecclesiastical doctrine but what has been called the European marriage pattern, namely, that young people, notably women, marry late, usually in their mid or late twenties and that a relatively high percentage – 10–15 per cent – never marry at all.[17] The normal pattern in other densely populated parts of the world is early and almost universal marriage, for women in the early teens or even earlier. Late marriages of course increase the possibility for a woman to decide for herself. The reason for this pattern is in turn the importance of the nuclear family. People marry when they have the possibility of taking over a farm or a profession, namely, when their parents die or retire. In some cases, they will also need to earn money by working as farm hands or servants before marrying.

In addition to heresy and marriage, the ecclesiastical courts dealt with a number of different cases, varying from country to country. It demanded that clerics be judged by ecclesiastical courts, a claim that led to conflict in many countries. As ecclesiastical courts were not allowed to pass the sentence of death, stubborn heretics and others whom the Church found deserved the death penalty were delivered to secular courts, which had to pass the death sentence or risk excommunication.

Moreover, the Church largely controlled two important sectors which in modern society usually belong to the state, namely, health and welfare and teaching and learning. Hospitals were mostly run by monasteries, which, together with the parish organizations, provided some relief for the poor. The importance of doctrine in Christianity made learning an important task for the Church and gave it a dominant position in intellectual and cultural life. With the general decline of learning in the Latin West after the fall of the Roman Empire, the Church became the main intellectual centre, not only in the field of theology, but also regarding secular learning. Schools were run by monasteries and other ecclesiastical institutions, and institutions for higher education, the universities, developed from the late twelfth century onwards.[18] The universities north of the Alps were originally founded by the Church and were for some time and in various degree under the control of the bishops. Even when they became largely independent, much of what they taught was derived from ecclesiastical doctrine. The universities south of the Alps formed some exception to this, as they were often founded by the towns and to a greater extent catered for the interests of the laity. The learning developed in the ecclesiastical schools and universities contributed to the formation of an intellectual elite, cultivating basically the same religious and secular learning all over Europe, expressed in a common language, Latin, in which its members could easily communicate in writing or conversation.

In this way, the Church not only controlled most of the learning and education at the time but also most of the intellectual framework. The French historian Lucien Febvre wrote a famous and much-discussed book on whether it was possible to be an atheist in the sixteenth century – and by implication of course also in the Middle Ages – and gave a negative answer.[19] Not all his arguments for this are convincing but he points to an important difference from today, when even many Christians will admit that God's existence is a matter of faith rather than reason and that Christianity only to a limited extent is able to explain the world. In the Middle Ages and largely also the early modern period, Christianity not only had an institutional but also an intellectual hegemony; it was not possible to develop a satisfactory interpretation of the world without assuming the existence of God, and the Christian religion was regarded not only as morally but also intellectually superior. It was possible to oppose the pope or individual prelates but not faith in itself. On the contrary, such opposition largely had to be based on interpretations of the faith.

Finally, in addition to the many particular sectors controlled by the Church, it held the key to the eternal fate of all Christians. Life on Earth is only a short period during which humans are put to the test regarding their fate in the next and real life, eternity, whether they will live forever in bliss together with God and his angels or in pain in hell with the devil. The road to salvation is obedience to the Church and its dogmas, living according to its moral demands or, if not, atoning for one's sins through confession and penance. Although we should not imagine that this doctrine determined the life of the whole population, few rejected it and most people sought reconciliation with the Church when death was approaching.

The Church created a largely similar administrative system all over Western Europe. The basic organization was the diocese, a term derived from the Late Roman administration. This unit was later, from the Carolingian period onwards, divided into parishes, each headed by a parish priest. In principle, this meant that every member of the Latin Church, which included the whole population of Western Christendom except the Jews, had a fixed place within the ecclesiastical organization. This organization also formed a clear hierarchy. Parish priests were subordinated to the bishop, who were in turn subordinated to the archbishop and ultimately to the pope. Apart from the parish priests, the bishops had a number of other subordinates, who might form separate hierarchies within the diocese: there was the cathedral chapter, the official (the bishop's substitute in various capacities) and judicial and administrative functionaries like archdeacons and provosts who often had their separate districts within the diocese. In addition to the secular clergy, there were the monasteries and the religious orders, originally consisting of men and women who worshipped God in isolation from the rest of society, later also organizations for pastoral or social work or learning, such as the Franciscans and Dominicans, both founded in the early thirteenth century. The leader of the whole organization, the pope, was originally one of many bishops, which is still expressed in the fact that the pope addresses other bishops as 'brother', whereas all others, including kings and queens, are addressed as 'son' or 'daughter'.

The development of papal supremacy is largely parallel to the development of secular monarchy.[20] In the same way as his secular counterpart, one of the main expressions of the pope's power was in the field of justice and legislation. The pope became the supreme judge of the Church, not only in complicated issues between high-ranking prelates but also in relatively trivial matters. His court attracted a large number of litigants once it became possible to appeal to it from lower ones.[21] An increasing number of cases from all parts of Europe reached the papal court from the twelfth century onwards, to the extent that the popes complained that they were hardly able to do other things than settle disputes, although of course only a minority of the cases were decided by the pope in person. Also like the king, there was a short step from judgment to legislation. Most popes from the twelfth century onwards were educated lawyers and formulated their decisions in individual cases in the awareness that they might later become general law. In 1234, Pope Gregory IX issued the *Liber Extra* (= additional, i.e. to Gratian), consisting of legislation based on his own and his predecessors' decisions, which was followed by the *Liber Sextus* by Boniface VIII (1298) and the *Clementinae* by Clement V (1311–12, revised and promulgated by John XXII in 1317), which together were recognized as canon law until they were replaced by a new law in 1917.

The supreme power of the pope, his *plenitudo potestatis*, was a central tenet in papal doctrine from Gregory VII onwards and reached a climax under Innocent IV (1243–54) and Boniface VIII (1294–1302). However, some canonists also developed a doctrine of collegiality in the Church, where the power of the pope was limited by that of the council, a meeting of the leading representatives of the whole Church, mostly bishops.[22] There had been altogether seven such councils, common to the eastern and western Church, from that of Nicaea in 325 to Constantinople in 869, all taking place in the East. In 1054, connections between the two parts of the Church were broken at the central level through mutual excommunications, after which the pope developed his supremacy in the Western Church. Seven new councils then took place in the West between 1123 and 1311–12, four in Rome and three in France. In the same way as in the kingdoms, these assemblies were summoned at the initiative of the leader in order to gain assent for his proposals. However, like their secular counterparts, the councils might also develop into bodies of opposition, as was the case in Lyon in 1274 and Vienne in 1311–12, where increasing opposition to papal centralization and demands for reform were voiced.[23] The opposition reached a climax in the first half of the fifteenth century, at the councils of Konstanz (1414–18) and Basel (1431–38/47). Before the Council of Konstanz, the papacy had been weakened by the previous schism which the council managed to end. The council was therefore in a strong position and carried out a number of provisions that increased its power and limited that of the pope. The Council of Basel was summoned to deal with the Hussite problem and the relationship to Byzantium and the Ottomans. It came to represent the climax as well as the defeat of the Conciliar movement. There was increasing disagreement between moderate and radical delegates. In 1438, Pope Eugenius IV summoned an alternative council in Ferrara that was later moved to Florence. The Lateran Council of 1512–17 achieved little, while the Council of Trent (1545–63) led to increased power of the pope. Then there was no council until the Vatican Council of 1869–70, which proclaimed the infallibility of the pope.

The defeat of Conciliarism forms some parallel to the defeat of constitutionalism in most kingdoms in the early modern period. However, the period of strength of the movement was shorter than that of similar ones in most kingdoms. The reason for this is probably the size of the territory of the Church. Generally, the pope as well as secular rulers had the advantage of a well-developed administration, of being in the centre and of running the daily government. The larger the unit, the greater this advantage. As the Church covered the whole of Europe and thus had a far larger territory than any kingdom, the victory of the centre comes as no surprise.

'Our predecessors have not understood how to be popes', declared Clement VI (1342–52). His own understanding is expressed in the magnificent papal palace in Avignon, where he invited prelates, princes, poets and musicians to lavish banquets and cultured entertainment. After a decline during the schism and a period afterwards, Clement's understanding of his office was once more applied in Rome by his successors from the mid-fifteenth century onwards. The best architects of Europe, including Michelangelo and Bernini, worked on the new St Peter's Church in Rome, finished in its main outline in 1626 and by far the largest in Europe. The numerous tourists who today crowd the enormous Vatican Museum, mostly aiming at the Sistine Chapel, hardly notice that they are actually in the old papal palace which was steadily extended over the centuries, to which the Sistine Chapel was attached to serve as the church for the pope and his entourage. The popes restored and rebuilt the old Roman aqueducts which gave the population of Rome clean water, streaming out of a number of fountains decorated by great artists. Numerous squares, arranged and decorated by great architects and sculptors, churches and palaces for the pope and his cardinals and higher officials fill the old centre of the city. Despite the loss of around half of Western Christendom at the Reformation, the pope increased his power as an Italian prince as well as his control of the ecclesiastical organization.

So far, the comparison between the Church under the leadership of the pope and the secular states ruled by kings has shown the similarity between the two as well as the superiority of the Church in several respects: a more professional bureaucracy, the greater power of the head of the organization and the greater size of its territory, in addition to the direct claim of the pope to be the national kings' superior. However, the papal monarchy also had weaknesses.

As we have seen, one of the first problems European kings had to solve was that of succession. This was an even greater problem for the pope, for whom the usual solution, hereditary succession, was of course impossible. Popes therefore had to be elected, and at the election there was no candidate with an obvious claim. The traditional rule about elections of popes as well as other bishops was by 'the clergy and people'. Although the clergy insisted on having the decisive vote, powerful laymen often dominated the election. With the development of a local aristocracy in Rome, the control of the papacy became an important aim in the numerous factional struggles. The restoration of imperial power through Otto I's coronation in 962 led to a number of popes elected through imperial influence. Many of these came from north of the Alps and were influenced by the reform movements there, particularly the one originating in Cluny in Burgundy. This resulted in the decree about papal elections issued by the Lateran Synod in Rome at the initiative of Pope Nicholas II in 1059, a reform-minded pope from Burgundy. The election was now left to a purely ecclesiastical body, namely, the College of Cardinals, consisting of the clerics in churches in Rome and its surroundings who acted as the pope's council. The people were only supposed to acclaim the election. After some conflicts over the exact procedure and the degree of outside influence, the College of Cardinals was eventually recognized as the elective body.

However, this did not eliminate pressure from outside, either the local popula-tion of Rome or powerful kings and princes, while the small number of electors increased the risk of bribery. Until the mid-fifteenth century, there were therefore a series of schisms, when two popes competed for loyalty, and a number of occa-sions where the election was delayed for up to two or three years. The origins of the most severe crisis, the great schism of 1378–1417, illustrate some of the pro-blems.[24] Since the election of Pope Clement V in 1305, the popes had resided in France, most of the time in Avignon. However, there was increasing pressure for the popes to return to Rome. Finally, Gregory XI decided to do so and arrived there on 17 January 1377. He died only a year later and was succeeded by an Ita-lian, Urban VI, with whom the majority of cardinals soon became dissatisfied. They claimed that his election had been the result of pressure from the Roman population and they elected a new pope, Clement VII, who returned to Avignon. The schism lasted until 1417, when it was brought to an end by the Council of Konstanz (1414–18), where two of the three popes at the time – one had been elected in the hope that he would replace the two others – were deposed and the third agreed to resign. The last schism took place shortly afterwards, in 1439, in connection with the conflict between Pope Eugenius IV and the Council of Basel. The anti-pope, Felix V, resigned in 1449 in return for being appointed cardinal.

Since the decline of the Roman Empire, the pope had in practice been the ruler of Rome and since the eight century also of the former Lombard kingdom in central Italy, conquered by the Carolingians. In practice, however, he had little control of this territory until the late fifteenth and early sixteenth century, approximately the period when the papal schisms came to an end. It may thus seem that a consolidated territory was a necessary condition for avoiding inter-ference in the elections from outsiders, including secular rulers. On the other hand, the existence of such a territory and the popes' interest in consolidating and extending it created new problems. The territory never became strong enough to make the pope really independent of secular rulers. The main limits to the power of the papacy lay in the fields of war and finance. Despite the numerous complaints about the pope's financial greed, his revenues in the middle ages, only 1/15 of those of the king of France, were inadequate, considering the territory he ruled as a religious leader. With the exception of the Peter's penny, a small tax paid by the inhabitants of some countries, he had no regular taxes. Most of his incomes came from payments from litigants and petitioners to the curia, which mostly went to the people who dealt with them, and from incomes in connection with papal appointment to ecclesiastical offices. From the second half of the thirteenth cen-tury, he also at regular intervals demanded extra taxes from the clergy, allegedly to finance new crusades but actually to cover his normal expenses, including wars against his Italian rivals.

Although the pope recruited an army in the early sixteenth century (the Swiss Guard), he never commanded a strong military power; he depended on secular rulers as allies. This in many cases made it difficult for him to maintain his claim to be a spiritual authority, independent of secular rulers, the more so as he often used his spiritual power against his secular enemies by excommunicating them, which of course weakened the respect for his spiritual sanctions. The many conflicts with the German Emperor between the late eleventh and the mid-thirteenth century can largely be understood in this way. In the sixteenth century, the pope's obvious ally against the Protestants was the Emperor Charles V and his son, Philip II of Spain, but as they also controlled most of Italy, the popes often intrigued against them and joined their enemies. The strengthening of the pope's secular power must therefore be regarded as a mixed blessing. In hindsight, the popes would seem to have had every reason to be grateful to Victor Emmanuel II and Garibaldi for conquering the Papal States in 1860 and 1870 – the papacy enjoys greater international prestige today than in the eighteenth century.

Was the Church, headed by the pope, ever a realistic alternative to the state as the dominant power in Europe? The answer to this question is clearly no. Despite the remarkable increase in papal power from the late eleventh century onwards, the pope never came close to realizing this aim – if it actually was his aim. There are papal proclamations that can be interpreted in this direction, notably the ones that the pope had highest moral authority and the right to define the border between the two organizations. However, despite the fact that the Church was the richest institution in medieval Europe, only a fraction of this wealth was at the disposal of the pope. Nor had he any proper army; his military successes, notably his victory over the emperor in the thirteenth century, were the result of aid from other princes.

Here, however, it is necessary to distinguish between the pope and the Church as such. When kings during the later Middle Ages were able to gain considerable control of the church in their countries and in some cases even to defeat the pope in a conflict, it was not because of increasingly secular attitudes in the population but rather because the kings could gain the loyalty of the clergy in their countries by acting as defenders of the faith. By the early fourteenth century, the Cathars had been suppressed in most of France; Montaillou was one of their last strongholds. However, Philip IV managed to emerge as the champion of orthodoxy by finding another heresy, that of the Templars.[25] The Order of the Templars had been founded as a crusading order in the Holy Land but by the early fourteenth century had as its main purpose to raise money for Crusades, which led to the accumulation of great wealth. Philip's motive was most probably to appropriate this wealth, as he was in a difficult financial situation when he launched the attack on the order in 1307. Philip had all the members of the order arrested and under torture extracted evidence of various kinds of misbehaviour: lack of chastity and homosexual acts, blasphemy, including spitting on the Cross and renouncing Christ, and various kinds of heresy. Philip achieved his aim; the Grand Master of the Order and several others were burnt at the stake and the order was suppressed by the pope, despite some misgivings by Pope Clement V. Philip got his money as well as a reputation for orthodoxy and defence of the faith.

In this respect, Philip continued the tradition from his grandfather St Louis, whose piety was nevertheless more genuine and whose motives were more purely religious. Mostly, the Church had the support of the kings in its defence of orthodoxy in this as well as the following periods. Several crusades were launched against the Hussites in the fifteenth century and Henry IV of England and his successors persecuted the Lollards, Wycliffe's followers. The Catholic kings of Spain, Ferdinand and Isabella, took a further step in this direction when they introduced the Inquisition in the country and received papal permission to control it themselves (1478). It thus became an important instrument, not only for religious but also for political control. When competing with the pope, the king's policy was not to separate politics from religion but, on the contrary, to gain the loyalty of his lay as well as clerical subjects by emphasizing his orthodoxy and suppressing heresy. This largely continued to be royal policy in the following period, although eventually, more than one variety of religious orthodoxy was introduced.

States without a king: principalities and city republics

In his history of Frederick Barbarossa's deeds, Bishop Otto of Freising includes an account of the Italian city republics as the introduction to Frederick's first expedition to Italy in 1154–55 in order to receive the imperial crown.[26] Socially and politically, the Italians are widely different from other peoples, preferring elected consuls for short periods to princes and strong government, so that the whole country is divided into city states. Even nobles have to submit to these, while artisans and men of low origin may be promoted to noble status. In this way, the Italian city states are wealthier and more powerful than other cities in the world. However, the Italians retain remains of their barbarian origin in refusing to obey the laws and show princes the respect due to them, unless they are forced by the use of arms. Thus they have to be subdued, and their rebellious nature makes them and not the prince responsible for the violence necessary for this purpose. The aristocratic German bishop's contempt for this country governed by merchants and artisans is unmistakable and is further confirmed by the account of Frederick's rejection of the representatives of the city of Rome who turn up when he approaches the city: These merchants and artisans do not represent the Roman republic; on the contrary, the real republic is now north of the Alps, with Frederick's own people, the Franks. The contemporary Romans have no right to set conditions for Frederick's imperial coronation; they only have to obey their lawful ruler.[27]

Frederick eventually discovered that it was not easy to suppress the rebellious Italians. Otto's successor, Rahewin lets Frederick express himself in more diplomatic terms to the Italians;[28] and in the end (1177 and 1183), Frederick had to conclude a peace treaty with them, which largely accepted their right to govern themselves. The king of Germany continued to claim the title as Roman emperor and Frederick's successor, Frederick II (1212–50), came closer to controlling northern Italy, but after his death, the cities became independent, although some of the later emperors still travelled to Rome to receive the imperial crown. Only in the sixteenth century did the claim to rule Italy become a reality.

While the European system of kingdoms in mutual competition over a long period of time seems to be exceptional in a global context, similar claims can be made about the European town. The Arab and Ottoman Empires, as well as China, were more urbanized than Europe in the Middle Ages and trade and manufacture were equally important or even more so, but towns as organized and largely self-governed communities mostly seem to have been specific to Europe. Their independence was particularly strong between the eleventh and sixteenth centuries, to the extent that many of them can be regarded as states. We thus have to deal with a third category of political units in addition to the Church and the kingdoms.

From the Roman expansion into the Eastern Mediterranean in the second century BC until the Arab invasions from the 630s, the Mediterranean or most of it had been part of one empire and served as the main artery for trade and communication within it. The Arabs managed to conquer the largest part of the area, including the wealthiest countries, Syria and Egypt. They also conquered many of the islands. However, the Byzantine Empire continued to exist and various western rulers held parts of Italy, from which a western revival began in the eleventh century, but in the form of independent city states rather than a great empire. These cities once more united the Mediterranean and controlled the trade between east and west. Admittedly, the difference from Roman conditions was less than it would immediately seem. The Roman Empire was less centralized than its Chinese counterpart and the cities retained much of their independence.[29] Nevertheless, trade was to a considerable degree controlled by the Empire and the urban elites were mostly landowners rather than merchants. The rise of the Italian city republics therefore represents a radical novelty. In the eleventh century, Italy was probably the most divided part of Europe. In the following period, strong kingdoms developed in the south, while the division continued in the north.

A new European Sea developed north of the Alps, consisting of the North and Baltic Seas with the Low Countries as its centre. This latter area had the advantage of rich soil which could support a large population, proximity to the wealthy kingdoms of England and France and communication with the inner parts of the Continent on the great rivers which had their estuaries there, including the Rhine. Later, new centres emerged along the Baltic Sea with the European expansion there.

Both the Low Countries and Northern Italy belonged to the central kingdom formed through the division of the Carolingian Empire in 843, but while the rest of it was included in either France or Germany, these areas maintained a considerable degree of independence. Both had good natural conditions for becoming centres of trade and manufacture, but their political independence probably owes much to the division of the Carolingian Empire. Their independence was important for their commercial success.

The Italian cities were the largest and most important in Europe. Of the five largest cities around 1300, four were in Italy, namely, Genoa, Venice, Milan and Florence. The fifth was Paris. These five may have had as many as 100,000 inhabitants each before the Black Death. The wealth of the cities made them strong enough to be independent, while independence in turn contributed to wealth. They could conduct a policy that served the interests of the merchants without paying taxes to any external authority. They could raise armies, often larger than those of the kingdoms; they had an elaborate political organization and independent courts of law. They suppressed feuds and solved conflicts between their inhabitants. Most of them were republics in the beginning, although many eventually came to be ruled by a lord, normally a member of some aristocratic family, who managed to suppress the republican institutions. Milan was ruled by the Visconti family from 1277, as dukes, 1395–1447. After the extinction of the Visconti, the Sforza took over and ruled the city until it was conquered by the French in 1500.

The most important Italian cities became centres of relatively large territories, but did not develop into homogeneous states; their republican constitution was not extended to the countryside or the dependent towns. This meant less stability and loyalty from the subordinate population. With the exception of Venice, the cities often experienced rebellions, coups and changes of constitution. The lords of the cities usually tried to establish dynasties, but generally had less success in this than the kings and were more often overthrown or murdered. In many ways, the Italian cities served as models of administration and finance for the kings north of the Alps, who often recruited Italian experts, but the states themselves proved to be vulnerable to foreign invasion to which most of them succumbed during the first half of the sixteenth century.

The most important trading towns in Italy were all in the north or middle of the country.[30] The little town of Amalfi in the south became an important centre of trade at the same time as Venice, but later lagged behind. Capitals like Naples and Palermo remained important but less so than the northern towns. As subjects to the Norman Kingdom and its successors, their merchants had to pay taxes and tolls to the king and risked blockades or confiscations when he was at war with their trading partners. By contrast, the independent towns could conduct their own policy in accordance with their mercantile interests. At the same time, they had to develop a strong military power to protect their trade, keep their enemies out of the market and secure their interests in negotiations with their trading partners. For this purpose, the two most important actors in the Mediterranean trade, Venice and Genoa, formed regular trading empires.

Today Venice is crowded by tourists, a favourite place for cruises, honeymoons and film festivals, full of luxurious and expensive hotels and restaurants, cold and foggy in winter, too hot in summer, but incredibly beautiful on a sunny day when rising over the golden sea and with the ancient buildings reflected in the canals.

In contrast to most Italian cities, Venice did not exist in Roman times.[31] It was founded on some islands in the lagoon by refugees from the troubled conditions on the mainland after the fall of the Roman Empire and was in the beginning subject to the Byzantine Emperor. Eventually, it became an important partner in the trade between Byzantium and the West, later also on the trade routes with the east. The relationship to the emperor deteriorated in the twelfth century, and in 1204, Venice struck back, diverting the Fourth Crusade from the Holy Land and orchestrating the sack of Constantinople. The spoils from this victory consisted of three-eighths of the city of Constantinople and a series of trading posts on the way between this city and Venice. Venice, together with Genoa, formed the first example of the trading empires later developed on other continents by the Portuguese, the Dutch and the British.

From far back in classical antiquity, various caravan routes linked East and West and served to bring attractive commodities, like silk and spices, to Europe. In the early Middle Ages, the trade on the Mediterranean between Western Europe and the East had declined, mainly because poverty in the West reduced the demand for luxury goods from the East. The trade that did exist was mainly carried out by Jewish and Arab merchants. From the tenth and eleventh centuries onwards, population increase and greater wealth made the West a more important market and the trade was increasingly carried on European ships, mainly Italian ones. This eventually also led to European military superiority at sea. Characteristically, the army of the First Crusade went over land through Asia Minor, whereas most of the later Crusades went by sea. From Italy, the merchandise was transported over the Alps to Northern Europe. From the second half of the thirteenth century, after the Castilian conquest of the southern coast of Spain, it became more usual to transport the merchandise by sea, through Gibraltar, which served to link Italy to the Flemish towns.

Venice and Genoa played a leading part in the trade on the Mediterranean between East and West, transporting their merchandise from Constantinople, Cairo, Damascus, later also from the Black Sea, to Italy or to northern Europe. The luxury goods from these areas was paid for by timber, metals, weapons and slaves from the northern shores of the Mediterranean and the Black Sea. In addition, wine, grain and salt were transported between various Mediterranean ports. Sicily and Puglia in southern Italy, later also the Black Sea coasts, were important suppliers of grain to Venice and other Italian cities.[32] With population growth and greater wealth among the elites north of the Alps, trade between North and South increased. In addition to the luxury commodities from the East, the Italians exported textiles, glass and arms to the North in return for metals, furs and wool, which were more abundant in the North. The Italians also produced valuable merchandise themselves, fine cloth of wool or silk and products of metal, including arms. The general pattern was raw material from the North in return for manufacture from the South, with the textile production in Florence as the main example. There was also an increased import from the Far East in the thirteenth century, because the Mongol Empire, covering most of Asia, had eased the communication[33] and several Europeans had visited China in the thirteenth and fourteenth centuries, including Marco Polo, whose report from his twenty-seven years in China in the late thirteenth century has been preserved.

The character of trade changed from the thirteenth century onwards.[34] Originally, most merchants travelled in person to the markets and sold their commodities;

great fairs, such as the one in Champagne in northern France, were centres of this trade. Eventually, when contacts had been established and communications had become somewhat better and safer, the goods were transported by professional transporters and contact with the customers was kept in writing. This also led to the introduction of double-entry book-keeping from around 1300. Finally, single merchants were to some extent replaced by trading companies, often with permanent representatives abroad. Thus, a step was taken in the direction of the modern firm. Admittedly, most companies were family-based, but they might have numerous partners and last over several generations. Moreover, there were some possibilities to attract capital from passive partners. The Venetian *commenda* gave wealthy people the opportunity to invest in trade by letting poorer partners do the travelling. The stationary partner invested the capital in return for ¾ of the profit, while the traveller received ¼. Moreover, in 1408, a Florentine statute allowed the creation of a *società in accomandita* in which dormant partners were liable only to the extent of their investment.

The Venetian Empire reached its climax in the late fourteenth and early fifteenth centuries. In the first half of the fifteenth century, it also became a leading power on the Italian mainland with the conquest of a large part of Northern Italy. Venice, Genoa and other Italian cities had in the previous period profited from political division and weak rulers in the Eastern Mediterranean. Although the Byzantine Empire was restored after the sack of 1204 and even reconquered the old capital in 1261, it never regained its old strength, and a disastrous civil war in the mid-fourteenth century reduced it to a petty principality. Eventually, however, it was replaced by a far stronger power, the Ottoman Empire, which conquered Constantinople in 1453 and in the following period also most of the Middle East – Egypt fell in 1517 – and then expanded into Eastern Europe, conquering most of Hungary and besieging Vienna in 1529. The Ottomans also developed a strong sea power and conquered several Venetian possessions in the Mediterranean, including Cyprus (1569) and Crete (1669). Admittedly, the Ottomans had the same interest in trade between East and West as their predecessors in the area, but it was of course more difficult to negotiate with a strong trading partner than with a weak one.

Venice is the most state-like of the medieval city states. It was ruled by the *doge* (from Latin *dux* = leader; cf. duke in English), whose power was eventually severely limited by other institutions. The city developed a very elaborate constitution, which remained almost unchanged from around 1300 to the fall of the republic in 1797. A stroll in the city gives an impression of its constitutional arrangements. Its centre, in the past as well as in the present, is the enormous square of St Mark, surrounded by numerous public buildings, including the cathedral, the Doge's palace and a number of other buildings, today mostly museums but earlier housing various offices of the state. Not far from St Mark's Square is the Arsenal, where the galleys of the republic were built and maintained. They could be rowed as well as sailed but because of their large crews, they were expensive to run and thus mainly used for transporting precious goods. In addition, they were used for military purposes until the early sixteenth century, when the use of cannons made them obsolete.[35] The rest of the city seems like a labyrinth where tourists can easily get lost, but the narrow streets are regularly interrupted by squares which formed centres for trade as well as for local government.

The main 'street' of the city, the Canal Grande, is surrounded on both sides by the palaces of the merchant aristocracy in different styles, from Gothic to Baroque. An address at Canal Grande was essential for aristocratic status; poor members of the aristocracy would sacrifice much before they gave up this. The names of the palaces are those of the ancient families of the city whose members often served as doges: Contarini, Dandolo, Loredan, Mocenigo, Vendramin-Calergi. Of course, all medieval and early modern cities were ruled by some kind of aristocracy but the Venetian one was nevertheless more dominant and more stable than those of others and the political institutions more developed and more permanent.

Venice was exceptional in being almost a monarchy from the beginning. The office of doge goes back to 697, and 120 men held the office until it was abolished in 1797. The doge was elected for life but the office was not hereditary. Consequently, there was the same problem as with the papacy about succession, but the Venetians seem to have been more successful in solving it than the clergy and people of Rome. Although there were a number of disputed successions and killings or depositions of doges in the eighth and ninth centuries, this became an exception in the following period, when only 4 of 102 were deposed. The greater stability reflects a clearer limitation of the doge's power as well as the consolidation of the ruling class of Venice in the constitution that was developed after the *serrata* (closure) in 1297, when membership to the Great Council was limited to men belonging to 200 families. The Great Council was not a particularly important body in itself, but it was essential to belong to it because all officials in the service of the republic were elected from its members. In addition, members of the council also enjoyed trade privileges. From now on, the doge had to share his power with various elected bodies, the most important of which was the Council of Ten, which could veto the doge's decisions and in addition had wide powers to prevent conspiracies against the constitution, including the right to arrest, depose and execute the doge. Outside the Doge's Palace an opening in the wall is still to be seen with the inscription that anonymous letters accusing people of conspiring against the constitution can be posted there.

The constitutional reform of 1297 and the following years created a remarkable stability but at a price; international trade largely became a privilege for the nobility and free competition was reduced. In addition, the state interfered more in trade and economic exchange in Venice than in other places. Favouring economic liberalism, Acemoglou and Robinson describe the development of Venice under the headline 'How Venice became a museum'.[36] Eventually, this did happen, but not until the second half of the seventeenth century. Until then, Venice was not the most economically dynamic of Italian cities, nor were the greatest fortunes created there – both Genoa and Florence were more successful in this respect – but, as a state, it survived much longer than both these rivals. Internally, it not only managed to create peace between the members of the aristocracy, not an easy task under medieval and early modern conditions, but also to keep the rest of the population reasonably satisfied through effective jurisdiction and a certain amount of welfare provisions. Externally, it managed to hold together its Mediterranean Empire despite some substantial losses, as well as survive the struggle for Italy between the European great powers in the sixteenth century, even keeping intact its early fifteenth-century conquest of part of the Po Valley on the Italian mainland. Despite the fact that its military power was weaker than that of its main competitors, notably the Ottoman Empire, it had experienced politicians and was the first European state to develop a professional diplomatic service. Reports from Venetian diplomats have for a long time been an important source for historians working on international relations in the sixteenth and seventeenth centuries.

By contrast, Genoa's economic dynamism corresponded to almost constant internal struggles. Its defeat against Venice in 1381 proved a turning-point. Soon afterwards, it came under French domination and was then conquered by Milan. From the sixteenth century onwards, it was under Spanish suzerainty, although with considerable internal independence and profited greatly from the Spanish conquest of America. The general point is therefore that what is good for trade is not necessarily good for society as a whole and that some balance between regulation and liberty needs to be found. Moreover, although Venice did not allow free competition among its citizens, this hardly means that its merchants did not face competition on international markets.

Finally, in the sixteenth and seventeenth centuries, Venice became an important centre of art, painting, architecture, music and opera. Titian was the favourite painter of the Habsburgs and his paintings, together with those of Veronese, Tintoretto and Tiepolo, are in all the great museums of Europe, while the music of Monteverdi and Vivaldi has a similar status. And for those who could not afford the greatest masters, there is always a Canaletto – is there any English country-house without one? Renaissance architecture came late to Venice but one of the most famous architects of the period, Andrea Palladio (1508–80) worked there. His works, notably his villas, including the Villa Rotonda in Vicenza, became a model for the Renaissance north of the Alps ('Palladian style'), in England through Inigo Jones and his Banqueting House in Whitehall in London (1619–22). Venice also became one of the most important centres of book printing in Europe, both because of competent technicians and because it for a long time was a centre for relative religious tolerance and free thinking in a country increasingly dominated by the intolerance of the Counter-Reformation. The University of Padua, under Venice since 1405, became the great intellectual centre of Italy until the first half of the seventeenth century, sought by students from all over Europe, regardless of confession, and known particularly for its studies of medicine and the natural sciences. Galileo was a professor there until 1610 when he left it for a better offer from Florence, his native town.

Moving from Venice to Florence, we are in a different world.

And when the plebs entered the palace, one Michele di Lando, a wool carder, had in his hands the ensign of the Gonfalonier of Justice. This man, barefoot and scantily clothed, climbed up the stairs with the whole mob behind him, and as soon as he was in the audience chamber, he said, 'You see: this palace is yours and this city is in your hands. What do you think should be done now?' To which all replied that they wanted him to be Gonfalonier and lord, and to govern them and the city however seemed best to him.[37]

In this way, Machiavelli describes the turning-point in the *Ciompi* rebellion in Florence. The *ciompi*, the unskilled textile workers who carded the wool before it was spun and woven into textiles, worked in large factories with low salaries and under bad conditions – the first industrial proletariat in Europe. In 1378, they rebelled against the government, together with other labourers, and in a short time managed to take control of the city. Machiavelli makes a point of the total collapse of the government and the power vacuum resulting from this, which made it possible for anyone to take control, including a half-naked proletarian who turned out to be a better ruler than the numerous wealthy, well-educated and experienced members of the elite. Although Machiavelli exaggerates Michele's inexperience as well as the breakdown of the Florentine government, he does describe a situation that would hardly have occurred in Venice. Florence was more dynamic as well as more democratic than Venice but also more unstable. A series of rebellions and changes of government took place between the formation of the Florentine Republic in the early thirteenth century and its fall in the early sixteenth century.

Florence's rise to one of the greatest and wealthiest cities in Europe began in the second half of the thirteenth century, when Florentine merchants became collectors of papal taxes of ecclesiastical revenues in Europe north of the Alps. The substantial surplus from this business was then invested in textile production. Wool was bought in Flanders, England and, to some extent, Spain – although the best quality wool comes from countries with a cold and wet climate. The wool was then brought to Florence where it was prepared, woven and coloured to be used as clothes for wealthy people all over Europe. The fourteenth century was a period of more luxurious dress and faster shifts in fashion than had been the case previously, which of course made textile production even more profitable. Florence also became a centre for the production of other commodities: silk, metal, arms, etc. but cloth was the most important and the guild of the cloth merchants and producers (*Arte della Lana*) was the most powerful of the originally seven guilds that formed the basis of the Florentine constitution.

In contrast to Venice before the fifteenth century, Florence was an inland city with some control over the surrounding countryside.[38] This meant that there was also a nobility with landed estates, although these nobles were often also engaged in business. The formation of a city republic dates back to the first half of the twelfth century, when consuls are mentioned for the first time. During most of the thirteenth century, the main political division was between the Guelphs and the Ghibellines, the adherents respectively of the pope and the emperor, both led by nobles. In 1267, the Guelphs came to power, after the defeat of the Staufen Manfred by Charles of Anjou in the previous year. In the following period, a new division emerged, between the nobles and the 'people', the latter dominated by great merchants. In the 1290s, strict rules forbidding feuds and barring the nobles from holding public office were introduced under the leadership of Giano della Bella, himself a noble. A new constitution was also introduced, based on the seven major guilds. The constitution underwent some revision in the following period, including participation by the fourteen lesser guilds in 1343. Most officials were elected by lots, in order to prevent particular people or factions from monopolizing power, but the sortation was preceded by scrutiny of the candidate's qualifications. Most offices were held only for a short time without possibility of immediate re-election. It has been suggested that as much as one-third of the adult male population of the city held some office in the course of their lifetime. Informally, however, the members of the mercantile elite had considerable influence.

Formally, this constitution existed until 1537, but eventually, one family, the Medici, emerged as the leaders of the republic. Cosimo di Medici gained power by a coup in 1434 and his descendants ruled the city until 1494, although formally maintaining the republican constitution. The Medici were expelled in 1494 but returned in 1512 with Spanish aid. Except for a brief republican interlude in 1527–30, they ruled the city in the following period, from 1537 as dukes. When the Medici became extinct in 1737, Florence was taken over by the Habsburgs.

A visit to the old centre of Florence gives an impression of a medieval or Renaissance city in the same way as in Venice but one with a different character. Take the political centres of the two cities: the Doge's Palace in Venice, finished in 1419, is in late Gothic but with clear associations to the Orient. It is not fortified and has no sign of military purposes. The Palazzo Vecchio or Palazzo della Signoria in Florence is older, built around 1298–1314, also in the Gothic style, and has the character of a fortress, with high walls, small windows only in the upper stories and an enormous tower, so that it might easily be defended, although the Ciompi managed to conquer it in 1378. Most of the private palaces were changed or rebuilt in the Renaissance style in the fifteenth century but earlier, they were strongly fortified to protect the family in internal struggles.

The two cathedrals are equally different. That of Venice, San Marco, dating from the eleventh century (consecrated 1094), is built in the Byzantine style and decorated with mosaics inside, also in the Byzantine style, although dating from various periods of the Middle Ages. The cathedral of Florence was begun in 1296 and took 150 years to complete. Most of it is in the Gothic style. Its most characteristic feature is the cupola, which is enormous, the largest until then in Western Europe after the fall of the Roman Empire. Its size was planned already in the fourteenth century, although nobody then knew how to construct such a large cupola; no beam would be big enough to support it during the building process. The architect Filippo Brunelleschi solved the problem, not by long beams but by arranging the stones so that they balanced until finally the whole cupola was covered. In 1436, the present cupola was in place, as the main monument of the Renaissance in art as well as in learning which at the time had its centre in Florence.

The new style in painting, sculpture and architecture was inspired by classical art and aimed at clarity and simplicity. Painting aimed at precise representation of the external world, notably through anatomically correct representations of the human body and the introduction of the central perspective which gave the illusion of three dimensions in a painting. Psychology and the representation of emotions were also important, combined with austerity in colours and use of detail. Portraits, particularly from the early fifteenth century, were inspired by Roman republican art. Politicians and intellectuals were portrayed in a straightforward, matter-of-fact way, showing precise individual detail and emphasizing republican virtue through simplicity in dress and faces expressing intelligence and determination. Finally, the new architecture expressed in the Renaissance churches of San Lorenzo (the Medici's parish church) and Santo Spirito, combined symmetrical and harmonious forms with extreme simplicity and lack of decoration. Both were designed by Brunelleschi but not finished until after his death in 1446. The style of palaces developed at the same time emphasized the same qualities. Characteristically, when Venice became a centre of painting in the late Renaissance, the style was far more lavish, above all in Veronese and Tintoretto but also in Titian.

Common to Venice and Florence as well as a number of other towns, particularly Italian ones, is the greater use of art and architecture for secular purposes. Of course, there are plenty of churches, which, however, were mostly erected at the initiative of the city or some of its prominent inhabitants, but there are also a number of monumental secular buildings. In addition to the many patrician palaces, there are the monumental town halls, which are also to be found in the leading cities of the North. They are often combined with large and well-planned squares, as in both Venice and Florence. The Italian cities also developed a political iconography. A famous early example is the *Buon Governo* (the Good Government) in the town hall of Siena from 1338, depicting the peace, concord and prosperity resulting from a good government and the disasters resulting from a bad one.

A considerable urbanization also took place in the rest of Europe from the twelfth century onwards as the consequence of increased population and clearing of new land and increased wealth among the landowners. The majority of the new towns were small and mostly centres of local trade. Only Paris, which was the capital of the largest kingdom in Europe, could compete in size with the largest Italian cities. Other large and important cities were London, Cologne, Bruges, Ghent and later Antwerp and further east and along the Baltic coast among others Bremen, Hamburg, Lübeck, Gdansk (Danzig), Riga and Tallin (earlier Reval). The main areas for distant trade were the Low Countries, the Baltic coast and cities along the main trade routes between North and South, such as the Rhine. Most important northern cities were in the beginning governed by bishops. This was also the case with the Italian cities, but Italian bishops were weaker than their counterparts north of the Alps, so there the cities easily managed to gain independence, with a few exceptions, such as Rome. North of the Alps, bishops were stronger and wealthier and the cities therefore often had to fight hard for their independence. In 1074, such a struggle broke out in Cologne, one of the richest and most important cities along the Rhine, and was shortly afterwards reported by the chronicler Lampert of Hersfeld.[39]

Archbishop Anno of Cologne's servants laid hold of a ship belonging to a wealthy merchant to serve the archbishop's guest, the bishop of Münster, as transport on his journey home. This action led to a general rebellion in the city. The mob attacked the archbishop's palace, took the archbishop himself captive, and detained him in the church of St Peter, while they plundered the palace and its chapel, not even respecting the altars and the sacred ornaments. The archbishop was saved from death at the last moment, being smuggled out of the church in disguise at night through a narrow passage. These events shocked the whole province, where the archbishop's saintly life and kindness to the poor were well known. An army was quickly gathered, and already on the fourth day, the archbishop was outside the gates of the city. The burghers surrendered, and the saintly archbishop was willing to forgive them, only imposing ecclesiastical penance on them. However, some of the richest burghers secretly escaped to the king, asking him to intervene, while the rest failed to appear before the archbishop, even after three days of waiting. This exhausted the patience of the archbishop's men and, without his consent, they took up arms to punish the rebels. Despite his respect for the archbishop's clemency, Lampert is not without sympathy for this action: 'a more serious illness demands a more serious medicine'. Lampert ends his account of the rebellion in Cologne by pointing to the subsequent decline of the city, and by describing the portents before the events which indicate that the city has been delivered to the Devil but been liberated thanks to the intervention of St George.

Lampert was a monk in the wealthy and aristocratic monastery of Hersfeld and sympathized with the aristocratic rebellion against the Emperor Henry IV. Actually, his detailed description of the rebellion in Cologne is probably intended to show the contrast between a just rebellion, that of the Saxon nobles, and an unjust one, that of the burghers who have to respect the authority of their lord, who, in addition, is Lampert's great hero. While modern readers would tend to sympathize with the merchant who suddenly finds his ship being requisitioned for the sake of the archbishop's guest, to Lampert, such an action is obviously the archbishop's right. Who are these merchants to complain when their betters require what they need for their comfort?

The archbishop of Cologne was one of the two most high-ranking and powerful prelates in Germany and the city of Cologne was the largest and wealthiest in the country. The conflict in 1074 was neither the first nor the last between the two parties. The result, however, was mainly in favour of the city, which became largely independent with its own government. The archbishop was even allowed to enter the city only on special occasions. Instead, he founded his own capital in Bonn nearby, where his palace, built in the eighteenth century, is now the university.

Northern cities also differed from their Italian counterparts in not becoming centres of larger territories and generally achieving less independence. On the other hand, once they became independent or almost independent, they were governed by burghers, as the nobles here lived in the countryside, not in towns.

The relative weakness of the northern cities made it more natural for them to join each other in leagues. There may also have been a financial reason for this. The northern cities mostly traded in bulky commodities that gave little profit, which meant that they might increase prices by organizing in leagues. By contrast, the Italians had less incentive to this because their merchandise was more costly.[40] The best-known of the leagues is the Hanseatic one, which consisted of a large number of towns and merchant communities from Novgorod in the east to Bruges and London in the west.[41] The League established and eventually dominated a large trade network from Flanders and England in the west to Novgorod in the east, with links to Scandinavia in the north. In this way, its merchants could profit from transporting the widely different commodities produced in the whole area to the markets. Already at this time, there was a difference between products of handicraft and industry in the West, notably textiles, and raw materials and agricultural products from the East and North, grain and timber from the Baltic area and fish, butter and hides from Scandinavia. The League was loosely organized; the various towns had various forms of connection with it and they did not always stand together; they might even wage war between them. The League was not intended as a kind of state; it existed to protect the commercial interests of its members. But it was powerful enough to fight against kings and princes; one of its greatest triumphs was the victory over the Danish King Valdemar IV in the war of 1367–70.[42]

The Hanseatic League was strongly involved in the conquest of the Baltic Area from the twelfth century onwards. The new towns founded in this area were populated by German merchants. Germans also played an important part in the territorial expansion. German farmers received land in the conquered areas and above all, German nobles created estates and principalities with the local population as serfs and labourers. Politically, the first phase of the conquest, from 1150, led to the formation of Pomerania and Mecklenburg, two of the larger German principalities. The next phase, from around 1200, was dominated by the German Order, whose territory covered most of the coastal area between Pomerania and Novgorod. This was a military order, consisting of armed monks who were supposed to fight for Christianity during the Crusades. The order was founded in the Holy Land, but moved to the Baltic area in 1230. Its power was reduced after its defeat against the Polish-Lithuanian Union at Tannenberg (Grünwald) in 1410.

Leagues of towns were common also elsewhere in the North. Cities along the Rhine, with Cologne as the most important, formed the Rhine League, and there was a union of the Flemish cities. Flanders was the most important trading area north of the Alps and included a number of important towns, in particular, Bruges and Ghent, later also Antwerp. The German emperor interfered little in the area after the thirteenth century, but the French influence was felt more strongly. The king of France claimed suzerainty over Flanders. There was frequent rivalry between the towns and the count of Flanders, who usually appealed to the king of

France for aid. During the Hundred Years War, the towns mostly sided with the English, while the count supported the French.

The development of stronger states from the sixteenth century onwards led to the decline of many smaller principalities and city republics. In particular, Italy succumbed to a military revolution to which it had itself made a major contribution. Of the more important city states, only Venice survived intact until 1797. The most successful cities in the early modern period, however, became united in the Dutch Republic which will be dealt with in greater detail below.

The medieval foundations of the European state

As we have seen, the basic division of Europe into kingdoms can be traced back to around 1200 and the military revolution in the sixteenth and seventeenth centuries made little difference in this respect. The changes are greater in the field of internal organization. The court and administration developed significantly from the thirteenth century onwards, regular or almost regular taxation was introduced, largely in connection with the growth of assemblies of popular and aristocratic representatives, the size of armies and the cost of warfare increased, the king took significant steps in the direction of a monopoly on justice, the aristocracy became more closely linked to the king, the problem of royal succession was largely solved and a theory of monarchy was developed which distinguished more clearly between the eternal royal office and its mortal and temporary incumbent. In all these fields, there is a strong continuity between the Middle Ages and the early modern period until the end of the ancient regime with the French Revolution.

Nevertheless, towards the end of the Middle Ages, it would still seem that the two organizations discussed in the present chapter might be able to compete with the state. The Italian city republics, and, in addition, many of their counterparts north of the Alps, must also be regarded as states in the sense that they were self-governing units; in many respects, they even had a stronger state character than the kingdoms. The Church also has many of these characteristics, although it is further from the essential criterion of monopoly of violence within a clearly defined territory than the contemporary kingdoms.

However, these categories of state differed regarding their fundamental purpose. The Church aimed at teaching the people the true religion and lead them to salvation in the next life, after death. Its organization and political power were in principle the means to this aim. The city was essentially a community of merchants and artisans whose political power was a means to secure the commercial interests of its inhabitants. Only the 'states', kingdoms and principalities, had government as their main purpose, defined as solving conflicts between its inhabitants, defending the community against foreign powers and increasing the territory and the status of the kingdom in question. Thus, the ability to conduct wars was the main characteristic of a kingdom but in principle only a means to an end for the Church and the cities.

In practice, the difference between the three was less. Means and ends are not easily distinguishable. The pope insisted that all his wars were fought for the sake of God and Christendom but found it difficult to convince people of this. The Venetians built up a large empire and even conquered a substantial territory on the Italian mainland, all with the explicit purpose of protecting their trade, but there were discussion within as well as outside the city on whether this was actually true. Nevertheless, there was a difference. Although the pope was far from peace-loving, there was a gap between his organizational and spiritual power and his military one. There are many examples of the cities regarding warfare as a necessary evil and that they deliberately abstained from war and conquest if it was against their commercial interests. Most importantly, city republics were more cautious regarding spending, for war as well as for cultural purposes, than kingdoms were.

Thus, more physical power was concentrated in kingdoms than in the two other kinds of organization. The consequences of this were to be seen in the following period. Although the military revolution had limited consequences for the relationship between the kingdoms, it did contribute to the victory of kingdoms over the two other kinds of organization.

In the Middle Ages, kingdoms and city republics mostly seem to have had opposite interests. Northern Italian cities were more successful than their southern counterparts because of their political independence. North of the Alps, the most successful cities were to be found in the areas with the weakest royal power, in the Low Countries, Germany – mainly along the Baltic coast and the main rivers from south to north, notably the Rhine. French towns were often allied with the king in the early phase of the expansion of royal power but later lost much of their independence. The capitals of large kingdoms, notably London and Paris, form an exception to this rule. They had some governmental institutions, but were clearly subordinated to the king, whose presence, however, added substantially to their wealth. Rome belongs to the same category as the capital of the pope.

The development from the sixteenth century onwards went in the direction of reduced independence for the cities. Most of the Italian cities lost their independence in the sixteenth century and the same largely happened to the cities north of the Alps. Admittedly, a number of German cities retained their independence until the unification of Germany in 1866–70, but both in Germany and its neighbouring countries, the power of territorial principalities increased at the cost of the cities. The greatest continuity is to be found in the Netherlands but even here, the cities became subordinated to a state, although its government was elected by the provinces, in which the cities had had great influence. At the same time, trade and manufacture became increasingly important to kings and princes, which meant that subordination to them did not necessarily harm the commercial interests of the cities. On the contrary, the support of a strong state might be a competitive advantage, as it had been to the Venetians in the Middle Ages. As we shall see, much depended on the kind of state to which the towns were subordinated. Eventually it turned out that the most successful states were those with a strong class of burghers, like the Dutch Republic and England.

Whereas in most monarchies, the king is the head of religion, European kings faced a strong religious organization claiming independence of secular powers and even superiority in matters defined as belonging to the strictly religious sphere, a definition that the head of this organization, the pope, claimed was his to make. Although the pope recognized the distinction between a religious sphere, ruled by the pope, and a secular one, ruled by the king, he claimed that the religious one was superior and that it was up to him to define the border between the two. To later ages, the picture of King Henry IV of Germany standing barefoot and dressed in penitential clothes before Pope Gregory VII in Canossa in 1077 forms the clearest expression of this relationship: to Catholics, expressing the age of belief and the power of religion over secular institutions, to Protestants and non-religious, the arrogance of the clergy and religion as an obstacle to the development of a secular state.

Another, equally famous scene represents a contrast to that of Canossa, namely Pope Boniface VIII being taken captive by the troops of King Philip IV of France in Anagni in 1303, an episode that ended the conflict between the two and eventually led to the pope moving to Avignon in 1308, where he was subject to French influence. Henry IV's defeat by Gregory is regarded as the introduction of the period of greatness for the papacy, while Boniface's defeat by King Philip IV of France signals the end of this period and the introduction of increasing royal control of the Church. The reality is somewhat more complicated than this. The episode in Canossa was not a total victory for the pope, nor was that of Anagni a total victory for the king. Henry's humiliation aimed at splitting his adversaries and the pope's victory was only temporary. Philip IV apparently aimed at bringing Pope Boniface to France and have him judged there, but had to release him shortly afterwards. Had he not died after a few weeks, King Philip might have faced difficulties.

However, King Philip had both theoretical and practical resources for defence against the pope. He had considerable, although not unanimous, support from intellectuals at the University of Paris who used Aristotle's theory of the political community based on human nature as an argument for the king's independence of the Church. Thus, in the so-called *Disputation between the Priest and the Knight*, one of the royalist pamphlets from the conflict, the priest points out that the Church has a higher authority than the secular power. To this the knight answers: 'Quite right, reverend, but your power is theoretical, ours is real.'[43] The truth of the latter observation is confirmed both by the fact the revenues of the king of France were 15 times greater than those of the pope and that the king had the advantage of proximity to the national church, which made most of the bishops support his cause. Thus, the conflict between Philip and Boniface shows the increasing strength of the monarchy in the period from the late eleventh to the early fourteenth century.

The papacy emerged as a universal power and a promoter of ecclesiastical reform in the late eleventh century, while the kings increased their power over the national churches from the early fourteenth century. From the point of view of state formation, the ecclesiastical organization represented an advantage as well as a challenge. The expansion of the Church led to a greater bureaucratization than would otherwise have been the case; it is difficult to imagine any other field than religion being bureaucratized to the same extent under medieval conditions. The ecclesiastical bureaucracy and territorial divisions served as models for the royal ones, in addition to the fact that ecclesiastics played an important part in the royal bureaucracy. Thus, despite frequent struggles, the king and the Church had basically common interests during most of the Middle Ages.

Moreover, the Church emphasized the king's sacred character through unction and coronation. Admittedly, this character became less pronounced after the Gregorian Reform, when the pope insisted on the difference between the clergy and the laity and firmly placed the king in the latter category, which in turn forced the king to develop a secular legitimation. Such a legitimation occurs already during the Investiture Contest and was further developed through the reception of Aristotle's political thought and by fourteenth-century authors like Marsilius of Padua. Thus, an increasing emphasis on the secular foundation of the king's power can be traced in the theoretical literature from the thirteenth century onwards.[44] However, this did not really reduce the king's sacred status which, as we have seen, was continued and even strengthened in rituals, courtly ceremonials and popular propaganda.

By the fifteenth and sixteenth centuries, the state in many European countries had reached a stage where it was possible to challenge the independence of the Church. This forms part of the background for the Reformation. Although the pope continued to claim superior power over the kings, this power was clearly reduced from the sixteenth century onwards, of course particularly in Protestant countries, which did not recognize any papal power, but also in Catholic ones, where the king largely gained administrative control of the Church in his country. Despite wide-reaching theoretical claims, the pope did not really attempt to become the ruler of the whole of Christendom. If he had, however, he would inevitably have been faced with the problem that his territory was too large to be governed effectively.

Concerning the victory of the state, there is more to say in favour of the military explanation of state formation regarding internal consolidation than the relationship between the states. Military mobilization did lead to greater bureaucratization and to some extent greater royal control but it might also work in the opposite direction, as illustrated by the widespread venality of offices in France, Spain and other countries. A better explanation seems to be the one suggested by Spruyt, of the comparative advantage of the state in satisfying the needs of its inhabitants, which in turn has to do with size. States were smaller than the Universal Empire and the Universal Church but larger than most cities. Compared to the city leagues, they mostly had the advantage of shorter distances between their borders. They covered larger areas than the cities and controlled these areas better than the universal powers. Spruyt's main examples of this concern trade and communications. States had formal borders where similar rules applied to all its inhabitants, where there was some freedom of communication and trade, a standard mint and standard measures of size and weight. There were also legislation, courts of law, some kind of police force and general rules of behaviour applicable to the whole population.[45]

Admittedly, what would have struck us if we could return to, say, early modern France, would be the absence of most of these features. There were a bewildering number of courts of law with different kinds of jurisdiction, there were internal toll stations and neither mint nor weights and measures were standardized for the whole country. Relatively, however, there was more unity in these respects within France than between this country and others, and it was easier to move around and do business in France than, for instance, in Germany, where one constantly had to cross borders and pay a toll, and where each of the around 400 units had their own law and currency. With the increase of trade, manufacture and communication, the state had obvious advantages over its competitors. Concerning the cities, their limited territory was an obstacle. In addition, the most advanced and important of them, the Italian ones, which did rule relatively substantial territories and for a long time were wealthier and administratively more advanced than most states, had the disadvantage that they were not homogeneous. They were ruled by the elite in their capital city, whereas the countryside and the dependent cities had little or no political influence and did not enjoy equal rights regarding trade and production. They, therefore, had little incentive to fight against foreign invaders.

On the other hand, the patriotic fervour of the inhabitants of early modern states should not be exaggerated. The armies at the time were not composed of men who longed to fight and die for their beloved fatherland but either of conscripts recruited against their will or men who had no other opportunity in life; in both cases, subject to drill, command, strict discipline and horrible punishments for dis-obedience and desertion. To the wealthier part of the population, however, the state offered a certain amount of safety and stability, made it easier to move and do business and to solve conflicts. Even the peasants, who paid most of the taxes and benefited least from the state, had some safety against arbitrary treatment and might appeal to the courts of law against their superiors, in addition to the mostly erro-neous belief that the king was their friend and protector and that all problems would be solved if they could reach him directly. Nevertheless, despite the burdens the state imposed on them, its breakdown was a worse evil. Although the devel-opment of the state certainly involved the use of force, this was not the only explanation. Its success was also due to some support from the population which saw their needs served in this way. Moreover, as we shall see, the most successful states were the ones that offered the best conditions for their inhabitants and thus received most support from them.

Conclusion

In accordance with the title of this chapter, the relationship between the state, on the one hand, and the Church and the city, on the other, may be understood as a competition that was finally won by the state. The period considered so far, from the early Middle Ages until the seventeenth century, shows a significant develop-ment in this direction, particularly through the Reformation and the conquest of Italy in the sixteenth century. However, we must also consider the importance of influence and cooperation. The royal administration was in many ways influenced by the ecclesiastical one; churchmen played an important part in the king's service;

ecclesiastical law became a model for royal legislation and the kings found legitimation for their rule in the Christian idea of the king as God's representative on Earth and the defender of Christian orthodoxy. Cities were an important source of income for most kings and experts from the Italian cities played a significant part in the royal administration as well as in exploiting the wealth of the Spanish colonies after the Great Discoveries. Moreover, the most successful states in the early modern period, the Dutch Republic and England, in many ways continued the practices and ideas that had developed in the medieval cities. Thus, the ancestor of the early modern state is not only the medieval kingdom but also the medieval Church and city.

Notes

1 For the following, see Ladurie, *Montaillou*, pp. 14–21.
2 Ibid., p. 432.
3 Ibid., p. 37.
4 Eisenstadt, *The Origins and Diversity*; Goldstone, *Why Europe?*, pp. 34–51.
5 Moore, *The War on Heresy*. For a criticism of Moore and other revisionists, see Taylor, *Heresy in Medieval France*, pp. 76–80, and Biller, 'Goodbye to Waldensianism', and '[Review of] R.I. Moore' and 'Heresy and Dissent'. For the traditional view, see Hamilton, 'Religion and the Laity' and 'The Albigensian Crusade and Heresy'. The recent general account by Ames, *Medieval Heresies*, pp. 28–78, does not express any opinion on the issue.
6 Reynolds, 'Social Mentalities'; van Engen, 'The Christian Middle Ages'; Biller, 'Popular Religion'; Arnold, 'Histories and Historiographies'; Yarrow, 'Religion, Belief and Society'; and Forrest, *Trustworthy Men*, p. 7.
7 Riley-Smith, 'The Crusades 1095–1198', pp. 539–40.
8 For the following, see Stow, 'The Church and the Jews'; and Bartlett, *England*, pp. 346–60.
9 Joinville, *Life of St Louis*, p. 175.
10 Smalley, *The Study of the Bible*, pp. 149–72.
11 Southern, *Western Views*, pp. 37–9.
12 For the following, see Levack, *The Witch Hunt*; Sallman, 'Sorcière'; Thomas, *Religion and the Decline of Magic*, pp. 520–3, 553–60; Rowlands, 'Witchcraft and Gender'; and Hutton, *The Witch*, pp. 147–211.
13 Christensen-Nugues, 'Och de skal vara ett hjärta', pp. 9–14; The bishop's objections are referred to in a letter from Margaret Paston, Margery's mother, to her husband, *Paston Letters*, vol. I, p. 341.
14 *Diplomatarium Norvegicum*, vol. V, no. 72.
15 Brundage, *Law, Sex and Christian Society*, pp. 333–7.
16 Duby, *Medieval Marriage*, pp. 25–81; L'Hermite-Leclerq, 'L'ordre féodal (XI–XIIe siècles)'.
17 Dyer, *Making a Living*, pp. 155–60.
18 Cobban, *The Medieval Universities*, pp. 3–121.
19 Febvre, *The Problem of Unbelief*.
20 The development of the medieval papacy has been subject to considerable discussion, of a confessional as well as scholarly character. Walter Ullmann, *The Growth of Papal Government*, regards it as a consistent attempt to put into a practice a doctrine of hegemony going back to late antiquity, whereas others, like R.W. Southern, *Western Society and the Church*, and Barraclough, *The Medieval Papacy*, have a more pragmatic approach, paying greater attention to circumstances and emphasizing the parallel to the growth of secular government. See, most recently, Cushing, 'Papal Authority'.
21 Southern, *Western Society and the Church*, pp. 109–25.

22 On constitutional thought in canon law and the Church, see Tierney, *Religion, Law* and *The Origins of Papal Infallibility*.

23 Barraclough, *The Medieval Papacy*, pp. 135–8.

24 Kaminsky, 'The Great Schism', pp. 674–8.

25 See Strayer, *The Reign of Philip the Fair*, pp. 285–97 and Barber, *The Trial of the Templars*, pp. 283–311, with a discussion of a series of previous accounts. There is general agreement among historians that the accusations against the Templars were false or at least vastly exaggerated, but opinions differ about Philip's motives. He obviously wanted to appropriate the Templars' great wealth but religious motives may also have played a part, either Philip's wish to gain a reputation for orthodoxy or some belief in the truth of the accusations, as suggested, among others, by Strayer.

26 Otto of Freising, *The Deeds of Frederick*, pp. 144–9.

27 Benson, 'Political *Renovatio*'; Bagge, 'Ideas and Narrative', pp. 356–60.

28 Otto of Freising, *The Deeds of Frederick*, pp. 234–5; cf. Bagge, 'The Model Emperor', p. 72.

29 For example, Brown, *Through the Eye of a Needle*, pp. 4–8.

30 For the following, see Waley, *The Italian City Republics*.

31 For the following, see Ferraro, *Venice*, pp. 1–25.

32 McNeill, *Venice*, pp. 48–56.

33 Frankopan, *The Silk Roads*, pp. 140–69, 175–86.

34 For the following, see de Roover, 'The Organization of Trade', pp. 70–105.

35 McNeill, *Venice*, pp. 5–6, 49–51.

36 Acemoglou and Robinson, *Why Nations Fail*, pp. 154–6.

37 Machiavelli, *Florentine Histories*, vol. III.16, p. 127.

38 Najemy, *History of Florence*, pp. 63–95.

39 Lampert, *Annales*, pp. 185–93; Bagge, *Kings, Politics*, pp. 266–9.

40 Spruyt, *The Sovereign State*, p. 149.

41 Bartlett, *The Making of Europe*, pp. 167–96; Dollinger, *The German Hansa*.

42 Olesen, 'Inter-Scandinavian Relations', pp. 718–19.

43 *Disputatio inter clericum et militem*; cf. Tierney, *The Crisis*, pp. 193–210.

44 Strayer, 'The Laicization'; Oakley, *The Mortgage*, pp. 39–41 and *The Watershed*, pp. 1–50.

45 Spruyt, *The Sovereign State*, pp. 153–80.

4

THE REVOLUTIONS OF THE SIXTEENTH CENTURY AND THEIR CONSEQUENCES

On 2 January 1492, the Spanish royal couple Ferdinand and Isabella received the surrender of Granada, the last Muslim principality in Western Europe. On the same occasion, a Genoese adventurer, Christopher Columbus, finally managed to persuade the two rulers to finance an expedition to approach India from the west.

The year 1492 is one of several used to mark the exact date of the transition between the Middle Ages and the early modern period, pointing to the Great Discoveries as the beginning of a new epoch, the European dominance of the rest of the world, which has lasted until the present. The conquest of Granada may be regarded in the same way, marking the beginning of Spain's era of greatness and forming an example of a second revolution, the military one, already discussed, that led to this result: the formation of a professional infantry army equipped with muskets and cannons. Receiving the capitulation, Ferdinand and Isabella were dressed in Moorish attire and the enemy were also given generous terms, both in accordance with the traditional multiculturalism in Spain. The following period, however, showed that this attitude had come to an end; from now on, Spain joined the common European intolerance and became the centre of Catholic orthodoxy, directed at Islam as well as against Christian heresy.

To the two Catholic monarchs, the conquest of Granada and the following discovery and exploitation of America probably represented a further step towards the expansion of Catholic Christendom. However, less than three decades later, a third revolution occurred that resulted in a deep split in Christendom and the loss of most of its northern part by the Catholic Church. In 1517, Martin Luther directed his first attack on the Church and in a few years created a movement that rejected papal primacy and the central tenets of Catholic doctrine.

Four years before Luther attacked the indulgences, in 1513, the Florentine Niccolò Machiavelli composed *The Prince*, which may be considered equally revolutionary in the political sphere as Luther's theses in the religious one, although it did not have the same immediate effect. It marks the beginning of the 'realistic' understanding of politics, emancipating it from religion and ethics, and introduces a new empirical approach to knowledge which eventually found parallels in other fields as well.

Although the distinction between the Middle Ages and the early modern period is more open to discussion today than it used to be in the nineteenth century and we have already dealt with several aspects of the early modern development, the changes listed above are important and will form the theme of this chapter. It will deal with the Renaissance movement and its intellectual and political consequences, with the religious divisions and their background in the previous development of the various kingdoms and with the Great Discoveries, which in turn will address the discussion of the relationship between Europe and the rest of the world.

The Renaissance

Beginning with internal European matters, we may note that the Great Discoveries and the overseas conquests coincided with cultural changes within Europe, the most obvious of which is the Reformation, which, however, is preceded by another movement, namely, the Renaissance. 'Renaissance' means re-birth and is a French translation of the original Italian 'Rinascimento', which referred to the rebirth of classical antiquity, its language, culture and art.[1] The poet Petrarch (1304–74) is usually regarded as the founder of the movement, wanting to renew poetry under inspiration from the Latin classics. Later, the idea was applied to art and architecture. The basic idea of the movement is clearly expressed in Giorgio Vasari's (1511–74) introduction to his book on famous Italian artists of 1550.[2] Here he sketches the history of art since Classical Antiquity, its decline after the fall of the Roman Empire and its renewal in Italy from the fourteenth century onwards. This periodization has been subject to much discussion in the following centuries and few scholars today will accept the picture of the dark Middle Ages and the bright Renaissance. Nevertheless, we find a number of important inventions during the Renaissance, not only in art and literature. In the present context, they can be summarized under four headings: (1) Greek language and literature; (2) the printing press; (3) the renaissance of science and learning; and (4) a new 'realistic' understanding of politics and the state.

Greek language and literature

The first is most directly related to the original Renaissance movement. A new and more systematic search for ancient texts occurred from the fourteenth century onwards, as recently exemplified by Poggio Bracciolini's discovery of Lucrece's *De rerum natura* in an early medieval manuscript.[3] However, the most important was not the discovery of Latin literature – not many previously unknown Latin texts were discovered during the Renaissance – but of Greek. Very few scholars knew

Greek in Western Europe in the Middle Ages and important authors, such as Homer, Herodotus, Thucydides and most of Plato's works were completely unknown. The main exception to this was Aristotle – in the Middle Ages usually referred to as 'the Philosopher' – whose work were known in Latin translation and who was regarded as the great authority. Even the New Testament was mostly read in Latin. Now the Greek texts became known and scholars began to study Greek.

The printing press

The knowledge of texts was further extended through the invention of printing.[4] Although it can hardly be considered part of the original Renaissance movement – it was invented in Germany and many leading Renaissance humanists preferred handwritten books, as in Classical Antiquity – it was of great importance for the new cultural trends. Most medieval libraries, even those of large and rich monasteries or cathedrals, were small by our standards. Printing made possible a drastic increase at a relatively low cost. It now became possible to compare the ancient texts to a greater extent and for the first time since classical antiquity to develop a concept of classical Latin style. Printing was also important for the development of textual criticism. New editions were now made on the basis of more manuscripts than before and methods were developed to trace the relationship between them so at to arrive at the reconstruction of the original version. Most importantly, printing not only made ancient texts more available but presented entirely new opportunities to spread new knowledge and ideas.

The consequences of these novelties can be illustrated through the founder of the new picture of the universe, Copernicus (Mikolaj Kopernik, 1473–1543), who had studied at Krakow and Bologna and had a degree in canon law.[5] Copernicus had an excellent knowledge of both Greek and Latin and was familiar with a number of Greek scientists, some of whom he mentions in his preface as adherents of the moving Earth. Moreover, Copernicus' theory was not based on observation; he had not proved that the Earth moved around the sun, but he had found that this theory gave a more economical and elegant explanation of the existing observations than the alternative one. Here we immediately see the importance of the knowledge of Greek, which made available alternative theories to the dominating one of Aristotle. Finally, considering the resistance to Copernicus' theory in the following period, we might ask what would have happened if printing had not been invented. Even if the new theory had not been suppressed, it is likely to have taken considerably longer to become accepted.

The renaissance of science and learning

We can also point to other examples of the combination of Renaissance humanism and science and technology. The great painter, Leonardo da Vinci was, in addition, a brilliant engineer, who constructed advanced weapons for his various patrons, including Francis I of France. Italy was also for some time the centre of the study of astronomy. Machiavelli was interested in medicine and tried to explain social phenomena by medical theory. Finally, the disciplines of astrology and alchemy must be mentioned, neither of which is regarded as science today but which were both subjects of great interest during the Renaissance.

Copernicus' theory formed the first step towards a scientific revolution. In the following period, his theory was confirmed by observations by Kepler (1571–1630) and particularly Galileo (1564–1642) and finally led to Newton's (1642–1727) theory of gravitation. This not only led to a more exact knowledge of the universe but also meant a methodological revolution in science, which was followed by others. The consequences of this will be discussed in the following.

A new 'realistic' understanding of politics and the state

Whereas the development of science from Copernicus onwards should most probably be regarded as a revolution, the relationship between the Middle Ages and the Renaissance is more open to discussion in the fields of historiography and political and social thought.[6] The founder of Italian Renaissance historiography is Leonardo Bruni, who wrote *Historia Florentini Populi* (History of the Florentine People) in the first half of the fifteenth century. Although writing in a terse and matter-of-fact style, Bruni celebrates the Florentine republic from its foundation until 1402, the year when the city was saved from conquest by Milan by the sudden death of Giangaleazzo Visconti, Duke of Milan, who at the time had conquered the surrounding cities and was preparing for the final assault on Florence itself. Particularly the last part of the work depicts the heroic defence of the city against tyranny.[7] Despite its seemingly neutral style, the work is strongly patriotic and it also tries to interpret the main lines of development in the history of the republic, from its foundation by Sulla – i.e. during the Roman Republic – until the present. Patriotic historiography was no novelty in the fifteenth century; Florence and other Italian cities has a long tradition of urban history from the thirteenth century onwards. However, Bruni differs from this tradition on several important points. He preferred Latin to the Italian of his predecessors. He is also strongly influenced by classical historians, not only Livy but also Greek historians like Thucydides, Polybius and Plutarch, who were unknown to his predecessors. He mostly avoids legend and religious explanation, to a greater extent attempts a critical assessment of his sources and seeks to explain the development of Florence in secular terms.

The fall of the Florentine republic gave rise to a new and more sombre kind of political reflection in Machiavelli's and Guicciardini's works. In his best-known work, *The Prince* (1513), Machiavelli departs from the traditional medieval genre of mirrors for princes, which is based on moral rules, and addresses the question of how to succeed as a ruler and remain in power. The book contains a series of strikingly cynical remarks, such as that it is better for a prince to be feared than to be loved – directly in contrast to the traditional doctrine – and that people more easily forgive the killing of their father than the loss of their property. However, the importance of *The Prince* and other of Machiavelli's works does not consist in such statements but in his attempts to build a theory of politics and society on systematic analysis of examples of actual behaviour from the present as well as the past. It also implies a more cynical and individualistic theory of human nature. Most people act to serve their own interests and political theory must be based on this fact, although in other contexts, Machiavelli is concerned with patriotic virtue and how this can be promoted in society. Both in *The Prince* and his other works, he takes his point of departure in concrete situations which he develops into analyses of more complex and long-term phenomena, such as the causes of the rise and decline of Florence and the Roman Empire and of the relative merits of princely and republican government. In principle, Machiavelli prefers the latter but he admits that it will not always work in practice. Machiavelli's theories are based on extensive reading of Roman authors, notably Livy, and contemporary and earlier Italian historical writings but also on his own career as an official of the Florentine republic, which had given him considerable practical experience; he was responsible for organizing and training the popular levy and he participated in diplomatic missions to foreign powers.

Modern democratic readers may find Machiavelli's cynicism, particularly in *The Prince*, less attractive than the medieval Aristotelian tradition and may have good arguments for this. Although we may easily oppose Machiavelli's cynicism and political opinions, however, he is a pioneer in sociology. He starts from empirical observations rather than norms and he shows great understanding of political behaviour. Thus, his analysis of the reasons for the *Ciompi* rebellion has been celebrated as a brilliant piece of sociology; the example from it discussed in Chapter 3 shows an excellent understanding of political psychology.[8]

Machiavelli's younger contemporary, Francesco Guicciardini (1483–1540), belonged to one of the most prominent families in Florence and spent most of his life as an administrator and military officer in the service of the pope. He became the governor of Florence after the defeat of the republic in 1530 but was dismissed when Cosimo I took power in 1537 and spent the last years of his life writing the history of Italy from the first French invasion in 1494 to 1534, largely based on his own experience. As the story of Francis I's captivity, discussed in Chapter 1, indicates, Guicciardini has a similar pessimistic view of politics and human folly as Machiavelli but is less concerned with general theories. His main contribution to the understanding of history and society are his meticulous analyses of decision-making processes, to reveal exactly why the actual events took place, in most cases, why things went wrong.

Modern historians who use Machiavelli and Guicciardini as sources find much to criticize in their accounts, particularly those of Machiavelli, who often deliberately changes the information he has received from his predecessors in order to make some political point. Nor did these writers or other humanists of the fifteenth and sixteenth centuries make any important scientific observations. Nevertheless, there seems to be some connection between the combination of an empirical and generalizing approach to society and human actions and the experimental science that

developed in the sixteenth and seventeenth centuries. There is also a clear connection between the Renaissance and the contemporary religious movement, the
Reformation.

The Reformation

In April 1521, the newly elected Holy Roman Emperor Charles V held his first
Diet with his new subjects in Worms. One of the items on the agenda was the case
of an Augustinian friar, Martin Luther, who had challenged the authority of the Church.
It had begun with an attack on indulgences in 1517, occasioned by the aggressive campaign by the Dominican friar Johann Tetzel to collect money for the building of the
new cathedral of St Peter's in Rome. During a series of debates with various theologians,
Luther had expressed his view on other aspects of theology, until, in 1519, he had
openly admitted his support for John Hus' teaching, thus, implying that the Council of
Konstanz, which condemned him, had been wrong. He had been excommunicated by
the pope in 1520, but had burnt the papal bull together with the writings of his adversaries and the collection of canon law. In the same year, he had published three books
that attacked various aspects of Catholic doctrine and demanded a thorough reformation
of the Church. These actions had had an enormous impact in Germany and had created
a movement in favour of the reform of the Church. On his way to Worms, Luther had
been hailed by masses of people along the road.

The emperor was and remained a staunch Catholic but was willing to listen to
Luther's arguments. At the meeting, Luther recognized his authorship of the books
that had been brought to the council and was then asked if he would recant. He
asked for one day's grace to make an answer. On the next day, he gave his answer
in a speech. Acknowledging his authorship of the books, he admitted that some of
them were polemics against the papacy which 'reflected the experience and the
complaint of all men'. He continued:

> If then, I revoke these books, all I shall achieve is to add strength to tyranny;
> and open not the windows but the doors for this monstrous godlessness for a
> wider and freer range than it has ever dared before.

Finally, he stated that without a conviction from 'scripture or plain reason (for I
believe neither in Pope nor councils alone)', he could recant nothing. This statement was later summarized by one of Luther's editors in the most famous of his
alleged utterances: 'Here I stand and can do no other.'[9]

In this way, Luther replaced a tradition many centuries old, supported by learned
theologians and high-ranking prelates, by his own conviction, based on his reading
of the Bible.[10] Luther's proclamation was revolutionary, but it also had its background in earlier intellectual and religious developments. The Reformation can to
some extent be regarded as a further development of the lay piety of the previous
period, often referred to as *Devotio moderna*, which emphasized personal piety and
the inner life rather than institutions and ceremonies.[11] In the case of Luther, his

religious development has usually been depicted as the result of a deep personal crisis, the experience of himself as a sinner who was unable to atone for his sins, whatever he did to obtain God's grace. The solution was to trust in Christ's redemption. No human being can satisfy God, but Christ has died for the sins of humankind and the only way to salvation is to accept the grace God bestows on completely undeserving sinners. This picture of an existential crisis is based on Luther's own account later in life and may possibly be exaggerated, but the doctrine and the personal experience of it were nevertheless central to Luther and his followers as well as to other reformers, although its intensely personal aspect may have been less prominent in them. The reformers rejected good works as a means to deserve God's grace, in particular, the many ceremonies and devotional practices of the Catholic Church. The logical consequence of this rejection of human ability to contribute to salvation was the doctrine of predestination: the whole humankind is condemned to perdition, but God has from eternity selected a few to be saved. The doctrine was particularly prominent in Calvinism, but was also shared by Luther, largely also by his followers. A particularly important source for it was Augustine, who was one of Luther's favourite authors and central to the other reformers as well.

In contrast to the Catholics, the Protestants regarded the Bible as the only source of God's revelation and Christian doctrine, an opinion that shows the close connection between the Reformation and Renaissance Humanism. In accordance with the latter, the study of the Bible in the original languages began in the fifteenth century. In 1516, Erasmus of Rotterdam (1466–1536), one of the leading humanists at the time, published an edition of the New Testament in Greek with comments. Luther was professor at the University of Wittenberg, which became one of the first centres of the new movement. The new emphasis on the Bible corresponded to a new attitude to tradition. There is a close parallel between the Protestant view of the Bible as a text that should be read independently of its long history of interpretation and the Renaissance humanists' perception of Classical Antiquity as a lost golden age which had to be recovered by pushing aside the intervening period, 'the Middle Ages'. Thus, Luther and the reformers did with the Bible what Machiavelli did with Livy and the Roman republic and Vasari with classical art. On the other hand, the reformers rejected the humanists' optimistic view of human nature and their attempts, which go back to the Middle Ages, to find a synthesis between Christianity and ancient philosophy. The difference on this point explains the increasing distance between Luther and Erasmus. Erasmus sympathized with Luther in the beginning but reacted against his radical attack on Catholicism and his pessimistic view of human nature. In 1524, he published a book on free will, to which Luther responded with one on the unfree will, proclaiming the doctrine of predestination (1525).

The Reformation thus had a solid basis in the intellectual innovations of the period. In addition, it had a broad popular appeal, and in a short time spread over large parts of Europe. This is in marked contrast with earlier religious movements, such as the Albigensian and Valdensian heresies in the thirteenth century and the

Lollards in England and Hussites in Bohemia in the fourteenth and fifteenth centuries. Whereas the Lollards, the adherents of John Wycliffe, had been suppressed relatively easily, the latter had resisted several crusades by Catholic powers and still existed in the country. However, neither of them had led to mass movements outside their country of origin. An important factor in explaining this difference is the invention of printing. Books and leaflets could easily be produced in many copies and spread over the Continent and these means were systematically exploited by the reformers – eventually also by their adversaries. More than 10,000 pamphlets were produced in Germany in the period 1500–1530, the overwhelming majority of them between 1517 and 1527.

Although we should not neglect the importance of individual conviction, religion was a matter of eternal salvation or damnation about which individuals might make different choices whatever their background, the different outcome of the religious competition in various parts of Europe and between various social layers is great enough to demand an explanation. The usual observation is that Protestantism appealed to the urban population and to the intellectuals and educated classes, a fact reflected in the importance of books and pamphlets, although these might also be read aloud or form the basis for preaching or other oral appeals. The fast spread of the movement to the towns of Germany, Switzerland, the Netherlands and to some extent France, is an example of this. By contrast, the peasants usually remained Catholic, although the Reformation did influence the German peasant rebellion of 1524–25. An important part of the explanation of this is the integration of Catholicism into peasant life, with feasts and rituals, related to community life and fertility of the soil and the animals as well as humans themselves. Most peasants were also illiterate and thus less susceptible to propaganda in the form of books and pamphlets. By contrast, the urban population was more likely to be influenced by the new forms of devotion, focusing on the inner life and rejecting or paying little attention to outward rites and ceremonies. In addition, the Church owned a large part of the ground in most German towns and was a serious competitor to the merchants and artisans. Thus, in Mainz, the residence of the most high-ranking archbishop in Germany, up to a quarter of the male population were clerics in the fifteenth century. Following an attack on some monasteries, the burghers were so heavily fined over a whole century that it led many of the wealthiest citizens to leave the town.[12]

According to these criteria, we might expect the Reformation to have had a great impact in Italy, which was the most urbanized country in Europe and the centre of Renaissance humanism. Actually, the movement was known in the country from early on and had considerable influence in intellectual circles. More influential, however, was a movement within clerical circles in favour of reform of the Church from the inside, accepting parts of the Protestant doctrines.[13] For a long time, there was little persecution of religious deviation; popes like Clement VII (1523–34) and Paul III (1534–49) were more interested in extending their territorial power and the influence of their families than in religious orthodoxy. Paul III, in addition, sympathized with the moderate reformers. This attitude changed with Paul IV (1555–59), who was violently anti-Protestant and initiated systematic persecution of heretics.

In the following period, Protestantism seems to have been suppressed in Italy. In contrast to Germany, Italy in the sixteenth century was no longer dominated by independent cities and principalities. Most of it was under the control of the pope, the Emperor or Spain, and particularly the Spanish influence led to religious conformity. Nevertheless, there seems have been no mass movement in favour of Protestantism in Italy, in contrast to Germany. A political explanation of this may be the different role of the Church in Italian urban society. The bishops had lost their leadership of the towns long ago, were only moderately wealthy and the Church was no serious competitor for the merchants. The town governments also controlled the local churches to a considerable extent. There were, therefore, no political or financial incentives for burghers or city councils to embrace Protestantism.

Concerning the other country in the south, Spain, the king and the nobility were staunchly Catholic, while the Church was largely under royal control. Moreover, contemporary, united Spain could be regarded as the result of a continuous struggle for Catholic Christianity against the Muslims, a struggle that had ended in victory with the conquest of Granada in 1492. In the following period, the king, the nobility and most of the people were united in the suppression of the Jews and the Moors and the Inquisition was under royal control. Although Protestantism did have some adherents in Spain, it is difficult to imagine that it would have any chance to influence significant parts of the establishment.

In the northern part of the Continent, Scandinavia, the relatively easy acceptance of Protestantism is striking.[14] The key country is Denmark, which was culturally closely linked to Germany. Since 1448, the dynasty had been German and the king ruled several German principalities. Already Frederick I (1523–33) sympathized with the Reformation and broke the ties with the papacy. His son, Christian III (1534–59) was a convinced Lutheran, who had heard Luther at the Diet of Worms in 1521. The Lutheran movement gained ground during the 1520s, particularly in the two leading towns, Copenhagen and Malmö, although there was also resistance from the Catholics. While all the bishops were Catholics, many priests converted and Lutheran sermons and religious services were held in many places in the country. When the Catholic clergy complained, the king answered, like many of the German princes, that he would not forbid anyone to practise his religion. A civil war over the succession broke out in 1534, but both candidates were Protestant. After his victory in 1536, Christian III arrested the bishops and made the country officially Lutheran. The new church was organized in close contact with Luther. As the king of Denmark was also king of Norway, the Reformation was introduced in this country during the following year. Here the population was little influenced by the new movement and probably remained Catholic for a long time, although there was little open resistance.

In Sweden, the Reformation was introduced by King Gustaf Vasa at a Diet in 1527, mainly for pragmatic reasons. The king wanted to tax the Church and confiscate some of its estates to pay for the costly war he had fought to chase the Danes out of the country and become king (1521–23). Here no alternative Church organization was introduced at the time and the Catholic bishops remained in their offices but were replaced by Protestants when they died. A series of later Diets took further steps in the direction of Protestantism, but the Reformation was less radical here than in Denmark. An attempt to reintroduce Catholicism or at least in the direction of a more positive attitude to the Catholic Church took place under John III (1568–92), who had married a Polish princess and wanted his son Sigismund to succeed to the Polish throne. However, the attempt failed. As a Catholic, Sigismund was deposed and replaced by his uncle, the staunchly Protestant Charles IX (1598–1611), whose son, Gustaf II Adolf (1611–32) became the saviour of the German Protestants during the Thirty Years War.

Concerning Scandinavia, there is some evidence of the factors that are usually regarded as decisive for the introduction of the Reformation. Both Denmark and Sweden had universities, although both were small and relatively new; Uppsala University in Sweden was founded in 1477 and Copenhagen University in Denmark in 1479. There was relatively little urbanization, although more in Denmark than in the two other countries, and this country also had a Reformation movement of the kind to be found in Germany and the Low Countries. It would nevertheless seem that the decisive factor was the king in all three countries. In addition to the Reformation movement in Denmark, he could exploit reactions against the financial burdens imposed by the Church and the greed of the secular aristocracy, which profited from the confiscation of Church lands.

Turning to the crucial middle zone, we find strong tension in all countries and widely different outcomes: Protestant victory in England and Scotland but with small Catholic minorities, Catholic victory in Ireland, despite the English conquest; Catholic victory in France after a long struggle, but with the survival of a Protestant minority; division between the two confessions in Germany, Catholic victories in Poland and Hungary but with Protestant minorities, and, finally, Catholic victory in Bohemia with Protestantism largely wiped out.

England resembles Scandinavia in becoming Protestant, although the process took longer and was more complicated in this country. There is little to indicate widespread support for the Reformation at the time when Henry VIII broke with the pope in 1533. This was not a direct consequence of Lutheran influence; Henry was a Catholic, who had even composed a treatise against Luther which earned him the title *Defensor fidei* (Defender of the Faith), bestowed by the pope, a title still used by British rulers. The reason was his unsuccessful attempts since 1527 to have his marriage to Catherine of Aragon annulled, so that he could marry again and secure the succession to the throne. Despite a number of pregnancies, Catherine had only borne him one daughter, Mary (born 1516), who later succeeded him. Finally, Thomas Cranmer, a Cambridge scholar of Protestant persuasion, convinced the king that he had no need of a papal dispensation; as king, he was also the superior of the Church and thus entitled to decide on his marriage.

Henry's original idea in 1533 was probably to remain head of a church that was Catholic in all respects except obedience to the pope. However, since most sincere Catholics disapproved of his divorce, he came to rely more on people with Protestant sympathies, in particular Thomas Cromwell, who became Chancellor and leading minister in 1534. During the rest of Henry's reign, various steps were taken in a Protestant direction, including the suppression of the monasteries (1535–39), the reform of the ecclesiastical calendar, abolishing a number of saints' days, and the destruction of various relics. There was also a reform of doctrine, although no consistent move in the direction of Protestantism, but rather in both directions, depending on the influence of people of different persuasion in the king's surroundings. Religious persecution also worked in both directions. Thus, on the same day in August 1540, three Catholic priests were hanged, drawn and quartered and three Protestants burnt as heretics – a demonstration that, regardless of confession, the most important was obedience to the king.[15]

The country became officially Protestant under the regency for Henry's son, Edward VI (1547–53), when a new, Protestant Church of England was founded and local churches were systematically purged of relics, vestments, statues and pictures. Then Catholicism returned under Henry's daughter, Mary (1553–58), when 273 Protestants, including four bishops, are known to have been burned at the stake. Most of them were ordinary people; Protestant members of the elite had mostly left the country. The final solution came under Henry's younger daughter, Elizabeth (1558–1603).

Personally, Elizabeth was clearly a Protestant, although her precise religious opinions are not easy to discern or to distinguish from political considerations; politically, she was bound to be a Protestant, because the Catholics did not recognize her as born in legitimate marriage and thus denied her right to the throne.[16] She was cautious in the beginning, partly because of England's alliance with Spain until the Peace of Cateau-Cambrésis in 1559. In 1559, Parliament passed the Supremacy Bill, which made the Queen Head of the Church. More precise rules for the English Church were passed in the Thirty-Nine Articles of 1563, which outlined the dogmas, organization and rituals of the new church, partly building on and partly revising earlier Protestant rules. Dogmatically, the Church of England received stronger influence from Calvinism, largely at the initiative of Marian exiles returning from Geneva or the Netherlands. This included the doctrine of predestination. On the other hand, a vague compromise was sought regarding the hotly contested issue of the Eucharist. Much of the Catholic liturgy and organization were retained, including the episcopal office and liturgical vestments, which provoked hard-core Protestants. The new church was in this way designed to include as many varieties of Protestants as possible. Participation in Anglican services every Sunday was made compulsory and failure to attend in principle and, to some extent, in practice punished by fines. In this way, Anglicanism became the only lawful religion, although there was no persecution of people with different religious opinions, as long as they showed external obedience to the Anglican Church.

Nevertheless, there was opposition. A large part of the population remained Catholic, although their numbers diminished during Elizabeth's long reign. However, since the pope had excommunicated Elizabeth in 1570, releasing her subjects from their obedience to her, Catholic priests were forbidden entry to the country and punished as traitors. Particularly during the conflict with Spain after 1587, Catholics were suspected of disloyalty, a suspicion that was in most cases unfounded; English Catholics were loyal to their country and did not wish a Spanish conquest. From the opposite side, the radical Protestants, eventually called Puritans, wanted to get rid of the remaining elements of Catholic liturgy, doctrine and organization.[17] They did not establish a separate religious community at this time, but formed an opposition within the established Church. Elizabeth reacted particularly strongly against their rejection of the ecclesiastical hierarchy, which she considered a danger to the organized hierarchy of society. This conflict did not end by Elizabeth's death but continued in the following period and, as we shall see, exploded during the Civil War in the 1640s.

During three decades in the middle of the sixteenth century, England had undergone four major religious changes without an open civil war. There had been some popular rebellion, but nothing like what happened in Germany or in France at around the same time. The reforms were carried through Parliament, which apparently calmly accepted to have Protestants burnt at the stake as well as Catholic priests hanged, drawn and quartered. It would immediately seem that the explanation of this must be that people in England were less religious than in other parts of Europe, or at least that the Catholic Church had little support in the country in the period before the Reformation. This has also been the view of a number of scholars.[18] More recently, however, this view has been challenged, particularly by Eamon Duffy who, having examined in detail popular religion in England, concludes that there was a great attachment to the Catholic cult both before and after the introduction of the Reformation and that there was widespread popular support for Mary's restoration of Catholicism. The decisive shift did not take place until Elizabeth's long reign.[19]

Protestantism probably had a stronger position among the elite than among the general population, similar to the situation in other countries. And the elite certainly had great material interests in the Reformation; in particular, lay landowners profited immensely from the suppression of the monasteries. Even Mary did not dare to try to reverse this process. Whatever our opinion of the religious fervour in Reformation England, however, there can be little doubt that the explanation for the series of religious transformations without open civil war must be the strength of the royal government. Even in the sixteenth century, however, neither Henry VIII, Mary, nor Elizabeth were able to introduce whatever reforms they wanted but had to juggle between various interests and religious opinions. The explanation for the religious development in England is therefore not that the king had full control of religion but rather a high degree of centralization which meant that the religious controversies played out on the central level in the form of factions and intrigues at court rather than in struggles between various parts of the country. No

English king has executed more nobles than Henry VIII. This is not only the result of Henry's cruelty and ruthlessness but also, and probably mainly, because of the factional rivalries at court.

The situation was somewhat different in Scotland. Here the Catholic Queen Mary Stuart was deposed by the Protestant nobility and the Reformation was introduced. The deposition may partly have been the consequence of Mary's behaviour; she was suspected of having murdered her husband, but it probably also reflects the weaker position of Scottish kings. A series of prolonged regencies during the later Middle Ages had strengthened the power of the aristocracy. Two previous kings had also been murdered, James I in 1437 and James III in 1488. Ireland was conquered by England and an Anglican Irish Church introduced. However, the majority of the population continued to be Catholic, which in the following period actually served to strengthen the English control of the country, by banning Catholics from holding public office, receiving education, etc.

In Germany, the Reformation became a strong movement from the 1520s onwards. Its introduction, particularly in towns, was also largely the result of popular initiative;[20] the great wave of conversions among the German princes came as late as the 1550s and 1560s. Only two major territories, Electoral Saxony and Hessen, adopted the new doctrine during the 1520s, both in 1526. However, few princes tried to suppress the movement. Frederick the Wise, Elector of Saxony, 1486–1525, protected Luther and tolerated his adherents but did not himself leave the Catholic Church. It was his brother and successor John who introduced the Reformation in Electoral Saxony.

Bavaria, later a Catholic bastion, had a large Protestant population, although its duke remained Catholic. The same applies to Austria, which was mainly Lutheran in the sixteenth century; thus two-thirds of the population of Vienna were Protestants. In Hungary, the Catholic population was reduced to around 10–15 per cent, while the majority were Reformed Protestants.[21] Further east, Transylvania, a country with a considerable German population, which from 1570 was a largely independent principality under Ottoman overlordship, became a centre of Reformed Protestantism.[22] Finally, Protestantism had a strong position in Bohemia, a country with a long history of religious dissent; only around 5 per cent of the population of Prague was Catholic in the sixteenth century.[23] When Ferdinand I was elected king of Bohemia in 1526, he had to guarantee religious tolerance. For the next century, this country was characterized by an extraordinary religious diversity: Utraquist Hussites,[24] radical Hussite Bohemian Brethren, Lutherans and Reformed Protestants.

The Reformation also spread from Germany to Poland and the Baltic region, particularly to the German-speaking merchants in the towns.[25] A great number of nobles converted to Protestantism, in addition to the fact that part of the population in the east belonged to the Orthodox Church. Already in 1544, a Lutheran university had been founded in Königsberg in Prussia, an area largely surrounded by Polish territory, which attracted Polish students. The country also had an anti-Trinitarian or Arian community, as well as a Russian-Orthodox Church in

Ukraine, which had existed before the Reformation. In contrast to further west, the Poles favoured religious tolerance. This may have had something to do with the strength of the nobility, which was also religiously divided, although the Polish monarchy was considerably stronger in the sixteenth century than it became later. Later, in the seventeenth century, there was a movement in the direction of Catholicism, particularly among the nobility, largely thanks to the Jesuit schools and universities, but Protestants were not persecuted. A union with parts of the Orthodox Church was achieved in 1596 through a compromise. The Orthodox were allowed to keep their Slavonic liturgy and married priests in return for recognizing the primacy of the pope.

During most of his reign, Charles V was too preoccupied with other enemies to launch a frontal attack on the Lutherans. Moreover, Germany was not his main field of interest; he actually delegated most of his power in this area to his younger brother Ferdinand as king of the Romans in 1530. Like Charles, Ferdinand was clearly a Catholic, but he was both more moderate and a cleverer politician than Charles, and tried to come terms with the Lutherans without war. The war that broke out in 1547 was the direct result of Charles' intervention.[26] He was successful at first, winning the famous victory at Mühlberg, immortalized by Titian, but his victory led the princes to unite against him and the war ended with the Peace of Augsburg in 1555, a compromise that was largely the result of Ferdinand's initiative. Here the religious question was settled according to the principle 'cuius regio eius religio', i.e. that the prince of the country should decide its religion. Those of his subjects who had a different religion than the prince should be allowed to emigrate. The episcopal principalities formed an exception to this. They were to remain Catholic; if the bishop converted to Protestantism – which happened in some cases – he had to resign. This settled the issue for a long time; despite much tension, there was no open war over religion until the Thirty Years War broke out in 1618.[27]

In the meantime, however, a general revival of Catholicism had taken place. This led to the reform of the Catholic clergy and the foundation of new religious orders, notably the Jesuits, founded by the Spaniard Ignatius Loyola in 1540. The Council of Trent (1545–63) was a victory for hard-core Catholicism, rejecting any theological compromise with the Protestants but also introducing a number of reforms: a standardized liturgy, compulsory for the whole Church, although with some exceptions, improvement of the education of the clergy as well as the laity, stricter enforcement of the rule of celibacy and the duty of the bishops and other clergy to reside in their districts. From the 1560s onwards, Catholicism managed to reconquer large parts of southern Germany and the Habsburg Empire, largely through preaching and education – the schools and universities run by the Jesuits were important in this – to some extent also through persecution by staunchly Catholic princes, the Dukes of Bavaria and the Habsburg princes in southern Germany and Austria. By contrast, the emperors were mostly tolerant.

This changed with the accession of the staunchly Catholic Emperor Ferdinand II in 1619 which led to the Thirty Years War (1618–48).[28] Religion was not the only factor but nevertheless an important one. The war began in Bohemia, where the estates refused to elect Ferdinand, replacing him with the Reformed Protestant, Frederick, Count Palatine of Rhineland, who arrived in Prague in autumn 1619 ('the Winter King'). However, the forces of the emperor and the Duke of Bavaria defeated the Bohemians at the Battle of the White Mountain outside Prague and conquered the city (1620). Twenty-seven Protestant nobles, considered responsible for the rebellion, were executed in the great square in Prague in 1621 and in the following period, Protestantism was brutally suppressed. Next, the emperor moved against the Count Palatine's territories in Rhineland and replaced him as an elector with the Catholic Duke Maximilian of Bavaria, who, like his predecessor, was a Wittelsbach. Eventually, a number of other powers were involved in the war, Spain, the Dutch Republic, Denmark, Sweden and finally France. The end result was that the emperor kept his control of Bohemia and the south, but failed in his attempt to reintroduce Catholicism in the north. Religiously, this resulted in a clearer difference between the Protestant north and the Catholic south in Germany, although with exceptions, such as the Catholic ecclesiastical principalities of Cologne and Münster in the north and the Protestant Württemberg in the south. Politically, the Peace of Westphalia formalized the division of the country into more than 400 units, around half of them principalities and the rest towns.

The importance of the Reformation for this result is open to question. It seems unlikely that the war would have broken out if it had not occurred. The reign of Maximilian I immediately before (1493–1519) shows some development in the direction of increased imperial power, but above all more cooperation between the emperor and the princes. However, it was hardly the emperor's main aim to suppress the princes, but rather to receive their aid in various imperial projects, notably in Italy and against the Turks. Without the Thirty Years War, the power relationship between the Empire and France would have been a different one – as Richelieu understood very well when he supported the Protestants, subsidized the Swedes and insisted on continuing the war in 1635 – but the character of the Empire would hardly have been very different. The Reformation was not the cause of the political division of Germany; on the contrary, the political division resulted in a religious division because the princes rather than the emperor decided the religious adherence of the inhabitants. Once a prince had converted and established a Protestant Church in his lands, it was difficult for the emperor to interfere; as shown in the war of the 1550s, this might easily lead even Catholic princes to resist the emperor.

In the sixteenth century, the religious conflict was more dramatic in France than in Germany. Here the Reformation, in its Calvinist version (Huguenots), was introduced at about the same time, but more gradually. Individual preachers were to some extent tolerated in the beginning, but later in his reign, Francis I took a stricter attitude, which was followed by his successors. The movement spread to large parts of the country, particularly in the south. In 1562, open civil war broke out, which lasted intermittently until 1598, when the former Huguenot leader, King Henry IV, who had converted to Catholicism in 1594, had become king and issued the Edict of Nantes, which allowed the Huguenots to practise their religion and gave them a number of fortified places as a guarantee.

Protestantism was weaker in France than in Germany; the number of Huguenots at the beginning of Henry IV's reign has been calculated at around 1/20 of the population.[29] Nevertheless, it was strong enough among the nobility as well as in the towns to create considerable problems for the central power and divide the country for 30 years or even longer, if we include the war in the 1620s to suppress the Huguenot strongholds. The religious division affected the very top of the French aristocracy; two of the five leading families, the Condé and the Coligny, were Huguenots, whereas the very influential Guise were staunchly Catholic. From this point of view, the conflict was not exclusively religious. It is significant that it broke out during a regency; traditionally a period likely to lead to internal divisions. At his death in 1559, Henry II was succeeded by Francis II (1559–60), aged 15, who in turn was succeeded by Charles IX (1560–74), aged 10. The minorities resulted in the dominance of the strictly Catholic Guises, which in turn provoked the reaction of the Calvinist nobles and eventually the civil wars.

Catherine of Medici, Henry II's widow, who ruled the country during her sons' minorities in the 1560s and played a central part in the government even later, tried to achieve compromises between the two factions to limit the influence of the Guise. Eventually, she found it necessary to get rid of Coligny, which in turn led to the St Bartholomew's Massacre of the Huguenots in 1572.[30] When finally a Huguenot ascended to the throne, it proved impossible to convert the country as a whole. Whatever the personal attitudes of the French kings before Henry IV, they all supported the Catholic cause. In contrast to the situation in Germany, the King of France had extensive control of the Church. In the recent Concordat of 1516, he had received the right to appoint bishops and abbots as well as some right to tax the Church. Consequently, he had little to gain by embracing the Reformation. In addition, during the wars over Italy until 1559, the pope was a valuable ally – mostly an enemy of the Habsburgs – which it would be dangerous to alienate. In the later phase of the struggle, from around 1570 onwards, the Counter-Reformation played an important part, mobilizing the people against the Protestants.

France in the sixteenth century was not the unified, bureaucratically organized state it became after the Revolution and Napoleon, and was also significantly less unified than under Louis XIV. Although the number of independent principalities had been greatly reduced since the late fifteenth century and the royal administration had expanded, the king still depended on a small number of great nobles with extensive estates as provincial governors, but in contrast to Germany, these nobles were not territorial princes with independent power bases; they were not able to divide the country according to the principle of 'cuius regio eius religio'. The religious issue had to be decided centrally. The solution became particularly complicated on the death of Henry III in 1589, when the Catholics had emerged as the stronger party, while the nearest heir was a Huguenot. The Catholics tried to find an alternative candidate, but with little success; hereditary monarchy was too well established in France. Henry IV's conversion solved the problem, in addition to the fact that he was a clever politician and an efficient and popular ruler.

Historians and historical sociologists have generally emphasized the importance of the Reformation for European state formation, which is correct enough. Particularly in Protestant countries but also to some extent in Catholic ones as well, the Reformation increased the power of the state: confiscation of Church lands, education of the population, the doctrine of obedience and the victory of the central power in the internal struggles over religion contributed to this. However, we should also consider how previous state formation can explain the spread of the Reformation and the different outcome of this in various parts of Europe. The easy introduction of the Reformation in Scandinavia is difficult to explain without a relatively strong monarchy, perhaps stronger at the time than most Scandinavian historians have assumed. Germany comes into the same category, although here the strength lies with the princes who had sufficient control over their territories to introduce religious reform, to some extent also to resist the central power. Concerning this country, we nevertheless have to take into account that the pressure from the people may have been stronger than in England and Scandinavia. Moreover, the division into principalities was also a weakness which almost enabled the emperor and Spain to suppress Protestantism during the Thirty Years War. Finally, the frequent shifts in religious belief without leading to open civil war form impressive evidence of the development of the state in England in the previous period.

We may also note that there is only one example of the introduction of the Reformation in a monarchy against the will of the ruler, namely, Scotland. Here the monarchy was relatively weak, not least because of the many previous periods of regency, when the aristocracy had ruled the country. Mary Stuart also had a weak position; she had spent 13 years in France, 1548–61, from the age of 5 to the age of 18, and had been married to King Francis II of France. She returned to Scotland at his death in 1561, at a time when the Reformation was well under way. She also committed some blunders which made her easy to outmanoeuvre.

The difference between England and France confirms the impression from the comparison between the two countries in the Middle Ages. France had reached a level of consolidation where it was impossible to divide the country into territories with different religion as in Germany but where the king could not to the same extent determine the religion of his subjects. France forms the only example of the failure of a king to introduce the Reformation, which may immediately seem to indicate a relatively weak monarchy in this country. However, Henry IV was the only Protestant king in the country, whereas all his predecessors had defended the Catholic cause. Moreover, at the time of his accession in 1589, Catholicism in France, as in most other places, had been strengthened by the Counter-Reformation, and there was a broad popular movement in favour of the traditional religion, led by the Jesuits and other reformed orders. Two regicides by Catholic fanatics, of Henry III in 1589 and Henry IV in 1610, the only ones in France in the post-Carolingian period, in addition to a number of attempts, may be regarded as the expression of this. On the other hand, the idea of dynastic succession was sufficiently strong in France to make it difficult to get acceptance for an alternative candidate to Henry IV. In the end, Henry's pragmatism solved the problem.

The Peace of Westphalia settled the religious division of Europe in its main outlines. The following wars mostly had less to do with religion,[31] although there was still a division between Catholic and Protestant Europe and most countries had an official religion to which their inhabitants had to adapt or risk persecution. Catholic and Protestant countries had in common that religion was largely governed by the state. The king was the head of the Church in Protestant countries or there was a republican constitution which subordinated religious and secular matters to the same authority in most Reformed countries. Catholic countries still recognized the doctrinal leadership of the pope, but the king usually governed the Church in his country and appointed the bishops.

With some exceptions, the Reformation would seem to have strengthened the power of the kings and eased the transition to absolutism. On the other hand, the movement also led to new debates about the right to resistance and opposition against unjust rulers.[32] Initially, the reformers had rejected the right of resistance, insisting on St Paul's command of obedience to secular powers, who, although pagan, were instituted by God. Luther was the first to change his opinion, under the influence of attempts to suppress the Reformation in the 1530s. One argument for resistance became particularly important in a German context, namely, the distinction between ordinary subjects and princes subordinated to the emperor. The argument was first put forward by the legal experts of Philip of Hessen, one of the leading Lutheran princes, who claimed that the German princes were not ordinary subjects but rulers in the Pauline sense, although subordinated to the emperor.[33] Thus, St Paul's words about respect for lawful rulers must also include the princes, who then could not be bound to the same loyalty to the emperor as ordinary subjects to them. In this way, the problem was largely solved for the German Lutherans, as the country in practice came to be divided according to confession so that the prince decided the faith of his subjects. By contrast, this argument was less relevant to the Calvinists, who rarely had the support of princes. Whereas Calvin himself continued to reject resistance, although with some modifications towards the end of his life, Calvinists in more exposed conditions, John Knox in Scotland and the Dutch during the war of independence against Spain, embraced active resistance, which they supported largely with secular arguments, going back to Classical Antiquity and the Scholastic reception of Aristotle.[34] In the seventeenth century, these arguments played an important part among the English Puritans during the Civil War. Similar arguments were still used in Catholic circles, although there was an increasing tendency here to embrace absolutism.

The Reformation and state formation

The social aspect of the religious division of Europe has been discussed in a famous book by Max Weber on the connection between Protestantism and capitalism.[35] According to Weber, Protestantism introduced a strong work ethic. The Christian's duty was not to leave the world to worship God in a monastery but to realize Christian ideals by living an ordinary life in the world. In particular, Calvinism insisted on this with its doctrine of predestination, according to which it is impossible for humans to know whether they belong to the saved or to the damned. Psychologically, a believer in the doctrine would face a horrible dilemma: what if he or she belonged to the damned and was thus unable to do anything to gain salvation? In practice, the solution would be a strict Christian life, not in order to gain God's grace but in order to show the signs of being elected. As Calvinism accepts no 'professional' religious life in the form of monasticism and recognizes no sharp distinction between clergy and laity, the only way to conduct such a life is to live according to God's commandments in an ordinary secular profession and to practise this to the best of one's ability. Consequently, there was a strong incentive for Calvinists to be hard-working and diligent and accumulate wealth, the surplus of which was supposed to be used for good purposes. In practice, Calvinism was particularly strong among burghers and businessmen and the good Christian life could thus easily be identified with success in this profession. Eventually, this pattern of behaviour became internalized and continued despite increasing religious indifference in the nineteenth and twentieth centuries.

Weber's thesis is still being discussed and attempts are made to present statistical evidence for or against it. Concerning the sixteenth and seventeenth centuries, there is no doubt that the most successful trading and colonial countries were Protestant but it is an open question whether they were capitalist because they were Protestant or vice versa. Both the Netherlands and England were more commercial than Spain and Portugal already before the Great Discoveries. By contrast, Reformed Protestantism was introduced in Hungary, Transylvania, Austria and Scotland without any trend towards capitalism; Calvinist nobles behaved in the same way as their Catholic counterparts.[36] It has also been pointed out that a strict work ethics is not sufficient to produce modern capitalism; science is also necessary, although a case can be made for Protestantism in this field as well.[37] Possibly the strongest argument in favour of Weber's thesis is Italy, which was the centre of trade and manufacture in the Middle Ages but was replaced by cities in the North in the early modern period. However, this may also have a political explanation; most of Italy became ruled by princes, largely under Spanish dominance, in the early modern period and merchants were hampered by various kinds of restrictions.

It may also be objected that Weber focuses too exclusively on the doctrinal aspect of religion compared to the institutional one. From an economic point of view, Catholicism was a more expensive religion than Protestantism. Most obviously, as we have seen, the Catholic Church was the greatest landowner in most countries and in addition received a tax from the inhabitants, the tithe, as well as incomes from its jurisdiction. At the Reformation, this wealth was largely taken over by kings or other secular powers. Thus, more capital became available for kings, nobles and burghers, which may have had political as well as economic consequences. In addition, Protestant, and particularly Calvinist, businessmen had less incentive than Catholic ones to spend money on altars, masses, pilgrimages, church buildings, and so forth.

The organization of the new churches had similar consequences. Lutheranism replaced the bishops by superintendents who were royal officials with far lower salaries than their Catholic predecessors, to the extent that the offices were no longer attractive to members of the higher nobility. In some countries, like Sweden and later (from 1660) Denmark-Norway, the title was still used but the office had changed character. A number of other Catholic prelacies and offices, cathedral chapters, archdeaconries, and so forth, also disappeared, as did the monasteries. By contrast, ordinary priests increased their status and also their income. Their education was also greatly improved; university studies eventually became compulsory for ordination. Despite the original Lutheran doctrine that every Christian was a priest, so that there was no difference between clergy and laity, the Lutheran pastors were distinguished by their learning and became prominent members of the local elites. The numerous portraits from the seventeenth and eighteenth centuries in Scandinavian churches of pastors with their families give a clear impression of their status – there is nothing similar in Catholic churches. Pastors and superintendents were royal officials and may even be regarded as the prototype of such officials, with clearly defined districts, education and duties. The latter not only included preaching, baptism and pastoral care but also a number of administrative duties on the king's behalf. Finally, the kings in Protestant countries not only took over the estates of the Catholic Church at the Reformation but they were also able to use the Church for royalist propaganda.

By contrast, the changes were less radical in the Church of England. Ickworth House in Suffolk is a large, rotund building in the classical style, inspired by Palladian and ancient Roman architecture and decoration. It was built in the period 1795–1829 for the Right Honourable and Right Reverend Frederick Hervey, Fourth Earl of Bristol and Bishop of Derry (1730–1803). As the building indicates, Bishop Hervey was fascinated by classical architecture and the ancient world, far more than by his clerical duties. He had a large art collection, which was one of his reasons for building Ickworth. He was a great traveller and spent most of his life in Italy, where he died in 1803. When many hotels nowadays are called Bristol, it is an indirect reference to him: a place sufficiently luxurious for the Fourth Earl of Bristol to stay there. He had a good education and intellectual interests, but was apparently not very religious and once even declared himself an agnostic. He is said to have appointed vicars by organizing a running competition between his curates and appointing the winner.

Frederick Hervey is of course not the typical English bishop but he illustrates some features of the Church of England in the early modern period. One is the close connection to the nobility. Most bishops belonged to aristocratic families, although they were more often younger sons than titled lords[38] – Hervey inherited the title from his elder brother after he had become bishop. It was also his wealth as a lord that enabled him to build Ickworth. Although the revenues of the Church of England had been reduced after the Reformation, the bishops still retained much of the wealth and status of their Catholic predecessors, including their membership of the House of Lords. Concerning his life-style and religious opinions, Hervey was not directly representative, but the higher clergy, not only in England but also in other countries were often strongly influenced by the Enlightenment and critical of many of the dogmas.

By contrast, ordinary ministers were often poor; some found it necessary to have more than one parish to gain a decent living. Moreover, the medieval system of patronage was upheld, only that the patrons were no longer monasteries. Only one-fourth of the parishes were controlled by the Church. Around half of them were held by private individuals and could be bought or sold. Around a tenth belonged to the Crown, while the rest was controlled by bodies like the Oxford and Cambridge colleges.[39] The practice with absent officeholders who let vicars take care of their duties continued, as expressed in the fact that 'vicar' is the usual term for the head of a parish.

From this point of view, the Reformation was less radical in England than in most other Protestant countries. On the other hand, the Church of England was far from the religious monopoly of the Lutheran Churches in the German principalities and Scandinavia. In 1662, a number of Puritan clerics broke out of the Church of England and founded their own religious community, 'chapel' versus 'Church'. In the following century, the Methodist movement started within the Church of England but became a separate religious organization in 1791, after the death of its founder, John Wesley.

Concerning Calvinism, the doctrine of predestination is not the only factor of political importance. Confiscations of ecclesiastical lands may have had the same importance in Calvinist countries as in England. In addition, as also noted by Weber, Calvinism created tight communities with strict supervision of the behaviour of their members, as did also the parallel movements in England. It may be added, however, that Jansenism, which was influential in some Catholic countries, notably France and the Southern Netherlands, represented similar moral principles and may have had similar effects.[40] Families and neighbours controlled behaviour more efficiently than did bureaucratic authorities. Based on these observations, there seems to be a connection between Calvinism and republicanism or constitutional government and between Catholicism and Lutheranism and absolutism, with the distinction between the two latter that the Lutheran version of absolutism is likely to have been more effective. However, there are also a number of individual differences between the various countries, which do not always conform to this pattern and which will be discussed later.

The Great Discoveries and the development of European trade

Having received the necessary financing from the royal couple in Granada, Columbus later in 1492, on 3 August, sailed from Palos de la Frontera with three ships and arrived at the Bahamas on 12 October. Six years later, the Portuguese Vasco da Gama arrived in the real India. These expeditions mark the beginning of what may be called the Europeanization of the world, which reached its climax in the nineteenth and twentieth centuries. However, they are not only a beginning but have their background in a gradual expansion of Europe during the previous centuries. Parts of this expansion have already been dealt with, namely, the conversion of Northern and Eastern Europe, which, as we have seen, largely took place by peaceful means. From the late eleventh century onwards, the Europeans started an offensive against pagans and Muslims that resulted in a substantial expansion of Western Christendom.

The Far East had played an important part in the Middle Ages, both as a kind of fairy-tale area of incredible wealth and beauty, including gold and silver, and as the place of origin of attractive merchandise, such as spices. Both the long and costly transport and the near monopoly of Venice and Genoa of this trade made these commodities very expensive and formed an incentive for trying to find an alternative route. When this became a reality in the fifteenth and early sixteenth century, the main explanation must be sought in the gradual development of the ship-building technology from the thirteenth century onwards.[41] The rudder replaced the long oar that had earlier been used for steering the vessel in the northern seas in the thirteenth century and was later adapted in the Mediterranean. The compass, originally a Chinese invention, was introduced from the end of the century. In the following period until the fifteenth century, the classical sailing ship used for military as well as commercial purposes was created, based on a combination of elements from northern and Mediterranean models. Thus, the new ship had three masts which combined the northern square sails with the Mediterranean ('Latin') triangular ones, increasing the possibility of crossing against the wind. An elevated platform at the rear end could form a protected spot for archers firing on enemy ships, while it might also be used to build living quarters for the crew so that they could cross long stretches of open sea without going ashore at night.

Finally, as we have seen, the ship was large and strong enough to be equipped with cannons, which made it into a floating fortress. On the other hand, it was smaller than the Chinese ship and thus easier to manoeuvre and more difficult to hit with cannons. These warships proved superior to the traditional galleys used in the Mediterranean and gradually replaced them. Thus, the warship that dominated the seas until it was replaced by the steamship of iron in the nineteenth century was fully developed in the fifteenth century; later changes were mainly adjustments, including increased size and heavier cannons. The development of studies of astronomy and cartography was also important for the Great Discoveries. Columbus' idea of reaching India from the west was based on such studies but he was wrong about the size of the Earth.

Before Columbus, Portugal was the pioneer in exploring the routes across the Atlantic. Prince Henry, nicknamed the Navigator, although he never personally took part in any expedition, began by sending ships south along the coast of Africa. The initial stimulus was the conquest of Ceuta in North Africa from Aragon in 1415, an end-point on the trade route across the Sahara, which suggested that greater wealth might be found further south. The journeys in the following period led to the discovery or rediscovery of Madeira (1420), the Azores (1427), and the Canary Islands (fourteenth century), the two former uninhabited, while the latter was inhabited by indigenous peoples who were suppressed and largely exterminated by the Spaniards after prolonged and bloody wars from 1402 until the end of the century. The expeditions, mainly by the Portuguese, continued further south until Bartolomeu Diaz reached the southern tip of Africa, named the Cape of Good Hope, in 1486. This paved the way for Vasco da Gama's arrival in India. Nevertheless, Columbus continued to believe that he had reached India until his death in 1506. Eventually, a Florentine explorer, Amerigo Vespucci (1451–1512) sailed along the coast of South America and discovered that the new lands were not a number of islands off the coast of India but a new continent which was shortly afterwards named after him.

The motive for the discoveries was greed. Europe lacked a number of attractive commodities such as gold, silver and spices, and Europeans were fascinated by the allegedly fabulous wealth of the East. In the following period, they gained great wealth from the trade in spices and other valuable commodities from the East and from gold and silver from America. Mines were opened and the native population was forced to work in them, under terrible conditions. When this labour force eventually proved insufficient because of high mortality, partly due to the work itself and partly to the new diseases the Europeans brought to America, slaves were imported from Africa, a trade that became very lucrative. In addition to the metals, the cultivation of sugar on large plantations, worked by slaves, was also very profitable.

To a greater extent than the Dutch and the British, the Spaniards introduced government and institutions in the colonies modelled on their homeland. New towns were founded and the previous ones, such as Mexico City, were rebuilt according to Spanish models, with monumental churches, monasteries and universities.[42] The centres of many Latin American towns are still largely dominated by early modern colonial architecture. A number of religious orders were introduced. The Franciscans were particularly important in the beginning but were surpassed by the Jesuits from the second half of the sixteenth century. Massive attempts were made to convert the indigenous population, which should in principle have given them equal rights with the colonists, although this only to a limited degree happened in practice. However, they were allowed to become priests and enter religious orders, although this often met with resistance from some of the colonists. Women from the old elites might also be married to prominent Spaniards. Several of the missionaries, like the Spanish Dominican Bartolomeo de las Casas, were genuinely concerned about the way the native population was treated and sought to protect them.[43] He also received some support from the Spanish authorities, including the victory in a famous debate about whether the Native Americans were really human beings. Later, the Jesuits were particularly concerned with the welfare of the indigenous population. They learnt their languages and tried to protect them from abuses by the colonists. Later, they received delegated authority from the king over a separate province, Paraguay, where they governed the local population with benevolent authoritarianism.[44] The Spanish authorities also in principle favoured protection of the native population, but their possibility to interfere in local conditions was limited. In addition, they became increasingly dependent on the surplus from the American mines.

America was regularly conquered by the Spaniards. The inhabitants of South America had great empires and densely populated cities, but their military technology was backward compared to that of Europe. They not only lacked firearms but they did not use metals at all and they had no horses or other animals that might have been used to develop a cavalry. The result was that the whole Aztec Empire could be conquered by 630 Spaniards and the Inca Empire by 168, admittedly in both cases aided by far larger numbers of rebels within the empire.[45] The importance of the latter has often been underestimated; the Europeans would hardly have succeeded without it, but neither would the indigenous peoples have succeeded without the Europeans. However, both the easy conquest and the aid the Spaniards received from rebels and enemies of the American Empires seem an indication of the weakness of the latter.[46] Finally, the entirely new diseases the Europeans brought to America are a crucial factor. Although it is difficult to know exactly by how much the American population was reduced, there is no doubt that we are dealing with a demographic disaster.[47]

By contrast, the technological difference was less in the East. Here the result was not conquest of large territories but the foundation of smaller colonies serving to transmit the trade to Europe. A mixture of negotiation and violence was used for this purpose. On his second voyage to India, Vasco da Gama bombarded Calicut and mutilated the crews of captured vessels. Later, in 1513, the Portuguese governor in India wrote to the king that all the native ships vanished and even the birds ceased to fly over the water at his coming.[48] If not the birds, the sailors had certainly learnt their lesson. In both places, the Europeans behaved differently from at home; there was no rule about chivalrous warfare and respect for treaties. The way the Dutch took over the trade on the South Asian Islands is characteristic. They replaced the Asian intermediaries by force and took over the leadership of the production. When this was not possible on the island of Banda in present-day Indonesia, they simply massacred the population, except for a few skilled artisans who were forced to teach them how to work.[49]

The main pattern in Europe from the sixteenth century onwards was the decline of centres along the Baltic and the Mediterranean and the rise of those along the Atlantic. This had both political and economic reasons. Venice was the great loser from the opening of the sea route to the East, as this city had previously controlled the trade from the end of the caravan routes to Europe. Nevertheless, Venice was soon able to compete. The land route across Asia was after all shorter than the sea route and the sea voyage along the Mediterranean was better protected. Therefore, more than half the trade from the East continued to be carried over land by caravans. The price difference between spices transported along the two alternative routes therefore soon disappeared.[50] Only in the first half of the seventeenth century did the sea route take over most of the trade. When Venice eventually declined, the causes were more complex than the Great Discoveries. Politically, the most important factor was the rise of Ottoman sea power and economically it was increasing competition from the Dutch and the English Companies which proved to be more effective and profitable than the Spanish and Portuguese trade organizations.[51] The rest of northern Italy continued to be an important urbanized region, but lost its dominant position as a centre of trade. The main exception was Genoa, whose merchants participated in the Spanish conquest and trade in America.

The discovery of America explains the rise of Spain to the leading power of Europe in the sixteenth century but also largely its decline in the following period. The main aim of the Spaniards in America was to find gold and silver, which they succeeded in doing after some disappointment in the beginning. The Spaniards were the earliest colonizers and seemingly took the most profitable colonies. In contrast to the southern part of America, the northern one was not rich in gold and silver and could only to a limited extent be exploited for plantations. The native population consisted of hunters and gatherers and was less numerous than the one further south and in addition warlike and little suited to forced labour. The colonizing powers, England, France, the Dutch Republic and others, had the same aims as the Spaniards, to make the colonies a source of profit for the homeland, but had little possibility to achieve this aim. The colonies were settled by farmers, in many cases, people leaving their native countries for religious reasons, who created their own environment and gave little surplus to their homelands. The different natural conditions go a long way towards explaining the different development of North and South America: capitalism and democracy among the white population of the North in contrast to a white elite of great landowners ruling a large native population in the South. Only Argentina and Chile form exceptions to this pattern, showing some resemblance to the North.[52]

In Spain, colonial trade was a Castilian royal monopoly and strictly controlled.[53] Only for short periods of time were foreigners allowed to participate, mainly in the beginning, when capital was needed to develop the resources in America. Aragonese merchants were also excluded. In 1503, a company for the trade with America, the *Casa de Contración*, was set up in Seville, which became the only harbour for trade with America until 1680, when Cadiz took over. Seville thus became extremely wealthy and increased its number of inhabitants from 60,000–70,000 around 1500 to 150,000 by 1588. In practice, due to the risk and difficulties in exploiting the American mines, the Crown rented out its rights over them to private merchants in return for a proportion of the profit, finally fixed at one-fifth. The Crown's incomes from America included this rent plus taxes from the continent. In principle, the trade with America ought to have stimulated the Castilian economy, as the exports to America equalled the imports. The colonists, possibly around 118,000 in 1570, wanted familiar goods from home: arms, horses, clothes, grain and wine. Some European crops were introduced to America but they were slow to grow, so a considerable market for European export remained. Nevertheless, the demand from the colonies failed to stimulate the Castilian economy. The peasants were too burdened by taxes and rents to be able to exploit the new opportunities and invest in increased production and the textile industry was of low quality because of lack of skilled workers. The result was that other countries than Spain, notably England and the Dutch Republic, profited from the increased demand in the colonies. Nor was the gold and silver used for investment; it served the government, above all its wars. However, a large amount of gold and silver created inflation, so that the state was constantly in debt despite the regular influx of wealth. In addition, the imports from America, combined with the monopolistic policy of the government, destroyed trade and industry within the country, which had had a revival in the fifteenth and early sixteenth centuries in what is usually regarded as the golden age of Spain, the reign of Ferdinand and Isabella.

The Portuguese colonization differed significantly from the Spanish one. Portugal was a smaller country with only around 1.4 million inhabitants whereas Spain had around 8 million.[54] Although the Portuguese were also settled in America, in Brazil, their most important colonies were in the Far East. After the discovery of the sea route to India, they quickly established settlements and fortifications in order to control the essential trade routes. Their main strategic points were Malacca, on the narrow sound between Thailand and Sumatra, Goa, on the western coast of India, and Ormuz, at the mouth of the Persian Gulf, which, together with some other harbours and fortresses along the way to Europe, secured the shipping of valuable spices from the East. Later, the Portuguese also managed to extend their trade links to China, where they established a colony at Macao, and for a period also to Japan. However, they had no chance of becoming the dominant power in the East; they were one of several actors in the lucrative trade in the area. In Brazil, they behaved in a similar way to the Spaniards, establishing plantations worked by slaves, partly indigenous people and partly people imported from Africa. Economically, however, Brazil was less attractive than the main Spanish colonies in America, so the settlements here were relatively small. Like the Spaniards, the Portuguese were also engaged in the spread of Christianity to the New World, mostly in contrast to the Protestant powers. In particular, the Jesuits were important in this and contributed to the fact that the Portuguese were less unpopular with the indigenous population than the Dutch and the British.

Despite being surpassed financially by the Dutch and the British, the Spanish kept their American Empire until the colonies made themselves independent in the early nineteenth century. By contrast, most of the Portuguese possessions in the East were lost to the Dutch in the seventeenth century. The global expansion of the Dutch Republic had started in the 1590s, during the war of independence against Spain.[55] As early as in 1600, there were more merchants from the Dutch Republic in the Far East than from any other nation. Amsterdam eventually became the leading centre of trade in Europe, surpassing the cities in the South, as well as the German and Italian ones. The number of its inhabitants increased from 30,000 in 1570 to 60,000 in 1600 and 140,000 in 1647. In the first phase, the reason for this was partly the great number of Protestant merchants who had left the areas under Spanish rule. The Dutch Republic became the main European power in the Far East, with Batavia (= Jakarta) on Java as the main centre. Somewhat later, with the conquest of Curaçao from Spain in 1634, they established colonies in America and participated in the transatlantic trade, including the slave trade. In addition, Dutch trade expanded in the Baltic area and in Russia; Dutch merchants sailed to Russia both across the Baltic Sea and along the northern route via Norway.

The trade between the Baltic area and Western Europe was largely taken over by the Dutch, while the Hanseatic towns declined. The change in Dutch trade was not only quantitative but also qualitative; there was a shift from the traditional bulk-carrying traffic in grain, timber, salt and fish to 'rich trade' in luxury goods. The former trade continued, but did not expand greatly, whereas there was a great expansion in the latter, which gave far greater profit. The Dutch Republic also became an important centre of production of textiles, brickwork and pottery, of tobacco processing and sugar refining, breweries and distilleries, shipbuilding and sawmilling. Finally, agriculture there was more efficient than in the rest of Europe, with some exception for England, and produced significantly larger crops, which made it possible to manage with less than 50 per cent of the population working on the land, whereas the corresponding figure in most other countries was 80 per cent or more. The fisheries were also of considerable importance; the Dutch caught fish inland, along the coast and on the great seas, the North Sea banks, around Spitsbergen, Greenland, Newfoundland and Novaja Semlja where they also caught whales. In the mid-seventeenth century, the Dutch Republic was the greatest shipping nation in Europe, with a merchant fleet of around 2,000 vessels.

England had begun its overseas expansion in the late fifteenth century, when the Venetian Giovanni Caboto (English: John Cabot) in the service of Henry VII explored North America in 1497.[56] Later, during the conflict with Spain, English pirates attacked Spanish ships in America and the Atlantic. As a late arrival in America, however, England in the beginning had to confine itself to North America, although it later succeeded in gaining colonies in the far more lucrative Caribbean. The English East India Company was founded in 1600, two years before its Dutch counterpart, but was for a long time was of less importance. During most of the seventeenth century, the Dutch Republic was a more important colonial power than England.

Both the Dutch and the English also had colonies similar to the Spanish ones, in the West Indies and in East Asia. The plantations, slave trade and the treatment of the local population were largely similar to that of the Spanish colonies, but the role of the state was different. The Dutch and British companies were essentially trading companies. As the use of military power, against the native population as well as against competing Europeans, was an essential part of the colonial expansion, a state monopoly combined with warships and troops was necessary, but was strictly a means to an end, to make profit for the shareholders. Costly investments in war and fortifications were avoided as much as possible. In this way, the companies could expand their wealth and activities, while the profit from their trade increased the wealth of their countries. In addition to the big companies for colonial trade, joint-stock companies, particularly for overseas trade, became more common and made it possible for passive partners with capital to invest in business.[57] Consequently, England – from 1707, Great Britain – and the Dutch Republic increased their wealth through the colonies whereas Spain was actually impoverished. Both the former countries followed the examples of the Venetians and Genoese, conquering territory to the extent that it was necessary for trade and production of merchandise, not to build large empires.[58]

The conquests of colonies overseas and the profit from trade and production there contributed to increasing the wealth of the Dutch and other colonial powers. However, this is not the whole explanation for the 'European Miracle' in the early modern period; trade and production within Europe were of far greater importance. Thus, in the 1650s, the Dutch exports to other European countries amounted to 115 million guilders and the one outside Europe to 5 million. The corresponding numbers for imports are 140 and 15 million. The percentage for extra-European trade increased in the eighteenth century but was still far less than the European one. Only in Britain did colonial trade, with 49 per cent, equal the European one by this time; the corresponding percentage for France is 38 and for the Dutch Republic 20.[59] Finally, the expansion of Dutch trade made Amsterdam the financial centre of Europe. This meant that it was not only the leading trading city internationally, but also a centre for credit, negotiations and information about markets and prices.

However, the period of the Dutch Republic as the centre of the European economy was of short duration; the decline had already begun towards the end of the seventeenth century. A series of factors contributed to this, including the strain resulting from the great power status of the republic which led to a series of costly wars and competition from Britain, which had greater natural resources and became the leading maritime and commercial power in the eighteenth century. There is also a natural tendency for merchant elites to become less bold and dynamic as the result of greater wealth. Finally, the many partners in the great Dutch trading network began to develop their own shipping, in which they were aided by the English Navigation Act of 1651, which decreed that all maritime transport to the British Isles should be carried either on British ships or ships from the country of origin.

Why did Europe conquer the world?

Why did the Europeans (including the North Americans) conquer the world? There is a long tradition in historiography, going back to the nineteenth century or even earlier, about European uniqueness, superior skills regarding technology, political and economic organization, culture and science which are said to have made the European supremacy inevitable. Such ideas were often used as legitimation for the Europeans or they might be more or less explicitly racist: the European race has always been superior and will continue to be so. Not surprisingly, decolonization and criticism of European behaviour in the past, combined with the increasing strength of non-European or non-western countries during the last decades, have led to a reaction. The so-called revisionist school has claimed that the European dominance was far from inevitable and should more be considered an episode in global history.[60] Thus, in a detailed comparative study of the economy of the main civilizations in the eighteenth and nineteenth centuries, Kenneth Pomeranz concludes that Europe had no decisive comparative advantage until around 1800 and that the advantage that eventually developed was not inevitable but depended on a few lucky circumstances, such as the proximity of coal and iron in England and the easy conquest of America.[61]

The revisionists are clearly right in rejecting the idea of a permanent European superiority and, above all, its racist implications. However, hardly any serious historian will defend such ideas today.[62] Attempting to find long-term or deep-rooted factors explaining European dominance does not imply that Europe is inherently superior and will remain so forever or that no other civilization can compete with or surpass it. Today, China and East Asia are modernizing rapidly and may well overtake the West in the near future. With this modification, there is much to be said in favour of long-term factors as the explanation of the European dominance during the last centuries. Admittedly, this is a difficult project, necessitating great knowledge of Europe as well as the rest of the world. Claims for European superiority in specific fields may be refuted by reference to non-European parallels or at least equivalents. Major increases in population size, standard of living or agricultural production may turn out to be temporary, to be replaced by decline at the next stage.[63] Nevertheless, it would immediately seem that a shift as fundamental as the one that took place in the relationship between Europe and the rest of the world in the eighteenth and nineteenth centuries cannot be the result of pure coincidence but must have some deeper explanation. This is also the conclusion of Ian Morris' comparative study of East and West, not only during the last centuries but back to around 14,000 BC. Civilization began in the west, i.e. the lands surrounding the Mediterranean, including the Euphrates-Tigris area, while the east (China, India and surrounding areas) came later. This changed around 550 AD, with the fall of the Roman Empire, after which the East took over until the late eighteenth century. The criteria for this comparison are: (1) energy capture; (2) urbanization, which serves to measure administrative capacity; (3) information technology, in practice, writing; and (4) military capacity.[64] Thus, Morris replaces the revisionists' idea of the basic superiority of the East with a more balanced view, while on the other hand, he accepts their late date for the revival of the West, the beginning of which, however, he traces back to the fourteenth century, with increasing likelihood for dominance during the following centuries. He also agrees with them in the explanation of the European superiority, rejecting cultural factors in favour of geography – the proximity to America – and basic material conditions.[65]

Concerning the chronology of European dominance, it must be admitted that the most striking example, America, is less relevant. Due to the previous isolation of America, the technological gap between the two civilizations is obvious, and a similarly easy conquest did not take place in Asia. It must also be added that the Europeans were better placed for discovering and conquering America than any others; the sea route across the Atlantic is far shorter than the one across the Pacific.

By contrast, the territorial conquests in Asia were modest in the sixteenth and seventeenth centuries. However, the reason for this is at least partly that Europeans were more interested in trade than in territorial conquest. The attraction of these areas was spices and textiles, which in most cases were bought from the producers, not gold and silver, which had to be extracted from mines in the mountains, thus necessitating extensive territorial conquest and suppression of the native population as forced labourers. Nevertheless, the Europeans did not monopolize the trade in these areas but became an additional participant, in some cases, as we have seen, suppressing local competitors.

The Muslim world had been a competitor as well as a source of inspiration for the Europeans since the early Middle Ages. Scientific and philosophical texts, partly translations from ancient Greek and partly original contributions by the Arabs, were an important impulse for the intellectual revival in Europe from the twelfth century onwards. Politically, the Muslim world had been in decline since the gradual dissolution of the Abbasid Caliphate, beginning in the tenth century. The Ottoman Empire represented a revival and formed an even greater threat to Europe than the Arab Empire had done, conquering most of the Balkan area and twice attacking Vienna (1529 and 1683). Although Europe was technologically superior already in the late fifteenth and early sixteenth century, when the Ottomans used European experts to develop their artillery,[66] the Ottomans were well organized and had the advantage that the Europeans were divided. The technological gap increased in the following period, while at the same time the Ottomans lost parts of their organizational superiority. The attack in 1683 was their last great offensive against Europe. In the following period, the Ottoman Empire declined and eventually became 'the sick man' of Europe and subject to various, largely unsuccessful attempts at reform. One of the reasons for this decline was religious. In contrast to its early period, Islam became increasingly sceptical of science and secular knowledge from the late eleventh century onwards. As God had created the universe and ruled it according to His will, it was presumptuous of humans to attempt to explain it. This extended even to practical inventions, like the printing of books, which was forbidden in the Ottoman Empire until the early eighteenth century. The same applied to the translation of books from foreign languages.

Admittedly, the relationship between science and Christianity was not unproblematic either. As we have seen, however, religious persecution within Christendom was primarily directed at religious movements, whereas intellectuals had some freedom to draw their own conclusions. Moreover, the distinction between religious and secular knowledge was clearer within Christianity. The Church did not try to monopolize all knowledge; Christianity had a long tradition of coming to terms with secular knowledge. Finally, the division of Europe is important in this respect as well; those who were persecuted in one country could move to another. Of course, the negative attitude to scientific speculation in Muslim countries did not directly extend to practical innovations, particularly not in the military field. However, the problem was that such innovations increasingly came to depend on scientific knowledge, which, as we have seen, can be illustrated by the development of artillery.

The Ottoman Empire was clearly not a serious competitor to Europe for world dominance. By contrast, another empire, the Chinese, was for a long time the most advanced civilization in the world and forms the main alternative to Europe in the 'Why Europe' discussion.[67] Marco Polo's account of his experience of China in the late thirteenth century is full of admiration for the large and well-organized cities and the superior technology of the Chinese. He gives a detailed description of a city called Quin-sai, which actually means capital and has been identified with Linngan, now Hangzhou.[68] The city is situated within a circle of around 50 kilometres.[69] It has broad streets which give room for waggons, large squares that serve as market places and where all kinds of food and other commodities can be bought. A large number of canals serve as transport arteries and to remove all kinds of waste, which is transported to the sea. Over the canals, there are more than 12,000 bridges. There are numerous shops, often situated on the ground floor of large houses with apartments. Wealthy people and imperial officials live in beautiful houses along the lake. There are hospitals, fire brigades, police and an efficient administration and people solve their conflicts without violence. Marco Polo is also deeply impressed by the imperial palace in Kambalu (= Bejing), its size, beauty and the ceremonies taking place there.[70] As Marco Polo observed, Chinese cities were clean; all waste from humans and animals was gathered and transported to the countryside where it was used as manure. By contrast, in Europe, it filled the streets so that one could smell cities from a distance. In contrast to European states, China had a proper bureaucracy resembling the Weberian model, with formally appointed and salaried officials with clearly defined duties and a uniform education. They were educated at institutions resembling universities and had to pass extremely severe examinations before they could be employed. The Chinese also excelled in many fields of learning; the great encyclopaedia composed by 2,000 scholars on Yongle's orders remained the largest in the world until surpassed by Wikipedia in 2007.

For a long time, China was also ahead of Europe technologically. The compass, gunpowder, the printing press, paper and the mechanical clock were invented in China and probably gradually made their way from there to Europe, where they were introduced during the last centuries of the Middle Ages. Some inventions, such as spectacles, were possibly originally European, others were further developed after their introduction, such as firearms. Some, like the mechanical clock, invented in China in the early eleventh century, were more or less forgotten in the following period, at least not developed further.[71] The Sung Period (960–1279), when China was divided, was more dynamic than the Ming (1368–1644), particularly after Yongle's death. The Ming represented a reaction against foreign conquest after the fall of the Mongol Yuan Dynasty and an increasing tendency towards isolation, as expressed in the ban on foreign travel. This was at least partly continued under the next dynasty, the Manchu or Qing (1644–1912).

Nevertheless, the picture of stagnation and despotism has been too negative; early modern China has in many respects an impressive record of efficient government and, by pre-industrial standards, relatively good living conditions for the population.[72] It was also fairly advanced regarding trade, industry and technology. No doubt, the Europeans made little impact on Chinese trade before 1800, and the European superiority was also far less by this time than it became later. A comparison between the populations of the two areas is also in favour of China, which had around 300 million inhabitants in 1800. The corresponding number for Western Europe was around half of this. Moreover, the two leading nations involved in Chinese trade at the time, Britain and the Dutch Republic, numbered only a fraction of this, around 15 million together. The number of merchants from these nations that actually visited China was negligible and they bought more from the Chinese than they sold, paying in silver. However, when we consider that trade outside Europe before the eighteenth century was only a fraction of the total volume of European trade, combined with the dominant position of the two leading trading nations, Britain and the Dutch Republic, the picture becomes different. At least these two countries must have been commercialized to a far greater extent than China, well before 1800, whereas the political importance of the merchants was also greater. China was governed by bureaucrats, and merchants had little political influence. By contrast, they largely governed the Dutch Republic and had considerable political influence in Britain, partly directly through membership of the House of Commons, partly indirectly through the fact that the landed aristocracy also had commercial interests. Whatever the exact chronology of the European dominance, the commercial development in Europe, particularly from the late sixteenth century onwards, has to be taken into account.[73]

Moreover, a recent study of the problem, based on extensive statistics, directly contradicts the revisionist claims on most points.[74] Average real wages and living standards for workers were significantly higher in North-West Europe than in China and India already in the sixteenth century and throughout the eighteenth, while the difference increased sharply from the mid-nineteenth century. Here, however, it has been objected that salaried workers were far less numerous in China than in Europe and in addition belonged to the poorest sector of the population.[75] The difference in living standard is also reflected in similar differences regarding height. Although urbanization was considerable in both China and India, even the most urbanized parts of these countries were below England and the Netherlands around 1800. It is also likely that conditions for trade and business were better in Europe, because of formal contracts and court of laws that could be used to solve conflicts, while the Chinese equivalents were kin-based organizations and decisions by magistrates which largely took the form of mediation. However, the importance of this may be open to discussion; there are indications that the Chinese system actually worked quite well.[76] The two fields in which the Chinese may possibly have equalled the Europeans are literacy and numeracy. A study estimates the former at 30–45 per cent for men and 2–10 per cent for women in eighteenth-century China. As we shall see, this is far below the Dutch Republic at the same time and approximately similar to France for men, but lower for women. Of course, there are uncertainties in a comparison like this and it hardly gives a complete explanation of the European dominance but it does suggest that it goes further back than the period around 1800.

In the first half of the fifteenth century, the Chinese eunuch admiral Zheng He led an expedition to Africa. The Chinese had both the technology and the navigational skills necessary for such expeditions, which were nevertheless discontinued in the following period because the emperor banned them. He even forbade the building of ocean-going ships.[77] It did not occur to any European ruler to impose such a ban, not because they were more enlightened but because they were poorer. Nor would a ban have had any effect; there would always have been another ruler willing to try his luck in expeditions across the sea. Thus, Columbus approached various kings and princes until he was lucky enough to be on the spot when Granada surrendered to Ferdinand and Isabella. Admittedly, as Morris points out, the end of the Chinese expeditions can also be explained by the fact that they were unnecessary. The Chinese had no need for import from other continents. Moreover, the Ming emperors had no incentive to maintain a large and costly fleet; their main military power was directed against the nomadic peoples on the eastern border.[78] Here, however, it must be added that the same would probably have been the case in Europe as well, if this continent had been one empire; fighting the Ottomans in the east would certainly have had higher priority than crossing the Atlantic.

The discovery of America forms an important part of the revisionists' argument. Europe was lucky enough to be closer to America than any other civilization and the conquest of this continent added vast amounts of land for cultivation, in addition to gold, silver and various valuable commodities like sugar and cotton. The emigration to America prevented overpopulation in Europe and increased wages which in turn gave an incentive to technological innovation. However, this argument has been rejected by a series of scholars. There is no evidence that high wages were one of the reasons for the Industrial Revolution.[79] Generally, the world would have been a better place if every need resulted in a new invention. Nor would it seem likely that the Industrial Revolution would have taken place if the Spaniards rather than the English had settled in North America. Admittedly, the examples of Argentina and Chile show that a Spanish conquest of North America might have resulted in a similar mode of settlement as the existing one. On the other hand, although America was a potential market for Spanish exports, it did not actually become one. There is no reason to believe that further emigration from Spain would have changed this. A Spanish America without interference from rival countries would in all likelihood have increased Spanish military power in Europe. Maybe it would have resulted in Europe becoming one Empire with the same conservative attitude as its counterpart on the other side of the Continent. In any case, nothing suggests that it would have developed in the way it actually did. The same applies to the Chinese conquest of a large part of Central Asia under the Qing dynasty in the seventeenth and eighteenth centuries,[80] which, like the

European conquest of America, increased the amount of land available for cultivation but otherwise had no effects similar to those the European expeditions. Consequently, the conquest of America was of limited importance in itself; its significance lies in its combination with the specific economic, political and cultural development in Northern Europe.

The development of trade and industry in England and the Dutch Republic, combined with the division of Europe, is therefore an important factor. As we have seen, the more or less constant wars between established states in Europe were an important stimulus to technological innovation, primarily in the military field but also in a number of others. In addition, the relative backwardness of Europe for a long time and the lack of attractive commodities like gold, silver and spices made the Europeans more willing to visit other peoples and learn from them – for good and for bad. On the one hand, this led to conquest and plundering of other continents, on the other to scientific and technological development which resulted in Europe surpassing China in these fields in the seventeenth and eighteenth centuries.

In 1793, a British Embassy arrived in China in the hope of persuading the Chinese to reopen trade, bringing examples of the most advanced British technology at the time, a planetarium, advanced lenses and electrical machines, but the emperor was completely uninterested. Later, he replied to King George III: 'There is nothing we lack. We have never set much store on strange or ingenious objects, nor do we need any more of your country's manufactures.'[81] Pomeranz points out that this example is not necessarily representative of early modern China, presenting various examples of Chinese interest in European imports, although adding that Europeans were more interested in Chinese commodities that vice versa.[82] However, he does not address the main point, which is not to what extent the Chinese bought European commodities but their interest in science and technology. Here various Europeans, notably the Jesuits in the seventeenth century, introduced European inventions but met with little response.[83]

Generally, when discussing the power relationship between the Europeans and the indigenous peoples, the revisionists tend to forget that the Europeans fought with small forces far from home, that they fought each other as much as the local rulers and that there was never any question of a Chinese or Indian invasion of Europe. Against this background, it is not surprising that it took time for the Europeans to achieve a dominant position. Considering the distance between Europe and the Far East and the time it took to reach the colonies and trading posts from Europe – about half a year each way – the European expansion in this area was impressive already in the sixteenth century.

The eighteenth century saw a parallel to the Spanish conquest of America, namely, the British conquest of India.[84] Here there were no previously unknown diseases decimating the native population nor any shock of a completely unknown people nor a big technological gap. Still, the British conquerors were not more numerous than their Spanish predecessors – no more than around a thousand men were employed in the British civil service at any time in the period 1857–1947.

Moreover, their main competitors were not the Indians themselves but the French. The British army mainly consisted of Indian soldiers, commanded by British officers. Admittedly, the Muslim Moguls who had conquered India in the sixteenth century were in decline and the British largely won by playing the various local princes off against one another, but they also mostly proved superior in direct military confrontation, even if greatly outnumbered. In the Battle of Plassey (1757) which is usually regarded as the breakthrough for British power in India, a British army of 1,100 Europeans and 2,100 Hindu Sepoys defeated a Moghul army of 50,000. The military technology was the same on both sides but the British won because of their superior tactics and discipline.[85] They fought in tight units in which all soldiers fired at the same time and kept firing continuously by changing places. Their success was the result of systematic training and drilling according to principles developed since the early seventeenth century.

As there was no military confrontation between China and the West in the eighteenth century, we cannot directly compare the two at this time, but the first war between them in the nineteenth century gives a similar impression as the case of India. This was the Opium War with Britain (1839–42), fought in order to force the Chinese to cancel their ban on the profitable import of opium from the British colonies.[86] From a moral point of view, this is far from being Britain's 'finest hour', but military and technologically, it shows the country's astounding superiority. China at the time had around 400 million inhabitants, England 13.6 million, some million more if we include the rest of Britain. The British force consisted of 15 barrack ships, carrying British Indian army troops, 4 steam-powered gunboats and 25 smaller boats that reached Canton from Singapore. Nevertheless, this force sailed along the whole coast of China from south to north and won a series of devastating victories over the Chinese. The British suffered some defeats ashore, but were totally superior at sea, thanks to their better ships. During the war, they conquered Canton and Nanking, sailed up the Yangtze and captured the emperor's tax barges, thus getting hold of most of the revenue of the imperial court of Beijing. When peace was concluded, the Chinese had to allow British trade with opium and other commodities and cede some ports, including Hong Kong for 155 years – it was returned in 1997. By contrast, a little more than a decade later, the performance of the British army and military organization in the Crimean War against Russia led to a devastating report by a Select Commission of Inquiry and a storm in the press, demanding an overhaul of the military as well as the civil service.[87] Britain thus did not enjoy the same superiority closer to home.

Here it may be objected that the main factor in the British success was the steam-powered gunboats which were a new invention at the time,[88] so that a similar success would not have been possible in the eighteenth century. On the other hand, the English victory initiated a period of long-term European superiority over China; not until the mid-twentieth century were the Chinese able to compete. Moreover, the case of India shows the trend in the direction of European superiority in the East already in the mid-eighteenth century.

According to Hoffman, European military superiority was actually the main reason for its conquest of the world. As we have seen, he seeks the explanation for this in the division of Europe. Only on this continent did the rulers fight 'tournaments' against one another over centuries without anyone winning a decisive victory. This led to a steady improvement in military organization and equipment, as has been pointed out by a number of scholars. As the example from India shows, the most important factor was better organization, drill and discipline and tactical leadership by competent and devoted officers but there was also a considerable technological development. By contrast, the typical military challenge for empires, such as China, were nomads along the borders who were technologically backwards but dangerous because of their mobility. They thus offered no stimulus to technological or organizational improvement.[89] Admittedly, Europe was not the only place in the world where rival kingdoms fought one another; this also applies to Persia, the Ottoman Empire and others.[90] Nevertheless, both the permanence of the division in Europe and the cultural unity despite the political division may have made a difference.

Hoffman regards these improvements as the result of trial and error and the loser learning from the winner, without any scientific basis. However, the development of fortifications from the sixteenth century and artillery from the eighteenth had a scientific basis in mathematics. Many of the famous scientists, like Galileo and Newton, were active in the arms industry as was also the painter Leonardo da Vinci in the early sixteenth century.[91] Generally, the improvement of arms was not only the result of trial and error in the field; there was an arms industry, located in specific areas, such as Liège in the Low Countries, where engineers competed to develop the best types which they sold for high prices to the warring parties. The development of a capitalist economy in the seventeenth and eighteenth centuries was therefore also an important factor in military development.[92] In addition, cartography advanced greatly in the eighteenth century and was crucial for navigation at sea as well as military operations on land.[93]

Science was particularly important in sea warfare. Mathematical principles were applied to the construction of warships from the sixteenth century onwards.[94] A further step was taken in England with the foundation of the Royal Observatory in Greenwich in 1675. The observatory was equipped with various instruments and served as the home of the royally appointed astronomer. The main reason for its foundation was the importance of astronomy for navigation, notably the problem of measuring longitude at sea, which might be a matter of life or death for sailors. A prize for solving this problem had been offered by the king of Spain in the early seventeenth century, which Galileo had aspired to win.[95] In the early eighteenth century, the British king promised £20,000 to the one who solved the problem. The solution was Harrison's longitude-finding chronometer (1761), a far more exact clock than any previous one. The current division of meridians was also developed here, with the zero meridian going through the centre of the building. This was also a short step from Newton's new understanding of the universe to Newcomen's and Watt's invention of the steam engine (1715 and 1764) and

Arkwright's water frame (1769). Scientific inventions were no longer the unexpected results of the brilliant idea of some genius; they were encouraged and planned and expected to happen through systematic research. The British government at the time had vital interests at sea and was willing to support scientific progress that improved navigation. This suggests that there was indeed a close connection between the military development, on the one hand, and scientific and the technological inventions, the commercial economy and state formation, on the other.

Nor is Hoffman's comparison between Europe and the Ottoman Empire entirely convincing.[96] Hoffman explains the continued predominance of cavalry in the Ottoman army with the need to fight nomads on the eastern borders of the empire, while at the same time admitting that the proportion of infantry to cavalry was the same as in the Austrian army along the border to this country. So why did the Ottomans not adapt the technology and organization of European infantry? Moreover, he explains the backwardness of the Ottoman navy by claiming that galleys were ideally suited to the Mediterranean. Admittedly, they were used longer in this area than in the North Sea and the Atlantic but they were no more superior there than elsewhere. The success of English and Dutch pirates in the Mediterranean in the sixteenth century was largely the result of their sailing-ships of the northern type. Although the Venetians were conservative, they eventually had to change to the new ship technology from the early seventeenth century onwards.[97] So why did the Ottomans not also change?

This finally raises the question of science.[98] Theoretically, the great breakthrough in European science came with the study of astronomy and the replacement of the geocentric world picture by the heliocentric one through a series of studies by scientists from Copernicus to Newton. The importance of this development lay not only in a new picture of the universe, reducing the Earth from its centre to one of more planets circling around the sun and later to a tiny spot circling around one of many billions of stars in an enormous universe. Even more important was its implication for the nature of knowledge, based not on pure thought but on systematic observation and experiment. The logical next step from the study of nature and the universe was to apply a similar method to phenomena on Earth, chemistry, medicine, zoology, botany and not least humans themselves and their society, i.e. history and the social sciences.

How can we explain the European success in this field? One possibility is, as Morris claims,[99] that it was simply a side-effect of European development in other fields, notably the expeditions across the ocean which necessitated precise measurement of time and space and in turn made European authorities more tolerant of eccentric intellectuals. According to the same logic, Ottoman authorities should have embraced European inventions with enthusiasm, but they didn't. Although intellectual development is not unconnected to social and material phenomena, there is still much to say in favour of it as an independent variable. Inventiveness is not a permanent characteristic of some peoples, in contrast to others, but certain inventions may nevertheless be more likely to occur under specific cultural and social conditions. Europe had the advantage over China that it had access to Greek science, probably the most advanced in antiquity, as well as the Muslim improvement of it in the early Middle Ages. Indirectly, the Europeans were probably also able to learn from China. By contrast, the Chinese were little influenced from the outside; they mostly regarded themselves as superior to all foreigners. When the Europeans surpassed the Muslims in the later Middle Ages, it was, as we have seen, mainly because of increasing distrust in science by Muslim rulers, notably the Ottomans.[100]

Admittedly, intolerance was also increasing in Europe in the sixteenth and seventeenth centuries, the period of the great breakthrough in science. When this did not lead to the same results as in China and the Muslim world, the explanation must partly be sought in stronger institutions, namely, the universities, and partly in the usual factor, the divided state system, which made it possible for people persecuted in one place to find refuge in another. Concerning the former, some scholars have traced the origins of the scientific discoveries back to the Middle Ages, when the universities had already received a considerable intellectual freedom despite general intolerance, while they were also able to preserve the progress that had been made. In addition, the study of law, logic and philosophy has been regarded as the theoretical foundation for the science that led to the heliocentric theory.[101] The institutional factor seems stronger in this case than the intellectual one; it can at least be argued that the development of science from Copernicus to Newton represents a radical novelty.[102] In addition to the universities, the relative intellectual freedom, open discussion and meeting of people from various parts of Europe in the Italian city republics and later in the Dutch Republic and England/Britain must have been an important factor.[103]

These observations of course only explain why the new science became dominant in Europe once it had occurred, not why it occurred in the first place. The occurrence of genius and its development are both unpredictable and inexplicable, but different intellectual traditions and thought systems may nevertheless give some clue to the kind of discoveries that may be expected in a particular culture. The classical study of this is Joseph Needham's great work, based on years of study of China and intimate knowledge of its language and culture as well as science in general.[104] Needham was full of admiration for Chinese science but was nevertheless clear about the decisive superiority of Europe from around 1600, with Galileo. In the previous period, he finds no decisive European advantage but great differences in modes of thought as well as in the fields in which the two cultures excelled. Nevertheless, he hints at an explanation in the European concept of law: 'We may ask perhaps whether the state of mind in which an egg-laying cock could be prosecuted at law was necessary in a culture which should later on have the property of producing a Kepler.'[105] In other words, the crucial difference does not necessarily consist in an obvious advantage, but might equally well be a mode of thought likely to lead to absurd consequences. The European notion of laws of nature by analogy to laws in society, given by a ruler, is totally alien to China. Although not more scientific, it might possibly have been more likely to have led to the scientific discoveries of Copernicus and his successors. In addition, as we have seen, increased knowledge of Greek science was a factor in Copernicus' formulation of the new theory. In the next stages, its verification by Kepler and Galileo was the result of observations through the use of better instruments.

It may be objected to this explanation that it is based on permanent features of the two cultures and thus underestimates the revolutionary changes that took place in Europe in the early modern period, with the Reformation, the Great Discoveries and various technological inventions, civilian as well as military.[106] Like China, Europe had its cultural canon, based on the Bible and the Christian tradition, on the one hand, and on the Greek and Roman classics, on the other. This canon was challenged from the sixteenth century onwards. The Reformation of course did not reject the Bible but, on the contrary, used it to attack the many dogmas and traditions introduced by the Catholic Church and restore what the Protestants regarded as original and authentic Christianity. The literary canon, based on the Greek and Roman Classics, was challenged during the debate between the Ancients and the Moderns in the late seventeenth century, in which the latter claimed that modern French literature, Racine, Corneille, Molière and others, was better than the Greek and Roman Classics.[107] The Great Discoveries established an entirely new picture of the world, showing that Aristotle and other ancient authorities had been wrong. Of the new Christian movements resulting from the Reformation, the Puritans were particularly important, with a strong attachment to scientific research, partly the result of the idea that God's works in the creation should be studied and known and partly because of the fact that many of them were active in business and practical activities. However, scientific research was not exclusive to the Puritans; despite the condemnation of Galileo, considerable scientific research was undertaken in Catholic countries. In addition, the invention of printing made it easier to communicate and discuss the results of research – the number of printed books in early modern Europe by far exceeded that of China. This can largely be explained by the different script systems in the two cultures. European alphabetic script demanded only a small number of types, which made printing easy, whereas the numerous Chinese signs gave printing little advantage over handwriting, except for short texts to be issued in numerous copies.

The connection between the scientific discoveries and the various practical inventions, such as the steam engine, has often been discussed and it has been pointed out that most inventors had limited theoretical education while the great scientists rarely tried to apply their science to solve practical problems. However, the gap between the two was certainly less from the eighteenth century onwards than it had been previously and, in the long run, it is difficult to imagine the Industrial Revolution without a connection to advanced science. In a similar way, technology contributed to the scientific discoveries. Kepler's and Galileo's arguments in favour of the Heliocentric Theory were based on observations by better instruments than those previously available. Europe also differed from China in this respect. Chinese education was exclusively focused on literary skill and knowledge, taught in private as well as public institutions, and aimed at preparing for a career in the imperial bureaucracy, although only a small minority of the graduates achieved this.[108] Thus, although the discussion about the rise of Europe and the scientific and industrial revolution will continue, it seems unlikely that these phenomena can be explained as chance events.

Moreover, once Europe – or parts of Europe – had taken this decisive step, it becomes of subordinate importance exactly when it overtook China according to the normal criteria of economic and political success, education, standard of living, and so forth. Although Europe in some respects lagged behind China for a long time, perhaps even until around 1800, it underwent a series of great changes in the centuries before which indicate a particular dynamism, while China seems to have reached a peak in its scientific and technological development already in the tenth and eleventh centuries. To compare with a running competition: the decisive moment is not when the winner overtakes the loser but when he starts to run faster.

China had been in contact with Europeans since the sixteenth century and must have had many opportunities to adopt their technology, but failed to do so. Nor did the disaster of the Opium War lead to reform, but on the contrary to further western dominance. Further, because of their relative backwardness in the earlier period, the Europeans were much more interested in China and other parts of the world than the Chinese were in Europe, and learned from other cultures. Finally, when the Industrial Revolution had taken place in England, it gradually spread to the rest of Europe – to the extent that Germany was ahead of England already in the 1880s – but only to one country outside Europe, namely, Japan. If the Chinese were close to doing the same as the Europeans in the late eighteenth century, why did they not make use of European technological and institutional improvements instead of becoming a battlefield for competing Western powers, the Europeans and the USA?

Conclusion

We have discussed three widely different topics which have often been regarded as marking a radical difference between the Middle Ages and the modern period. The Renaissance made Greek language and literature known to Europeans and made more texts available through the invention of printing, which in turn contributed to the scientific revolution. The Reformation ended the theological monopoly of the Catholic Church and increased the power of the state over religion. The Great Discoveries greatly extended the known world and introduced the Europeanization of other continents which has continued until the present.

Both contemporaries and later ages have regarded these novelties as the expression of a radical break between the medieval and early modern period, but there is also a certain amount of continuity. The great maritime discoveries have their background in the expansion of Europe from the ninth and tenth centuries onwards, partly militarily through the conquests of the Mediterranean and the Baltic Seas and some of the countries along them, partly technologically through improvements in navigation and ship-building and partly culturally through the spread of Christianity. The rich cultural and intellectual tradition of the Middle Ages, combined with the introduction of printing, contributed to the Renaissance, partly also the Reformation, which in addition has its background in the increasing control of ecclesiastical institutions by kings and other secular authorities. In addition, the Reformation forms a test of previous European state formation, which largely explains the success or failure of the movement in different parts of Europe. Finally, the discussion of the consequences of the Great Discoveries has led to the conclusion that the present-day European or rather Western dominance can hardly be the result of a sudden change around 1800 but must have its background in the development of European culture and society during the previous centuries.

Concerning the relationship between the three fields, there is a clear intellectual connection between the Renaissance and the Reformation. Criticism of tradition and the idea of a radical break with the past are common to both, while the knowledge of Greek and of textual criticism form a direct background to the Reformation. On the other hand, there is a radical difference between the largely optimistic view of humanity in the Renaissance and the dominance of original sin and predestination in the Reformation. The connection between the Great Discoveries and the two intellectual trends might immediately seem less obvious. The sailors, soldiers and merchants who took part in the former were hardly much influenced by the new intellectual trends. However, the result of the discoveries, i.e., the European dominance of the world in the following period, was not solely the result of long voyages and military conquest, but also of scientific discoveries and new ways of regarding the world. In practice, these discoveries led to major improvements in navigation and military technology and contributed to the Industrial Revolution. Although some of the intellectual trends can be traced further back in history than the fifteenth and sixteenth centuries, this period nevertheless represented a new dynamism, which laid the foundation for the period of European supremacy in a more direct sense.

There are also arguments in favour of the importance of the state for this supremacy. The competition between the European states was an important factor in the development of the military and naval technology and the political importance of merchants and capital was decisive in the success of English and Dutch colonialism. Some amount of intellectual freedom served to stimulate scientific discoveries in the first phase, while in the second one, it received active support through the formation of learned societies and awards to distinguished scientists.

Notes

1 For a brief introduction, see Burke, *The Renaissance*. See also Baker, *Italian Renaissance Humanism*.
2 Vasari, *Lives of the Artists*, pp. 3–6.
3 Greenblatt, *The Swerve*.
4 Mandrou, *From Humanism to Science*, pp. 40–9; Eisenstein, *The Printing Revolution*.
5 For the following, see Weinberg, *To Explain the World*, pp. 153–4 and Greengrass, *Christendom Destroyed*, pp. 216–26.

6   See e.g. Wilcox, *The Development*; Phillips, *Francesco Guicciardini*; Ianziti, *Writing History*, pp. 93–113 and Connell, 'Italian Renaissance Historical Narrative'.
7   Bagge, 'Medieval and Renaissance Historiography', pp. 1353–6.
8   Najemy, '*Arti* and *Ordini*', p. 175; Phillips, 'Barefoot Boy'; Bagge, 'Actors and Structures', pp. 56–62.
9   MacCulloch, *Reformation*, p. 131.
10 For the following, see ibid., pp. 70–123.
11 Mandrou, *From Humanism to Science*, pp. 66–82; Van Engen, *Sisters and Brothers of the Common Life*, pp. 238–304. For the influence of this movement on Luther and other sixteenth-century reformers, see ibid., pp. 306–8, 315–20.
12 MacCulloch, *Reformation*, p. 47.
13 Ibid., pp. 111, 214–17; Greengrass, *Christendom Destroyed*, pp. 356–9.
14 Schwarz Lausten, 'The Disintegration'; Grell, 'The Reformation in Denmark, Norway and Iceland'; Kouri, 'The Reformation in Sweden and Finland'.
15 Elton, *England under the Tudors*, p. 194; Shagan, *The Rule of Moderation*. By contrast, Ryrie, 'Moderation, Modernity and the Reformation', p. 273, is more sceptical of this explanation, pointing instead to Henry VIII's unpredictability.
16 For this and the following, see Smith, *The Emergence of a Nation State*, pp. 109–11, 140–54. Admittedly, this was hardly a definite obstacle, as there were hints from the pope that a dispensation might be possible.
17 For the development of this movement from the early sixteenth century onwards, see Gunther, *Reformation Unbound*.
18 Elton, 'The Reformation in England'.
19 Duffy, *The Stripping of the Altars* and *Fires of Faith*.
20 For this and the following, see Whaley, *Germany*, vol. I, pp. 168–89, 240–71.
21 Curtis, *The Habsburgs*, pp. 71–2.
22 MacCulloch, *Reformation*, pp. 57–64.
23 Curtis, *The Habsburgs*, p. 71.
24 The Utraquists (from *utraque specie* = in both species, namely, bread and wine) demanded that Holy Communion be given in this way to the laity, instead of the practice introduced by the Catholic Church from the thirteenth century, that the laity only received the bread. As a result of the reconciliation with the moderate Hussites in 1436, the Catholic Church accepted this practice.
25 MacCulloch, *Reformation*, pp. 340–4 and 358–65.
26 Nexon, *The Struggle for Power*, p. 173.
27 Wilson, *The Holy Roman Empire*, pp. 115–24.
28 On the war, see e.g. Burkhardt, *Der dreissigjährige Krieg* and Wilson, *The Thirty Years War*.
29 Skinner, *The Foundations*, vol. II, p. 241.
30 Ibid., vol. II, pp. 242f.; Collins, *From Tribes to Nation*, pp. 247–51.
31 However, Onnekink and Rommelse, *Ideology and Foreign Policy in Early Modern Europe (1650–1750)*, point to the continuous importance of religion in the following period.
32 For the following, see Skinner, *The Foundations*, vol. II, pp. 190–348.
33 Ibid., vol. II, pp. 195–6.
34 Ibid., vol. II, pp. 225–38 and van Gelderen, 'Liberty, Civic Rights'.
35 Weber, *Protestantische Ethik*.
36 Trevor-Roper, 'Religion'.
37 Mokyr, *Culture of Growth*, pp. 122–3; cf. also pp. 227–46.
38 Blanning, *The Pursuit of Glory*, p. 373.
39 Hoppit, *A Land of Liberty*, pp. 212–13.
40 Ladurie, *The French Peasantry*, p. 283.
41 For the following, see Cipolla, *Guns and Sails*, pp. 75–89; McNeill, *Venice*, pp. 48–51.
42 Thomas, *World without End*, pp. 39–86.
43 Goodwin, *Spain*, pp. 15–19, 98–106.
44 Mörner, *The Political and Economic Activities of the Jesuits*, pp. 194–216 ,with discussion of various views on their regime.

45 Thomas, *The Golden Age*, pp. 225–51.
46 Fukuyama, *Political Order*, pp. 248–52.
47 Ferguson, *Civilization*, pp. 99–102; Goldstone, *Why Europe?* pp. 61–5.
48 Ferguson, *Civilization*, p. 34.
49 Acemoglou and Robinson, *Why Nations Fail*, p. 248.
50 McNeill, *Venice*, pp. 127–8.
51 Steensgaard, *Carracks*, pp. 154–69.
52 Ferguson, *Civilization*, pp. 96–115; Acemoglou and Robinson, *Why Nations Fail*, pp. 7–40; Fukuyama, *Political Order*, pp. 242–58.
53 Elliott, *Imperial Spain*, pp. 172–91.
54 For the following, see Boxer, *The Portuguese Seaborne Empire*, pp. 45–105 and Ferguson, *The Square and the Tower*, pp. 73–6.
55 Israel, *The Dutch Republic*, pp. 307–27, 934–58; de Vries and van der Woude, *The First Modern Economy*, pp. 155–349.
56 For the following, see Ferguson, *Empire*, pp. 1–29.
57 Supple, 'The Nature of Enterprise', pp. 439–47.
58 Steensgaard, *Carracks*, pp. 114–53.
59 De Vries and van der Woude, *The First Modern Economy*, p. 499; O'Rourke *et al.*, 'Trade and Empire', p. 103.
60 Osterhammel, 'World History'; Vries, 'Global Economic History'.
61 Wong, *China Transformed*; Pomeranz, *The Great Divergence*, e.g. pp. 10–27, 43–68, 168–207, 279–97; Marks, *The Origins*; Goldstone, 'Efflorescence' and *Why Europe?*; Goody, *Capitalism*; Parthasarathi, *Why Europe Grew Rich and Asia Did Not*. Concerning the chronology, Pomeranz has later suggested a slightly earlier date for the European superiority (Pomeranz, 'Ten Years After').
62 Mokyr, *Culture of Growth*, p. 297, with reference to Goody's allegations.
63 Goldstone, *Why Europe?*, pp. 16–51.
64 Morris, *Why the West*, pp. 145–70.
65 Morris, *Why the West*, p. 168.
66 Cipolla, *Guns and Sails*, pp. 92–9; Ferguson, *Civilization*, pp. 50–9.
67 For the following, see Ferguson, *Civilization*, pp. 20–33; and Mokyr, *Culture of Growth*, pp. 287–341.
68 Marco Polo, *The Travels*, vol. II, Chapter 68.
69 The text has miles, which probably corresponds to Chinese *li*, a measure of length which varies but is usually around 500 metres.
70 Marco Polo, *The Travels*, vol. II, Chapters 5–25.
71 Huff, *The Rise*, p. 319, with reference to Needham.
72 Bin Wong, *China Transformed*, pp. 95–104; Goldstone, 'Efflorescence', pp. 348–53 and *Why Europe?*, pp. 52–119.
73 Ferguson, *Money*, pp. 286–8.
74 Gupta and Ma, 'Europe in an Asian Mirror'; cf. also Morris, *Why the West*, p. 502.
75 Pomeranz, 'Ten Years After', p. 23.
76 Mokyr, *Culture of Growth*, pp. 291–5.
77 Ferguson, *Civilization*, pp. 28–33.
78 Morris, *Why the West*, pp. 427–31.
79 Mokyr, *Culture of Growth*, pp. 288–9.
80 Spence, 'The K'ang-hsi Reign', pp. 150–60; Woodside, 'The Chi'en-lung Reign', pp. 268–82.
81 Ferguson, *Civilization*, p. 47.
82 Pomeranz, *The Great Divergence*, pp. 157–8.
83 Huff, *The Rise of Early Modern Science*, pp. 287–320. Cf. also Mokyr's comment on the episode. While admitting that one emperor's rejection is not necessarily evidence of general attitudes, he finds that it corresponds to other cases (Mokyr, *Culture of Growth*, pp. 334–6).
84 Ferguson, *Empire*, pp. 29–52, 163–92.

85 Keegan, *A History of Warfare*, pp. 346–7.
86 Ferguson, *The Ascent of Money*, pp. 290–3; Morris, *Why the West?*, pp. 7–8.
87 Fukuyama, *Political Order*, p. 132.
88 Goldstone, *Why Europe?*, p. 165.
89 Hoffman, *Why Did Europe?*, pp. 19–153.
90 Goldstone, *Why Europe?*, pp. 99–102; Mokyr, *Culture of Growth*, p. 291.
91 Frankopan, *The Silk Roads*, p. 261.
92 Ferguson, *Civilization*, pp. 70–1, 198–212. See also Lenman, *Military Engineers*.
93 Meyer, 'State, Roads, War', pp. 120–4.
94 Frankopan, *The Silk Roads*, pp. 244, 254.
95 Sobel, *Galileo's Daughter*, p. 81.
96 Hoffman, *Why Did Europe?*, pp. 90–1.
97 Abulafia, *The Great Sea*, p. 461.
98 Pomeranz 'Ten Years After', p. 21, admits that he has neglected this aspect in his book.
99 Morris, *Why the West*, p. 476.
100 Weinberg, *To Explain the World*, pp. 120–3.
101 Berman, *Law and Revolution*, vol. I, pp. 151–64, 271–94, 520–58; Huff, *The Rise of Early Modern Science*, pp. 119–48, 321–64.
102 Weinberg, *To Explain the World*, pp. 124–88.
103 Goldstone, 'Efflorescence', pp. 359–79 and *Why Europe?*, pp. 120–61, who is generally sceptical of the idea of a long-term European superiority, regards this as the decisive factor.
104 Needham's studies are published in a series of volumes, comparing European and Chinese science in various fields. The following is based on his discussion of the main differences and similarities in *The Grand Titration*.
105 Needham, *The Grand Titration*.
106 For the following, see Mokyr, *Culture of Growth*, pp. 247–83.
107 Monod, *The Power of Kings*, pp. 219–20; Mokyr, *Culture of Growth*, pp. 248–56.
108 De Weerdt, *Negotiating Standards*; Mokyr, *Culture and Growth*, pp. 303–7. Thanks to Hilde De Weerdt for sending me her book.

5

ABSOLUTISM AND CONSTITUTIONALISM

Capital versus coercion: England, the Dutch Republic and France

Winston Churchill introduces his account of the Battle of Blenheim, on the banks of the Danube, on 13 August 1704, in the following way:

> The wide plain, bathed in the morning sunlight, was covered with hostile squadrons and battalions ... But behind this magnificent array ... were the shapes of great causes and the destinies of many powerful nations. Europe protested against the military domination of a single Power. The Holy Roman Empire pleaded for another century of life ... The Dutch Republic sought to preserve its independence, and Prussia its kingdom rank. And from across the seas in England the Protestant succession, Parliamentary government, and the future of the British Empire advanced with confident tread. All these had brought their cases before the dread tribunal now set up in this Danube plain.[1]

In the battle, Churchill's ancestor, John Churchill, First Duke of Marlborough, and the imperial commander-in-chief Eugene of Savoy, inflicted a crushing defeat on the French-Bavarian army.[2]

In the period 1688–1714, France was at almost continuous war with a number of other countries, including England; there were only five years of peace (1697–1702). From a territorial point of view, the two wars resulted in relatively minor changes, despite the French success in the former and failure in the latter. The greatest change, Louis XIV's grandson succeeding to the Spanish Empire, was the result of the late king of Spain's will (1700). From an English point of view, the latter of the two wars marked the beginning of the country's rise to a leading power of Europe, surpassing France at sea and as a colonial power, while in addition, the Battle of Blenheim introduced a series of English victories over French armies that made Louis sue for peace at almost any price in 1709. Whether there was a real French recovery in the following years or disaster was avoided only because of increasing British passivity is disputed.[3] In any case, the peace treaties of Utrecht (1713) and Rastatt (1714) were not disasters from a French point of view. The real disaster was the financial consequences of the wars. There were periods of widespread hunger, particularly in 1709; the situation was still difficult at Louis' death in 1715; and the war debts burdened the French finances during the following decades. A number of later wars (1733–36, 1740–48, 1756–63 and 1778–83) added to the burden and eventually contributed to the outbreak of the French Revolution. By contrast, England participated in the same wars as France and continued to spend more resources on them, in absolute as well as relative terms, but without running into similar problems, despite the fact that the English population numbered less than one-third of that of France: 5 million against 18 million around 1700.[4]

Why this difference? The answer to this question leads us directly into a central debate on the rise of the modern state, notably the question of the contrast between absolutism and constitutionalism, which has played an important part in the discussion between modern historians and social scientists. Among the latter, the starting-point has often been Barrington Moore's attempt to trace the origins of democracy and dictatorship in the twentieth century, in which he strongly emphasized the urban origins of democracy.[5] As we have seen, this idea was then applied to early modern history by Charles Tilly, who distinguished between coercion and capital, and a series of later scholars. More recently, however, the term 'absolutism' has frequently been criticized and the limited power of kings of countries like Prussia, France and Spain been emphasized.[6] The king was still bound by the laws and his actual power over his kingdom was, in practice, limited. In particular, the difference between European absolutism and the stronger and more arbitrary power of rulers like the emperor of China and the Ottoman Sultan has been pointed out.[7] On the other hand, the assemblies usually represented only a small part of the population. Nevertheless, the difference between the two kinds of regime is significant enough to deserve a discussion.

The Dutch Republic

The ancestor of states based on capital, such as the Dutch Republic from the late sixteenth century and England from the late seventeenth century, was the medieval city state, which might mobilize far larger forces in proportion to its number of inhabitants than the contemporary kingdoms. When the Italian city states nevertheless succumbed to the invading great powers in the sixteenth century, the reason was their failure to unite against them. By contrast, their northern counterparts had been united, partly in city leagues and partly under imperial, royal or princely suzerainty. From the late fourteenth century onwards, altogether 17 cities and provinces of the Low Countries formed a union under the leadership of the Duke of Burgundy. These provinces also contributed substantially to the dukes' court and the various wars they fought, contributions that increased many times during the wars of their successor, Charles V, and, in the beginning, his son, Philip II.[8]

Various conflicts with the Spanish authorities, including reactions against attempts to introduce the Inquisition in order to suppress the strong Protestant movement in the country, led to the Dutch War of Liberation, which ended with seven of the provinces achieving independence from Spain, temporarily in 1609 and permanently in 1648. The independent provinces were all situated in the north, whereas the south, with cities like Ghent, Antwerp and Brussels, which remained under Spanish control, had earlier been those leading in trade and manufacture. The Southern Netherlands, later (from 1831) called Belgium, had considerable independence under Spanish rule. The Spanish aim was to eradicate Protestantism, not to make the Low Countries a Spanish province. Nevertheless, the Dutch Republic in the north was more successful commercially.

With less than two million inhabitants, the Dutch Republic became a European great power in the seventeenth century, able to field an army of 75,000 men, mostly mercenaries, during the Thirty Years War, which increased further during the wars against Louis XIV,[9] and at that time the largest and most efficient navy in Europe. When the war against Spain began again in 1621, after the end of a truce lasting 12 years, the Dutch suffered some defeats in the beginning but eventually turned the tables and extended their territory towards the south and east, in addition to conquering parts of the Spanish and above all the Portuguese colonies in America, Africa and Asia. Later in the century, the Dutch Republic repeatedly defeated England in naval wars and also managed to fight off a French invasion.

How was it possible for a country of two million inhabitants to mobilize such forces, almost continuously during 80 years (1572–1648, except the years 1609–21) when the much larger and more populous countries of France and Spain at the time were on the brink of bankruptcy during any prolonged war? Not only did the Dutch Republic manage to raise the troops but also pay them regularly and keep them in garrisons in the country without causing any harm to the civilian population. In 1673, the English ambassador Sir William Temple at least partly gave the answer with the following comment on the Dutch public debt:

> Whoever is admitted to bring in his money, [regards] it for a great deal of favour; and when they pay off any part of the principal, those it belongs to, receive it with tears, not knowing how to dispose of it to interest, with such safety and ease.[10]

Of course, a solid economy is necessary to make people invest their money in this way, but also a strong government. The Dutch Republic was the leading trading and colonial nation in Europe at the time, but also had an efficient tax system which in turn enabled it to introduce a permanent public debt.[11] The system was mainly based on the provinces. The Union determined the level of taxation and the percentage each province had to pay. The actual taxation was the responsibility of the provinces and varied between them; indirect taxes dominated in the urban and mercantile ones; direct taxes in the rural provinces. The Union also determined the weight and value of the mint while the provinces issued the coins. Like the Habsburgs, the Dutch Republic also resorted to borrowing but in the beginning, from the 1590s onwards, the financial boom resulting from the colonial trade made borrowing from the state unattractive. This changed from around 1640, when the confidence in Holland's public debt had increased so much that loans could be obtained at an interest rate of 5 per cent. This then introduced the public debt described by Temple.

Thus, for a long time the Republic had considerable economic freedom, could maintain a strong army and navy and engage in wars without imposing undue burdens on the taxpayers. In 1713, the total debt had increased to 378 million guilders which meant 14 million in interest or more than the total annual tax revenues. By this time, most of the debt was concentrated in relatively few Dutch families whose members largely had access to privileged political office; none of it was held by foreign governments. The consequence was a drastic reduction in military expenses which meant the end of the Republic's period as a great power.[12] Thanks to greater austerity in the following period, the debt was somewhat reduced but increased once more as a consequence of the war against Britain in the 1780s and then the internal conflict in 1787 and the Napoleonic Wars. By the end of the latter, the Republic in practice went bankrupt. Thus, as we shall see, there was some resemblance to the situation in France, although most of the other problems there were not to be found in the Dutch Republic. However, a basic problem was that the economy became less dynamic. There was more competition from abroad, many of the markets were lost and, owing to its lack of coal and iron, the Dutch Republic had little opportunity to participate in the beginning Industrial Revolution from the late eighteenth century.

Politically, the Dutch Republic was less consolidated than kingdoms like England and France; the provinces ruled themselves in most ways, but there was also a central executive power in the shape of the stadholder. He was originally the king's or duke's representative in each province. During the war against Spain, all the provinces elected the same stadholder, first William of Orange and, after his murder in 1584, his son, Maurits. He was in turn succeeded by his younger brother, Frederick Hendrik, and the office in practice became hereditary in the Orange family. In peacetime, the stadholder might have little importance, or the office might be vacant, but he acted as the leader in war. The stadholder normally represented military interests which often led to conflict with the civilian leaders, the most important of which was the elected leader of the Province of Holland. Two conflicts between these officeholders in the seventeenth century ended with the death of the latter. Eventually, in 1815, after a period of French occupation, the stadholder was elected king.

Each of the seven provinces had their own government. In addition, they were very different and often competed with each other. Holland was by far the largest and richest and profited most from the trade, with the other sea province, Zeeland, as its main rival in this field. The other provinces were less urbanized and without access to the sea, although they had some important towns. Moreover, the provinces were fairly decentralized internally; particularly the cities had great independence. Considering these conditions, the relative stability of the Republic seems remarkable. However, it had the advantage of great wealth and easy communications which made it possible to meet frequently and solve problems that occurred. Above all, the exposed position must have been a strong incentive to stick together, as a small country with no natural borders and threatened by powerful neighbours, England, France and Spain, the latter from 1713 replaced by Austria.

Frans Hals' portrait of the Lady Governors of the Old Men's Almshouse in Haarlem shows five elderly women, dressed wholly in black. Despite the immediate impression of monotony, they are highly individualized and seen from different angles. They give an impression of seriousness and responsibility. Black had been the usual colour in dress in the second half of the sixteenth century, but had long ago been replaced by bright colours in the rest of Europe. Its use by the Governesses may be due to their strict Calvinism; colours are to be found in other Dutch portraits of the period. In addition to the religious impression, we may note that the painting illustrates the strong position of women in Dutch society.[13] They often had public duties and could act independently in commercial life. This was combined with a certain puritanism; nude women are rare in Dutch art. Dutch painting generally does not excel in colour and lavish effects, in clear contrast to Rubens' works from the southern side of the border. Here we find drama, colour, pomp and circumstance, in portraits as well as in religious or mythological paintings: colourful dress alternating with the soft, white colour of women's skin, fighting heroes and giants, suffering saints and monumental palaces and temples. In particular, the Church was an important patron of arts. After the Spanish victory, the many churches that had been sacked by Protestant iconoclasts were redecorated to serve as monuments of Catholic Baroque piety at the border towards the heretics.

The simplicity and discreet colours of Dutch art are not only evidence of puritanism but also of the importance of the burghers as patrons. There is little religious art, not because the Dutch were not religious but because of the Calvinist ban on religious paintings. Although the republic did have a nobility of some importance and the Prince of Orange was sufficiently recognized internationally to be able to marry a king's daughter, members of the bourgeoisie were the main patrons of art. As the Dutch Republic was the richest country in Europe in the seventeenth century, there were plenty of patrons. Frans Hals' governesses form one of many examples of this, but there were also others, including the most famous of them all, Rembrandt's night watch, a dramatic picture of a troop of soldiers breaking up to march out, painted when the Republic was still at war (1642), although the troop in question was a social club rather than a military unit.

Thus, we are dealing with bourgeois art but a bourgeoisie sufficiently rich and confident in itself not to imitate the court and the aristocracy, but developing its own taste. It has been discussed, both in the seventeenth century and among modern historians, to what extent the wealthy burghers used their wealth exclusively for investment, in accordance with Max Weber's Protestant work ethic, or whether they spent it on luxury and comfort. Dutch cities, notably Amsterdam, where large areas dating from the seventeenth and eighteenth centuries have been preserved, give a more austere impression than, for instance, Venice and other Italian cities. The tall, narrow houses do not much resemble palaces, but of course we must bear in mind that in the rapidly expanding city of Amsterdam, the ground was very expensive, not only because the space was narrow but also because the soft and humid terrain made it very difficult to build there. Most of the houses, as well as the many monumental town halls, are built in a style often referred to as Renaissance, which was imitated in many other places in northern Europe, but which is closer to medieval architecture than the more classicizing Italian style. It would also seem that the Dutch gave priority to comfort rather than ostentation and of course also that they had to spend much on collective purposes, notably defence, because of the vulnerable position of the country. This is also confirmed by a comparison between Venice and Amsterdam.[14] Although austerity was also an ideal in the private lives of the Venetian elite, both the city and its leading citizens organized lavish and spectacular festivities on special occasions. In the seventeenth century, Venice was still an important commercial city, but many members of the elite at this time were rentiers rather than active businessmen. Whereas this reflects the reduced importance of Venice and other Italian cities in international trade, it is also a normal phenomenon that the number of rentiers increases with time in commercial cities. In the eighteenth century, there was a similar tendency in Amsterdam as well.

A frequent observation by foreign visitors is how clean everything was in the Dutch towns; the houses were dusted and cleaned regularly, and even the streets are said to have been clean:

> The beauty and cleanliness of the streets are so extraordinary that Persons of all ranks do not scruple, but even seem to take pleasure in walking them. As the streets were paved with brick and as clean as any chamber floor, a woman could even walk there in mules.[15]

A waste and garbage service was introduced in Amsterdam in the 1590s. Considering the filth and rubbish filling the streets in most European towns, the surprise and admiration of visitors to the Dutch ones are easy to understand. When entering the houses, however, some of them might find the cleanliness a little exaggerated. Sir William Temple tells of a magistrate visiting a house where the maid found that his shoes were not clean enough. Resolutely, she took him on her back, set him down at the bottom of the stairs, took off his shoes and gave him some slippers, after which she told him to go up to the mistress who was in her chamber.

Visitors also note the numerous charitable institutions, including the one already mentioned, and many others whose regents are also portrayed in art. A Venetian observer comments that the Dutch were able to practise this kind of charity because they had stolen the wealth of the Church, which suggests the difference from Catholic countries, that charity in Calvinist countries was almost the only way to spend money on religious purposes. Moreover, Calvinist ethics included care for the 'worthy poor'. All humans should work but it was the duty of society to support those who were not able to do so. This gradually became the attitude all over Europe, regardless of confession, partly replacing earlier ideas of poverty as an expression of virtue and the poor as particularly loved by God, but it was practised to a greater extent in Calvinist areas.[16] A further motive for this kind of charity was actually a constant lack of workers which formed an incentive to take care of poor children so that they might be of use to society later. Like all colonial powers, the Dutch exploited their colonies and profited from the slave trade. The conditions on board Dutch ships were no better than of those of other nations, which means that the voyages were dangerous and the mortality high. The surplus of the trade and shipping, however, seems to a greater extent than in most other places to have been invested in better living conditions, above all, for the bourgeoisie, but to some extent also for the rest of the population.

Coercion and capital

The Dutch Republic had many of the features occurring in Weber's account of the social importance of Calvinism. It would immediately seem that this confession was less useful from an organizational point of view. Here the original idea that all Christians were equal continued to be practised. There were individuals with greater learning and charisma who became ministers and preachers but no offices and no churches, except that former Catholic churches were taken over for practical reasons and used for assemblies. Nevertheless, it has been claimed that Reformed Protestantism was actually a very important factor in state formation and that it is therefore no coincidence that this religion was represented in two of the most successful early modern states, namely, the Dutch Republic and Prussia.[17] As we have seen, the Dutch Republic lacked many of the criteria that are usually said to characterize successful early modern states, such as a strong royal power and an extensive bureaucracy, but there is nevertheless no doubt of its success, militarily, economically and politically. The cleanliness and well-ordered cities as well as the low crime-rates form part of this picture but were not the result of extensive bureaucratization and control from above but of the mobilization of neighbourhoods and local communities to take responsibility for local order. Here small religious communities without sharp distinctions of rank may have been more efficient than the more hierarchical Lutheran and, above all, Catholic churches.

As normal in pre-industrial societies – and largely also in industrial ones – wealth was unequally distributed, most of the profit going to those who were already wealthy. Ordinary people nevertheless seem to have been better off here than in most other countries. Wages were high, due to great expansion and the need for workers. Although living costs were also high, they did not increase faster than the wages, in contrast to most other places.[18] Tax records from 1742 allow some conclusions about the distribution of income. The average income in the Dutch towns, which comprised 60 per cent of the population, was 654 guilders per year, while the minimum for survival is estimated at 200 guilders. The 20 per cent top earners together had 56 per cent of the total, against 43 per cent in the late twentieth century. However, the modern tax system, in which the richest pay a higher percentage, modifies this, so that the actual modern percentage becomes 37. Not surprisingly, income distribution was thus more unequal in the eighteenth than in the twentieth century. More interesting, of course, is the comparison with other countries in the eighteenth century, but here there is less data. In England, the top 10 per cent were better off than in the Dutch Republic, while the opposite was the case with the next 10 per cent. This corresponds to the general impression of the two countries, the more aristocratic character of English society. Despite the lack of exact comparative data, however, it would also seem likely that the distribution of wealth was less unequal in the Dutch Republic than in countries like France and Spain and probably most other countries in the early modern period.

The Dutch public credit is the obvious model for its English counterpart, introduced shortly after Temple's comment. The Bank of England was founded in 1694 and was able to borrow money on the international marked, with the English state as guarantee.[19] Whereas Charles II in 1671 had repudiated his debt of £1.3 million, loans were now guaranteed by the whole landed and commercial wealth of the country. By the middle of the eighteenth century, there were 60,000 public creditors which had increased to around half a million by the end of the century. The annual interest payment on the loans, 8 per cent, was guaranteed by Parliament. This meant the opportunity to borrow more money at a lower interest rate than was the case in France. The British national debt eventually became much larger than the French one. It was 100 per cent of the national income in the 1770s and nearly 200 per cent in the second decade of the nineteenth century, while the French one had been greatly reduced after the repudiation of two-thirds of it in 1797. The British expenses from the Napoleonic Wars were still not paid in 1914. With the expanding economy of the country, the debt, which in the nineteenth century gave an interest of 5 per cent, served as a good and safe investment for its wealthy inhabitants.[20]

Thus, England and the Dutch Republic clearly had a financial advantage over France from the second half of the seventeenth century, which also seems to imply the superiority of capital over coercion and the connection of the former with constitutionalism. The merchant aristocracies of England and the Dutch Republic needed military forces to protect and extend their trade and, in the case of the latter, to defend their very exposed borders against foreign conquerors, and were willing to pay for this. Both countries had the advantage that the wealthy part of the population, including the nobility, paid taxes, which not only brought substantial revenues but also enabled the country to get loans on favourable conditions. England was probably wealthier per capita than France in the eighteenth century, but its greatest advantage was the ability to tax the whole population. This was in turn the result of its constitutional government: the taxpayers were represented in Parliament. Thus, the key to success was not the use or threat of force, but involving the population, or at least the wealthier parts of it, in the government. This lesson was transmitted to France and several other countries from the French Revolution and the Napoleonic Wars onwards, where large armies were mobilized through participation in government and patriotic appeals.

Privileges and monopolies were characteristic of most absolutist states and led to great inefficiency in the economy. The economic success of England in the eighteenth century was to a considerable extent a result of the absence of such interventions.[21] Admittedly, England and the Dutch Republic also had their trading companies with monopolies, but they were not able to control trade in the same way. In particular, the Glorious Revolution in 1688 led to the abolition of a number of monopolies, which had been an essential part of royal policy under the Stuarts. Granting monopolies was profitable for the king and increased his power by making people dependent on him. For the same reason, Parliament was against them and tried to restrict or abolish them. A statute on monopolies was passed in 1623 and the Long Parliament (1640–53) abolished all domestic monopolies, but the king still retained the opportunity to grant overseas ones during the period of restauration. Thus, the Royal African Company had a monopoly, granted by Charles II in 1660, on the very lucrative slave trade across the Atlantic, but this was frequently infringed by other traders. In 1689, the company seized the cargo of one such merchant, named Nightingale, who brought the matter to court. The judge ruled that the seizure was illegal because the company was exercising a monopoly right created by royal prerogative, i.e. not by Parliament – this was just after the Glorious Revolution. The question of overseas monopolies became hotly debated, with numerous petitions to Parliament, which finally, in 1698, abolished the monopoly of the African Company.

Thus, monopolies had now become a matter for Parliament which received a number of petitions from various people and organizations either to abolish or introduce them. Producers and businessmen often wanted monopolies or bans against competition and in some cases succeeded. Thus, the wearing of lighter cloth, cotton or silk imported from India, was banned in the early eighteenth century to protect English wool production, but the ban was abolished in 1774. However, the many diverging interests prevented the kind of monopolies that developed in Spain.

The English Parliament did not make the world a better place by liberating the slave trade but it did contribute to economic growth by abolishing privileges and allowing free competition. In a similar way, the commercialization of agricultural production led to economic growth and was probably also a factor in the later Industrial Revolution but had negative social consequences. As a consequence of the reduction of the population because of the Black Death in the later Middle Ages, many landowners turned to sheep farming instead of agriculture, thus reducing the areas cultivated by individual peasants, even after the population had begun to increase again. Later, landowners got hold of common land, earlier at the disposal of the village communities, through enclosure, i.e. that they became reserved for the owner himself or the one to whom he rented the land.[22] Gradually, many village communities consisting of small farms were replaced by large estates, cultivated by the landowner himself or more usually by one tenant with sufficient capital to rent the whole. The evicted farmers had to resort to a precarious existence as landless workers or as artisans or later industrial labourers in the towns. In a similar way, landowners in the Scottish Highlands evicted their tenants in order to use the land for sheep farming.

From an economic point of view, however, the effect was positive; agricultural production increased greatly; the production per agricultural worker is considered to have increased by 75 per cent during the seventeenth and eighteenth centuries. The introduction of new crops, such as turnips and clover, which enriched the soil rather than exhausting it, made it possible to avoid the long periods of fallow – of around one-third of the area – that had been necessary previously. The increasing size of cities and improved transport also formed an incentive to produce for the market. Thus, enclosure enabled the country to feed a larger population, added to the wealth of the landowners and created a workforce that could be employed by the new industries that developed from the late eighteenth century. Together with the Dutch Republic, where a similar development took place, England had by far the most productive agriculture in Europe. England and the Dutch Republic were thus wealthier than France and their wealth to a greater degree consisted in surplus from trade and manufacture in the form of ready money. Finally, English warfare largely served the interests of the commercial classes who were then willing to contribute to financing it. Thus, constitutional government by merchant aristocracies, at least those of the character of the English and Dutch ones in the seventeenth and eighteenth centuries, made coercion unnecessary. Their constitutional government increased their capital.

During the eighteenth century, England – from 1707, Britain – surpassed the Dutch Republic as the leading commercial nation of Europe. However, the country did not become dominated by the bourgeoisie to the same extent. England still had a strong nobility with a great influence on culture as well as politics. On the other hand, the court had a less central position than in France; there is no Versailles in England. Instead, the residences of the nobility and gentry dominate, particularly in the countryside, to some extent also in the cities, in the latter, together with those of the wealthy burghers. Since the breakthrough of Palladian architecture in the early seventeenth century, these residences are mostly built in the classicist style, from Blenheim Palace to a number of smaller houses all over the country and in cities like Edinburgh and Bath and large parts of London. Numerous portraits of elegantly dressed men and women give a more aristocratic impression than their counterparts in the Dutch Republic. However, it was relatively easy for wealthy burghers to get a title, at least to be knighted, but this did not mean that they gave up their trade. On the contrary, ideas of profit and investment largely penetrated the nobility and gentry, as expressed in the reforms in agriculture. Moreover, in most cases, the way to public office did not go through royal favour but through election or connections with the political establishment. In this way, social barriers were determined by wealth rather than birth. As Members of Parliament received no pay, only wealthy people or people with wealthy patrons could be elected. Commissions as officers in the army and navy also had to be bought, in addition to the fact that patronage was important for most positions in society. In contrast to France, however, there was no rule about noble birth.

Turning to France, we first have to observe that this was by no means a purely agrarian country. Particularly during Louis XIV's reign, France made great efforts to stimulate trade and commerce, including the abolition of some of the internal tolls, improvement of communications, notably the great Canal du Midi, 150 miles long, built at Colbert's initiative, and privileges for merchants. Like England, France also expanded overseas, with colonies in America, the Caribbean and India, some of which were lost to England in the wars of the eighteenth century. Even so, France remained an important colonial power, profiting greatly from sugar production in its colonies in the Caribbean and from the slave trade across the Atlantic. Bordeaux, the leading port of colonial trade, made a deep impression on two English visitors, respectively in 1775 and 1787.[23] Its quay extended on a straight line for more than 2 miles and had a range of regular buildings, and the city had the opulence which only wealth could confer. The latter of the two, Arthur Young, added that although Paris could not be compared to London, Bordeaux by far surpassed Liverpool. After the recent restoration of its eighteenth-century beauty – the product of its mercantile wealth at the time – it has become an attractive focus for tourists.

There was also an increase in agricultural production and some improvement of the conditions of the peasants in the eighteenth century, aided by longer periods of peace and good harvests in the mid-eighteenth century. As in England, but not to the same extent, there was a tendency in many parts of the country towards larger farms, rented by a few wealthy farmers who owned ploughs and other equipment and employed those with smaller plots as labourers. Nevertheless, strong control and intervention from the state made France lag behind England and the Dutch Republic. It is also difficult to imagine a different economic policy in a country like France, not only because of its absolutist doctrine but also because of the importance of patronage in the king's rule of the country. In contrast to Britain and the Dutch Republic, France did not institute a national bank. The explanation for this is probably the financial experiments introduced by the Scot John Law, which ended in bankruptcy in 1720. In principle, this was a useful reform, but Law was a ruthless speculator who exploited the unreserved trust he received from the regent, the Duke of Orléans, in a way that was bound to lead to disaster. There was a similar financial scandal in England at the same time, but less disastrous, because the parliamentary system made it more difficult for one person to get the same position there as in absolutist France.[24] The lack of a national bank contributed to the problems later in the century that led to the Revolution, although it is an open question whether such an innovation would have been sufficient to solve the country's financial problems.

Culturally and socially, the court dominated in France to a greater extent than in England and the Dutch Republic in the seventeenth and eighteenth centuries. The centre of the country was Versailles, which was also the model for noble residences all over the country, as well as for art and literature in general. The nobles also had greater privileges in France than in the two other countries. They still retained some governmental rights in local society and in the eighteenth century, they had an exclusive right to commissions as officers, to the extent that noble descent in four generations was demanded for admission to cadet schools. The fact that this rule was not applied to artillery officers made it possible for many of the great generals of the Revolution, including Napoleon, to get their education. On the other hand, it was not difficult for wealthy people to obtain noble status. They were then included in the *noblesse de robe* ('robe' nobility, after the long robe which distinguished the holders of certain offices), whereas the more exclusive *noblesse d'épée* (sword nobility) was reserved for the ancient families. The difference from England, however, was that ennoblement was not compatible with a bourgeois profession. It has been pointed out that successful businesses only remained for one generation in the same family; success was an incentive to buy an office or seek ennoblement. In addition, institutions like tax farming were a strong incentive for wealthy people to invest in office and royal patronage rather than pure business. The French bourgeoisie actually consisted more of rentiers and administrators than of businessmen.

The wars of 1688–1714 partly confirm Tilly's observation about coercion and capital. Although Tilly classifies both England and France as combinations of the two, coercion was clearly more prominent in France while capital dominated in England. France was ruled by an absolute king, whereas the Dutch Republic and England were constitutional countries, in which the executive power was limited by that of elected assemblies. The difference between France, on the one hand, and England and the Dutch Republic, on the other, in the seventeenth and eighteenth centuries is obvious and the comparison seems in most respects to be in favour of the latter. England and the Dutch Republic were enormously successful and clearly demonstrate that capital had now become the main path to political success. Another question is the causal relationship between capital and constitutionalism and to what extent the difference can be traced further back in history. In the case of the Dutch Republic, both phenomena are already to be found in the Middle Ages, which makes the causal relationship between them more difficult to decide. England, however, underwent great commercial changes in the seventeenth century, whereas it seems possible to trace its constitution back to the thirteenth century.

Towards absolute monarchy in France

Already in the mid-fifteenth century, the English political theorist Sir John Fortescue characterized France as a *dominium regale* and England as a *dominium regale et politicum*, in accordance with contemporary terminology, i.e. unrestricted versus restricted royal power.[25] The difference between the two countries was less at the time than it became later and the king of France can hardly be said to have been absolute as early as around 1450. Nevertheless, there were significant differences already then.

As we have seen, Philip Augustus' conquest of the English fiefs in 1202–6 marks one step in the process of centralization in France. This meant that Normandy and the other former English provinces were added to the royal domain, which in principle was governed directly by the king, through his appointed officials. However, an important factor in King Philip's success in this area was support from the local aristocracy, which evidently retained much of its influence even after the conquest. Moreover, the conquered provinces kept their laws and customs. This was probably the only way for the king to control the country, but it resulted in France becoming a kingdom composed of a number of provinces governed in very different ways until the centralization under the Revolution and Napoleon. By contrast, Edward I's conquest of Wales in the late thirteenth century led to a massive introduction of English law and administration.[26]

Several great principalities continued to exist in the following centuries and the king's position was seriously weakened for long periods during the Hundred Years War. In the long run, he nevertheless increased his control of the country, partly by taking over several of the principalities, partly by developing the central administration and the supreme court of appeal in Paris. French kings often married into princely families and in some cases inherited their principalities; most of the great princes were the king's relatives. Eventually, a series of important principalities came under the crown: the former English possessions in 1450–53 and later Brittany, Anjou and Maine. When the crown was inherited by members of side branches of the dynasty, their territories reverted to the crown. This happened with Louis XII in 1498, Francis I in 1515 and Henry IV of Navarra in 1589; the latter joined this originally Spanish kingdom to the French crown.

However, the formation of the kingdom of France should not only be regarded as a series of conquests that increased the territory under the king's direct control. As we have seen, the increasing links between the king and the leading nobles in the period until the building of Versailles were also crucial. In the thirteenth century, the long reign of St Louis was of particular importance. Louis was one of the last kings in Europe to be canonized, whereas previously, royal saints had been common, notably in England and in the newly converted countries.[27] Louis' sanctity was an important factor in the development of the French monarchy, notably the combination of saint and real knight, having twice been on Crusades and showing his personal skill and courage in fighting in a way that impressed his vassals, although some objections might be directed at his qualities as a general. Moreover, his possession of the main royal virtue, justice in judgement, is expressed by the picture of him, sitting outdoors and urging all who sought justice to approach him personally. In particular, the sources refer to a large oak at the palace at Vincennes, under which Louis used to sit – there is still an oak in the place today. Louis' reign also had a reputation for being a time of wealth and internal peace; concerning the former, it stands as a contrast to the many demands for money made by his grandson Philip IV. For his part, Philip exploited his grandfather for what he was worth. He was active in securing his canonization and during the following conflict with the pope, he used the piety and sanctity of the French kings, of course, including Louis, as an argument.

Already around 1300, there is a clear difference between English and French government. Whereas England had no royal saint comparable to St Louis – Edward the Confessor had died 250 years before – France had no institution comparable to the English Parliament. Admittedly, France also had an institution called Parliament with a continual existence until the Revolution but this was the highest court of law in the country. In the Middle Ages, there was a vague distinction between legal and political assemblies but the difference increased over the centuries. At no time, however, had the French Parliament (the Parliament of Paris) been a representative institution like the English one. Large assemblies of estates, divided into clergy, nobles and commoners, were summoned on various occasions, for instance, in 1302 and in 1329, after the change of dynasty from the Capetians to the Valois. However, as the French kings never managed to make their assemblies grant taxes, these bodies did not attain the same importance as the English Parliament and gradually disappeared from the fifteenth century onwards. After the assembly of 1484, the next one did not meet until 1560 – both took place during a regency, as did also most of the following ones. The period of the wars of religion meant a revival, but the assembly 1610–14, during the minority of Louis XIII, was the last before the one that led to the Revolution (1789). By contrast, regional assemblies were more frequent and important and some of them continued to meet until the eighteenth century.[28]

The various crises in France during the later Middle Ages and the early modern period and the largely decentralized character of the country until the age of the Revolution and Napoleon may serve as a warning against exaggerating the amount of state formation in the country during this period. However, neither should it be underestimated. Despite a series of setbacks, the king always regained his power and mostly increased it. Already in the early fourteenth century, the case of the Templars shows the remarkable strength of the royal administration. Almost all the members of the Order were arrested on the same day, on 13 October 1307, all over the country. As Strayer comments: 'No modern dictatorship could have done a better job.'[29] The development of the judicial system in this country as well as in England points in the same direction.

As the result of the Hundred Years War, the king of France managed to introduce a permanent tax to finance a standing army, first, under Charles V, and then later and permanently under Charles VII. At the time Fortescue compared the two countries, France seemed to have been better off financially than England and in addition more stable politically. As late as in the mid-seventeenth century, English taxes were significantly lower than the French; altogether, they amounted to less than one of the French taxes, the *gabelle*.[30] France was one of the first countries to introduce the military revolution, using artillery to conquer the English castles in 1450–53 and creating a standing army. When Henry VIII sought to imitate his predecessors by invading France in 1543, it ended in disaster; France was now militarily superior to England. As we have seen, the French king invaded Italy in

1494 and fought an almost continuous war against the king of Spain and the Holy Roman Emperor – from 1519 united in the person of Charles V.

Internally, the around 200 years from the end of the Hundred Years War to Louis XIV's accession to the throne made Fortescue's characterization of the French monarchy a reality. Two main factors brought about this, namely, the increased frequency and costs of war and internal conflicts. The traditional taxes were insufficient to finance Francis I's wars, even if they were increased drastically. As a result, he resorted to sales of offices on a large scale, a practice that continued and increased in the following period, during the wars of religion, 1562–98, and the participation in the Thirty Years War, and the war against Spain, 1635–59. The French local administration was transformed through the introduction of the venality of offices and a series of desperate means to finance the wars.

Venality of some offices goes back to the early Middle Ages but, as we have seen, the conquests in the thirteenth century introduced a system of local officers strictly controlled by the king. They were paid by a part of the revenues of their districts but they depended on the king and could be moved and deposed by him. The introduction of venal offices changed this. There was little control with the qualifications and character of the officers and eventually, they also became free to appoint their successors. This became firmly established by Henry IV in 1604. Until then, the rule had been that a royal officer who sold or transferred his office had to survive for 40 days for the transaction to be valid, which meant that it could only with difficulty be transferred to his heir by death. Henry introduced the *paulette*, a tax of 1/60 of the value of the office per year, which gave exemption from the 40-days rule. In this way, the king had given up most of his control of his officers in return for a fixed income. Admittedly, there were also non-venal officers called *commissaires* who were appointed and could be deposed by the king and who were supposed to control the venal officers. As there were around 45,000 venal officers under Louis XIV and only 300 full-time *commissaires*, it goes without saying that this control must have been very limited.[31]

Venality of offices was particularly important in France but is to be found in many other countries as well, mostly in southern Europe: Spain and Italy, in the latter with the exception of Florence and Venice. It did occur in northern Europe as well, e.g. Britain and Scandinavia, but only in shorter periods or to a limited degree. It was also rarely practised in Germany and Austria. The geographic distribution of the practice, mainly in Catholic countries, and its early introduction by the papacy may suggest the latter as the source of inspiration. It also seems that the legal forms were borrowed from this quarter.[32] However, the main explanation for the development of the practice in France and other countries must be sought in financial crises and the reluctance to use other means to gain money. It may also be added that despite the many bad consequences of the practice, it had the advantage of linking local elites closely to the monarchy.

Despite the venality of offices, taxes were also necessary and there were more than a hundred violent tax rebellions in the last decade of Richelieu's rule alone.[33]

Taxation increased drastically from the sixteenth century onwards: the net income of the state was 200 tons of silver around 1560, which increased to 400 between 1600 and 1630, to 500 in 1645 and 800 around 1690.[34] As the nobles and in practice also a number of other wealthy people were exempt from taxes, this meant a heavy burden on ordinary people, notably the peasants, in addition to limiting the sums that could actually be levied. Admittedly, indirect taxes were a considerable source of income, in addition to the possibility of levying extraordinary taxes on the nobles. At the same time, Richelieu and his successor, Mazarin, had amassed great wealth and created an extensive system of patronage, reactions against which were largely the cause of the Fronde, a series of rebellions during Louis XIV's minority, which made a deep impression on him; his style of government can largely be explained as an attempt to prevent a similar disaster from happening again. Constitutional government was not regarded as a realistic alternative in France, as it had never really worked.

When Louis took over, he was hardly in a position to reform the system root and branch. He may have found the sales of offices unsatisfactory and wished for a more efficient local administration but he could not afford to provoke the leading men of the local communities. The only way he could rule was by creating a system of patronage that involved most of the leading people in the country, which he did at Versailles. While Charles I provoked his subjects, including the nobility, by insisting on his absolute power, High Church Anglicanism and the attempt to rule without Parliament, Louis made the nobles his clients by gathering them around him in Versailles and securing the loyalty of local elites by continuing the system of venality of offices. In addition, his leading ministers, notably Colbert, created similar links through an elaborate system of patronage. Louis XIV had the largest and most modern army in Europe since Roman times; it may in periods have consisted of 300,000–400,000 men, which is approximately the same as the Romans mobilized from a far larger empire. However, this centralization of power came at a cost. The financial surplus from the mid-fifteenth century was long gone. After the reign of Henry IV (1589–1610), annual expenses most of the time exceeded the incomes.[35] Nor can the extensive bureaucracy be regarded as an instrument in controlling society but rather as a means to gain support from local elites.[36]

Fukuyama applies the term 'weak absolutism' to France and Spain, meaning the combination of the absence of formal limits to the king's power and inefficient government. At least regarding the reign of Louis XIV, this seems an exaggeration. An inefficient administration would hardly have been able to mobilize the largest and strongest army in Europe, and in times of crisis, Louis was also able to make the nobles pay taxes. He also mostly succeeded in appointing well-qualified people to the most important military and civilian offices.[37] On the other hand, there were limits to absolutism. The king was obliged to respect the fundamental rights of this subjects, notably that of property, and although he might legislate, he had to respect divine and natural law.[38]

The development of constitutional government in England

By the mid-fifteenth century, the English Parliament had met regularly for 200 years or more and the king needed its consent for taxation, in addition to the fact that it dealt with a number of other matters. The English Parliament had its background in similar assemblies dating back to the Anglo-Saxon period in the tenth century.[39] It was not an assembly of estates, as most other similar institutions, but consisted of only two parts or 'houses': the lords and the commons. It was also unique in its representative system, based on the shires, which meant that each part of the country sent its representatives to Parliament to promote its interests there. This gave the assembly a solid basis in local society. Finally, and perhaps most importantly, England differed from most other countries in that the nobles paid taxes. This goes back to the first general taxes in the country in the late twelfth century, the Crusading tax and the ransom for Richard I, and with a few exceptions continued in the following period. England also had a formal limitation of the king's power, in the form of the Magna Carta (the Great Charter), issued by King John in 1215 as the result of a rebellion against him. The Charter was renewed a number of times in the following period in a slightly revised form and became a kind of constitution for England. As we shall see, similar charters were issued in a number of other countries, although mostly without the same long-term importance.

When Parliament became a permanent and very important institution in the following period, it was to a considerable extent because of war. The traditional doctrine, in England as well as in other countries, was that the king 'should live from his own', that is the royal estates and manors and the various feudal aids his vassals were obliged to contribute. If he wanted more, he had to ask permission. For this purpose, Edward summoned his tenants-in-chief, i.e. the high nobility, and representatives from the commoners, who had to meet with power of attorney (*plena potestas*) from their constituents, according to contemporary legal doctrine.[40] This gave him relatively easy access to extra grants. Parliament met frequently, often more than once in the same year, and could be easily summoned in a small and densely populated country like England.

According to the understanding at the time, the king's demands were not simply suggestions that Parliament was free to accept or reject; the king could base his argument on a doctrine of necessity. It was the duty of the inhabitants of the realm to support the political community in the case of a necessity. Accordingly, the assembly was in principle bound to accept what the king demanded; the only way its members could reject the king's demands was by denying that there was a necessity. In practice, some criteria for this emerged; Parliament refused to pay for the suppression of rebels or to finance the king's debt, claiming that such expenses had to be covered by his regular revenues. Above all, it was an important principle that taxes were extraordinary, not something the king could claim as a matter of routine. Whereas the king's need for taxes was the original reason for the existence of Parliament, its duties and competence increased during the later Middle Ages and the early modern period. Parliament demanded concessions in return for its taxes in the form of new legislation and reform of administration and government.[41] New legislation had to be approved by the House of Commons. A number of petitions from individuals were also dealt with in Parliament. Policy-making and advising the king were for a long time a matter for the House of Lords, while the House of Commons presented petitions and gave assent. However, the importance of this body increased during the troubled periods in the fourteenth and fifteenth centuries. It was involved in the depositions of Edward II, Richard II and the various crises during the reign of the latter, as well as during the reign of Henry VI and the following periods of civil war, when it clearly had assumed the character of a political institution that it continued to have until suppressed by Charles I in 1629.[42]

England had the strongest monarchy in medieval Europe. The country had an elaborate judicial system and large tracts of land belonged to the king, feuds were forbidden and the Roman Law of Treason was implemented more harshly here than elsewhere in Europe. On the other hand, the courts of law and the local administration were run by the 'people' – namely, the nobility and gentry – to a far greater extent than they had been in the previous period. Thus, while the king of France had to pay the local elites to make use of their services, his English counterpart could use them without cost – at least, without direct monetary compensation, although of course, their positions gave prestige and influence and limited the king's possibility to intervene directly in local society. The common people might also in some cases have acted politically and have had a direct relationship to the king, but the aristocracy was clearly the most important class and in many ways acted as the link between the king and local society.

Despite the strength of the monarchy, however, no military revolution took place in England between 1450 and 1650.[43] In the Tudor period, the army consisted partly of local militias and partly of private retainers of the nobility. The latter formed more than one-third of the army of 45,000 men mobilized when the country was threatened by the Spanish Armada in 1588. As we have seen, English taxes also amounted to far less than the French ones until the mid-seventeenth century. When England could manage with a small army most of the time, only increasing it at particular periods of crisis, the explanation is largely to be sought in its protected location as an island, notably after having gained control of the whole of it, which happened in 1603, when King James VI of Scotland succeeded Elizabeth I as King James I. Even before, however, its neighbours were normally less dangerous than those of its continental counterparts, while on the other hand, the problem of Scotland was not eliminated with the union; Scotland played an important part later in the seventeenth century, notably during the Civil War.

This relatively peaceful period gives some impression of a reduced power of Parliament, which might seem to support the theory of war as the main reason for its existence. It met more rarely, and particularly during the reign of Henry VIII, the monarchy seems to have been almost absolute, more so than that of Louis XIV, with his numerous executions of nobles, his extensive use of the Law of Treason and his frequent introduction of religious changes, in either a Catholic or Protestant direction. There was one difference, however; in principle, Henry did not act arbitrarily, he always had the necessary legal support, either by a court of law or Parliament.

The Reformation strengthened the king by making him the head of the Church and increasing his wealth through the suppression of the monasteries but he also shared the spoils with his subjects, notably the nobility and gentry, whose members were given or allowed to buy the confiscated estates at favourable prices. On the other hand, the country was divided religiously and Henry needed allies to carry out his religious policy, which increased the importance of Parliament. Thus, despite an old-fashioned and inefficient army and the lack of a military revolution, the way the Reformation was introduced shows the strength of the monarchy. Moreover, the new dynasty, the Stuarts, which succeeded to the throne at the death of Elizabeth I in 1603, represented a further step in the direction of stronger monarchy, which led to the great conflicts between king and Parliament, ending with the 'Glorious Revolution' of 1688.

According to the 'Whig view' of English history, developed particularly in the nineteenth century, the victory of Parliament in the seventeenth century, notably in the Glorious Revolution of 1688, comes as the logical conclusion to a long development of English constitutionalism dating back to the Anglo-Saxon period. A number of revisionist historians have later opposed this view, pointing to significant constitutional differences between various periods and to the importance of contingent factors, which might easily have led to completely different results than the actual ones. Despite the truth of many of these observations, however, there is still much to be said in favour of the continuity of English constitutional history.

From the 1930s onwards, the English Civil War was often understood in social terms as a class struggle between the gentry and the burghers on the Parliamentarian side, while the high nobility supported the king.[44] These studies resulted in much valuable information on English social history in the sixteenth and seventeenth centuries but most scholars nowadays agree that it is very difficult to find consistent patterns regarding the social background of the two parties. By contrast, the clearest distinction between them is religious. Most Catholics and High Church Anglicans supported the king whereas most Puritans favoured Parliament. Otherwise, it is likely that the party division to a considerable extent was determined by patron–client relationships: influential local landowners or burghers formed networks joining one of the two sides. In addition, there were hard-liners and moderates on both sides and various aims and programmes.

Although long-term factors are clearly important for understanding the whole constitutional development in the seventeenth century, it therefore seems that the main explanation for the outbreak of the Civil War must be sought in short-term ones. In contrast to his predecessors, Charles I (1625–49) was inspired by Continental ideas of the absolute power of the king and systematically attempted to rule without Parliament, which he actually succeeded in doing from 1629 to 1640. He also, unsuccessfully, tried to establish a standing army. Moreover, he challenged the Puritans through his religious policy, formulated and carried out by William Laud, from 1633, the Archbishop of Canterbury.[45] Theologically, Laud supported Arminianism, a doctrine developed by the Dutch theologian Jacob Arminius which rejected predestination. This was clearly against the established teaching in the Church of England and particularly offensive to the Puritans. Organizationally, Laud sought to increase the power and revenues of the Church and restrict lay patronage over ecclesiastical appointments. Liturgically, he introduced reforms that many people found smacked of Catholicism and provoked the Puritans by imposing strict punishments against those who failed to obey his commandments.

The persecution of religious dissenters was sufficiently harsh to make thousands of people leave for America, but not harsh enough to suppress the opposition. On the contrary, the persecution led to grievances which came to the surface in the 1640s and resulted in Laud's imprisonment in 1640 and execution in 1645. Moreover, Charles' attempt to enforce Anglicanism in Scotland led to rebellion in that country in 1637, which eventually forced him to summon Parliament once more in 1640. In addition, the queen, Henrietta Maria, was a Catholic, the daughter of King Henry IV of France, which made people suspect that Charles really aimed to reintroduce Catholicism, a suspicion that was in all likelihood unfounded but which was nevertheless effective in anti-royal propaganda.

There was thus more than enough reasons for large sectors of the English people to oppose King Charles. When Parliament was once more summoned on 3 November 1640, only a small minority supported the king. Parliament now introduced a series of anti-royal measures, including the arrest and execution of the king's leading councillor, Lord Strafford. However, an increasing minority eventually found that the anti-royalist measures went too far and turned to support the king, who now made some, relatively minor concessions. When the Civil War broke out in summer 1642, a number of moderates who had earlier supported Parliament joined the king.

The Civil War led to the victory of Parliament, the execution of Charles in 1649, the proclamation of an English republic and the dictatorship of Oliver Cromwell, the leader of the Parliamentarian army, until his death in 1658. Already in 1660, the monarchy was restored without much resistance and without any firm guarantees from the new king, Charles' son Charles II, to respect the reforms that had been introduced since the deposition of his father. The king's defeat had not led to the victory of Parliament; on the contrary, Parliament became the object of repeated purges. There were also suggestions that Cromwell should become king but he refused. He was nevertheless the real ruler and managed to uphold some degree of stability, but his death in 1658 and the succession of his son Richard led to a breakdown, which paved the way for the restoration. The victory of Parliament after the Civil War was thus a mixed blessing. Cromwell apparently believed that Parliament would come to the 'right' conclusion without any suggestion from himself but was repeatedly disappointed and reacted by purging it. Thus, he showed even less skill in handling Parliament than the Stuarts had done.[46] The taxes also became heavier than they had been during Charles' reign, due to the money needed to pay for the Civil War. In short, royal government was replaced by military dictatorship, not by a republican constitution.

Charles II was the last real baroque ruler, with a lavish court, plenty of mistresses, heavy drinking and a lot of entertainment. As a person, he was very different from his father who was a devoted husband and led an impeccable private life. Charles II was said to have had Catholic sympathies, but generally does not seem to have been very religious, as illustrated by the following story told by the court chaplain. When he was preaching at court, most of the congregation, including the king, was asleep. The chaplain addressed Lord Lauderdale, one of the sleepers, in the following way: 'My Lord, I am sorry to interrupt your repose, but I must beg you that you will not snore quite so loud, lest you should awaken His Majesty.'[47] Politically, however, Charles held similar ideas as his father, but he was more flexible and showed greater skill in handling people. Charles was succeeded by his brother, James II, who was a Catholic and tried to make Catholicism tolerated. This led to his deposition and replacement by his daughter Mary and her husband William of Orange in 1688. Although no detailed constitution was proclaimed, the basic principles for the rights of Parliament and the limited power of the king were settled, notably in the Declaration of Rights of 1689.

There has been less discussion among historians about the events of 1688–90 than about the previous Civil War.[48] English society was also clearly less divided at the time; James had little support in England; his main adherents were the Scots and above all the Irish. Not surprisingly, his defeat introduced a long period of suppression of the Irish. In contrast to the Civil War, when the main division was between High Church Anglicans and Puritans, both groups were now united against Catholicism, which was hated by the majority of the English population. In addition, powerful London merchants – the ones who invited William to England – might have regarded the union with the Dutch Republic as a means to commercial success.[49]

In practice, the Glorious Revolution laid the foundation for the English parliamentary system that has lasted until the present. Once more, we are faced with the problem of causation. Was this the logical development of the English democracy back to the Middle Ages in accordance with the Whig view or the result of fortuitous circumstances in the late seventeenth century? There are some obvious arguments in favour of the latter view. In the 1640s, the country was divided between two parties of approximately equal strength, which resulted in a prolonged civil war. By contrast, the king was stronger in 1688 than he had been in the 1640s. Thanks to French subsidies, Charles II was able to rule without Parliament during the last five years of his reign and James II had at his disposal a strong standing army and navy.[50] Nevertheless, these forces turned against him and joined his enemies. The reason for this is most probably that he had converted to Catholicism. Thus, if he had remained a Protestant, he might have retained the loyalty of the army, prevented the victory of Parliament and made England an absolute monarchy according to the French model.[51]

The problem with this reasoning is that contra-factual theories can only to a limited extent be used to construct an alternative future. It is reasonable to assume that James II would not have been deposed in 1688 if he had not been a Catholic but apart from that, English history might have developed in a multiplicity of ways that cannot be easily predicted. To take one example: In 1685, Charles II's illegitimate son, the Duke of Monmouth, led a rebellion against James II which failed and led to his execution shortly afterwards. If he had succeeded, it would no doubt have led to a contra-factual theory to the effect that if he had failed, James would have remained on the throne until his death in 1701, which would have enabled him to introduce a number of changes. Further arguments against the idea of English absolutism in the period include that fact that James' Catholicism was largely the direct cause of his conflicts with Parliament; he tried to introduce some measures in favour of religious freedom, which were in practice intended to favour Catholics. Actually, it has been argued that his reign represented a liberal move against the strict Protestant orthodoxy of the previous period and not necessarily a step towards royal absolutism.[52]

Thus, if James had remained a Protestant, these conflicts might not have taken place. On the other hand, as most of his provocations of Parliament were results of his religious policy, he might also have had a better relationship to this body. Moreover, England at the time was developing into a great colonial power with a strong merchant aristocracy which resented royal privileges and which would hardly have been willing to accept absolutism according to the French model. Finally, it may be pointed out that increased militarization is hardly the only reason for French absolutism. More important is the fact that constitutional government had never worked in France. As demonstrated by the wars of religion, the Fronde and other internal conflicts, rebellion against the king led to chaos and internal division. By contrast, despite Cromwell's limited success, the English Civil War had not resulted in chaos, and England had repeatedly shown that there were alternatives to royal government and, above all, that opposition against the king did not automatically lead to regional division. Thus, despite the changes in the late seventeenth century, we have to take into account the long-term differences between England and France, going back to the thirteenth century.

The difference between France and England

In a short summary of English history from 1327 onwards, Charles Tilly lists a series of regicides and civil wars, concluding that 'armed struggles over the royal power and royal succession continued for three centuries, until the Glorious Revolution in 1688 set the House of Orange on the throne'.[53] Despite exaggeration of the amount of conflict in the period and the somewhat curious mention of the House of Orange as the last in the series of English dynasties, Tilly points to a characteristic feature of English history. More kings were deposed or killed in England than in any other country of Western Christendom during this period, seven altogether. Nevertheless, it does not follow from this that England was also more affected by internal struggles than other countries. On the contrary, despite only one example of regicide in Castile between 1252 and 1479, a large part of this period was marked by civil wars and struggles over the succession. In a similar way, France had considerably more dynastic continuity after 987 than England, but at least as much civil war, including the disastrous reign of the incapacitated Charles VI and the wars of religion. Thus, we must conclude that the absence of a king or conflict over the throne was less disastrous in England than in most other countries.

The new kings were approved by Parliament and were relatively soon able to take over the government. Even the period 1455–85, commonly referred to as the Wars of the Roses, only included shorter periods of open war and no long-term division of the country between two or more rulers. In a similar way, royal minorities, which were periods of crisis in most countries, were relatively peaceful. This is further confirmed by the almost sensational fact that four changes of religion took place over a period of 30 years in the mid-sixteenth century without a civil war. Admittedly, the changes were not without bloodshed; more nobles were executed during this period than at any time before or after, in addition to other victims of religious persecution. This, however, forms evidence in the same direction; a corresponding number of executions of nobles would probably have led to open war in most other countries. Finally, it must be considered even more remarkable that a radical change of religion took place during a period of regency, that of Edward VI, who died at the age of 16, having ruled for six years (1547–53). In this case, the regents did not confine themselves to keeping the government going until an adult king could take charge but introduced major reform, a sharper break with Catholicism than in the reign of Henry VIII. Thus, the regents acted on behalf of the monarchy as an institution in the absence of a fully capable king. Concerning the other regencies between 1200 and 1700, of Henry III (1216–32), Richard II (1377–82), Henry VI (1422–37), Edward V (1483), none of them were entirely peaceful but the adult reigns of the first three were significantly more troublesome than their minorities.

Finally, there is a parallel to the Civil War already in the mid-thirteenth century, namely, the Baronial Rebellion of 1258–67 against King Henry III. The barons, with considerable popular support, reacted against the king's costly foreign policy and forced him to accept a committee of barons to govern the country together with him, in clear conflict with normal practice.[54] The French king Louis IX, who acted as an arbiter between the two parties, but pronounced in favour of the king, is reported to have said that he would rather break clods behind a plough than to be king in this way.[55] The rebellion was ultimately unsuccessful but did show the barons' ability to govern the country, at least for a short time, under the leadership of Simon de Montfort (1264–65), and did not lead to a weakening of the central power. Moreover, it was an important factor in the development of Parliament in the following period.

Thus, whether or not England was more peaceful than France, the country was certainly more able to handle crises, notably that of the absence of a king or a divided monarchy. This in turn questions the idea that the survival of Parliament in the seventeenth century was just the result of some favourable accidents. The basic factor was the development of a national aristocracy closely linked to the king as well as to the local gentry and commoners, whose conflicts and struggles were always over the central power in the country, not aiming at creating separate regions outside royal control.

The explanation of the difference between England and France must to some extent be sought in geography and ecology. England was a small country with sufficient agricultural land to support a large population and with easy communications, which allowed considerable centralization. Situated on an island, it was also relatively protected against attacks from abroad. Even Anglo-Saxon England seems to have been remarkably centralized and William's conquest developed this centralization further by establishing a Norman secular and clerical aristocracy to rule the country together with the king. The following internal struggles were all about the central power in the country; there was no attempt to create a separate local power independent of the king.

By contrast, post-Carolingian France was largely a collection of principalities under the nominal suzerainty of the king, which is not surprising, considering the size of the country and the difficulties of its terrain. Compared to his German counterpart, the French king's success in converting this area into a real kingdom under his rule was remarkable and made France, despite its weaknesses, the leading country on the European Continent until the unification of Germany in 1870. Next to England, it was also the wealthiest; no other continental power had larger incomes and could muster a larger army in the seventeenth and eighteenth centuries. The Austrian monarchy, with about the same number of people as France, had only one-fifth of the French tax incomes. Spain, with less than half the population of France but with a colonial empire, also had around one-fifth, 110 million pounds *tournois* against 500 million.[56]

In this connection, we also have to point to the financial consequences of the fact that France was a Catholic country. Admittedly, the king of France had already achieved considerable control of the Church in the Middle Ages, which was further extended in the following period. The king controlled appointments to higher ecclesiastical offices, the clergy were normally his loyal supporters and the Church gave substantial contributions to the government in the form of 'gifts', while insisting on its freedom from taxation. Nevertheless, these payments amounted to considerably less than ordinary taxes and the clergy were not state functionaries in the same way as in Protestant, particularly Lutheran, countries. On the other hand, neither were the majority of royal officials. Finally, with the largely aristocratic character of the higher clergy, the Church served to strengthen the traditional character of French society based on landownership and prestigious offices. One of the most radical reforms introduced during the Revolution was the confiscation of ecclesiastical lands and the suppression of the monasteries in return for state salaries for the clergy, measures largely introduced for financial reasons. This led to papal condemnation and a bitter conflict during which many priests, who had been positive in the beginning, turned against the Revolution.

A comparison between England and the Dutch Republic, on the one hand, and France, on the other, in the late seventeenth and early eighteenth centuries seems to form a perfect confirmation of the thesis about capital and coercion. Thanks to their capital, the two former were able to finance their wars while retaining their constitutional government, whereas the latter had to develop absolute monarchy to raise the necessary sums. However, a more long-term perspective questions this conclusion. The constitutional difference between England and France can be traced back to the thirteenth century or even earlier, whereas the economic one is mainly a product of the seventeenth century. Even in the eighteenth century, the landed aristocracy largely dominated Parliament. Capital is thus more likely to have been the result of constitutionalism than vice versa. Moreover, England had a strong state during the whole period, despite the fact that it was weak militarily until the second half of the seventeenth century.

By contrast, the militarization of France from the sixteenth century onwards did not lead to a corresponding strengthening of the state. The king increased his power, the number of officials increased and the court at Versailles formed a visual expression of the king's glory, but the venality of offices resulted in an inefficient administration over which the king had little control. In the end, the regime broke down, largely because of financial problems for the king and his government. It would therefore seem that the French state would have been better off with less war and a smaller army. Concerning the question of capital, France did participate in the overseas expansion, but was less successful in this, largely because of its absolutism and venal bureaucracy. In both cases, we are therefore dealing with long-term constitutional differences, which influenced the relative success in building up capital.

Would a greater amount of direct taxation granted by central assemblies parallel to the English Parliament have been a realistic alternative to the sales of offices? Would assemblies where the nobles were represented have been willing to impose taxes that they were liable to pay themselves? If so, they would certainly have demanded a say in the use of those taxes and might have refused to support some of the wars the king wanted. Given the record of noble rebellions and Louis XIV's experience with the Fronde, it is also understandable that Louis XIV did not want such assemblies. However, then there was no alternative to the venality of offices.

It would seem that the best way for the king to improve his finances would have been to wage less war. As pointed out by many scholars, France did not have the advantage of England of being an island and was consequently subject to greater threats from its neighbours. On the other hand, with the possible exception of the wars of religion, when the country was divided, and the 1630s and 1640s, when a total victory of the Emperor in Germany, combined with the close alliance between the German and Spanish Habsburgs, might pose the threat of encirclement, it is difficult to see that France was under any great threat from abroad. As long as it avoided internal division, France was a strong country surrounded by weaker neighbours. The wars were therefore more probably the result of the king's search for wealth and glory by foreign conquest. Although the aim of historical research is to explain what people in the past actually did rather than what they ought to have done, we can at least question the current theory of the importance of warfare for state formation and conclude that an important explanation for the French king's relative failure in this respect was the frequency of his wars. Thus, the example of France shows that war might not only strengthen the state but also weaken it. The widespread sales of offices would seem to have resulted in a number of officers with little to do as well as to reduce the government's influence over its local representatives.

The examples discussed so far clearly point to the importance of capital in the seventeenth and eighteenth centuries. Colonial and inter-European trade and manufacture created great fortunes which enabled the Dutch Republic with two million inhabitants to mobilize military forces strong enough to defeat Spain and France with many times larger populations and even combining this with a higher standard of living for its inhabitants. Already before discussing the rest of Europe, we can conclude that a purely agrarian state would have had great difficulties in competing internationally during this period. It also seems likely that there was a connection between capital and constitutionalism, most probably in the sense that constitutionalism under certain circumstances would lead to capital accumulation by creating the conditions for free competition in the economic field. Whereas both seem to have been present from early on in the Netherlands, constitutional government is certainly older than capital in England.

The Spanish kingdoms

The difference between England and France has some parallel in the Iberian peninsula, where Aragon-Catalonia resembled England and Castile resembled France. Aragon-Catalonia had a strong assembly and limited monarchy.[57] Here burghers, notably those of Barcelona, played an important part together with the nobility, which led to the development of a reasonably effective constitutional government.

During the period of expansion in the twelfth and thirteenth centuries, a large part of the population of Castile had been militarily active and received corresponding political influence, notably through the governments of the towns. The country did have a medieval assembly of some importance, although the king was stronger here than in Aragon. After the great conquests in the first half of the thirteenth century, Castile was by far the largest kingdom on the Iberian Peninsula. It thus had similar problems as France. Moreover, it consisted of parts that had earlier been independent kingdoms and it was thinly populated, notably in the centre, the Castilian Plain, which consists of dry and barren highland, mostly used for sheep farming. This became even more dominant with the reduction of the population resulting from the expulsion of the Moors. The prolonged wars against them had necessitated a certain unity under the king's leadership, whereas the period after the death of the great conquering King Ferdinand III (1252) was marked by a series of inner struggles. Their cause was the increasing power and wealth of the nobles who appropriated most of the lands conquered from the Moors in the thirteenth century, combined with the absence of further foreign expansion. The troubled period continued until the reign of the two 'Catholic kings', Ferdinand of Aragon (1479–1516) and Isabella of Castile (1474–1504), who united the two countries in a personal union and whose reigns have traditionally been regarded as the most glorious in Spanish history.

Aragon was somewhat more peaceful in the Middle Ages, possibly because of a more expansive foreign policy, directed towards conquests in the Mediterranean area, Sicily, Sardinia, eventually also Southern Italy and the Byzantine Empire during its period of decline in the fourteenth century. Despite its internal troubles, however, Castile was the more successful of the two in the later Middle Ages. Aragon's expansion in the Mediterranean came to an end, partly as the result of the rise of the Ottoman Empire, whereas Castilian merchants profited from the trade with England and Flanders. In addition, Castile, together with Portugal, which had enjoyed internal peace under a strong monarchy during most of the period, began the expansion towards the west and south that eventually led to the Great Discoveries. The difference between the two countries survived the personal union between them in 1479 and continued until the defeat of Aragon during the War of the Spanish Succession (1702–14), when the country became integrated into the larger Spanish kingdom. Thus, when Aragon did not develop in the same way in the early modern period as England and the Dutch Republic, the explanation must largely be sought in the union with Castile, in which it was clearly the weaker partner, combined with the general weakening of the Mediterranean powers during this period. Nor did the country profit from the trade with America and was therefore probably too weak economically to develop in the same way as England and the Dutch Republic.

Constitutionally, the foundation of royal absolutism in Castile was laid during the troubled period of the fifteenth century. Both John II (1406–54) and Henry IV (1454–74), neither of whom was a particularly strong king, solemnly proclaimed royal absolutism and resisted any claims from the nobles or the *cortes* to share the power of the ruler.[58] Their successors, Ferdinand and Isabella and later the Habsburgs, made the claim a reality. As was the case in contemporary France, the inner struggles had demonstrated that only a strong monarchy was able to create stability in the country. Moreover, the king's main potential rivals, the members of the high nobility, discovered that they could live with royal absolutism; they retained their tax exemption and privileges and monopolized the high offices in the royal administration.

A curious feature of royal absolutism in Spain is the abolition of royal coronation. The last coronation in Castile was that of John I in 1379 and the last in Aragon that of Ferdinand I in 1414. The king also lacked the normal regalia, sceptre, crown and throne. A possible explanation for this is the Muslim influence; for Muslim rulers, such distinctions were blasphemy. Nevertheless, the king was clearly different from other humans, as expressed in the development towards absolute monarchy and in the strong emphasis on the Spanish king as the defender of the Christian faith.[59]

The revival of Spain in the following period seems to have been the result, partly of the political skill of Ferdinand and Isabella and partly of the new opportunities for the nobility resulting from the Great Discoveries and the ambitious foreign policy in the sixteenth and seventeenth centuries. However, when the Castilian *cortes* dwindled into insignificance in the sixteenth century whereas the English Parliament prospered, the reason was not that the king of Spain had plenty of gold and silver from America while the poor English monarch depended on taxes.[60] The Spanish king lived from hand to mouth and went bankrupt eight times in the period 1557–1680, because of costly wars and bad financial management, including the tax exemption of the nobles. In 1647–48, the estimated annual expenses amounted to four times the income.[61] Although the English king at the time was far from rich, he managed better financially than his Spanish counterpart, partly because he was less involved in war and partly because he could tax the nobility with consent from Parliament. Like France, Spain thus serves as an example of war weakening rather than strengthening the state.

In several respects, however, Spain faced greater problems than France. The Habsburgs, who inherited the Spanish throne in 1516, used Spain and its colonies as a base for an ambitious foreign policy that involved the country in an almost continuous war throughout the sixteenth century. Apart from the colonies, which were exploited in a way that gave the country significantly less surplus than its competitors, Spain was not a rich country, with relatively poor agricultural land and less than half the population of France. Spain was also more composite than France. In addition to the fact that the three main kingdoms on the Iberian peninsula, Castile, Aragon and Valencia, were largely independent units, only joined in a personal union, the king of Spain also governed various other largely separate units, like the Kingdom of Naples and other Italian units, the Low Countries and Franche Comté. The strict religious policy, including the persecution and eventual expulsion of Moors and Jews, weakened the country economically as well as intellectually. Finally, a series of weak kings after the death of Philip II (1598), notably Charles II (1665–1700), contributed further to the decline of the country. The new dynasty from 1700, the Bourbons, resulted in some improvement but the country never regained its position as a great power.[62]

Absolutism and constitutionalism in agrarian states: the case of Scandinavia

The comparison between Britain and the Dutch Republic, on the one hand, and France and Spain, on the other, has largely confirmed the theory of a connection between capital and constitutionalism and an agrarian economy and absolutism. Although not purely agrarian, France was clearly less commercialized than the two other countries. However, other cases are more difficult to fit in. Let us first consider Denmark and Sweden.[63]

These two countries, today regarded as largely similar and examples of Scandinavian democracy and welfare state, followed different paths in the early modern period. Sweden was one of the few countries where the medieval Diet continued into the nineteenth century – it was transformed into a modern parliament with two chambers in 1866 – whereas Denmark became the most absolutist country in Europe, actually the only one with a formal constitution granting the king absolute power. This does not correspond to any great social difference between the two countries. Both were largely agrarian, with a strong aristocracy, but Denmark was clearly more urbanized and commercialized than Sweden in the sixteenth and first half of the seventeenth century. Scania was the centre of the lucrative trade in herring and Bergen in Norway – at the time (1536–1814) a part of Denmark – played a similar part in the trade in stockfish. Moreover, timber and eventually also metal from Norway were important export articles. In addition, the king of Denmark profited from the control of the most important sea route in Northern Europe, through the Sound (Øresund) which until 1658 was surrounded by Danish land on both sides. The only comparable asset for Sweden was the export of iron from Dalarna, which, however, had the added advantage that it could be used in the country's own armament industry.

Thus, according to the theory, we should have expected the opposite result, constitutionalism in Denmark and absolutism in Sweden. The actual explanation must therefore be sought in the development of the two countries in the seventeenth century. This can be summarized in one sentence: Swedish success and Danish failure in war. Denmark had traditionally been the strongest kingdom in Scandinavia and in the later Middle Ages attempted to unite the three kingdoms in a union, originally entered in Kalmar in 1397. The union between Denmark and Norway became permanent, while Sweden after a series of conflicts finally left the union in 1521 and founded its own dynasty. From the second half of the sixteenth century, Sweden began to expand in the Baltic area, fought a long war against Poland after a short period of personal union between the two countries and in 1630 became involved in the Thirty Years War, which made it into a great power in the Baltic Area and Northern Germany. By contrast, Denmark most of the time conducted a more peaceful policy but eventually became alarmed by the Swedish success and tried to prevent it, both by getting involved in the Thirty Years War (1625–29) and by a series of wars against Sweden which led to the loss of all the Danish land north of the Sound and the south-eastern part of Norway. These defeats then led to the introduction of absolutism in Denmark (1660–61).

Denmark in the seventeenth century was a wealthy agricultural country where the nobles owned most of the land and shared the central power with the king through the council of the realm.[64] By contrast, the wider assembly of estates, dating back to the thirteenth century, was of little importance and met rarely. The council restricted the king's power in many ways and was generally reluctant to engage in war. Thus, Christian IV had to enter the Thirty Years War in 1625 as a German prince, not as king of Denmark, because the council vetoed the war. For this purpose, he was able to use the Sound toll, which amounted to around one-fourth or a little more of the royal revenues in the first half of the seventeenth century and which was available without consent from the Council.[65] The result of the war indicates that the council was right. Although Christian escaped without ceding land, Jutland was occupied by enemy forces for more than a year and the war was costly and destructive. The war against Sweden (1657–58), also the result of the king's initiative, was even more disastrous. It was shortly afterwards (1658–60) followed by a new one, in which Sweden was the aggressor and which ended with the return of some of the lands ceded in the previous one.

The introduction of absolutism in Denmark was the result of the critical financial situation after the wars of 1657–60. The war debt amounted to a sum so large that its interest exceeded the annual income of the kingdom. To deal with this problem, an assembly of nobles, burghers and clerics was summoned in Copenhagen on 10 September 1660, which ended in an unanimous decision to make the monarchy hereditary, to return the election charter to the king and leave it to him to organize the government of the realm. On 10 January 1661, the king issued a charter proclaiming absolute monarchy, which was then formally accepted by the assembly and later by assemblies summoned for the purpose in the other countries under the Danish crown.

The introduction of absolutism led to a series of reforms. The debt was largely repaid by massive sales of crown lands. The loss of revenues resulting from this nevertheless had to be compensated for by taxes which increased drastically and had to be paid by the whole population, including the nobility, although large estates were later exempted. Moreover, extensive and costly military reforms were introduced, which created a modern army and navy, partly based on conscription of the peasants, partly on mercenaries. The most important source of recruitment of soldiers was Norway, which had the same advantage as Sweden of peasants who produced relatively little surplus and thus were more easily available for military purposes. The new army and navy performed well in the next wars against Sweden in 1675–79 and 1709–20, although neither of them led to recovery of lost territory.

Finally, a number of administrative reforms were introduced, partly influenced by the French departmental system.[66] However, the administration did not consist of ministers responsible for particular sectors, but of colleges of officials who were supposed to prepare the cases for the king's decision. Each member was to present his own proposal, so that the king would not in practice be bound by unanimity among his councillors. Only very minor decisions were left to the members of the colleges; which of course meant a heavy burden for the king. The first three absolute kings nevertheless personally decided a large number of cases, notably Frederick IV (1699–1730), who was extremely hard-working. In the local administration, the old officials, appointed by the king, usually nobles, who governed their districts like a kind of mini-kingdoms, were replaced by specialists, responsible respectively for the military, judicial and general administrative sector. The appointment of officials was based on previous administrative experience and education and was subject to detailed control by the royal government.

The introduction of absolutism has often been regarded as the solution to Denmark-Norway's problems in the first half of the seventeenth century. Although most historians blame the kings for beginning the wars without sufficient preparation, they have usually explained the lack of military preparation by the noble council's unwillingness to spend money on the army and the stalemate between the king and the council. Apparently, Denmark therefore forms a perfect example of the inefficiency of constitutional government in agrarian states and absolutism as the solution to the problem. Recently, however, this interpretation has been questioned.[67] Both the size and capacity of the army and the bureaucracy increased gradually throughout the period, while the council actually strengthened its power in the 1640s and 1650s. Thus, a modernization might possibly have taken place even without absolutism. Whether Denmark would also have avoided war if the kings had followed the advice of the council, is an open question, as Sweden was clearly superior militarily and had an incentive to expand at the cost of Denmark–Norway. In any case, the blame for the actual, unsuccessful wars falls on the king. Concerning the country's relative success in the later wars, this was not exclusively the result of internal reforms but also of the fact that Denmark–Norway was now part of great coalitions of Sweden's enemies.

Rather than being the solution to the country's long-term problems, the introduction of absolutism may therefore be explained by specific events in 1657–60. The king had distinguished himself during the siege of Copenhagen in 1658–60 while the nobles were blamed for having been unwilling to make sacrifices for the sake of the country. The king's main supporters were the clergy and the burghers, in addition to the army, which was now less dominated by the nobility than previously. In addition, the king could exploit the resentment of the lower nobility against the higher nobility.

Turning to Sweden, the advantage of this country from a military point of view was that it was poor. It had some wealthy agricultural areas but large parts of the country consisted of forest and poor and thinly populated land. Thus, it had a relatively large agrarian population that could be used as soldiers without any great loss to agricultural production.[68] Most of the nobles were also relatively poor and more inclined to military adventure than their wealthier Danish counterparts. When Gustaf II Adolf landed in Germany in 1630 to join the German Protestants in their struggle against the Emperor, he commanded a small, but well-trained and experienced army from previous wars in Poland and the Baltic area. He was also a brilliant general and a charismatic figure who managed to involve the Swedish nobility and largely also the peasantry in the war effort. Sweden, in addition, had a long tradition, back to the fifteenth century, of political rhetoric addressed to the common people.

In the following years, the Swedish army was supplemented by mercenaries financed by French subsidies, although there was also a substantial recruitment of Swedes. During the Thirty Years War, its size was more than 100,000 men, an enormous number, considering that the population of the country was hardly more than 1 million. Around 20 per cent of the Swedish army at Breitenfeld consisted of native Swedes but this percentage declined in the following period. Native Swedes were also more often used for garrison duty and in addition formed an elite corps of the army.[69] When the French subsidies dried up later in the century, Charles XI

(1660–97) organized a new army based on conscription: the whole country was divided into districts in which a certain number of farms had to send one man to the army or navy – Sweden also had a strong navy, recruited from the population along the coast.[70] In this way, Sweden became the most militarized country in Europe in the seventeenth and early eighteenth century, a country in which around 30 per cent of all adult men died in war.[71] Sweden thus forms a clear counter-example to the theory of a connection between constitutional government and a strong commercial sector, the difficulty in making a landed nobility pay for war and the connection between militarization of an agrarian country and absolutism.

Both Sweden and Denmark are examples of the connection between warfare and state formation but differ regarding the constitutional consequences of this. The difference between the two countries can largely be explained by their previous history. The Danish council of the realm was a small and exclusive body with little contact with the rest of society, corresponding to the dominance of the aristocracy and the relative weakness of the common people. It could therefore easily be abolished during a period of crisis, with the support of the clergy, bourgeoisie and the lower nobility. By contrast, the internal and external struggles affecting Sweden in the fifteenth century show the importance of the common people, notably the gentry and miners of Dalarna, who were mobilized by the Sture at various assemblies. This in turn led to the formation of the Swedish Diet (Riksdag), which met for the first time with its later composition in 1527, but has its background in a series of meetings of popular assemblies in the previous period.[72] Sweden first established strong royal government in cooperation with the people and the nobility under Gustaf Vasa (1523–60) and then embarked on foreign conquest, although without introducing royal absolutism.

During the most successful of its wars of conquest, Gustaf Adolf's victories in the Baltic and Poland and the following participation in the Thirty Years War, the king and the regency after his death acted in close cooperation with the top nobility, which profited more than any other class from the country's new status as a great power. In particular, the Chancellor, Axel Oxenstjärna (1584–1654), one of the great statesmen of the seventeenth century, for a long time had held a central position in the government of the country. He was the leader of the first two regencies and played an important part in the adult reigns of Gustaf Adolf as well as his daughter Christina. Eventually, trade, industry, towns, intellectual life and universities expanded, which consequently increased the importance of burghers, clerics, civil servants and professionals of various kinds, but this was the consequence of strong government and military success, not its cause. Sweden thus shows that constitutional government could be as efficient as absolutism even in a largely agrarian society. The only way for a small and poor country like Sweden to become a great power was to mobilize the nobility and the people for this purpose – in addition to receiving subsidies from abroad. In the following period, however, there were tendencies in a similar direction as in Denmark. The Diet reacted against the dominant position of the aristocratic council and supported an increase in the king's power. Thus, the period 1672–1718 is often referred to as a period of absolutism, but the Diet still existed, although it met less often and was less important.

In the context of European power politics in the seventeenth and early eighteenth centuries, both Denmark and Sweden may be considered failures. Despite some military success, Denmark never managed to regain the lost provinces and Sweden's period as a great power came to an end with the defeat by Russia at Poltava (1709) and the Peace of Nystad in 1721. Both countries were ultimately too small to compete with the emerging great powers in the region, Prussia and, above all, Russia, in addition to the two great naval powers, Britain and the Dutch Republic. However, they would probably have managed better if they had been allies rather than enemies. Sweden, with its Baltic empire and Denmark with its control of the Sound would seem a formidable combination, but a long tradition of enmity and rivalry made such an alliance unlikely.

By contrast, if we consider the internal conditions in the two countries, the picture becomes different. Neither of them declared bankruptcy and both overcame the financial crises resulting from the wars. Both developed reasonably effective and competent bureaucracies with an increasing level of education and neither practised sales of offices. Although the importance of absolutism for the recovery of Denmark after 1660 is open to discussion, the regime that developed in this country in the following period must be regarded as reasonably efficient.

Both countries entered a more peaceful period after 1720. Denmark had almost continual peace until 1807, whereas Sweden was involved in some wars against Russia, although far less than in the previous century. Both were influenced by the Enlightenment in the second half of the century and introduced some liberal reforms regarding the economy, agriculture and freedom of expression. To what extent their different constitutions led to differences in this respect has been discussed in a great comparative project on the decision-making process, which concludes that the differences were not dramatic but that they did exist.[73] Absolutist Denmark was not arbitrary and constitutionalist Sweden was not democratic. As a matter of fact, Sweden had a more developed and efficient bureaucracy than Denmark. Whereas most of Sweden was governed directly from the capital in Stockholm, the Danish nobility still retained some administrative power over their peasants. Norway was from this point of view more absolutist in practice, as this country had only very few estates, but here the distance involved greater delegation to local officials. Both in Denmark-Norway and Sweden, the subjects had ample opportunity to influence the authorities through petitions. In both countries, these were most likely to favour wealthy and influential people, although peasants also made frequent use of them, sometimes with success. Here, however, the different constitutions led to significant differences. In Denmark-Norway, the subjects had to confine themselves to asking the authorities for a certain course of action, whereas in Sweden they had the opportunity to engage in a political process through their elected representatives. Thus, Sweden resembles England in having a strong tradition of popular representation and cooperation between the nobility and the commoners.

Absolutism and constitutionalism in agrarian states: Prussia, Austria and East Central Europe

Dresden is one of the most beautiful cities in Germany, now lovingly restored to its ancient glory after the bombing in 1945. Its beauty is largely the work of the Duke Elector Frederick Augustus II who was also king of Poland. He is usually referred to as Augustus the Strong, the latter because of his tall and strong body; he used to break horseshoes with his bare hands. He was cultured and had intellectual interests; he loved music and opera and built the largest opera house in Germany. He was a great lover of beauty in women as well as in buildings – he had at least eleven mistresses and numerous children; contemporary rumour lists more than 300. He is buried in the largest and most distinguished of his realms, Poland, but his heart rests in the Hofkirche in Dresden and legend has it that it beats every time a beautiful woman enters the church.

Saxony was one of the richest territories of northern Germany and during Augustus' reign it would immediately seem to have been the nearest to fill the power vacuum in the area after the Swedish defeat in the Great Nordic War (1700–21). The union with Poland seemed a step in this direction, as did also Augustus' success in dynastic marriages. In a conversation with his neighbour, Frederick William I of Prussia, notorious for his stinginess and austerity, Augustus is reported to have said: 'When Your Majesty collects a ducat, you just add it to your treasure, while I prefer to spend it, so that it comes back to me three-fold.'[74] There may have been something to be said in favour of this argument in the period of Baroque lavishness but in this concrete case, the comparison turned out to Frederick William's favour. When Augustus died in 1733, he left an enormous debt to his son and successor, whereas Frederick William seven years later left a full treasury and an army of 81,000 men, better trained and equipped than its Saxon counterpart, which only numbered 30,000. The difference between the two countries was then expressed dramatically under Frederick William's successor Frederick II.

In the mid-seventeenth century, Prussia consisted of three parts, separated by other countries, Brandenburg with the capital, Berlin, in the middle, Cleve, in the west, in Rhineland, and Prussia, in the east. Cleve was the most commercialized part but was small and not particularly wealthy; the two others were both agrarian and relatively poor. Although belonging to the larger German principalities with its ruler, the margrave, having the status of elector, he was the poorest of the four original secular electors. Prussia's rise to a European great power took place over a span of around 100 years under four rulers, three of whom were great statesmen, namely, Frederick William, called the Great Elector (1640–88), Frederick III (elector, 1688–1701 and king as Frederick I, 1701–13), Frederick William I (1713–40) and Frederick II (1740–86). By contrast, none of their predecessors had been particularly distinguished. Frederick II later described the Great Elector's predecessor George William (1619–40) as 'incapable of governing', whereas a modern historian has commented that his worst defect was not indecision of mind but the absence of any mind to make up.[75] The Elector himself created the strong Prussian state with permanent taxes, a well-trained standing army and the more or less absolute power of the prince. He also had some military successes, including the victory over the Swedes by Fehrbellin in 1675, and made some conquests of territory, notably that of Eastern Pomerania, which gave access to the sea. However, he had to return Western Pomerania to Sweden because of Louis XIV's intervention at the peace conference in 1679.

His successor was the least important of the four, but succeeded in gaining the royal title. Frederick William I was a strict, efficient and authoritarian ruler who greatly increased the army, created the system of compulsory conscription (1733) and forced the nobles to become officers.[76] On his accession to the throne, he drastically reduced the number of courtiers and sold off or gave away most of the jewels, gold and silver, fine wine and beautiful furniture collected by his father. Except for music, he had no cultural interests and the centre of his social life was the 'Tobacco College', a wholly masculine assembly consisting of councillors, senior officials, army officers or various visitors, including men of letters, who gathered in the evenings for conversation over strong drink and pipes of tobacco. Everybody was free to speak his mind and the tone was informal and often crude. Frederick William was cautious in his external policy and reluctant to risk his beloved army in warfare, but extended his country significantly thanks to Sweden's defeat in the Great Nordic War (1721).

By contrast, Frederick II was a gambler who fought two prolonged wars against numerically largely superior enemies and won a number of spectacular victories. He also conquered wealthy Silesia and joined the two eastern parts of his kingdom to each other in the first partition of Poland (1772). In contrast to his father, he was a great intellectual, loved arts and music, was a composer and a distinguished writer and a friend of artists and philosophers. He became a symbol of enlightened despotism, at least to foreign intellectuals, while his subjects might have found that the difference between him and his father was not too great; government and administration continued in much the same way, but Frederick attached greater importance to the general education of his administrators than his father had done. He also distinguished more clearly between himself and the state, regarding himself as the servant of the state and obliged to obey the rules by which it was governed. In particular, he reformed the courts of law and improved the education of judges and judicial personnel. Already at his accession to the throne, he abolished judicial torture. He also reduced the number of crimes to be punished by death and abolished the cruellest forms of execution.

He not only conquered new provinces but also tried to govern them in a way that made the conquest acceptable to the population. He went further than his predecessors in the direction of religious tolerance – he was religiously indifferent himself – and accepted the religion of his new subjects. He also allowed some freedom of expression, although he did not abolish censorship. He tolerated Jews and Catholics and even allowed the latter to build a cathedral in the centre of Berlin. Frederick built a palace for himself in Potsdam, Sanssouci, supported cultural activities and gathered intellectuals around him but generally spent little on luxury and courtliness; he regarded himself as a servant of the state.

Prussia's success must to a considerable extent be explained by the quality of its rulers until the late eighteenth century – the following ones were not remarkable, but by then, capable ministers, bureaucrats and generals took over. However, the circumstances are also important. Prussia would seem like a combination of Sweden and Denmark. Like Sweden, it was poor and like Denmark, it had suffered in war. It had been torn between the Protestants and the Emperor during the Thirty Years War and had suffered plunder and Swedish occupation. The Great Elector had spent his youth in Holland and wanted to transform his small country without natural borders into a great sea power in the way the Dutch had done. The experience of the Thirty Years War must also have made it somewhat easier to persuade the assembly of the need for a strong army, although this was not achieved without problems.[77] The Elector Frederick William I combined nego-tiation and bullying for more than 20 years to make the various assemblies grant the sums he demanded for his army and in the end succeeded in breaking their resistance and paving the way for absolute rule and further expansion of the army. Prussia thus becomes the only possible example of Finer's 'extraction–coercion cycle'.

However, some doubt has recently been raised about this conclusion. It has been suggested that the real issue between the Elector and the assemblies was religion rather than taxation.[78] Most of the country was Lutheran, but since 1613, the Elector, later King, had been a Calvinist. It seems that both the Elector Frederick William I and his namesake the king were genuinely engaged in Reformed Pro-testantism and that their austerity – particularly that of the latter – was inspired by this source. Both also actively promoted people who belonged to this confession, in addition to supporting the Pietistic Movement within Lutheranism, a movement more concerned with religious practice than with orthodoxy and therefore more open to cooperation with other confessions. Thus, while his predecessors had been content with the country remaining Lutheran, Frederick William actively propa-gated Calvinism and systematically appointed Calvinists to leading offices. Char-acteristically, he abolished the assemblies in his two Lutheran principalities, while he allowed the continued existence of the one in Calvinist Cleve. His namesake King Frederick William I continued the same policy, while going to extreme lengths in austerity.

Prussia would seem to be the very opposite of the Dutch Republic, agrarian and hierarchical rather than urban and democratic. As the majority of the population remained Lutheran, it cannot be regarded as an example of a Calvinist country, but it seems likely that Calvinism was of some importance for its political success. Another factor is geopolitics. There was a certain power vacuum in the east after the defeat of the imperial power in 1648, temporarily filled by Sweden, which, however, was vulnerable in the long run, as a small state on the other side of the sea than its German possessions. Another potential rival, Poland, also became more vulnerable from the mid-seventeenth century, partly because of a prolonged civil war, partly because of inefficiency. By modernizing according to the Swedish model, Prussia eventually defeated both these rivals and emerged as a great power in the mid-eighteenth century. In the next phase, however, Prussia underwent largely the same experience as Sweden. It turned out that the country's financial basis was inadequate and it was defeated by France both in 1795 and 1806. Only with the acquisition of the wealthy and commercialized Rhineland and internal reforms that involved larger parts of the population in the government could Prussia develop into a great power in the nineteenth century.

Together with Denmark, Prussia forms an example of successful absolutism. By contrast, East Central Europe presents examples of failed constitutionalism. Here the aristocracies during the later Middle Ages had reversed the situation described by Otto of Freising in the twelfth century, taking control of much of the local administration and restricting the king's power. The assemblies were therefore dominated by the nobility. From the point of view of state formation, these assemblies and their privileges can often be regarded as reactionary, preserving the privileges of the most prominent members of the hereditary nobility. Some of the countries in which the nobility had the greatest success in defending its privileges, later succumbed to more efficient neighbours or became dissolved into petty principalities. The Hungarian defeat against the Ottomans at Mohacs in 1526 and the following conquest of most of Hungary have been explained by the weakening of the monarchy after the death of Matthias Corvinus (1490), when the nobility took over the government and neglected the army, but this interpretation has been challenged in recent scholarship. Martyn Rady[79] has pointed out that the changes after Matthias' death were largely a natural reaction to his costly policy of conquest which had led to four times higher taxes than previously. Moreover, these changes, including a reduced level of taxation, did not make the country defenceless, nor did they lead to a full control of the country by an exclusive high nobility. The Diet was still active with broad participation by the gentry. The king still had a court of 650 persons and the army that suffered the disastrous defeat at Mohacs in 1526 was large, modern and well-equipped. It must also be admitted that the Ottoman Empire in the early sixteenth century was a formidable adversary which repeatedly defeated large European armies. In a similar way, Bohemia, which had also developed a constitutional government based on the nobility and the bourgeoisie, was defeated when it rebelled against the emperor in 1618–20. Once more, there is doubt about the relative importance of internal and external conditions.

By contrast, Poland presents the main example of a failed constitutional state.[80] After the union with Lithuania in 1386, the new kingdom was by far the largest in Western Christendom. It covered the whole of present-day Ukraine and reached from the Baltic to the Black Sea and in the east included Belorussia and a part of modern Russia. It goes without saying that such a large and thinly populated area could not form a centralized state.[81] In particular, the eastern areas that had earlier formed the Duchy of Lithuania were dominated by strong chieftains with little respect for the authority of the monarch. Nevertheless, there was little in the history of Poland in the fifteenth and sixteenth centuries to suggest the later fate of the country. Poland had several strong and efficient monarchs during this period. It managed the divisions of the Reformation better than most western countries and stayed out of the Thirty Years War. Culturally, Poland was strongly influenced by the Renaissance and had close contacts with intellectual milieus in Western Europe. It is no coincidence that one of the most important scientific discoveries in the period was made in Poland, namely, the formulation of the heliocentric theory by Copernicus. Although Copernicus had studied in Italy in his youth, he spent the last 40 years of life in Poland, where he developed his theories.[82]

Traditionally, Poland had a numerous and strong nobility, corresponding to the character of its army, where the cavalry dominated longer than in most other countries. The Diet, the Sejm, dominated by the nobility, traditionally had a strong position in Polish politics. Its basis was the king's usual need of support for his decisions, which from the early thirteenth century led to the formation of regional assemblies. The principles that no member of the nobility could be arrested without legal procedure and of assent as necessary for taxation became law in the fifteenth century, which increased the importance of the Sejms. In 1468, the regional Sejms decided to join in a national assembly which in 1493 was divided into two chambers, the Senate, consisting of 81 bishops, palatines and castellans (i.e. high nobles) and the ordinary Sejm which consisted of 54 representatives from the lower nobility (*szlachta*) and the largest cities. From now on, the Sejm demanded influence on the election of kings, even if the new king was the son of the previous one, and posed conditions for the election. In 1569, Poland formally became an elective monarchy. The direct cause of this was the need to preserve the union with Lithuania at a time when strict dynastic succession would have led to different rulers in the two countries, but it was also the expression of a general trend.

The Polish Sejm is best known for its rule of *liberum veto*, i.e. that one member had the right to veto all the assembly's decisions. The rule was based on the idea of equality between all nobles, combined with that of representation: an elected member did not speak only for himself but for a larger constituency. The principle was not unknown in other medieval assemblies; it was far from obvious that a majority had the right to bind a minority. However, most other assemblies either developed a rule of majority vote or disappeared. Although the principle of veto existed from early on in Poland, it did not have really serious consequences until the seventeenth century. Earlier, dissenting deputies were often convinced or pressured to withdraw their objections. Moreover, a veto only concerned one particular decision, whereas later, from the mid-seventeenth century, it led to all decisions of a particular session being cancelled. This happened more and more often from the second half of the seventeenth century. In the eighteenth century, when Polish politics was largely controlled by Russia, the veto became an instrument to block any Polish attempt at reform. Characteristically, this was a part of Polish liberty the Russians were willing to defend at any price.

A dysfunctional political system forms part of the explanation for Poland's decline but this system is, on the other hand, largely a symptom of deeper problems. After all, the king and the Sejm had been able to work together reasonably well until the early seventeenth century and even after that, Poland had had strong and efficient rulers.

A Polish noble in the seventeenth century was an impressive figure. Poland was still considered a great power at the time and Polish nobles abroad made sure that nobody forgot it. When Krsysztof Ópalinski and his followers entered Paris in 1645 to collect King Wladyslaw IV's bride, Louise Marie de Gonzague, his horses were intentionally loosely shod, so that their solid gold horseshoes dropped off, to the joy of the Parisian people. Polish ambassadors would arrive in foreign capitals with regiments of private troops, dressed in lavish liveries and with horses with gold-embroidered velvet adorned by precious stones. Concerning a Polish embassy to Turkey in 1677, one of the hosts commented that the ambassador had brought too many to sign a peace and too few to fight a war. Inventories from noble families and descriptions of the dress of kings and princes give the same impression: coats and dresses stiff with gold and jewels, large collections of gold and emeralds and surrounded by numerous servants, in addition to private armies. The greater the man, the more people surrounded him.

The seventeenth century was a period of pomp and circumstance all over Europe, but the ostentation was probably greater in Poland than in most other countries. Above all, the contrast between this ostentation and the real wealth of the country was certainly greater than elsewhere. Poland was not a wealthy country in the seventeenth century. The gap between the small minority of great nobles and the rest of the population, including the majority of the nobility, had increased since the previous century. An important factor in this was the increasing economic difference between eastern and western Europe: the expansion of trade and manufacture in the west in contrast to the exclusively agrarian economy in the east. Polish grain and other agricultural products, cultivated by poor peasants working for noble landowners, were exported to the west by German or Dutch merchants in return for various luxury and industrial commodities, which meant that the main surplus of the trade went to the west. Most of the land was divided between great landowners with almost absolute power over their peasants. Landownership also became increasingly concentrated in the hands of a small elite during the sixteenth and seventeenth centuries. The great landowners wanted as little interference as possible from the king, a purpose that was well served by the need for unanimity in the assembly. A prolonged internal war in the mid-seventeenth century made the situation worse, as did also increasing competition from powerful neighbours, first, Sweden, then Prussia and, finally and most importantly, Russia.

The Polish state was badly equipped for this competition. Like most other countries, its finances were inadequate, but in contrast to them, little attempt was made to improve them. In the first half of the seventeenth century, its revenues were only slightly higher than those of Bavaria, whose size was a fraction of that of Poland, and only one-tenth of those of France, whose revenues were also inadequate. There was apparently little attempt to increase these revenues, in contrast to the strong pressure of military mobilization on the financial resources of many other countries at the time. One reason for this was that Poland had managed reasonably well in earlier wars. It had suffered some defeats against the Swedes but had had considerable success against the Russians and the Turks. As long as it remained neutral in the Thirty Years War, it had also little to fear from the German Emperor. This situation changed quickly and drastically in the late seventeenth and early eighteenth century with the rise of Prussia and Russia as the new great powers and the great Austrian victories over the Turks which made this country more likely to expand towards the north and east.

After a brief revival of Poland's fortunes under the warrior hero Jan III Sobieski (1674–96), who defeated the Turks at the gates of Vienna in 1683, decline set in. If we want a particular event as the turning-point, a night in 1698 when two young men sat drinking together suggests itself. The two were Augustus the Strong, Duke Elector of Saxony, newly elected king of Poland, and Tsar Peter I of Russia. Both were tall and strong and known to be able to drink any competitor under the table. The winner of the drinking contest in 1698 is unknown but the political winner eventually turned out to be Tsar Peter. On the morning after the party, the two men agreed on a plan: they would attack Sweden, a country still holding valuable possessions along the south-eastern shore of the Baltic Sea, of interest to both rulers. The moment seemed favourable; King Charles XI had recently died (1697) and been succeeded by his 15-year-old son Charles XII, who seemed an easy victim. In 1699 the two rulers, together with King Frederick IV of Denmark–Norway, declared war on Sweden.[83]

Charles, however, was no easy mark. He quickly invaded Zealand and forced King Frederick to leave the alliance, after which he inflicted a crushing defeat on the Russians at Narva in November 1700. Then he turned against Poland, which, however, was technically not at war with Sweden; Augustus had declared war as duke of Saxony. Charles did not care about such technicalities; he invaded Poland and replaced Augustus with a native Pole, Stanislaw Leszynski. Then he invaded Saxony and forced Augustus to abdicate as king of Poland. When Charles once more turned against Russia, however, he was defeated in the Battle of Poltava on 8 July 1709, on his way towards Moscow. Sweden never recovered as a great power; its place was taken by Russia. Augustus was reinstated as king of Poland but spent the rest of his reign as a Russian client. He was succeeded by his son Augustus III, who had inherited only one of his father's qualities, namely, his fondness for drink. He reigned for 30 years, of which he spent only two in Poland. From a Russian point of view, he was the ideal ruler, as he did nothing. The Poles had originally elected Stanislaw Leszynski – the man who had earlier been Charles XII's candidate. This led to the War of the Polish Succession in 1733–36, in which Augustus had the support of Austria and Russia and Stanislaw that of France. After two years, France withdrew from the war in return for some concessions from Austria in Italy. Stanislaw was compensated with the Duchy of Lorraine, where the famous Place Stanislas in Nancy commemorates him.

The Russian dominance eventually led to a reaction in Poland, whose elites were increasingly influenced by the ideas of the Enlightenment. Several attempts at political reform were made in the second half of the eighteenth century but all were brought to a halt by Russian intervention. The introduction of a new constitution in 1791, inspired by the ideas of the French Revolution, led to intervention from the three neighbouring powers which had begun the division of the country in 1772 and ended with the extinction of Poland as a state and the division of its territory between Russia, Prussia and Austria in 1795.

Austria or the Habsburg Empire was the largest political unit in Western Christendom and, in addition, highly composite. The term Empire may refer to the hereditary lands the emperor ruled directly as king, prince or with various other titles as well as to the Holy Roman Empire which comprised the whole of Germany and some neighbouring countries. The latter has often been regarded as of limited importance, expressed in the fact that the emperor had little opportunity to intervene in these countries and that their princes might even wage war against him, as during the Thirty Years War and under Frederick II of Prussia. However, as the lands the emperor ruled directly by far exceeded those of any of his subordinates, his influence was nevertheless considerable and there was also idea of the Empire as a unit above the individual lands, as can be illustrated by the negotiations over the Peace of Westphalia. Moreover, the emperor had considerable success after the end of the Thirty Years War. The last Turkish attack on Vienna was repelled in 1683 and in the following period, the larger part of Hungary, previously occupied by the Turks, was conquered, together with Croatia and parts of Serbia. The attempt by Prince Charles, later the Emperor Charles VI (1711–40), to become king of Spain failed, but resulted in the acquisition of the Spanish Netherlands (now Belgium).

Austria, Bohemia, Hungary and the Southern Netherlands had strong assemblies with privileges that were difficult to abolish. With the rise of nationalism and the development of national and increasingly democratic states in the nineteenth century, the Empire was regarded as an anomaly, and in addition as a bastion of political reaction. More recently, with the development of the European Union, the evaluations have tended to be more positive: the Empire has been regarded as an important experiment in multinationality.[84] Of course, the Empire was not to the same extent an anomaly in the seventeenth and eighteenth centuries, when many countries were conglomerates of various territories and only a small minority of the population was involved in political decisions, whether the country in question was formally absolutist or constitutionalist. Nevertheless, the composite character of the Empire was stronger than elsewhere. After the Counter-Reformation and the Thirty Years War, the majority of its inhabitants were Catholic but there were also Protestant and Orthodox minorities, eventually also Muslim ones. Linguistically, there was great variety. German was the main language of administration but was spoken by only a minority of the inhabitants. Socially and economically, there was a great difference between wealthy and refined cities like Vienna or Prague and the numerous village communities in the Alps and on Balkan.

Conclusion: absolutism and constitutionalism: advantages and disadvantages

If we focus particularly on the seventeenth and eighteenth centuries, we have found two convincing examples in favour of the thesis about a connection between a commercial economy and constitutionalism, namely, England and the Dutch Republic, in addition to some examples of the combination of a more agrarian economy and absolutism: France, Spain, Denmark, Austria and Prussia, plus a number of German principalities. By contrast, Poland, Hungary and Sweden, as well as Denmark before 1660, combined an agrarian economy with constitutionalism, while there are no examples of the combination of a commercial economy and absolutism. Thus, constitutional countries include both the most and the least commercialized; England and the Dutch Republic, on the one hand, and Poland and Hungary, on the other. There are also differences between absolutist countries, with Denmark and Prussia more efficient than France and Spain. We can thus operate with a successful and an unsuccessful category of each.[85]

What the successful examples of constitutionalism seem to have in common is that the constitutional assemblies had a broader basis than just the high nobility which could easily be persuaded to give up the assemblies in return for privileges. This may in turn point to some degree of urbanization, as in Aragon-Catalonia with Barcelona and of course in the Low Countries, but peasant elites or the lower aristocracy may have had a similar importance, as in Sweden. However, size may also be a factor. It is easier for representative assemblies to meet frequently in small countries than in large ones and, in addition, small countries are likely to be more homogeneous, which makes it easier to make the representatives of such assemblies work together.

In the case of England and the Dutch Republic, we may ask whether constitutionalism is the explanation for their commercial success or vice versa. In the case of England, the chronology indicates that the former is the case, whereas the question is more open in the case of the Dutch Republic. In any case, there is considerable evidence in favour of the importance of constitutionalism for economic success, not least the many examples of enlightened kings trying to promote trade and industry with limited success, at least less than in these two cases. However, as the case of Poland shows, a constitutional state dominated exclusively by the nobility is no more likely to promote trade and industry than an absolutist one, rather the contrary, as illustrated by countries like Prussia and France.

It is also a question how significant the difference actually was between absolutism and constitutionalism. England was far from democratic by modern standards; only a small portion of the population had the right to vote and most decisions were taken by a narrow elite. On the other hand, the power of the absolute kings in France and other countries was often limited. They were celebrated as God on Earth in Versailles and other places but as we have seen, their power on the local level was restricted and the price of their absolute power was tax exemption and substantial privileges for the nobility. Moreover, although

European absolutism meant government on the king's sole authority, it was not arbitrary rule. Rather, it was combined with the rule of law: as a result, the inhabitants, particularly the upper classes, for the most part had a degree of security for both their lives and their property. The main problem of absolutist kingdoms was not tyrannical kings but weak kings; there was no Nero in early modern Europe.

Although the difference between European absolutism and constitutionalism should not be exaggerated, neither should it be neglected; it largely explains the success of the Dutch Republic in the seventeenth century and that of England in the eighteenth. The most important difference between these countries and most others was freedom of speech and writing and to engage in trade and business. Government could be criticized, scientific results openly discussed and books and newspapers published without censorship. Most economic privileges and monopolies were abolished and there was free competition in most respects. These countries therefore became very important not only commercially but also intellectually in the seventeenth and eighteenth centuries. By contrast, the granting of privileges was an important element in the king's power and the king controlled or tried to control the economy in all absolutist countries. Although both merchants and members of constitutional governments might want to do the same – merchants do not object to privileges as long as they are granted to them – a collective government dependent on a majority in Parliament would in practice have less opportunity to behave in this way.

The difference between more or less efficient absolutist states seems to correspond to the presence or absence of venal offices. Denmark, Prussia, Austria and many of the German principalities developed reasonably efficient bureaucracies based on appointment by the king or his advisors, while France and Spain relied on venality. As mentioned about, tradition may have had some importance in this, but a more important factor is probably the frequency of wars. Particularly Spain but also, to a large extent, France were involved in more costly and prolonged wars than other countries, at least until the eighteenth century, when England did the same, although with better finances. As we have seen, there is a direct connection between war and venality in France and the same is probably also the case in Spain. Prussia might seem to belong in the same category, but although this was the most militarized country in Europe, it was less involved in war than France and it also spent less on the court. There is no doubt that strong armies and navies were important factors in state formation, but they seem to have been most efficient when they were not used too often in active warfare. The venality of offices shows that war not only builds the state but might also weaken it.

Finally, one feature is common to all European states, whether constitutionalist or absolutist, namely, the ruler's dependence on support from his subjects. Evidently, no ruler can have absolute power in the sense that he can command without any consultation and without considering any other interest than his own. Attempts in this direction would often lead to dependence on bureaucrats or slave soldiers, as in the Arab or Ottoman Empires and in periods also in China. By contrast, most European bureaucracies were relatively weak and even if armies increased greatly in the early modern period, there was nothing resembling military dictators until the period of Napoleon. European rulers depended on the support of their subjects, admittedly mainly the upper classes, the nobility, gentry and bourgeoisie, in other words, largely the classes that continued to dominate until the introduction of mass democracy in the twentieth century.

Notes

1 Churchill, *Marlborough*, vol. I, pp. 843–4.
2 The date is occasionally given as 2 August, because England at the time still used the Julian calendar. When the country changed to the Gregorian one in 1752, 11 days had to be added.
3 Bluche, *Louis XIV*, pp. 551–72. By contrast, Rowlands, *The Financial Decline of a Great Power*, after a detailed examination of the French finances and their administration, argues that the French were in a desperate situation and were only saved because the British began to withdraw from the war.
4 Ertman, *Leviathan*, p. 220; Coward, *The Stuart Age*, pp. 8, 485.
5 Barrington Moore, *The Social Origins*, pp. 413–505.
6 The criticism began with Henshall, *The Myth of Absolutism*. See more recently Beik, 'Absolutism' and Durchhardt and Schnettger, *Barock und Aufklärung*, pp. 169–73. Reinhard, *Geschichte der Staatsgewalt*, pp. 113–22, points to Hobbes as a representative of the idea of the state rather than that of absolutism, and to the king's limited control of local society (ibid., pp. 183–209). On Hobbes and other theorists of the monarchical state, see also Skinner, 'From the State of Princes to the Person of the State'. On France, see Collins, *From Tribes to Nation*, pp. 403–14 and Bluche, *Louis XIV*, pp. 124–31. On the German principalities, see Vierhaus, *Staaten und Stände* and von Friedeburg, *Luther's Legacy*.
7 Kunt, *The Sultan's Servants*, pp.31–56; Fukuyama, *The Origins*, pp. 218–20, 296–8, 308, 331–2 and Imber, 'Government, Administration and Law', pp. 205–22.
8 For this and the following, see Blockmans, 'The Low Countries in the Middle Ages' and 't Hart, 'The United Provinces 1579–1806'.
9 t'Hart, 'The United Provinces', p. 311.
10 Ibid., p. 309.
11 For the following, see Israel, *The Dutch Republic*, pp. 285–91 and de Vries and van der Woude, *The First Modern Economy*, pp. 113–29.
12 De Vries and van der Woude, *The First Modern Economy*, pp. 673–87.
13 Schama, *The Embarrassment of Riches*, pp. 260, 407–12.
14 Burke, *Venice and Amsterdam*, pp. 113–24.
15 For this and the following, see Schama, *The Embarrassment of Riches*, pp. 375–86; Burke, *Venice and Amsterdam*, pp. 89–90 and Israel, *The Dutch Republic*, p. 329.
16 Gorski, *The Disciplinary Revolution*, pp. 125–37.
17 For the following, see ibid., pp. 39–113.
18 For this and the following, see Israel, *The Dutch Republic*, pp. 351–60 and de Vries and van der Woude, *The First Modern Economy*, pp. 561–71.
19 Ferguson, *Empire*, pp. 17–25.
20 Piketty, *Le capital au XXIe siècle*, pp. 206–14.
21 Acemoglu and Robinson, *Why Nations Fail*, pp. 182–212.
22 For this and the following, see Smith, *The Emergence of a Nation State*, pp. 169–71 and Hoppit, *A Land of Liberty*, pp. 352–65.
23 Blanning, *The Pursuit of Glory*, pp. 93–5.
24 Van der Wee, 'Monetary, Credit and Banking Systems', pp. 378–80; Collins, *From Tribes*, pp. 454–5; Ferguson, *The Ascent of Money*, pp. 139–58.
25 Dunbabin, 'Government', p. 508.

26 Given, *State and Society*, pp. 42–52.
27 Vauchez, *La sainteté*, pp. 187–215, 291–328; Le Goff, *St. Louis*, pp. 298–310.
28 Durand *et al., Des États dans l'État.*
29 Strayer, *Philip the Fair*, p. 286.
30 Aylmer, *The Struggle*, p. 55.
31 Collins, *The State*, pp. 24–5, 93.
32 Gorski, *The Disciplinary Revolution*, pp. 144–8.
33 Ardant, 'Financial Policy', p. 194.
34 Ladurie, *The French Peasantry*, p. 19.
35 Bonney, 'France 1494–1815', pp. 142–3; Collins, *From Tribes to Nation*, pp. 404–5.
36 Beik, 'Absolutism'.
37 Bluche, *Louis XIV*, pp. 144–6, 202–4, 432–6, 499–506.
38 Ibid., pp. 129–31; Collins, *From Tribes to Nation*, pp. 409–10. For an example of these limits, see e.g. Pitts, *Embezzlement and High Treason in Louis XIV's France*, on the process against Nicholas Fouquet.
39 For this and the following, see Maddicott, *The Origins*, pp. 1–105.
40 Post, *Studies in Medieval Legal Thought*, pp. 108–62.
41 Harriss, *King, Parliament, and Public Finance*, pp. 108–9, 254–69, 510–15.
42 Harriss, *Shaping the Nation*, pp. 66–74, 437–501, 650–3.
43 Finer, 'State and Nation Building', pp. 117–21.
44 For an overview of the discussion, see Coward, *The Stuart Age*, pp. 500–8.
45 Ibid., pp. 172–8, for the following. Cf. also Monod, *The Power of Kings*, pp. 103–10.
46 Trevor-Roper, 'Cromwell and his Parliaments'.
47 Coward, *The Stuart Age*, p. 296.
48 Vallance, *The Glorious Revolution*, pp. 1–20.
49 Ferguson, *Empire*, pp. 22–4.
50 Ertman, *Birth of the Leviathan*, pp. 209–22.
51 Cf. Goldstone, 'Europe's Peculiar Path', on the possible consequences for science if James II had succeeded.
52 Sowerby, *Making Toleration;* cf. also Pincus, *1688: The First Modern Revolution.*
53 Tilly, *Coercion*, p. 155.
54 Maddicott, *Simon de Montfort* (Cambridge: Cambridge University Press, 1994). On the popular support, see Valente, *The Theory and Practice*, pp. 90–9.
55 *Documents*, no. 37–8, pp. 252–89; Maddicott, *Simon de Montfort*, p. 295. On Louis' attitude as the expression of the traditional concept of monarchy, see also Le Goff, *Saint Louis*, pp. 264–7.
56 Ardant, 'Financial Policy', p. 200.
57 For the following, see MacKay, *Spain* and Hillgarth, *The Spanish Kingdoms.*
58 MacKay, *Spain*, pp. 136–42.
59 Monod, *The Power of Kings*, p. 43; Erkens, 'Thronfolge und Herrschersakralität', pp. 363–4.
60 Thus, Acemoglou and Robinson, *Why Nations Fail*, p. 105.
61 Elliott, *Imperial Spain*, index; Muto, 'The Spanish System', p. 258.
62 Monod, *The Power of Kings*, p. 129, with reference to Elliott, 'Self-Perception and Decline' and Kamen, 'The Decline of Spain'.
63 For a recent account in English of these countries in the period, see Jespersen, 'The Military Imperative', 'Fiscal and Military Developments', 'From Aristocratic Regime to Absolutism', and 'The Consolidation of the Nordic States', Rian, 'Centre and Periphery', and Grell, 'Religious and Social Regimentation'.
64 For the following, see Jespersen, *Danmarks historie*, vol. III, pp. 70–92, 181–211.
65 Gamrath and Ladewig Petersen, *Danmarks historie*, vol. II, p. 419.
66 For the following, see Jespersen, *Danmarks historie,* vol. III, pp. 212–37 and Lind, 'Den heroiske tid?'.
67 For the following, see Lind, *Hæren og magten*, pp. 383–401 and *Konger og krige*, pp. 429–67.
68 Lindegren, 'Men, Money and Means', pp. 150–5.

69 Roberts, *The Swedish Imperial Experience*, pp. 44–5, 56.
70 Ibid., pp. 123–43.
71 Lindegren, 'Men, Money and Means', p. 140.
72 Schück, *Riksdagen*, pp. 32–53.
73 For the following, see Gustafsson, *Political Integration*, particularly pp. 154–72.
74 Blanning, *Culture of Power*, p. 70.
75 Clark, *Iron Kingdom*, p. 26.
76 For the following, see ibid., p. 78–114.
77 Finer, 'State and Nation-Building', pp. 134–44; Clark, *Iron Kingdom*, pp. 53–64.
78 Gorski, *The Disciplinary Revolution*, pp. 85–92.
79 Rady, 'Rethinking Jagiello Hungary'; Watts, *The Making of Polities*, p. 360. Thanks to Martyn Rady for drawing my attention to this. For the older interpretation, see Engel, *The Realm of St Stephen*, pp. 345–71 and Fukuyama, *The Origins*, pp. 378–85.
80 For the following, see Zamorsky, *Poland: A History*, particularly pp. 125–88 and Davies, *God's Playground*, vol. I, pp. 125–385.
81 Nevertheless, the links between the two countries were stronger than most earlier scholars have assumed; see Frost, *The Oxford History of Poland-Lithuania*.
82 Weinberg, *To Explain the World*, p. 147.
83 For this and the following, see Frost, *The Northern Wars*.
84 Recent discussions of the Empire include Schmidt, *Geschichte* and Schmidt, 'Das früh-neuzeitliche Reich'; Schilling, 'Reich-Staat und frühneuzeitliche Nation der Deut-schen'; Wilson, 'Still a Monstrosity?' and Wilson, *The Holy Roman Empire*, pp. 655–86. The tension between the imperial power and the independence of the princes in the ritual field is explored elegantly in Stollberg-Rilinger, *The Emperor's Old Clothes*.
85 Ertman, *Leviathan*, pp. 28–34 distinguishes between a bureaucratic and a patrimonial version of each. Cf. also Fukuyama, *The Origins*, pp. 373–85.

6

THE STATE AND THE ENLIGHTENMENT

In 1856, the following text from 1784 was found on the steeple-ball on St Margaret's Church in Gotha:

> The days we spent on this earth constituted the happiest period of the eighteenth century. Emperor, kings and princes are philanthropically stepping down from their intimidating heights, disdain pomp and display and become the fathers, friends and companions of their people. Religion sheds its clerical vestments and emerges in pure godliness. Enlightenment marches forward with giant steps; thousands of our brothers and sisters who lived in sacred idleness now contribute to the community. Sectarian hatred and religious persecution diminish; philanthropy and freedom of thought win the upper hand ... Here you have a true portrayal of our age. Do not look down on us with arrogance, if you stand higher and see further that we did; rather appreciate from the picture we have given you just how much we elevated and supported your fatherland. Do the same for your posterity and be happy.[1]

This text forms a succinct contemporary proclamation about the Enlightenment: the ideas of freedom, equality and sense of community and the belief in progress, from the past to the present and from the present to the future.

In a famous book of 1969, Jürgen Habermas pointed to a fundamental change in the public sphere during this period, from the 'representative public' of the Middle Ages and the following period to the 'open public' of the Enlightenment. In the former, the result of a discussion was determined by the status of the participants, in the latter by rational arguments. In the new public sphere of coffee-houses, newspapers and magazines, status was awarded according to knowledge and argumentative skills.[2] As has often been pointed out, Habermas exaggerates the difference between the two epochs; public discussion can be found much earlier than the seventeenth and eighteenth centuries, for instance, in the intense discussion during the Investiture Contest.[3] Nevertheless, important changes had taken place.

Quantitatively, there were more fora for public debate and a larger debating public. More people were literate and there was now an educated middle class consisting of burghers, civil servants, teachers and free intellectuals who participated in various kinds of debate. Qualitatively, there had been a radical change during the previous centuries. In the Middle Ages, intellectual debate had taken place within the intellectual framework of Christian doctrine and ancient philosophy, notably Aristotle. The discussion within this framework was considerable and many changes had taken place, to the extent that Bernard of Chartres in the twelfth century could claim that contemporary scholars had surpassed the ancients in the famous statement that they were dwarves on the shoulders of giants.[4] However, this only meant a marginal addition to the contribution of the giants of the past. Now the ancients could be shown to have been wrong, not only because they lacked Christianity but also because it could be proved by strict empirical methods that the character of the universe was radically different from what even the greatest ancient philosophers had imagined. The Enlightenment represented the victory of critical thought, the idea that old traditions, the teaching of the ancients or appeals to divine revelation, were not sufficient reason to believe anything but that belief must be based on critical examination of the proposition in question. In a similar way, the scientific discoveries opened up attacks against the Church and Christianity, notably because the churchmen often rejected them.

Whereas with some exceptions, it had been usual to regard the present as inferior to the past, it was now increasingly regarded as better. The Enlightenment intellectuals believed in progress; the backwardness and superstition of the past were about to be surpassed and the future would be better than the present. The great scientific discoveries, the technological innovations and the increasing wealth in many countries pointed strongly in this direction. As we have seen, this also applies to the famous debate between the Ancients and the Moderns.

Intellectually, the background to the Enlightenment can be traced back to the Renaissance, with its emphasis on the human intellect and criticism of various accepted ideas, held by the Church and other authorities. A particularly important factor was the study of astronomy and the replacement of the geocentric world picture by the heliocentric one through a series of studies by scientists from Copernicus to Newton. In the eighteenth century, several important discoveries were made in electricity, mechanics and other fields which eventually led to practical inventions and in turn to the Industrial Revolution. From a methodological point of view, the scientific discoveries showed the importance of systematic observation and experiment for gaining knowledge, in contrast to speculation. Scientific theories must be based on evidence, which meant a rejection not only of the Aristotelian tradition from the Middle Ages but also of the great systems of Descartes and Leibniz from the seventeenth century.

The Enlightenment is far from being a homogeneous movement; it is a common term for a number of opinions and intellectuals in various parts of Europe. However, despite its late date, the following reflection by Alexis de Tocqueville on his discovery of American democracy in the 1830s expresses some central features of the political attitudes of the Enlightenment:

> 'Individualism' is a word recently coined to express a new idea. Our fathers only knew about egoism ... Individualism is of democratic origin and threatens to grow as conditions get more equal.
>
> Among aristocratic nations families maintain the same station for centuries and often live in the same place ... A man always knows about his ancestors and respects them; his imagination extends to his great-grandchildren, and he loves them. He freely does his duty both to ancestors and descendants and often sacrifices personal pleasures for the sake of beings who are no longer alive or are not yet born ...
>
> In democratic ages, on the contrary, the duties of each to all are much clearer, but devoted service to any individual much rarer. The bonds of human affection are wider but more relaxed.[5]

As de Tocqueville points out, 'individualism' was a new term at the time, the 1830s. It was also a term coined by its opponents, to whom Tocqueville himself largely belonged. The exact term was first used in 1820 by Joseph de Maistre, a conservative and Catholic opponent of the French Revolution, but it was a common objection to the Enlightenment and the Revolution that these movements celebrated individual freedom at the cost of social order, religion, hierarchy and the common good. Examples of such attitudes are Bossuet's criticism of the English Revolution and Edmund Burke's of the French.[6] By contrast, the adherents of these movements celebrated individual freedom, regarding thought and opinions as well as behaviour, as in the passage in the American Declaration of Independence about 'life, freedom and the pursuit of happiness'. To the adherents of these principles, there was no opposition between the individual and society. A good society consisted of free individuals; the old society was dominated by elites who suppressed individual freedom while at the same time manipulating governments in accordance with their own interests. Neither family or kindred nor estates or inherited positions should determine an individual's position in society; he or she (mostly he!) should be free to make his own choice and pursue a career in society. Moreover, this was not only an ideal; there was now a strong emphasis on the idea that society consisted of individuals who acted according to their own interests.

This also formed an argument for democratic reform, government based on popular election, even, during the most radical phase of the French Revolution, universal suffrage for men. Although there were also movements for the rights of women at the time, the democratic ideas of the Enlightenment did not very much favour women. To some extent, this may be the result of a reaction against women's considerable influence in courtly society, particularly under Louis XV, when the king's mistresses interfered in politics. It may also have to do with the difference between bourgeois and aristocratic society, the former based on the husband supporting the family through his business or career while the wife took care of the household and the children, whereas in the latter both spouses spent their lives in leisure and social activities.

Two central and very different political thinkers both take their point of departure in the individual. Thomas Hobbes (1588–1679) rejected Aristotle's idea of man as a social animal, replacing it with that of original anarchy. Life in the natural condition is 'solitary, poor, nasty, brutish and short'. Thus, man is a ruthless pursuer of his own interests, who has to be kept at bay by a strong government.[7] John Locke (1632–1704), who became the main apologist for the Glorious Revolution,[8] had an equally individualistic but different understanding of human nature, claiming that humans were born without any innate qualities. Individual freedom was no threat to society, whose main duty was to uphold the individual right to property which was the fundamental principle of society and granted by God. Despite the difference between Hobbes' pessimism and Locke's optimism, both take their point of departure in the individual. By contrast, Jean-Jacques Rousseau (1712–78) clearly placed society above the individual in his radical theory of popular sovereignty which was taken up by the extreme left during the French Revolution. Society should be ruled by the will of the majority, the individual seeking fulfilment by becoming part of the general will.[9] At the same time, Rousseau rejected the traditional ties that linked together the society of the *ancien régime*, estates, kinship and patronage. His individual relates directly to society and realizes his full opportunities by acting politically.

A more moderate approach was represented in the great work by Charles-Louis de Secondat Montesquieu (1689–1755), *L'Esprit des lois* [*The Spirit of the Laws*]. Montesquieu still uses Aristotle's division of constitutions into monarchy, aristocracy and democracy, current from the Middle Ages onwards, and advocates a balance between the three, largely in accordance with the constitution of contemporary Britain. In his work, he combines history with comparative sociology and political thought. He discusses numerous societies in the past and the present and the differences between them, in which he regards climate as an important factor. Montesquieu, like other theorists, was also interested in other civilizations, such as the Ottoman Empire and the newly discovered islands in the Pacific, which they compared to Europe, not only to the advantage of the latter. There were vivid discussions of laws and constitutions and concrete proposals of improvement in various fields.

A similar emphasis on the rational individual is expressed in the fields of law and economy. Cesare Beccaria (1738–94) criticized the contemporary penal laws for their harshness; not mainly for humanitarian reasons, but based on the argument that punishment should serve to prevent crime. Too harsh punishment, such as hanging for petty theft, would not do so, for most people would then not report the criminal in question. Killing people for their crimes was also counter-productive; it would be better to let them work to atone for what they had done. Thus, punishment is no longer a matter of justice or atonement for sin, but an instrument to reduce crime by appealing to people's self-interest. In the field of economics, the French physiocrats attacked the current theory of Mercantilism, which claimed that the wealth of a country depended on its surplus of gold or silver and that international trade was a zero sum game, in which the gain of one nation was the loss of another. The physiocrats replaced this with the idea of agriculture as the basis of the economy. This was further developed by the Scot Adam Smith (1723–90), who in *An Inquiry into the Nature and Causes of the Wealth of Nations* of 1776, claimed that the wealth of a country did not consist of its amount of precious metals, as the Mercantilists claimed, but of the commodities and services produced, not only the agricultural production, which meant that there was no limit to growth and the states might as well be allies as competitors. Based on British experience as opposed to the Continental one, Adam Smith developed the theory of free competition as essential for economic growth. The state should not organize or control the economy, but intervene in order to secure free competition – which, in fact, demanded a fairly strong state – and protect the life and welfare of its inhabitants. Here also the starting-point is the rational individual. Production is stimulated by self-interest, not by force or decree from the state.[10]

The study of history underwent great changes. A more critical examination of the sources had developed during the previous century. The great pioneers in were the Benedictine monk Jean Mabillon (1632–1707) in the monastery of St Germain des Prés in Paris and the Bollandists, a group of Jesuits in Antwerp, named after Jean Bolland (1596–1665). Both worked on ecclesiastical sources, notably the lives of saints, and made a great effort to trace the original versions and eliminate later distortions and fictions. In the eighteenth century, the study of history was increasingly based on the idea of progress, showing the emergence of the present enlightened age or, alternatively, recovery from a period of decline, such as Edward Gibbon's *The History of the Decline and Fall of the Roman Empire*, describing the whole period from Late Antiquity to the Renaissance as a deterioration of conditions from the second century AD, 'the happiest period in the history of mankind'. The typical example of a period of decline was the Middle Ages; the term itself became current in this period as the expression of the idea of a dark period between Classical Antiquity and the present. The origins of the division into three periods can be traced back to Leonardo Bruni in the fifteenth century and later to Machiavelli, but the term itself only became current with its use in a textbook by Michael Cellarius in 1688.[11]

In accordance with the development of political and economic thought, historical writing developed in a more sociological direction, aimed at understanding the different development of various countries and civilizations. Thus, Montesquieu compares constitutional and social conditions all over the world, tries to explain their origins and discusses their merits. Gibbon's work has similar features and is far more than a lament on the fall of the Roman Empire. Similar attitudes characterize the historical works of David Hume, Voltaire, Diderot and others, many of whom show great interest in societies outside Europe and are critical of the slave trade and other examples of European imperialism.[12]

Generally, the Enlightenment is characterized by a clear idea of how society should be organized and concrete proposals for reform, largely based on John

Locke's theory of the human mind as a '*tabula rasa*' that can be developed in any direction. Thus, during the French Revolution, there was a strong will to create, not only a new society but a new kind of humans. The Enlightenment was often critical of the Church and religion, notably in France. The best-known French intellectual of the period, Voltaire (1694–1778), believed in God but despised established Christianity, notably the Catholic Church, and used all his considerable wit to ridicule it. However, the strong connection between Enlightenment and anti-religious attitudes was mainly a French phenomenon. Doubt about the dogmas of the Church and outright rejection of them were to be found in other countries as well, but usually in a less aggressive form.[13] On the other hand, greater literacy and the increase in the production of books and papers also increased the amount of religious literature, and attempts to abolish or change traditional religious expression often met with strong popular protests, like Joseph II's religious reforms in Austria. Moreover, religion and the Enlightenment were not incompatible.

The authority of the king and the state was based less on religious arguments than previously. When Louis XVI became king in 1774, there were some suggestions about omitting the coronation. Although Louis was crowned, less people attended the ceremony than usual. Admittedly, as the example of Spain shows, the absence of a coronation is not necessarily evidence of lack of belief in the divine origin of kingship. However, there is no doubt that the religious legitimation of monarchy became less prominent in the eighteenth century, in France, as well as in other places, and was largely replaced by practical arguments about the necessity of a strong government. There was also a clearer distinction between the state and the king and a preference for using the former term instead of the latter. A French prelate even commented that it was no longer possible to say that one served the king, for then one would be taken for one of the chief valets at Versailles; it was therefore necessary to say, 'I serve the state.'[14]

Whereas the development of these ideas was the result of the scientific revolution and the philosophical thought based on it, an important factor in spreading them was the printing press. Admittedly, this was not a new invention in the eighteenth century, but books had now become cheaper and were produced in larger numbers, while at the same time a larger percentage of the population was literate. During the first decade of the sixteenth century, around 400 titles were published in Britain, a number that increased to 6,000 in the 1630s, 21,000 in the 1710s and 56,000 in the 1790s. There is less data on statistics from other parts of Europe, but the growth is likely to have been similar. In France, the number of titles seems to have been doubled between 1750 and 1789 and continued to rise in the following period. In the German world, around 175,000 titles were published during the eighteenth century, two-thirds of them after 1760. In addition, there were newspapers and magazines. A German periodical from 1780 reports that 60 years ago, only academics bought books, but 'today there is hardly a woman with some claim to education that does not read'.[15] Of course, these books not only contained the latest ideas of the Enlightenment; they also included novels, practical handbooks and, not least, religious literature. Newspapers and magazines also became more widespread and important. The first newspapers had already appeared in the early sixteenth century, but they just contained a few pages, mainly of announcements. In the eighteenth century, they had become important sources of information and discussion. Some of them, like *The Times* (founded in 1785), has had a continual existence since the eighteenth century.

Finally, one of the most important ways the ideas of Enlightenment were spread was the great *Encyclopédie*, edited by Denis Diderot, assisted by the better-known and prominent Jean le Rond d'Alembert,[16] and published in 17 volumes of text and 11 of pictures and paintings between 1751 and 1772. Its aim was to summarize all knowledge in a form that might be understood by the ordinary, non-professional reader. Moreover, the idea was not only to present what was usually regarded as knowledge, but knowledge gained by critical examination and intelligent understanding of nature and society. This meant that it attacked a number of ideas officially acknowledged in contemporary France, notably religious ones. Not surprisingly, the editors ran into trouble with the censorship, but the publication nevertheless continued. Altogether, the *Encyclopédie* sold 22,000 copies before the Revolution, about half of which were outside France.

In addition, the number of public meeting-places increased in the form of salons and coffee-houses, where people met for discussion and entertainment.[17] The aristocratic salons, which were particularly prominent in France, above all, in Paris, but were also imitated in other countries, were very often run by women. They were important expressions of the fact that women now to a greater extent took part in intellectual life and they stimulated friendship and conversation between married men and women without any sexual implications. They also contributed to a less professional and learned intellectual culture, conversations and writings in the vernacular, in contrast to the earlier view that serious knowledge had to be transmitted in Latin. The fact that women did not normally have access to the learned culture contributed to this change. On the other hand, women's involvement in this kind of intellectual culture may also be regarded as a compensation for the restrictions to which they were subject. Although some women did publish books and journals, this was not considered appropriate and might have bad consequences for their reputation.

This form of intellectual life was particularly prominent in the larger cities, like Paris, Vienna, Berlin and, above all, London, by far the largest European city in the eighteenth century, with more than one million inhabitants. In London and to some extent in Paris, it was possible to live from books and publications as a free intellectual. This was more difficult in Germany, with smaller towns and a smaller public for books and magazines. On the other hand, many German principalities, notably Prussia but also others, had well-educated bureaucrats and good schools and universities whose employees participated in an extensive literary production, which made the eighteenth century, notably its second half, the golden age of German culture and literature.

The spread of the ideas of the Enlightenment of course implies a rise in the rates of literacy, of which there is clear evidence. In France, the literacy rate is estimated to have increased from 29 per cent to 47 per cent for men and 14 per cent to 27 per cent for women between 1680 and 1780. These numbers hide great regional variations, with much higher rates in the north and around Paris. In Amsterdam, 87 per cent of Protestant men and 69 per cent of Protestant women could sign their names in the marriage register. The corresponding rates for Catholics were 79 and 53. Literacy rates are usually believed to have been higher in Protestant than in Catholic areas, which may be true on average, but the geographical differences were more significant. Literacy was most widespread in northern and western Europe, regardless of confession; in Catholic areas, it was particularly high in northern and eastern France, Belgium, the Rhineland and parts of northern Italy. However, there was no general agreement that common people should learn to read. A pastor in Scania in the seventeenth century complained that the peasants had been taught to read in order to learn religion but used their skills to read the ordinances about land lease, so that they became impossible to deal with. The writer Bernard Mandeville put the problem like this in *The Fable of the Bees*: 'If a horse knew as much as a man, I would not sit on it.'

These latter observations point to the social and economic background of the Enlightenment. As indicated by the comparison between East Asia and Europe, there was some improvement in living conditions in the eighteenth century. There was less war and greater protection of the civilian population in war, an increase in population and somewhat higher living standards, some slight improvement in health care, including vaccination against smallpox, better education, an increase in literacy and the number of professions and thus the emergence of a more numerous and wealthy middle class. From a modern point of view, the changes were not dramatic; they were less from the seventeenth to the eighteenth century than from the eighteenth to the nineteenth. Still, they were important enough to produce the expression of optimism quoted above.

Enlightened despotism and parliamentary government

Visits to the great European art galleries give an impression of how early modern European monarchs presented themselves to the world – there are relatively few portraits of medieval monarchs and most of them seem to be of types rather than real persons. As we have seen, the individualized portrait was the product of the Italian Renaissance, with Florence as its centre. This also formed the point of departure for the later portraits of kings, notably Titian's of the early Habsburgs. Charles V and Philip II are easily recognized, both with the characteristic Habsburg chin, whether they are portrayed on horseback, standing or sitting and with some symbolic object in their hands, but their expression is blank; the whole portrait indicates distance. The same applies even more to Rigaud's portrait of Louis XIV where the king's body is almost completely hidden under the big robe and the face is equally blank. By contrast, Louis XVI, even when wearing his coronation robe, is shown as a stout young man, with round cheeks, half-closed eyes and a bene-volent expression. Nothing, apart from the robe, indicates royal majesty. This applies even more to Goya's portrait of the Spanish royal family from 1800–1. The royal couple, surrounded by children, grandchildren and in-laws, looks exactly like any bourgeois family. The portraits of Frederick II of Prussia, notably those of the elderly king, are in one sense different, showing his worries as well as his intelli-gence, but from the point of view of genre fall into the same category: they depict the man rather than the king.

There is now an emphasis on different qualities in rulers than previously: humanism, intellectual interests, building the country in peace rather than in war, although unfortunately, the latter may occasionally be necessary. Of course, this change does not necessarily correspond to any change in the character of the kings but it does tell us something about ideology and how the kings wanted to appear. They emphasized the proximity to their subjects rather than their distance from them. The portraits may also indicate a clearer distinction between the person and the office and thus between the state and the king in person.

Moreover, the Enlightenment had obvious consequences for governments. Ear-lier, ecclesiastical and secular bureaucracies, combined with courts and palaces, had been sufficient to attach the elites to the king and secure the obedience of the common people. As we have seen, Louis XIV of France was very skilful in this field. Now, a real public opinion was emerging and a far larger number of people began to have political opinions and propagate them to others. They might even criticize kings and governments. In a few countries, like Britain, such criticism was a normal feature; there was a constant debate between the government and the opposition and all politicians had to make use of the new media to win elections and gain influence. Most countries, however, were ruled by more or less absolute monarchs who had to deal with the new situation. The most obvious remedy was of course censorship, which existed in most countries, but this was rarely sufficient. There were a number of indirect ways to express opinions. A better method was therefore to combine censorship with active participation in the debate.

The virtuoso in this was Frederick II of Prussia.[18] He began his reign by abol-ishing censorship, although he soon had to reintroduce it (1743). However, he did not stop there; he used the new media actively. From the beginning of his reign, he systematically used foreign newspapers and publishing houses to defend his war against Austria, often writing articles himself that would be published anon-ymously. He also addressed the British public and later, during the Seven Years War, became a great hero in this country, as the defender of German Protestantism against Catholic Austria and France. The German market was supplied with various objects, snuff-boxes, knives and bracelets, with Frederick's portrait. He often appeared in public, even raising his hat to people he met, in a period when no one raised his hat to a social inferior. Despite some ambivalence regarding great crowds, he might on occasion be very clever at handling them. Finally, he was an active participant in a number of cultural activities, despite his lack of appreciation of contemporary German literature. Several other princes in the German-speaking world showed similar skills, such as Maria Theresa of Austria and her two sons and successors. Her appeal to the Hungarian nobility, referred to in Chapter 2, was a first-rate performance and she continued to show herself to the public. Joseph II's residence in an ordinary house in Vienna also served to gain him popularity. It has been suggested that this forms part of the explanation why Austria avoided a revolution in the late eighteenth century. By contrast, the king of France's lack of skill in this respect may have contributed to the outbreak of the French Revolution.

The natural starting-point for a discussion of the practical consequences of the ideas of the Enlightenment is the Glorious Revolution in England.[19] This was not only a change of dynasty and a defeat for the attempts to reintroduce Catholicism but also the beginning of a new form of government which eventually developed into the parliamentary system that later became current in most Western democracies. This development has three main aspects: (1) the increased importance and frequency of Parliament; (2) the formation of political parties; and (3) the formation of cabinet government.

The first point was expressed already in the Declaration of Rights, issued by William and Mary on their accession to the British throne on 13 February 1689, in which the king's power was explicitly restricted on several points and that of Parliament increased. The king is no longer allowed to suspend or dispense with the laws, levy money or maintain a standing army without the consent of Parliament; elections to Parliament are to be free and various restrictions on individual freedom are to be abolished.[20] Parliament now met annually, was in session for longer than previously and demanded more work from its members. The party system can be traced back to the conflict over the succession in the 1680s, when the Tories supported the king, whereas the Whigs represented the opposition. Both names are originally derogatory. 'Tory' is derived from Middle Irish *tóraidhe*, meaning outlaw or robber, Whig is an abbreviation of *whiggamor* = cattle driver, referring to the western Scots who came to Leith for corn. Both terms refer to religious sympathies, the Tories for Irish Catholics, the Whigs for Scottish dissenters. They were not organized parties in the modern sense, but became more formalized from the late eighteenth century. There were frequent divisions between them and defections from one to the other. The issues dividing them shifted over time. The Tories were originally considered more royalist than the Whigs, but after the deposition of James II, the rulers mostly relied on the Whigs, who had been the main force behind the Glorious Revolution.

Originally, the ruler was in principle free to choose his or her councillors. However, something resembling a modern government had gradually developed from the Elizabethan Privy Council in the sixteenth century and the king normally had a first minister as his second-in-command. The cabinet was originally a committee of the Privy Council, a body that still exists but has little political importance. With the increasing power of Parliament, it became important for the king to have the support of this body. This was the origin of the modern cabinet and its leader, the prime minister. Robert Walpole is usually considered to have been the first British prime minister, holding the office in the period 1721–42. His official title was First Lord of the Treasury, which is still the official – but rarely used – title of the British prime minister. It is no coincidence that the office originated under the first two Hanoverians who interfered little in politics and were happy to leave much of their duties to an indigenous politician. Walpole was also, like all his successors, a Member of Parliament. He sat in the House of Commons and refused to be made a lord in order to be able to influence this assembly. He was the most prominent and clever politician during the long period of Whig dominance.

Whereas Charles II had been able to rule without Parliament during the last years of his reign, this was no longer possible, as Parliament controlled the finances. Nor could the king any longer veto a Bill from Parliament; the last time this happened was in 1708. At the same time, this control increased the power of the cabinet, as it was decided informally in 1706 and formally in 1713 that Parliament could not vote for money for any purpose except on a motion of a Minister of the Crown. With the increasing importance of Parliament, the prime minister had to relate to this body, persuading it to agree to the king's policies and transmitting the opinion of Parliament to the king. This eventually led to the present parliamentary system, in which the king or queen – who still formally appoints the government – has to appoint one that is acceptable to Parliament. The last time a king tried to appoint a prime minister without support from Parliament was in 1834, when he had to give up. William III (1688–1702) appointed cabinets with members from both parties, but the normal practice in the following period was that only one party was represented.

Eighteenth-century Britain was far from democratic according to modern standards. Not only was one of the Houses of Parliament, the House of Lords, composed of non-elected members, the bishops and the greatest lords, but in addition, the lower one, the House of Commons, only to a very limited degree represented the people. Only a minority of the population had the right to vote, 400,000 of a population that increased from 7 to 10.5 million during the eighteenth century. Actually, Parliament had become increasingly less representative over the centuries. The districts with the right to elect had been the same since the Middle Ages, which meant that the new cities based on trade and industry in the north were largely without representation, while small villages in the south had a disproportionate influence ('Rotten boroughs'). Moreover, elections were often controlled by local lords; in some cases seats were hereditary or a certain landowner had the right to appoint the representative. Such rights might also be bought and sold. To a considerable extent, the members of the House of Commons were the clients of aristocratic patrons, often the same people who sat in the House of Lords. Personal links and patronage were still an important part of the political system.[21]

Nevertheless, the country had introduced a series of changes in the modern direction, to the extent that Fukuyama regards it as the first example of accountable government.[22] The courts of law were independent of the king and Parliament; if the government wanted to punish its critics, it had to approach a court of law which might come to another conclusion. The acceptance of the party system with a government and an opposition is also an important expression of a new understanding of politics. Since classical antiquity, the word 'party' had a bad sound. A politician was supposed to act in the interest of the community as a whole, not of a special class or group. The same was the case in the Middle Ages and the Renaissance, except for some steps in the modern direction in Machiavelli. In the eighteenth century, there was still no idea of parties as the expression of clearly defined social groups or classes. As the electorate was very limited and almost all politicians belonged to the elite, there was little incentive in that direction; but there were different opinions on important political or religious issues, such as the relationship between the Church of England and respectively Catholics and Protestant dissenters, Stuart or Hanoverian succession, war or peace or, in the case of the former, which alliance? Whereas earlier, there had been a thin line between opposition and treason, opposition now became a normal and necessary part of the political system, expressed in the term His/Her Majesty's loyal opposition.

The parliamentary system also had its advantages from point of view of political efficiency. As already Aristotle put it, government by one good and wise man might be excellent, but in practice, this will happen so rarely that it is better to have an elected government consisting of more than one person. Britain entered a period of greatness when ruled mostly by mediocre kings, whereas weak kings had disastrous effects on France and Spain during the same period. On the other hand, the British system was a demanding one. It is not easy to get a minority to respect the rule of a majority and there is no guarantee that the system will produce capable rulers. There is also the additional problem of making people obey somebody not unlike themselves; although in this case, it was an advantage for Britain to be a monarchy; the king's importance as formally the highest authority should not be underestimated. By contrast, the prime minister only became a public figure in the first half of the nineteenth century. Earlier, he mainly acted within Parliament. He did not conduct election campaigns and he rarely addressed the general public.

In the eighteenth century, the closest parallel to Britain was Sweden.[23] As we have seen, the Swedish Diet had existed in largely the same form continuously since 1527, with predecessors some centuries further back in history. In the same way as in Denmark, an unsuccessful and costly war (1675–79) increased the power of the king. Also similar to Denmark, the king received support against the nobility from the commoners, who were represented in three of the four houses of the Diet. A new and greater military disaster, the defeat in the Great Nordic War (1700–21) led to a reaction against the royal regime. After Charles XII's sudden death from an enemy bullet during the siege of Fredriksten in Norway on 11 December 1718,[24] the king's power was strictly limited. The Diet assumed a position similar to the British Parliament and the king was no longer free to elect his councillors, but depended on the will of the Diet. As in Britain, this also led to the development of political parties, called the Hats and the Caps – the names were first used during the Diet in 1738–39. The main division between them was based on foreign policy. The Hats were more in favour of war and wanted an alliance with France, the Caps wanted peace and an alliance with Britain. Socially, the Hats were dominated by the high nobility, while the lower nobility and the burghers often supported the Caps. However, like the British parties, they were held together more by personal loyalty and ambition than by a consistent political ideology or organization.

Another difference from Britain was the composition of the Diet which conformed to that of the medieval estates. In was divided into four houses, respectively of the nobles, the clergy, the burghers and the peasants. The house of nobles was the largest, consisting of the heads of all the noble kindred or their deputies, more than a thousand altogether. The three others mainly consisted of elected representatives. As each house had one vote, however, the three non-noble estates were able to outvote the nobles, which explains the alliance of the king and the Diet against the noble council.

The sudden outburst of a something resembling parliamentary government after more than 40 years of almost absolute royal power seems surprising and very different from contemporary Britain. Nevertheless, as we have seen, the situation around 1720 has parallels further back in history and the changes seem a natural reaction against the disastrous consequences of the king's policy in the previous period. However, the Period of Liberty proved to be briefer than in Britain. Gustaf III's coup in 1772 increased the king's power, abolished the party system and once more made the king free to choose his own councillors, although he did not gain absolute power. Gustaf's murder in 1792 led to a new regency for his son, Gustaf IV Adolf, who was later (1809) deposed as the result of the defeat in the war against Russia that led to the loss of Finland. This led to a new and more modern constitution, although not to a government dependent on a majority in the Diet. This was not introduced in Sweden until the early twentieth century.

The development of a modern bureaucracy

Apart from particular sectors, the army and particularly the navy, Britain was late in developing an efficient bureaucracy; for a long time, most of the local administration was run by amateurs and the educational system was also backwards. The distinction between political offices and purely administrative ones was also less clear in practice than in theory; access to offices, particularly higher ones, was often the result of patronage, as may be illustrated by the account of the Church of England in Chapter 4. The now prestigious universities of Oxford and Cambridge were intellectual deserts in the eighteenth and well into the nineteenth century, while the German universities flourished. Whereas the electoral system was reformed in 1832, making Parliament more representative and extending the number of voters to around 650,000, it took longer to introduce a reform of the civil service. A proposal regarding this, the Northcote-Trevelyan Report of 1854, proposing higher educational standards and abolishing patronage, was a first step, but the reform was not really carried out until 1870.[25]

By contrast, the formation of a professional bureaucracy came much earlier in Germany. A large part of Germany and particularly Prussia went through a substantial modernization from the mid-eighteenth century onwards but this was a modernization of the bureaucracy rather than the political sector. We have already traced part of this development under Frederick William I and Frederick II. The next step came after Prussia's defeat by Napoleon in 1806 and was led by Prince Karl August von Hardenberg and Baron Karl vom und zum Stein. Already in 1770, Prussia had introduced a reform of the civil service with examinations as the basis for promotion.[26] Now the education of civil servants was improved and the bureaucracy in practice took over much of the king's power. While Prussia had become a great power largely because of a series of exceptionally competent rulers, its further development took place under fairly mediocre kings but under the leadership of well-educated and competent bureaucracy. The Prussian ministerial system worked in a similar way as the British cabinet but gained its power from the king, not from the people. It eventually developed considerable independence; although formally, the king might reject its advice, it was not easy for him to do so when the ministers controlled the whole bureaucracy and were united behind their decision, as they normally were; they had voted on the issue before it was presented to the king.

In Austria, the reign of Maria Theresa marks an important epoch. She not only saved the Empire from dissolution; she carried out a number of important reforms. Despite being basically conservative, a staunch Catholic, anti-Protestant and anti-Jewish, she is one of the most prominent representatives of enlightened despotism in contemporary Europe. She reformed the army and the bureaucracy – often inspecting the units on horseback – increased the revenues of the government, improved the bureaucracy, eased the conditions of the peasants and restricted the power of the landowners. She introduced compulsory education for the whole population and reformed court procedures. Although she was personally against the reform, she was persuaded by her counsellors to abolish judicial torture in 1774. Generally, she was clever in finding good counsellors and willing to listen to advice even if it went against her original opinions. The reforms were continued during the reigns of her two sons, Joseph II (1780–90) and Leopold II (1790–92). Joseph II closed down Schönbrunn, the Austrian equivalent of Versailles, and converted the old palace in the centre, the Hofburg, into offices, while living himself in a house in the Augarten, described by his biographer as 'no bigger, and much plainer and less ostentatious than a Victorian suburban villa'.[27] Like his older contemporary Frederick II, he regarded himself as a servant of the state. Joseph was a stronger adherent of enlightened despotism than his mother but lacked her skill in handling people and proceeding cautiously, which led to several rebellions against him. Only his death and succession by his brother, who had basically the same aims but was more diplomatic, saved the situation. Leopold had distinguished himself through his enlightened rule as Duke of Tuscany (1765–90), where he had introduced a number of reforms to stimulate the economy and increase the personal freedom of the inhabitants and had even, as the first European ruler, abolished the death penalty. During his short reign, he managed to calm the opposition against his predecessor. However, he was succeeded by his son, Francis II (1792–1835, from 1806 Francis I of Austria), who did not continue his predecessors' reforms.

The Austrian Empire shows a combination of absolutism and constitutionalism, an absolute ruler making decisions for the empire as a whole but with limited possibilities to interfere in each country because of ancient privileges and strong opposition from local elites. The influence from the Enlightenment in the eighteenth century did not come from constitutional assemblies but on the contrary was imposed on them by the absolute emperor. Generally, the example of Austria points to a significant difference between medieval and early modern constitutionalism and contemporary democracy. The former is based on privilege, whereas the latter is based on a fundamental equality between all citizens. Thus, the French revolutionaries were as much against the remains of constitutional government, the Parliament of Paris and the privileges and relative independence of various provinces, as against absolute monarchy. Even the English Parliament was largely an assembly of and for the privileged, which was heavily criticized and finally, after much conflict, was reformed in 1832. Nevertheless, as we shall see, there is some connection between ancient privileges and modern democracy.

The Danish kings were absolute throughout the eighteenth century, but their personal qualities made it necessary to leave more to the colleges. This applies particularly to the reign of Christian VII, who was mad, probably from schizophrenia, and during most of his long reign (1766–1808) was entirely incapable of governing. Characteristically, this meant that political power passed to his immediate entourage, first, his medical doctor, then his teacher. The former, the German Struensee, launched an ambitious reform programme and in addition had an affair with the queen, which led to a coup against him and his execution in 1772. The latter, Ove Høegh Guldberg, a professor and a classical scholar, ruled as the head of a regency government until he was deposed by the crown prince in 1784.

Whereas Guldberg had been basically conservative, the new government, led by A.P. Bernstorff, inaugurated a series of liberal reforms, partly resembling those of Struensee, including the abolition of censorship. It also introduced a major agrarian reform (1788), which abolished the manorial system and allowed the farmers to buy their own land from the landowners. Although the reform was controversial, it was not a stroke against the noble landowners, nor was it intended as such.[28] Bernstorff was a noble and the greatest landowner in the country. The reform was introduced at a period of boom in agricultural prices and was accepted by many landowners who regarded it as an opportunity to make their farms more profitable and get rid of their administrative duties.[29] A similar reform was introduced in Sweden at around the same time. In both countries, there was a change from peasants subordinated to the lord of the manor to free farmers who either owned their own farm or leased it against a fixed rent. Typically, these farmers formed the basis of the democratic movements in both countries as well as in Norway in the nineteenth century, in contrast to many other countries, where agrarian parties were often reactionary and anti-democratic.

However, the reform shows the advantage of the Danish system once government had decided for reform; there was no assembly that had to be convinced and no possibility of protesting against the king's decision. By contrast, the system was not quite as successful when the rather mediocre Frederick VI had restored government by the king in person, formally when he succeeded his father in 1808 but in reality earlier. Ministerial government was introduced once more, together with a thorough revision of the whole administration, when absolutism was abolished in 1848.[30]

Although Denmark was formally and largely also in reality the most absolute kingdom in Europe, the scholarly evaluation of its regime has often been positive. Despite a series of wars in the beginning, the country enjoyed a period of almost permanent peace between 1720 and 1807, its wealth increased, there were no great conflicts, education and learning improved and censorship was abolished or at least relaxed from the late eighteenth century onwards. When Norway was ceded to Sweden in 1814, the country had an enlightened elite which in a short time succeeded in composing a constitution, influenced by many similar documents that were produced in the years after the French Revolution. Despite financial problems in the beginning, it also managed to establish an efficient government. Denmark itself also managed a peaceful change from absolute to constitutional government in 1848, although the process was complicated by the composite nature of the monarchy, with a large German-speaking population in the duchies in the south. This relatively harmonious transition from absolutism to constitutional rule has given rise to a theory, with some support from contemporary evidence, that the king and the government ruled largely in accordance with public opinion.[31] This is probably exaggerated, as freedom of expression during most of the time was limited, although various suggestions for the government might be expressed and the numerous petitions sent to the king gave information of the needs and interest of a number of individual people. Generally, however, there can be no doubt that public opinion had become a far more important factor in the eighteenth century than earlier, in Denmark as well as in other countries, and was able to influence governments.

Despite considerable individual variation among kings and reforms that were more on paper than in reality, Enlightened Despotism is no empty phrase. The ideas of the Enlightenment did influence kings and governments and a number of reforms were attempted, more or less successfully. Most dramatic were the ones of Joseph II which were about to lead to disaster when he died. These reforms are also evidence of the problems of limited monarchy. Joseph suffered his worst defeats in countries with constitutional assemblies, like Hungary and the Southern Netherlands. By contrast, Denmark, where the king was really absolute, was able to introduce far-reaching and successful agrarian reforms in the late eighteenth century. In Sweden, the king was also the driving force in the reforms and was resisted by the nobility, whereas he received some support from the non-noble estates. Prussia was more absolute than Austria as well as more homogeneous; Frederick II's reforms were also reasonably successful, although they went less far than those of Joseph II in Austria.

France was central in the Enlightenment, but more in the form of discussions and publications by intellectuals than of concrete reforms introduced by the king and his ministers. Despite censorship, which might be troublesome but was as inefficient as most other aspects of government in this country, there were vivid debates on various aspects of politics, government and religion. The ideas of the Enlightenment also had political importance. The nobility was neither isolated nor reactionary; many of its members were well read and were positive to reform, at least within certain limits. Some of the ministers, notably under Louis XVI, were influenced by the Enlightenment. Some reforms were also introduced, including greater religious freedom and the abolition of judicial torture and of the cruellest forms of execution. However, there was no Frederick II or Joseph II and, apart from a long tradition of loyalty to the king, the French monarchy in the eighteenth century did little to appeal to the general public.

France is actually the great exception among the major powers of Europe regarding the position of the king and the court. Here the rules laid down by Louis XIV continued to be observed until 1789. Versailles had been functional in the seventeenth century, but now became increasingly obsolete. Paris became the centre of culture and political debate, while the king was isolated in Versailles and without contact with the new ideas. And while Louis XIV was able to create respect and admiration for himself not only by virtue of his office but also because of his personal qualities, his successors were unable to do so. Louis XV was surrounded by mistresses, who, in addition, had great political influence and, although he was intelligent, he was a weak and lazy ruler. Louis XVI led a respectable private life and was a man with the best intentions, but was weak and indecisive as a ruler and with little political understanding. It would seem that the people still had a good opinion of the king in 1789–90 and that a more energetic and charismatic ruler than Louis XVI might have exploited this position to carry out moderate reform. However, this did not happen; instead, the Old Regime in France broke down, and despite a number of different constitutions in the following period and various attempts to restore it, it never returned.

Could France have developed differently?[32] The answer to this question depends on whether the French crisis can be explained as the result of purely technical problems or it has to do with more fundamental, structural factors. Here historians disagree. Although the royal revenues in France were significantly lower than the ones in Britain, there was no acute financial crisis until the steep rise in the debt resulting from the American War of Independence, which had been financed entirely by loans. As we have seen, the British debt was larger at the time and continued to rise in the following period without causing similar problems, but the trust in the French economy was less. At the same time, the French minister of finance, Necker, had tried to increase the efficiency of the financial administration and reduce superfluous expenses, such as the many pensions and sinecures to members of the nobility. He also stopped the sales of offices. However, the situation deteriorated further as the result of a series of bad harvests which eventually led to peasant rebellions in 1789. Here it must also be added that most of France had not undergone the modernization of agriculture that took place in England and the Dutch Republic in the seventeenth and eighteenth centuries. Most farms were too small and were easily divided; property rights were often unclear and there was a considerable increase in population, from 20 million around 1700 to 28 million in 1789, as well as a greater difference between the few wealthy and the many poor peasants.

We can fairly easily identify the financial problem as inadequate revenues rather than too high expenses, as illustrated by the comparison with Britain. Although England was wealthier per capita than France, this difference cannot in itself explain the problem of managing the burden. The average burden on the French taxpayer was less than the one on his English counterpart, that is, the burden would have been easy, if all Frenchmen had paid taxes. The problem, of course, was that the wealthiest people in France, the nobles and the clerics and a large number of other wealthy people, most of the time did not pay direct taxes at all, so that the burden was heavy on peasants and poor people. Moreover, even this burden was distributed unequally; there were great differences between the regions, with the heaviest burden on those around Paris. Even so, it might be thought that a debt of this size might be increased relatively easily, as in Britain, but here the problem was that France had no national bank which could attract capital from the international market. Most of the creditors were French, to a great extent, the king's officials. The French government also had to pay a higher rate of interest than the English. After the Revolution, France also introduced a national bank (1800), abolished the venal offices and the tax exemption. Still, however, the French state incomes were lower than the British ones.[33]

There thus seems to have been a 'technical' solution to the financial problem in the form of a national bank that was able to extend the credit and a reform of the tax system that increased the revenues. In the crisis in 1709, during the War of the Spanish Succession, Louis XIV had managed to raise a new army by imposing new taxes. Although this was more difficult to do in peacetime, it would not seem impossible for a more determined and energetic government to have solved the financial crisis of the 1780s. However, there were also more deep-rooted problems: extreme inefficiency in the administration, increasing tension between the social classes, a public opinion increasingly critical of the court and the monarchy and the isolation of the latter in Versailles. Fundamentally, the problem was that to have any effect, a reform would have to go against important interests in society. The nobility had various local privileges as well as a monopoly on commissions as officers in the army and navy. The bourgeoisie consisted largely of people who profited from the venality of offices or were employed in the very inefficient tax-farming system, which greatly reduced the net surplus from the taxes. The many privileges and monopolies that hampered economic progress were, of course, highly profitable for the people who enjoyed them. 'Creative destruction' is usually regarded as necessary for economic progress, which, of course, means that it can hardly take place without meeting resistance. The last twenty years before the Revolution were characterized by a series of attempts at reform by a large number of ministers who were mostly deposed after a short time because of court intrigues or protests from influential groups. In addition, the Enlightenment movement had resulted in a public opinion increasingly critical of the court and the government and a strong demand for reform. From this point of view, it has been claimed that the decisive shift that eventually led to the Revolution must be dated to around 1760, after the defeats in the Seven Years War and Louis XV's political incompetence and moral failures had undermined its authority.[34]

This, however, raises a new question: why did the changes in the eighteenth century lead to revolution in France, while the rest of Europe were either subject to moderate reforms or underwent few changes? Here we can point to the fact that the new ideas were particularly strong and widespread in France, while their practical impact was less than in many other places because of the weakness of its kings and the low competence of the bureaucracy. Prussia, Austria, many German principalities and Scandinavia performed better in both respects. Considering the opposition to reform in many countries, notably France and Austria, we may ask whether the problem in the eighteenth century was that the king was too absolute or that he was not absolute enough. Although France had no Diet operating between 1614 and 1789, there were numerous institutions that limited the power of the king, in addition to the fact that he had little control of the bureaucracy. A stronger king might possibly have been able to reform the system or at least improve it. By contrast, the Danish and Prussian governments succeeded in introducing major reforms because the king was absolute and there was no assembly that might restrict his power. In the case of Sweden, it is at least possible to claim that Gustaf III carried out reforms that the previous 'parliamentary' system had proved unable to introduce. However, the problem with absolutism was that so much depended on the king's personal qualities. Thus, the solution, even in countries that remained formally more or less absolute, was ministerial government based on a strong and competent bureaucracy, as in Prussia. In the nineteenth and twentieth centuries, this also became a fundamental factor in democratic states. This has led to tension and problems, as caricatured in the popular television series, *Yes, Prime Minister*, in which the smiling and affable Sir Humphrey depicts himself as the humble servant who carries out the prime minister's orders, while manipulating him to act according to the interests of the bureaucracy. It is nevertheless difficult to imagine that government by the people through their elected representatives can function without a strong element of educated professionals, recruited according to merit, who solve practical problems and give the elected leaders the necessary information.

The first examples of democracy in the modern sense in the western world were the Constitutions of the United States of America of 1789 and of France of 1791. The former was probably at the time too distant to have been very important as a model, whereas the latter created strong reactions abroad, positive as well as negative. Despite its resemblance to modern constitutions, it can hardly be regarded as a great success, as it was soon abolished and led to a period of terror and internal struggles, followed by military dictatorship. In the long run, however, the ideas of the French Revolution proved victorious, in some countries after revolution or internal or external wars, in other gradually and peacefully, the latter notably in Britain and the Scandinavian countries. A series of changes in the political, cultural and economic fields led to this result: the Industrial Revolution, greater wealth, higher living standards, better education, scientific progress and the mobilization of larger and larger parts of the population to fight for their interests and demanding a say in the government of the country. To this must be added the introduction of compulsory military service and the great mobilization during the two World Wars. However, the beginning of this process lies in the eighteenth century, with the Enlightenment and the reform processes that started in constitutional as well as absolutist countries.

Conclusion

'Intellectually, Voltaire is our contemporary, but his daily life was radically different from ours.' These words by Fernand Braudel seem an apt characterization of the Age of Enlightenment. Despite the scientific discoveries and other changes that have taken place since the eighteenth century, we can identify with Voltaire and other intellectuals at the time, while we can hardly imagine their daily life, the number of servants needed for a comfortable bourgeois life, the absence of lavatories, showers, electric heating, cars, railways and planes, the stinking streets and the general poverty, the exposure to diseases and the lack of what we would consider elementary medical care. In other words, little had changed regarding social and economic conditions from the Middle Ages to the eighteenth century compared to what happened later, while a great deal had happened in the intellectual field: increased literacy, an enormous increase in the publication of books and papers and the formation of a public opinion. Politically, something corresponding to modern parliamentary government had been introduced in two countries, Britain and Sweden. In most others, some modifications of absolutism had taken place, in the form of Enlightened Despotism, including increased freedom of expression, judicial reforms and in some countries, notably Prussia, a more efficient and professional bureaucracy. In the leading country on the Continent, France, this clearly proved insufficient and the Revolution led to the destruction of the Old Regime. It remains an open question whether reform would have continued in other parts of Europe; in any case, the reaction against the French Revolution put an end to it for a long time.

Notes

1 Blanning, *The Pursuit of Glory*, p. 294.
2 For the following, see Habermas, *Strukturwandel* and Blanning, *The Pursuit of Glory*, pp. 456–521.
3 See e.g. Melve, *Inventing the Public Sphere*, vol. I, pp. 1–42.
4 Southern, *The Making of the Middle Ages*, p. 194. The attribution to Bernhard stems from John of Salisbury.
5 Tocqueville, *Democracy in America*, pp. 652–3.

6 Lukes, *Individualism*, pp. 1–9.
7 On Hobbes and other theorists of the monarchical state, see also Skinner, 'From the State of Princes' and *Visions of Politics*, vol. III, *Hobbes and Civil Science*.
8 Monod, *Power of Kings*, pp. 269–71.
9 Riley, 'Social Contract Theory and its Critics', pp. 362–9.
10 Winch, 'Scottish Political Economy'.
11 Hankins, 'Preface', pp. xvii–xviii.
12 Mason, 'Optimism, Progress and Philosophical History'; Richter, 'The Comparative Study'; O'Brien, 'English Enlightenment'; cf. Abbatista, 'The Historical Thought' and Alan, 'Scottish Historical Writing'.
13 Blanning, *The Pursuit of Glory*, pp. 385–92.
14 Ibid., p. 286.
15 Ibid., p. 478.
16 Roche, 'Encyclopedias and the Diffusion of Knowledge'.
17 Dalong, 'De la conversation à la création'.
18 For the following, see Blanning, *Frederick II*, pp. 342–66.
19 Hoppit, *Land of Liberty*, pp. 13–50; Goldie, 'The English System of Liberty', pp. 40–78.
20 Hoppit, *Land of Liberty*, p. 24.
21 For a detailed case study of the political system in the early eighteenth century, see Graham, *Corruption*.
22 Fukuyama, *The Origins*, pp. 321–35.
23 For the following, see Rosén, *Svensk historia*, vol. I, pp. 540–716; Carlsson, *Svensk historia*, vol. II, pp. 91–203 and Hein, 'Cultural Europeanization', pp. 604–5.
24 In Sweden, the usual date is 30 November, as Sweden at the time still used the Julian calendar. It was the last country in Western Europe to change, in 1753, one year after Britain.
25 Fukuyama, *Political Order*, pp. 126–34.
26 For the following, see Clark, *Iron Kingdom*, pp. 312–44 and Fukuyama, *Political Order*, pp. 66–80.
27 Blanning, *The Culture of Power*, pp. 430–1.
28 Thus, Fukuyama, *Political Order*, p. 433, who credits the king with the reform and points to fierce resistance from the landowners.
29 Feldbæk, *Danmarks historie*, vol. IV, pp. 146–94 and 'Vækst og reformer', pp. 302–8.
30 Knudsen, 'Ministerialsystemet', pp. 465–75.
31 Seip, *Det opinionsstyrte enevelde*; more critical is Rian, *Sensuren*, pp. 575–628.
32 For the following, see Bonney, 'France 1494–1815'; Blanning, *The Pursuit of Glory*, pp. 337–43; Ladurie, *The Ancient Regime*, pp. 494–513; Collins, *From Tribes to Nation*, pp. 481–537; Doyle, *The Ancien Regime*, pp. 1–36 and *French Revolution*, pp. 1–85.
33 Blanning, *The Pursuit of Glory*, pp. 348–9.
34 Collins, *From Tribes to Nation*, pp. 481–92.

CONCLUSION

The state of the Old Regime and its legacy

On the night between 4 and 5 August 1789, the members of the assembly at Versailles, having recently declared themselves to be the Constitutional Assembly of France, met to discuss demands from the peasants for the abolition of the 'feudal dues', i.e. the various duties and payments the peasants owed to their lords. The first speaker was the Viscount of Nouailles who proposed that all the dues should be abolished, largely without compensation. For Nouailles, this was an easy sacrifice, as he was a younger son, with no substantial property. However, he was followed by the Duke of Aiguillon, the greatest landowner in the country, who stood up and resigned all his feudal rights. Then the avalanche was let loose. During the night one nobleman after the other resigned his rights and were joined by clergy and burghers, all renouncing their ancient privileges. By dawn, France had become a different country.[1]

The event seems almost like a miracle and was often regarded as such at the time. Two factors make it less miraculous. First, a major peasant revolt had broken out in the summer of 1789, instigated partly by a series of bad harvests and partly by the meeting in Versailles. To use military power against the peasants meant that the army might next be used against the assembly itself; consequently, the peasants had to be pacified. Second, the minutes from the meeting, issued on 11 August, contained the provision that compensation should be paid to those who had renounced their privileges, which, however, proved impossible to enforce. Nevertheless, the element of idealism should not be underestimated, nor the symbolic importance of the act: it was the beginning of a new society of freedom and equality – the latter not in the sense it is often used today of equal conditions, but in the sense of equal opportunities, no formal rules or institutions preventing individual choice. These principles were further developed in the Declaration of Human Rights of 26 August, their classical formulation but anticipated by and influenced by the similar declarations from the American Revolution, notably the

Declaration of Independence of 2 July 1776. The French Declaration of 1789 contains 17 articles, opening with the following two:

1. Men are born and remain free and equal in rights. Social distinctions can be founded only on the common good.
2. The goal of any political association is the conservation of the natural and imprescriptible rights of man. These rights are liberty, property, safety and resistance against oppression.

The following articles deal with popular sovereignty, liberty to do anything that does not harm others, the foundation of law in the popular will, safety against unjust accusation and the rule of law, freedom of thought and expression, consent to taxation and the right to private property. Later declarations of human rights, from 1948 onwards, represent further developments of the ones from the eighteenth century.

More than 200 years later, we recognize the declarations as containing the fundamental ideas on which our own democracy is built, but also know that their proclamation in 1789 did not lead to a smooth transition to a new society. The French Revolution introduced a period of terror, violence and war, a civil war in France as well as a general European war that lasted almost continuously from 1792 until 1815. A number of constitutions, modelled on the American and French ones, came into being during this period but most of them were abolished by its end. In the long run, however, the ideas of 1789 have won, not only in Europe but also in other parts of the world, to the extent that Francis Fukuyama in a short period of extreme optimism in 1992, just after the fall of Communism, could publish a book entitled *The End of History and the Last Man*.

The ideas of the American and French Revolutions were new and radical and were deliberately aimed at replacing the old structures and ideas, the ones we have dealt with on the previous pages. Their direct ancestry is to be found in the Enlightenment. It was no longer an argument in favour of an institution or a practice that it had existed for a long time; to be acceptable, it had to be based on reason. Thus, the American Declaration of Independence opens with the words: 'We hold these truths to be self-evident, that all men are created equal, that they are endowed by their Creator with certain unalienable Rights, that among these are Life, Liberty and the pursuit of Happiness.' Until 1789, in Europe, these principles were mainly promoted by intellectuals, but, as we have seen, they also to some extent influenced practical politics, through the idea of 'Enlightened Despotism'. Some countries introduced freedom or partial freedom of expression of religion, abolished privileges and reformed justice by abolishing judicial torture and the cruellest forms of punishment. Britain took some steps towards democracy through the greater influence of Parliament, the institution of a cabinet and the abolition of economic privileges. It may also be added that the British path to democracy was more successful than the French one. Although regarded as reactionary by the most radical French revolutionaries, Britain gradually developed in a democratic direction, first, with the Parliamentary Reform of 1832, then with gradual extension of the vote, until all adults gained this right in 1928.

A more fundamental question is the relationship between the society we have considered during most of the previous pages and the one developing after the French Revolution. Is there continuity, despite the dramatic rejection during the Revolution? The key to this continuity is the concept of rights. When Margaret Thatcher, on the 200th anniversary of the French Revolution in 1789 claimed that England had done the same as France long before, pointing to the Magna Carta, she was clearly wrong. The Magna Carta is a list of established or allegedly established rights for specific people, not of rights common to all men. Even the most famous paragraph, the ban against arresting a free man without legal procedure, originally only applied to a minority; the majority of the English population was unfree. Only later did it receive a wider application.[2] Moreover, most of the other paragraphs favour the nobility; the charter is thus largely in support of the society which the Declaration of 1789 wanted to destroy. A closer parallel is the Declaration of Rights of 1689 which proclaims a series of rules for the government of England, but nevertheless has a more pragmatic character without any reference to fundamental rights for all men.

Nevertheless, such rights formed an important part of medieval political thought, notably after the reception of Aristotle's political ideas in the thirteenth century, although they were not expressed in any political proclamation. Their practical consequences were therefore limited and, as we have seen, inequality and hierarchy were fundamental elements of European society from the Middle Ages until the French Revolution. Thus, it is not difficult to recognize the targets of the criticism during the Enlightenment and the French Revolution. The society of the Old Regime was often oppressive, unjust and inefficient but it was not arbitrary. The rights of property and inheritance were respected; there was a kind of rule of law, although the laws might be harsh and there was no equality before the law; the privileged had better rights than ordinary people. Rulers might be more or less bound by formal rules but, in contrast to the great eastern empires, they depended on support from a larger society, normally the elites. They had no slave soldiers or bureaucracies independent of the local population; they had to base their government on cooperation with local elites, particularly the nobility, eventually also the bourgeoisie and, to some extent, even the peasants. The concept of rights was thus an important fact during the Old Regime. The aim of the French Revolution and other reactions against it were therefore largely to extend these rights to the whole population.

The division into smaller kingdoms and the competition between them increased the king's dependence on his subjects. This division was established already around 1200. It would seem that the initial weakness of the state after the fall of the Roman Empire was an important factor in this, combined with the lack of invasions, which in turn was partly the result of the poverty of Europe at the time and partly of its distance from the main areas of nomads. The development of dynasties in the following period made the division permanent, although reducing it somewhat through unions caused by dynastic marriages. A gradual development of political institutions then took place during the following centuries. In this way, the state eliminated competition within its borders, while increasing it across them. From the sixteenth century, it also largely managed to subdue its external competitors, the city and the Church – the latter mainly in Protestant countries but also, to some extent, in Catholic ones. However, this was achieved by integrating the competitors rather than suppressing them. The nobles became part of national elites, surrounding the rulers in places like the Palace of Versailles or Westminster Hall. The ecclesiastical bureaucracy increasingly served the state, particularly in Protestant but also in Catholic countries. The independent cities largely disappeared but their merchants formed an essential element in the most successful states, England/Britain and the Dutch Republic. There was a considerable element of violence and suppression in European state building, but this is not the whole explanation. The state had to appeal to the population, admittedly mostly its leading members, and it had to make itself useful by conflict solution and protecting trade and communication within the country.

Not only the division itself but also the competition between the states was an important factor in their further development. Whereas the purely military development is of limited importance in explaining the borders between them, it is certainly important in explaining their internal development. Warfare led to internal reforms, the development of bureaucracies and, in some cases, the increased importance of constitutional assemblies and popular participation. It served to unite the national aristocracy under the king's leadership to fight foreign enemies. However, it might also lead to less efficiency, such as the venality of offices in France and Spain and the financial crises in both countries. By contrast, the development of Parliament and local government in England was only to a limited extent the result of military mobilization. State formation was therefore also the result of internal consolidation, law and justice, aristocratic participation in government and the courtly culture. In short, state formation was not exclusively the result of force; it was also largely based on cooperation, although with the elites rather than with the common people.

In contrast to the claims by Tilly and some other scholars, it seems unlikely that a great European empire was a realistic option at any time before Napoleon. Charles V's limited success against one of his European competitors, France, as well as his problems in getting any real control of the petty principalities in Germany, enable us to dismiss this idea in his case. Concerning Louis XIV, there is no evidence that he had any plans in this direction and even if he had, it is difficult to see that he would have been able to establish effective control of the whole of Europe, considering the limited control he had of his own country. Moreover, both rulers were hampered by legal and ideological factors. The dynastic state, ruled by a hereditary king, had internal as well as external legitimacy. Open disregard for this principle might endanger one's own position, externally and possibly even internally. No doubt, both Napoleon and Hitler – both of whom could afford to disregard this and other principles – came closer to this aim. Both, however, were stopped by forces outside the European Continent; Britain and Russia, in the case of the former, Britain, Russia and the USA, in the case of the latter. Regarding both, it may, in addition, be pointed out that their 'empires' took the form of the old state system – in Napoleon's case, including substantial changes in Germany and Italy – with puppet or dependent rulers. Concerning the most recent, voluntary attempt at a European union, whatever one's view of its success, it must be admitted that we are still far from the United States of Europe. Thus, despite the many and great changes that have taken place between the late eighteenth century and the present, Europeans still live in a world that to a considerable extent was shaped before that date.

For a period of more than a thousand years after the fall of the Roman Empire, East Asia was probably the most advanced part of the world, with a larger population, more intensive agriculture, larger and better organized cities and stronger states and empires. This changed at some stage in the early modern period, and during the last 200 years, Europe and the USA have dominated the world in a way that has never occurred before. The reasons for this have been much discussed, but there are at least indications that the story told in the previous pages is of some relevance to this answer. The organization and technological innovations in the military field were clearly results of the competition between the European states. The great scientific discoveries from the sixteenth century onwards have been explained in different ways but at least from the time when they had practical applications, the importance of the state must have been great. This includes both active support, as in England/Britain from the late seventeenth century onwards, and the competition between states, which made it possible to escape persecution by moving across the border and find a more stimulating environment. Such environments were to some extent to be found at the medieval universities, in the Italian cities during the Renaissance, and later notably in the Dutch Republic and England. Whether actively or passively, the European state thus played a part in the scientific revolution.

Thus, despite the many deficiencies of the European state of the Old Regime, it seems to have been based more on support from at least a portion of its subjects than most kingdoms and empires in other parts of the world, which in turn forms part of the explanation for later Western dominance.

Notes

1 Doyle, *The French Revolution*, pp. 112–18.
2 Holt, *Magna Carta*, pp. 327–31.

REFERENCES

Abbatista, Guido. 'The Historical Thought of the French Philosophes', in José Rabasa, Masayuki Sato, Edoardo Tortarolo, and Daniel Woolf, *et al.* (eds), *The Oxford History of Historical Writing*, vol. III (Oxford: Oxford University Press, 2012), pp. 406–427.

Abulafia, David (ed.) *The New Cambridge Medieval History*, vol. V (Cambridge: Cambridge University Press, 1995).

Abulafia, David. *The Great Sea: A Human History of the Mediterranean* (London: Penguin, 2012).

Acemoglou, Daron and James A. Robinson. *Why Nations Fail: The Origins of Power, Prosperity and Poverty* (London: Profile Books, 2013).

Adamson, John (ed.) *The Princely Courts of Europe: Ritual, Politics and Culture Under the Ancien Regime, 1500–1750* (London: Weidenfeld and Nicholson, 1999).

Adamson, John. 'The Making of the Ancien-Régime Court, 1500–1700', in John Adamson (ed.), *The Princely Courts of Europe: Ritual, Politics and Culture Under the Ancien Regime, 1500–1750* (London: Weidenfeld and Nicholson, 1999), pp. 7–42.

Adamson, John. 'The Kingdoms of England and Great Britain. The Tudor and Stuart Courts', in John Adamson (ed.), *The Princely Courts of Europe: Ritual, Politics and Culture Under the Ancien Regime, 1500–1750* (London: Weidenfeld and Nicholson, 1999), pp. 95–118.

Airlie, Stuart. 'The Aristocracy', in Rosamund McKitterick, Timothy Reuter, Paul Fouracre, *et al.* (eds), *The New Cambridge Medieval History, c. 900–c. 1024*, vol. II (Cambridge: Cambridge University Press, 1995), pp. 431–450.

Alan, David. 'Scottish Historical Writing of the Enlightenment', in José Rabasa, Masayuki Sato, Edoardo Tortarolo, and Daniel Woolf (eds), *The Oxford History of Historical Writing*, vol. III (Oxford: Oxford University Press, 2012), pp. 497–517.

Allmand, Christopher (ed.) *The New Cambridge Medieval History*, vol. VII, *c. 1415–1500* (Cambridge: Cambridge University Press, 1998).

Althoff, Gerd. *Freunde, Verwandte und Getreue. Zum politischen Stellenwert der Gruppenbindungen im früheren Mittelalter* (Darmstadt: Wissenschaftliche Buchgesellschaft, 1990).

Althoff, Gerd. 'Die Beurteilung der mittelalterlichen Ostpolitik als Paradigma für zeitgebundene Geschichtsbewertung', in Gerd Althoff (ed.), *Die Deutschen und ihr Mittelalter* (Darmstadt: Wissenschaftliche Buchgesellschaft, 1992), pp. 147–164.

Althoff, Gerd. *Kaiser Otto III* (Darmstadt: Wissenschaftliche Buchgesellschaft, 1996).

Althoff, Gerd. *Spielregeln der Politik im Mittelalter* (Darmstadt: Wissenschaftliche Buchgesellschaft, 1997).

Althoff, Gerd. *Die Macht der Rituale. Symbolik und Herrschaft im Mittelalter* (Darmstadt: Wissenschaftliche Buchgesellschaft, 2003).

Althoff, Gerd. *Heinrich IV* (Darmstadt: Primus, 2006).

Althoff, Gerd. 'Establishing Bonds: Fiefs, Homage, and Other Means to Create Trust', in Sverre Bagge, M.H. Gelting and T. Lindkvist (eds), *Feudalism: New Landscapes of Debate* (Turnhout: Brepols, 2011), pp. 101–114.

Althoff, Gerd. *„Selig sind, die Verfolgung ausüben". Päpste und Gewalt im Hochmittelalter* (Darmstadt: Wissenschaftliche Buchgesellschaft, 2013).

Althoff, Gerd. *Kontrolle der Macht. Form und Regeln politischer Beratung im Mittelalter* (Darmstadt: Wissenschaftliche Buchgesellschaft, 2016).

Ames, Christine Caldwell. *Medieval Heresies: Christianity, Judaism, and Islam* (Cambridge: Cambridge University Press, 2015).

Andersen, Per, Mia Munster-Swendsen, and Helle Vogt (eds) *Law and Power in the Middle Ages: Proceedings of the Fourth Carlsberg Academy Conference on Medieval Legal History* (Copenhagen: DJOF Publishing, 2008).

Anderson, Perry. *Passages from Antiquity to Feudalism* (London: NLB, 1975).

Anderson, Perry. *Lineages of the Absolutist State* (London: NLB, 1975).

Ardant, Gabriel. 'Financial Policy and Economic Infrastructure of Modern States and Nations', in Charles Tilly (ed.), *The Formation of National States in Western Europe* (Princeton, NJ: Princeton University Press, 1975), pp. 164–242.

Arnold, John. 'Histories and Historiographies of Medieval Christianity', in John Arnold (ed.), *The Oxford Handbook of Medieval Christianity* (Oxford: Oxford University Press, 2005), pp. 23–41.

Arquillière, Henri. *L'augustinisme politique* (Paris: 1934).

Aylmer, Gerald. *The Struggle for the Constitution, 1603–1689* (London: Blandford, 1963).

Bachrach, David S. *Warfare in Tenth-Century Germany* (Woodbridge:Boydell Press, 2012).

Bagge, Sverre. *The Political Thought of the King's Mirror* (Odense: Odense University Press, 1987).

Bagge, Sverre. *Society and Politics in Snorri Sturluson's Heimskringla* (Berkeley, CA: University of California Press, 1991).

Bagge, Sverre. 'Ideas and Narrative in Otto of Freising's Gesta Frederici', *Journal of Medieval History* 22(1996): 345–377.

Bagge, Sverre. 'Medieval and Renaissance Historiography: Break or Continuity?' *The European Legacy* 2. 8(1997): 1336–1366.

Bagge, Sverre. *Kings, Politics, and the Right Order of the World in German Historiography c. 950–1150* (Leiden: Brill, 2002).

Bagge, Sverre. 'Actors and Structures in Machiavelli's Istorie fiorentine', *Quaderni d'italianistica* 28(2007): 45–87.

Bagge, Sverre. *From Viking Stronghold to Christian Kingdom: State Formation in Norway c. 900–1350* (Copenhagen: Museum Tusculanum Press, 2010).

Bagge, Sverre. 'The Model Emperor: Einhard's Charlemagne in Widukind and Rahewin', *Viator* 43(2012): 49–78.

Bagge, Sverre. *Cross and Scepter: The Rise of the Scandinavian Kingdoms from the Vikings to the Reformation* (Princeton, NJ: Princeton University Press, 2014).

Bagge, Sverre. 'The Decline of Regicide and the Rise of European Monarchy from the Carolingians to the Early Modern Period', *Frühmittelalterliche Studien* (forthcoming).

Bagge, Sverre, M.H. Gelting and T. Lindkvist (eds) *Feudalism: New Landscapes of Debate* (Turnhout: Brepols, 2011).

Baker, Derek (ed.) *Medieval Women* (Oxford: Blackwell, 1978).

Baker, Patrick. *Italian Renaissance Humanism in the Mirror* (Cambridge: Cambridge University Press, 2015).

Balázs, Nagy and Frank Schaer. *Karoli IV Imperatoris Vita ab Eo Ipso Conscripta/Autobiography of Emperor Charles IV*, ed. and trans. Paul W. Knoll and Frank Schaer (Budapest: Central European University Press, 2001).

Baldwin, John. *The Government of Philip Augustus: Foundations of French Royal Power in the Middle Ages* (Berkeley, CA: The University of California Press, 1991).

Barber, Malcolm. *The Trial of the Templars* (Cambridge: Cambridge University Press, 2006).

Barraclough, Geoffrey. *The Medieval Papacy* (London: Thames and Hudson, 1968).

Barth, Fredrik. *Ethnic Groups and Boundaries: The Social Organization of Culture Differences* (Oslo: Universitetsforlaget, 1969).

Barthélemy, Dominique. 'Vassaux et fiefs dans la France de l'an mil', in Sverre Bagge, M.H. Gelting and T. Lindkvist (eds), *Feudalism: New Landscapes of Debate* (Turnhout: Brepols, 2011), pp. 57–75.

Barthélemy, Dominique. *Nouvelle histoire des Capétiens* (Paris: Seuil, 2012).

Bartlett, Robert. *Trial by Fire and Water: The Medieval Judicial Ordeal* (Oxford: Oxford University Press, 1986).

Bartlett, Robert. *The Making of Europe: Conquest, Colonization and Cultural Change* (London: Penguin, 1994).

Bartlett, Robert. *England under the Norman and Angevin Kings, 1075–1225* (Oxford: Oxford University Press, 2000).

Bayley, David H. 'The Police and Political Development in Europe', in Charles Tilly (ed.), *The Formation of National States in Western Europe* (Princeton, NJ: Princeton University Press, 1975), pp. 328–379.

Becher, Matthias (ed.) *Die mittelalterliche Thronfolge im europäischen Vergleich* (Ostfildern: Jan Thorbecke, 2017).

Beik, William. 'The Absolutism of Louis XIV as Social Collaboration', *Past and Present* 188 (2005): 195–224.

Bellamy, John G. *The Law of Treason in England in the Later Middle Ages* (Cambridge: Cambridge University Press, 1970).

Benson, Robert L. 'Political Renovatio: Two Models from Roman Antiquity', in Robert L. Benson and Giles Constable (eds), *Renaissance and Renewal in the Twelfth Century* (Toronto: University of Toronto Press, 1991. [orig. 1982]), pp. 339–386.

Berend, Nora (ed.) *Christianization and the Rise of Christian Monarchy: Scandinavia, Central Europe and Rus' c. 900–1200* (Cambridge: Cambridge University Press, 2007).

Berend, Nora, Przemyslaw Urbanzyk and Przemyslaw Wiszewski. *Central Europe in the Middle Ages: Bohemia, Hungary and Poland c. 900–1300* (Cambridge: Cambridge University Press, 2013).

Berger, Stefan. 'The Invention of European National Traditions in European Romanticism', in Stuart Macintyre, Juan Maiguashca, and Attila Pok (eds), *The Oxford History of Historical Writing*, vol. 4 (*1800–1945*) (Oxford: Oxford University Press, 2011), pp. 19–40.

Berman, Harold. *Law and Revolution: The Formation of the Western Legal Tradition* (Cambridge, MA: Harvard University Press, 1983).

Berman, Harold. *Law and Revolution*, vol. II, *The Impact of the Protestant Reformations on the Western Legal Tradition* (Cambridge, MA: The Belknap Press of Harvard University Press, 2003).

Bernhardt, John W. *Itinerant Kingship in Early Medieval Germany, c. 936–1075* (Cambridge: Cambridge University Press, 1993).

Beumann, Helmut. 'Zur Entwicklung transpersonaler Staatsvorstellungen', in *Das Königtum. Seine geistigen und rechtlichen Grundlagen. Vorträge und Forschungen*, vol. 3 (Lindau: Thorbecke, 1956), pp. 185–224.

Biller, Peter. 'Popular Religion in the Central and Later Middle Ages', in Michael Bentley (ed.), *Companion to Historiography* (London: Routledge, 1997), pp. 221–246.

Biller, Peter. 'Goodbye to Waldensianism?', *Past & Present* 192(2006): 3–33.

Biller, Peter. 'Heresy and Dissent', in R.N. Swanson (ed.), *The Routledge History of Medieval Christianity* (London: Routledge, 2015), pp. 251–264.

Biller, Peter. 'Goodbye to Catharism', in Antonio Sennis (ed.), *Cathars in Question* (Woodbridge: Boydell Press, 2016), pp. 274–313.

Biller, Peter. 'R.I. Moore. The War on Heresy: Faith and Power in Medieval Europe'. Available at: www.history.ac.uk/reviews/review/1546

Bisson, Thomas. 'The Feudal Revolution', *Past and Present* 142(1994): 6–42.

Bisson, Thomas. 'The Feudal Revolution', *Past and Present* 155(1997): 208–225.

Bisson, Thomas. *The Crisis of the Twelfth Century* (Princeton, NJ: Princeton University Press, 2009).

Blanning, T.C.W. *The Culture of Power and the Power of Culture: Old Regime Europe 1660–1789* (Oxford: Oxford University Press, 2002).

Blanning, T.C.W. *The Pursuit of Glory: Europe 1648–1815* (London: Penguin, 2007).

Blanning, T.C.W. *Frederick the Great, King of Prussia* (London: Allen Lane, 2015).

Blickle, Peter (ed.) *Resistance, Representation and Community* (Oxford: Clarendon Press, 1997).

Blickle, Peter. 'Conclusions', in Peter Blickle (ed.), *Resistance, Representation and Community* (Oxford: Clarendon Press, 1997), pp. 325–338.

Blickle, Peter, Steven Ellis and Eva Österberg. 'The Commons and the State: Representation, Influence and the Legislative Process', in Peter Blickle (ed.), *Resistance, Representation and Community* (Oxford: Clarendon Press, 1997).

Bloch, Marc. *Les rois thaumaturges* (Paris: Gallimard, 1983 [orig. 1924]).

Blockmans, Wim. *A History of Power in Europe* (Antwerp: Fonds Mercator, 1997).

Blockmans, Wim. 'Representation (Since the Thirteenth Century)', in Christopher Allmand (ed.), *The New Cambridge Medieval History*, vol. VII, *c. 1415–c.1500* (Cambridge: Cambridge University Press, 1998), pp. 38–47.

Blockmans, Wim. 'The Low Countries in the Middle Ages', in Richard Bonney (ed.), *The Rise of the Fiscal State c. 1200–1815* (Oxford: Oxford University Press, 1999), pp. 281–308.

Bluche, François. *Louis XIV* (Oxford: Oxford University Press, 1990).

Bonney, Richard. *The Rise of the Fiscal State in Europe c. 1200–1815* (Oxford: Oxford University Press, 1999).

Bonney, Richard. 'France 1494–1815', in Richard Bonney (ed.), *The Rise of the State in Europe c. 1200–1815* (Oxford: Oxford University Press, 1999), pp. 123–176.

Boxer, C.M. *The Portuguese Seaborne Empire 1415–1825* (Harmondsworth: Penguin, 1969).

Braudel, Fernand. *La Méditerranée et le monde méditerranéen à l'époque de Philip II* (Paris: Armand Colin, 1949).

Breuilly, John. *Nationalism and the State* (Manchester: Manchester University Press, 1993).

Broekmann, Theo. *Rigor iustitiae. Herrschaft, Recht und Terror im normannisch-staufischen Süden (1050–1250)* (Darmstadt: Wissenschaftliche Buchgesellschaft, 2005).

Brooke, Zachary N. *The English Church and the Papacy from the Conquest to the Reign of King John* (Cambridge: Cambridge University Press, 1931).

Brown, Peter. *The World of Late Antiquity* (London: Thames and Hudson, 1971).

Brown, Peter. 'Society and the Supernatural: A Medieval Change', in Peter Brown, *Society and the Holy in Late Antiquity* (London: Faber and Faber, 1982).

Brown, Peter. *The Rise of Western Christendom: Triumph and Diversity, A.D. 200–1000* (Malden, MA: Blackwell, 2003).

Brown, Peter. *Through the Eye of a Needle: Wealth, the Fall of Rome, and the Making of Christianity in the West, 350–550 AD* (Princeton, NJ: Princeton University Press, 2012).

Bruijn, Jaap R. 'States and their Navies from the Late Sixteenth to the End of the Eighteenth Centuries', in Philippe Contamine (ed.), *War and Competition between States* (Oxford: Clarendon Press, 2000), pp. 69–98.

Brundage, John. *Law, Sex and Christian Society in Medieval Europe* (Chicago: University of Chicago Press, 1987).

Brunner, Otto. *Land und Herrschaft. Grundfragen der territorialen Verfassungsgeschichte Österreichs im Mittelalter* (Darmstadt: Wissenschaftliche Buchgesellschaft, 2005).

Bryant, Chris. *Parliament: The Biography*, vol. I (London: Doubleday, 2014).

Buc, Philippe. *The Dangers of Ritual: Between Early Medieval Texts and Social Scientific Theory* (Princeton, NJ: Princeton University Press, 2001).

Burckhardt, Jacob. *Die Kultur der Renaissance in Italien* (Leipzig: Kröner, 1928 [orig. 1860]).

Burke, Peter. *The Renaissance* (Basingstoke: Macmillan, 1987).

Burke, Peter. *History and Social Theory* (Cambridge: Polity Press, 1992).

Burke, Peter. *The Fabrication of Louis XIV* (New Haven, CT: Yale University Press, 1992).

Burke, Peter. *Venice and Amsterdam* (Cambridge: Polity Press, 1994).

Burke, Peter. *Varieties of Cultural History* (Cambridge: Polity Press, 1997).

Burkhardt, Johannes. *Der Dreissigjährige Krieg* (Darmstadt: Wissenschaftliche Buchgesellschaft, 1997).

Burns, J.H. (ed.) *The Cambridge History of Medieval Political Thought* (Cambridge: Cambridge University Press, 1988).

Cantor, Norman F. *Inventing the Middle Ages: The Lives, Works, and Ideas of the Great Medievalists of the Twentieth Century* (New York: Quill, William Morrow, 1991).

Carlsson, Sten. *Svensk historia*, vol. II (Stockholm: Svenska bokförlaget/Bonniers, 1961).

Carpenter, Christine. *The Wars of the Roses: Politics and the Constitution in England, c. 1437–1509* (Cambridge: Cambridge University Press, 1997).

Carpenter, Christine. 'Resisting and Deposing Kings in England in the Thirteenth, Fourteenth and Fifteenth Centuries', in Robert von Friedeburg (ed.), *Murder and Monarchy: Regicide in European History, 1300–1800* (London: Palgrave Macmillan, 2004), pp. 99–121.

Carpenter, David. 'The Plantagenet Kings', in David Abulafia (ed.), *The New Cambridge Medieval History*, vol. V (Cambridge: Cambridge University Press, 1995), pp. 314–357.

Castan, Nicole. 'Criminelle', in Natalie Zemon Davis and Arlette Forge, *Histoire des femmes*, vol. III, *XVI–XVIIIᵉ siècles* (Paris: Plon, 1991), pp. 470–496.

Chaline, Olivier. 'The Kingdoms of France and Navarre: The Valois and Bourbon Courts c. 1515–1750', in John Adamson (ed.), *The Princely Court of Europe: Ritual, Politics and Culture Under the Ancien Regime, 1500–1750* (London: Weidenfeld and Nicholson, 1999), pp. 67–93.

Cheyette, Frederic. 'Suum cuique tribuere', *French Historical Studies* 6(1970): 287–299.

Christensen-Nugues, Charlotte. 'Och de skal vara ett hjärta', in *Konsensusdoktrinene i medeltida kanonisk rätt* (Lund: Lund University, 2003).

Churchill, Winston S. *Marlborough: His Life and Times*, vols I–II (London: Harrap, 1947).

Cipolla, Carlo. *Guns, Sails and Empires: Technical Innovation and the Early Phases of European Expansion 1400–1700* (London: Collins, 1965).

Clanchy, Michael T. *From Memory to Written Record: England 1006–1307* (London: Edward Arnold, 1979).

Clark, Christopher. *Iron Kingdom: The Rise and Downfall of Prussia, 1600–1947* (London: Penguin, 2006).

Cobban, Alan. *The Medieval Universities: Their Development and Organisation* (London: Methuen, 1975).

Cohen, Meredith. *The Sainte-Chapelle and the Construction of Sacral Monarchy: Royal Architecture in Thirteenth-Century Paris* (Cambridge: Cambridge University Press, 2015).

Coleman, Janet. 'Property and Poverty', in J.H. Burns (ed.), *The Cambridge History of Medieval Political Thought* (Cambridge: Cambridge University Press, 1988), pp. 607–648.

Coleman, Janet (ed.) *The Individual in Political Theory and Practice* (Oxford: Oxford University Press, 1996).

Coleman, Janet. 'The Individual and the Medieval State', in Janet Coleman (ed.), *The Individual in Political Theory and Practice* (Oxford: Oxford University Press, 1996), pp. 6–34.

Collins, James B. *The State in Early Modern France* (Cambridge: Cambridge University Press, 1995).

Collins, James B. *From Tribes to Nation: The Making of France 500–1799* (Toronto: Wadsworth, 2002).

Connell, William. 'Italian Renaissance Historical Narrative', in José Rabasa, Masayuki Sato, Edoardo Tortarolo, and Daniel Woolf, *et al.* (eds), *The Oxford History of Historical Writing*, vol. III (Oxford: Oxford University Press, 2012), pp. 347–363.

Contamine, Philippe. *War in the Middle Ages* (Oxford: Oxford University Press, 1984).

Contamine, Philippe (ed.) *War and Competition between States* (Oxford: Clarendon Press, 2000).

Contamine, Philippe. 'Introduction', in Philippe Contamine (ed.), *War and Competition between States* (Oxford: Clarendon Press, 2000), pp. 1–7.

Contamine, Philippe. 'The Growth of State Control. Practices of War, 1300–1800. Ransom and Booty', in Philippe Contamine (ed.), *War and Competition between States* (Oxford: Clarendon Press, 2000), pp. 163–193.

Coward, Barry. *The Stuart Age: England, 1603–1714.* 3rd edn (London: Longman, 2003).

Crossley, P. and Zoe Opačić, 'Prague as a New Capital', in Jiří Fajt and Barbara Drake Boehm (eds), *Prague, the Crown of Bohemia: Art and Culture under the Last Luxembourgs, 1347–1437* (New Haven, CT: Yale University Press, 2005), pp. 58–73.

Croxton, Derek. *Westphalia: The Last Christian Peace* (New York: Palgrave Macmillan, 2013).

Curtis, Benjamin. *The Habsburgs: The History of a Dynasty* (London: Bloomsbury, 2013).

Cushing, Kathleen G. 'Papal Authority and its Limitations', in John H. Arnold (ed.), *The Oxford Handbook of Medieval Christianity* (Oxford: Oxford University Press, 2014), pp. 515–530.

Cuttino, G.P. *English Diplomatic Administration, 1259–1339* (Oxford: Clarendon Press, 1971).

Cuttler, S.H. *The Law of Treason in Later Medieval France* (Cambridge: Cambridge University Press, 1981).

Dabringhaus, Sabine. 'The Monarch and Inner-Outer Court Dualism in Late Imperial China', in Jeroen Duindam, Tülay Artan and Metin Kunt (eds), *Royal Courts in Dynastic States and Empires: A Global Perspective* (Leiden: Brill, 2011), pp. 265–287.

Dalong, Claude. 'De la conversation à la création', in Natalie Zemon Davis and Arlette Forge, *Histoire des femmes*, vol. III, *XVI–XVIIIe siècles* (Paris: Plon, 1991), pp. 403–425.

Davies, Norman. *God's Playground: A History of Poland in Two Volumes*, vol. 1, *The Origins to 1795* (Oxford: Oxford University Press, 2005).

Davies, Rees. 'The Medieval State: The Tyranny of a Concept?', *Journal of Historical Sociology* 16(2003): 280–300.

Davies, Wendy and Paul Fouracre (eds) *The Settlement of Disputes in Early Medieval Europe* (Cambridge: Cambridge University Press, 1986).

Davis, Natalie Zemon. 'La femme au politique', in Natalie Zemon Davis and Arlette Farge (eds), *Histoire des femmes*, vol. III, *XVI–XVIIIe siècles* (Paris: Plon, 1991), pp. 175–190.

Davis, Natalie Zemon and Arlette Farge. *Histoire des femmes*, vol. III, *XVI–XVIIIe siècles* (Paris: Plon, 1991).

Davis, Norman (ed.) *Paston Letters and Papers from the Fifteenth Century*, vols I–II (Oxford: Clarendon Press, 1971).

Debax, Hélène. *La Féodalité langedocienne. Serments, hommage et fiefs dans le Languedoc des Trencavel* (Toulouse: Presses Universitaires du Mirail, 2003).

Debax, Hélène. 'L'aristocracie languedocienne et la société féodale: Le témoignage des sources (Midi de la France: XIe et XIIe siècles)', in Sverre Bagge, M.H. Gelting and T. Lindkvist (eds), *Feudalism: New Landscapes of Debate* (Turnhout: Brepols, 2011), pp. 77–100.

De Roover, R. 'The Organization of Trade', in M.M. Postan, E.E. Rich and Edward Miller (eds), *The Cambridge Economic History of Europe*, vol. III (New York: Cambridge University Press, 1963), pp. 42–118.

De Vries, Jan and A.M. van der Woude. *The First Modern Economy: Success, Failure and Perseverance of the Dutch Economy, 1500–1815* (Cambridge: Cambridge University Press, 1997).

De Weerdt, Hilde. *Negotiating Standards for the Civil Service Examinations in Imperial China (1127–1279)* (Cambridge, MA: Harvard University Asia Center, Harvard University Press, 2007).

Diamond, Jared. *Guns, Germs and Steel: A Short History of Everybody for the Last 13,000 Years* (London: Vintage, 1998).

Diamond, Jared. *The World until Yesterday: What Can We Learn from Traditional Societies?* (London: Allen Lane, 2012).

Dolezel, H. 'Die Gründung des Prager Slavenklosters', in F. Seibt, *Kaiser Karl IV, Staatsmann und Mäzen* (Munich: Prestel-Verlag, 1978), pp. 112–114.

Dollinger, Philippe. *The German Hansa* (London: Routledge, 2000).

Downing, Brian. *The Military Revolution and Political Change: Origins of Democracy and Autocracy in Early Modern Europe* (Princeton, NJ: Princeton University Press, 1992).

Doyle, William. *The Ancien Regime* (Basingstoke: Macmillan, 1986).

Doyle, William. *The Oxford History of the French Revolution* (Oxford: Oxford University Press, 2002).

Duby, Georges. *Les trois ordres ou l'imaginaire du féodalisme* (Paris: Gallimard, 1978).

Duby, Georges. *Medieval Marriage: Two Models from Twelfth-Century France* (Baltimore, MD: Johns Hopkins University Press, 1978).

Duby, Georges and Michelle Perrot (eds) *Histoire des femmes*, vol. II, *Le moyen âge* (Paris: Plon, 1990).

Duffy, Eamon. *The Stripping of the Altars: Traditional Religion in England 1400–1580*, 2nd edn (New Haven, CT: Yale University Press, 2005).

Duffy, Eamon. *Fires of Faith: Catholic England under Mary Tudor* (New Haven, CT: Yale University Press, 2009).

Duffy, Seán. *Ireland in the Middle Ages* (Basingstoke: Palgrave Macmillan, 1997).

Duggan, Anne (ed.) *Kings and Kingship in Medieval Europe* (Exeter: Short Run Press, 1993).

Duggan, Anne (ed.) *Queens and Queenship in Medieval Europe* (Woodbridge: Boydell Press, 1997).

Dunbabin, Jean. 'Government', in J.H. Burns, *The Cambridge History of Medieval Political Thought* (Cambridge: Cambridge University Press, 1988), pp. 477–519.

Dupont-Bouchat, Marie-Sylvie. 'Guilt and Individual Consciousness: The Individual, the Church and the State in the Modern Era, Sixteenth-Seventeenth Centuries', in Janet Coleman (ed.), *The Individual in Political Theory and Practice* (Oxford: Oxford University Press, 1996), pp. 123–148.

Durand, Stéphane, Arlette Jouanna and Elie Pélaquier. *Des États dans l'État: Les États de Languedoc, de la Fronde à la Révolution* (Geneva: Dros, 2014).

Durchhardt, Heinz and Matthias Schnettger. *Barock und Aufklärung* (Oldenburg: De Gruyter, 2015).

Dyer, Christopher. *Making a Living in the Middle Ages: The People of Britain 850–1520* (London: Penguin, 2003).

Eisenstadt, Shmuel N. *The Origins and Diversity of Axial Age Civilizations* (Albany, NY: State University of New York Press, 1986).

Eisenstein, Elisabeth. *The Printing Revolution in Early Modern Europe* (Cambridge: Cambridge University Press, 1983).

Eisner, Manuel. 'Long-Term Trends in Violent Crime', *Crime and Justice* 83(2003): 83–142.

Eisner, Manuel. 'Killing Kings: Patterns of Regicide in Europe, AD 600–1800', *British Journal of Criminology* 51(2011): 556–577.

Elias, Norbert. *Über den Prozess der Zivilisation*, vols I–II (Frankfurt: Suhrkamp, 1976).

Elias, Norbert. *The Court Society* (Oxford: Oxford University Press, 1983).

Elliott, John H. *Imperial Spain, 1469–1716* (London: Edward Arnold, 1969).

Elliott, John H. 'Self-Perception and Decline in Early Seventeenth-Century Spain', *Past and Present* 74(1977): 41–61.

Elliott, John H. 'A Europe of Composite Monarchies', *Past and Present* 137(1992): 48–71.

Elton, Geoffrey R. 'The Reformation in England', in G.R. Elton (ed.), *The New Cambridge Modern History*, vol. II (Cambridge: Cambridge University Press, 1990), pp. 262–287.

Elton, Geoffrey R. *England under the Tudors*, 3rd edn (London: Routledge, 1991).

Engel, Pál. *The Realm of St Stephen: A History of Medieval Hungary, 895–1526* (London: I.B. Tauris, 2001).

Englund, Peter. *Poltava. Berättelsen om en armés undergång* (Stockholm: Atlantis, 1988).

Erickson, Norma N. (ed.) '*Disputatio inter clericum et militem*', *Proceedings of the American Philosophical Society* 111. 5(1967): 294–309.

Erkens, Franz-Reiner. 'Thronfolge und Herrschersakralität in England, Frankreich und im Reich während des späteren Mittelalters: Aspekte einer Korrelation', in Matthias Becker (ed.), *Die mittelalterliche Thronfolge im Europäischen Vergleich* (Ostfildern: Jan Thorbecke, 2017), pp. 359–448.

Ertman, Thomas. *Birth of the Leviathan: Building States and Regimes in Medieval and Early Modern Europe* (Cambridge: Cambridge University Press, 1997).

Esmark, Kim, Lars Hermanson, Hans Jacob Orning and Helle Vogt (eds) *Disputing Strategies in Medieval Scandinavia* (Leiden: Brill, 2013).

Febvre, Lucien. *The Problem of Unbelief in the Sixteenth Century: The Religion of Rabelais* (Cambridge, MA: Harvard University Press, 1982).

Feldbæk, Ole. *Danmarks historie*, vol. IV (Copenhagen: Gyldendal, 1982).

Feldbæk, Ole. 'Vækst og reformer', in *Dansk forvaltningshistorie*, vol. I (Copenhagen: Jurist- og økonomiforbundets forlag, 2000), pp. 227–340.

Ferguson, Niall. *Empire: How Britain Made the Modern World* (London: Penguin, 2004).

Ferguson, Niall. *The Ascent of Money: A Financial History of the World* (London: Penguin, 2008).

Ferguson, Niall. *Civilization: The West and the Rest* (London: Allan Lane, 2011).

Ferguson, Niall. *The Square and the Tower: Networks, Hierarchies and the Struggle for Global Power* (London: Allan Lane, 2017).

Ferraro, Joanne M. *Venice: History of the Floating City* (Cambridge: Cambridge University Press, 2012).

Finer, Samuel E. 'State- and Nation-Building in Europe: The Role of the Military', in Charles Tilly (ed.), *The Formation of National States in Western Europe* (Princeton, NJ: Princeton University Press, 1975), pp. 84–163.

Firnhaber-Baker, Justine. *Violence and the State in Languedoc, 1250–1400* (Cambridge: Cambridge University Press, 2014).

Fletcher, Richard. *The Conversion of Europe: From Paganism to Christianity 371–1386* AD (London: HarperCollins, 1997).

Forrest, Ian. *Trustworthy Men: How Inequality of Faith Made the Medieval Church* (Princeton, NJ: Princeton University Press, 2018).

Fössel, Amalie. 'The Political Tradition of Female Rulership in Europe', in Judith M. Bennett and Ruth Mazo Karras (eds), *The Oxford Handbook of Women and Gender in Medieval Europe* (Oxford: Oxford University Press, 2013).

Fossier, Robert. 'Rural Economy and Country Life', in Timothy Reuter (ed.), *The New Cambridge Medieval History*, vol. III (Cambridge: Cambridge University Press, 1999), pp. 27–63.

Foucault, Michel. *Surveiller et punir. Naissance de la prison* (Paris: Gallimard, 1975).

Fouracre, Paul (ed.) *The New Cambridge Medieval History*, vol. I (Cambridge: Cambridge University Press, 2005).

Fourquin, Guy. *The Anatomy of Popular Rebellion in the Middle Ages* (Amsterdam: North-Holland, 1978).

Frankopan, Peter. *The Silk Roads: A New History of the World* (London: Bloomsbury, 2016).

Freedman, Paul. 'Rural Society', in Michael Jones (ed.), *The Cambridge Medieval History*, vol. VI (Cambridge: Cambridge University Press, 2000), pp. 82–101.

Freedman, Paul and Gabrielle M. Spiegel. 'Medievalisms Old and New. The Rediscovery of Alterity in North American Medieval Studies', *The American Historical Review* 103(1998): 677–704.

Fried, Johannes. 'Gens und regnum. Wahrnehmungs- und Deutungskategorien politischen Wandels im früheren Mittelalter: Bemerkungen zur doppelten Theoriebindung des Historikers', in Jürgen Mietke and Klaus Schreiner (eds), *Sozialer Wandel im Mittelalter: Wahrnehmungsformen, Erklärungsmuster, Regelungsmechanismen* (Sigmaringen: Jan Thorbecke Verlag, 1994), pp. 92–104.

Fried, Morton. *The Evolution of Political Society* (New York: Random House, 1967).

Froissart. *Chronicles*, trans. Geoffrey Brereton (London: Penguin, 1978).

Frost, Robert I. *The Northern Wars: War, State, and Society in Northeastern Europe, 1558–1721* (London: Routledge, 2014).

Frost, Robert I. *The Oxford History of Poland-Lithuania*, vol. I, *The Making of the Polish-Lithuanian Union, 1385–1569* (Oxford: Oxford University Press, 2015).

Fryde, E.B. and M.M. Postan. 'Public Credit, with Special Reference to North-West Europe', in M.M. Postan, E.E. Rich and Edward Miller (eds), *The Cambridge Economic History of Europe*, vol. III (New York: Cambridge University Press, 1963), pp. 430–553.

Fryde, Natalie. *The Tyranny and Fall of Edward II* (Cambridge: Cambridge University Press, 1979).

Fukuyama, Francis. *The End of History and the Last Man* (London: Hamish Hamilton, 1992).

Fukuyama, Francis. *The Origins of Political Order: From Prehuman Times to the French Revolution* (New York: Farrar, Straus and Giroux, 2011).

Fukuyama, Francis. *Political Order and Political Decay: From the Industrial Revolution to the Globalisation of Democracy* (New York: Farrar, Straus and Giroux, 2014).

Gamrath, Helge and Erling Ladewig Petersen. *Danmarks historie*, vol. II (Copenhagen: Gyldendal, 1980).

Ganshof, F.L. *Feudalism* (New York: Harper, 1964).

Geary, Patrick. 'Living with Conflicts in Stateless France: A Typology of Conflict Management Mechanisms, 1050–1200', in Patrick Geary, *Living with the Dead in the Middle Ages* (Ithaca, NY: Cornell University Press, 1994), pp. 125–160.

Geary, Patrick. *The Myth of Nations: The Medieval Origins of Europe* (Princeton, NJ: Princeton University Press, 2002).

Gellner, Ernest. *Nations and Nationalism: New Perspectives on the Past* (Oxford: Basil Blackwell, 1983).

Gelting, Michael. 'Marriage, Peace and the Canonical Incest Prohibitions: Making Sense of an Absurdity?', in Mia Korpiola (ed.), *Nordic Perspectives on Medieval Canon Law* (Helsingfors: Matthias Calonius Society, 1999), pp. 93–124.

Gillingham, John. '1066 and the Introduction of Chivalry into England', in John Gillingham, *The English in the Twelfth Century: Imperialism, National Identity and Political Values* (Woodbridge: Boydell Press, 2000), pp. 209–231.

Gillingham, John. 'Enforcing Old Law in New Ways: Professional Lawyers and Treason in Early Fourteenth Century England and France', in Per Andersen, Mia Munster-Swendsen, and Helle Vogt (eds), *Law and Power in the Middle Ages: Proceedings of the Fourth Carlsberg Academy Conference on Medieval Legal History* (Copenhagen: DJOF Publishing, 2008), pp. 199–220.

Given, James. *State and Society in Medieval Europe: Gwynedd and Languedoc under Outside Rule* (Ithaca, NY: Cornell University Press, 1990).

Goetz, Hans Werner. 'Regnum: Zum politischen Denken der Karolingerzeit', *Zeitschrift der Savigny-Stiftung für Rechtsgeschichte. Germanistische Abteilung* 104(1987): 110–189.

Goetz, Hans Werner. 'Social and Military Institutions', in Rosamund McKitterick, Timothy Reuter, Paul Fouracre, et al. (eds), *The New Cambridge Medieval History, c. 900–c. 1024*, vol. II (Cambridge: Cambridge University Press, 1995), pp. 451–480.

Götzmann, Jutta. 'Weihen – Salben – Krönen. Die vormoderne Kaiserkrönung und ihre Imagination', in Gerd Althoff, Jutta Götzmann, Matthias Puhle and Barbara Stollberg-Rillinger (eds), *Spektakel der Macht. Rituale im alten Europa, 800–1800* (Darmstadt: Wissenschaftliche Buchgesellschaft, 2008), pp. 21–26.

Goldie, Mark. 'The English System of Liberty', in Mark Goldie and Robert Wokler (eds), *The Cambridge History of Eighteenth-Century Political Thought* (Cambridge: Cambridge University Press, 2006), pp. 40–78.

Goldie, Mark. [rev. of] 'Scott Sowerby, Making Toleration: The Repealers and the Glorious Revolution, Cambridge, MA: Harvard University Press, 2013', *The English Historical Review*, 129(2014): 971–972.

Goldie, Mark and Robert Wokler (eds) *The Cambridge History of Eighteenth-Century Political Thought* (Cambridge: Cambridge University Press, 2006).

Goldstone, Jack A. 'Europe's Peculiar Path: Would the World be "Modern" if William III's Invasion of England in 1688 Had Failed?', in Ned Lebow, et al. (eds), *Counterfactual History* (New York: Columbia University Press, 2002).

Goldstone, Jack A. 'Efflorescence and Economic Growth in World History: Rethinking the "Rise of the West" and the Industrial Revolution', *Journal of World History*, 13(2002): 323–389.

Goldstone, Jack A. *Why Europe? The Rise of the West in World History, 1500–1850* (New York: McGraw-Hill, 2008).

Goodwin, Robert. *Spain: The Centre of the World, 1519–1682* (London: Bloomsbury, 2015).

Goody, Jack. *The Development of the Family and Marriage in Europe* (Cambridge: Cambridge University Press, 1983).

Goody, Jack. *Capitalism and Modernity: The Great Debate* (Cambridge: Polity Press, 2004).

Gorski, Philip. *The Disciplinary Revolution: Calvinism and the Rise of the State in Early Modern Europe* (Chicago: University of Chicago Press, 2003).

Graham, Aaron. *Corruption, Party and Government in Britain, 1702–1713* (Oxford: Oxford University Press, 2015).

Greenblatt, Stephen. *The Swerve: How the Renaissance Began* (London: Vintage Books, 2012).

Greengrass, Mark. *Christendom Destroyed: Europe 1517–1648* (London: Penguin, 2015).

Grell, Ole Peter. 'The Reformation in Denmark, Norway and Iceland', in E.I. Kouri. and Jens Olesen (eds), *The Cambridge History of Scandinavia*, vol. II, *1520–1870* (Cambridge: Cambridge University Press, 2016), pp. 44–59.

Grell, Ole Peter. 'Religious and Social Regimentation', in E.I. Kouri and Jens Olesen (eds), *The Cambridge History of Scandinavia*, vol. II, *1520–1870* (Cambridge: Cambridge University Press, 2016), pp. 416–440.

Guenée, Bernhard. *States and Rulers in Later Medieval Europe* (Oxford: Blackwell, 1985).

Guibernau, Montserrat and John Hutchinson. *Understanding Nationalism* (Cambridge: Polity, 2001).

Guicciardini, Franscesco. *The History of Italy*, trans. Sidney Alexander (Princeton, NJ: Princeton University Press, 1984).

Gunther, Karl. *Reformation Unbound: Protestant Visions of Reform in England, 1525–1590* (Cambridge: Cambridge University Press, 2014).

Gupta, Bishnupriya and Debin Ma. 'Europe in an Asian Mirror: The Great Divergence', in Stephen Broadberry (ed.), *The Cambridge Economic History of Modern Europe*, vol. 1, *1700–1870* (Cambridge: Cambridge University Press, 2010).

Gustafsson, Harald. *Political Integration in the Old Regime: Central Power and Local Society in the Eighteenth-Century Nordic States* (Lund: Studentlitteratur, 1994).

Habermas, Jürgen. *Strukturwandel der Öffentlichkeit: Untersuchungen zu einer Kategorie der bürgerlichen Gesellschaft* (Darmstadt: Luchterhand, 1962).

Hallam, Elizabeth M. and Judith Everard. *Capetian France, 987–1328* (London: Longman, 2001).

Hamerow, Helena. 'The Earliest Anglo-Saxon Kingdoms', in Paul Fouracre (ed.) *The New Cambridge Medieval History*, vol. I (New York: Cambridge University Press, 2005), pp. 263–288.

Hamilton, Bernard. *The Medieval Inquisition* (New York: Holmes & Meier, 1982).

Hamilton, Bernhard. 'The Albigensian Crusade and Heresy', in David Abulafia (ed.), *The New Cambridge Medieval History*, vol. V (Cambridge: Cambridge University Press, 1995), pp. 164–182.

Hamilton, Bernhard. 'Religion and the Laity', in David Luscombe and Jonathan Riley-Smith (eds), *The New Cambridge Medieval History*, vol. IV.1 (Cambridge: Cambridge University Press, 1998), pp. 499–533.

Hankins, James. 'Preface', in Leonardo Bruni, *History of the Florentine People*, vol. I, ed. and trans. by James Hankins (Cambridge, MA: Harvard University Press, 2001), pp. ix–xxi.

Harriss, Gerald L. *King, Parliament, and Public Finance in Medieval England to 1369* (Oxford: Clarendon Press, 1975).

Harriss, Gerald L..'Political Society and the Growth of Government in Late Medieval England', *Past and Present* 138(1993): 28–57.

Harriss, Gerald L.. *Shaping the Nation: England 1360–1461* (Oxford: Clarendon Press, 2005).

Heimskringla: History of the Kings of Norway, trans. Lee M. Hollander (Austin, TX: The University of Texas Press, 2005).

Hein, Jørgen. 'Cultural Europeanization, Court Culture and Aristocratic Taste, c. 1580–1750', in E.I. Kouri and Jens Olesen (eds), *The Cambridge History of Scandinavia*, vol. II (Cambridge: Cambridge University Press, 2016), pp. 587–608.

Helle, Knut (ed.) *The Cambridge History of Scandinavia* (Cambridge: Cambridge University Press, 2003).

Henneman, John Bell. 'The Military Class and the French Monarchy in the Late Middle Ages', *The American Historical Review* 83(1978): 946–965.

Henshall, Nicholas. *The Myth of Absolutism: Change and Continuity in Early Modern European Monarchy* (London: Longman, 1992).

Hill, Henry B. (ed.) *The Political Testament of Cardinal Richelieu* (Madison, WI: University of Wisconsin Press, 1961).

Hillgarth, J.H. *The Spanish Kingdoms, 1250–1516*, vols I–II (Oxford: Oxford University Press, 1976–1978).

Hilton, Boyd. *Mad, Bad, and Dangerous People?: England 1783–1846* (Oxford: Oxford University Press, 2006).

Hilton, Rodney H. and H. Fagan. *The English Rising of 1381* (London: Lawrence and Wishart, 1950).

Hintze, Otto. *Staat und Verfassung*, ed. G. Oestreich (Göttingen: Vandenhoeck und Ruprecht, 1970).

Hirschman, Albert O. *The Passions and the Interests: Political Arguments for Capitalism before its Triumph* (Princeton, NJ: Princeton University Press, 1977).

Hobbes, Thomas. *Leviathan or, The Matter, Forme, and Power of a Common-Wealth, Ecclesiasticall and Civill* (Hamilton Hobbes, ON: McMaster University, 1999 [orig. 1651]).

Hobsbawm, Eric. *Nations and Nationalism since 1780: Programme, Myth, Reality* (Cambridge: Cambridge University Press, 1990).

Hoffman, Philip T. *Why Did Europe Conquer the World?* (Princeton, NJ: Princeton University Press, 2017).

Hollegger, Manfred. *Maximilian I (1459–1519): Herrscher und Mensch einer Zeitenwende* (Stuttgart: Kohlhammer, 2005).

Holt, James C. *Magna Carta* (Cambridge: Cambridge University Press, 1992).

Hoppit, Julian. *A Land of Liberty? England 1689–1727* (Oxford: Oxford University Press, 2000).

Housley, Norman. '*Pro Deo et patria mori*: Sanctified Patriotism in Europe, 1400–1600', in Philippe Contamine (ed.), *War and Competition between States* (Oxford: Clarendon Press, 2000), pp. 221–248.

Huff, Toby E. *The Rise of Early Modern Science: Islam, China, and the West* (Cambridge: Cambridge University Press, 1993).

Hui, Victoria Tin-bor. *War and State Formation in Ancient China and Early Modern Europe* (Cambridge: Cambridge University Press, 2005).

Hutton, Ronald. *The Witch: A History of Fear, from Ancient Times to the Present* (New Haven, CT: Yale University Press, 2017).

Hyams, Paul. 'Trial by Ordeal: The Key to Proof in Early Common Law', in Morris S. Arnold, *et al.* (eds), *On the Laws and Customs of England: Essays in Honour of Samuel E. Thorne* (Chapel Hill, NC: The University of North Carolina Press, 1981), pp. 90–126.

Hyams, Paul. *Rancor & Reconciliation in Medieval England* (Ithaca, NY: Cornell University Press, 2003).

Ianziti, Gary. *Writing History in Renaissance Italy* (Cambridge, MA: Harvard University Press, 2012).

Iggers, Georg G. *New Directions in European Historiography* (Middletown, VT: Wesleyan University Press, 1975).

Imber, Colin. 'Government, Administration and Law', in Suraiya N. Faroqhi and Kate Fleet (eds), *The Cambridge History of Turkey*, vol. II (Cambridge: Cambridge University Press, 2012), pp. 205–222.

Imsen, Steinar and Gunter Vogler. 'Communal Autonomy and Peasant Resistance in Northern and Central Europe', in Peter Blickle (ed.), *Resistance, Representation and Community* (Oxford: Clarendon Press, 1997), pp. 18–27.

Ioannis Saresberiensis. *Policraticus*, ed. K.S.B. Keats-Rohan (Tournhout: Brepols, 1993).

Israel, Jonathan. *The Dutch Republic: Its Rise, Greatness and Fall, 1477–1806* (Oxford: Oxford University Press, 1995).

Jaeger, C. Stephen. 'Courtesy and Treachery: The Double Life of Royal Courtiers', in Øystein H. Brekke and Geir Atle Ersland (eds), *Håkonshallen 750 Years: Royal Residence and National Monument* (Oslo: Dreyer, 2013), pp. 199–218.

Jespersen, Knud J.V. *Danmarks historie*, vol. III, *Tiden 1648–1730* (Copenhagen: Gyldendal, 1989).

Jespersen, Knud J.V. 'The Military Imperative', in E.I. Kouri and Jens Olesen (eds), *The Cambridge History of Scandinavia*, vol. II (Cambridge: Cambridge University Press, 2016), pp. 310–325.

Jespersen, Knud J.V. 'Fiscal and Military Developments', in E.I. Kouri and Jens Olesen (eds), *The Cambridge History of Scandinavia*, vol. II (Cambridge: Cambridge University Press, 2016), pp. 326–342.

Jespersen, Knud J.V. 'From Aristocratic Regime to Absolutism', in E.I. Kouri and Jens Olesen (eds), *The Cambridge History of Scandinavia*, vol. II (Cambridge: Cambridge University Press, 2016), pp. 343–369.

Jespersen, Knud J.V. 'The Consolidation of the Nordic States', in E.I. Kouri and Jens Olesen (eds), *The Cambridge History of Scandinavia*, vol. II (Cambridge: Cambridge University Press, 2016), pp. 370–391.

Joinville. *Life of St Louis, King of France*, trans. P.J. Kennedy (New York: Excelsior Catholic Publishing House, 1903).

Joinville and Villehardouin. *Chronicles of the Crusades*, trans. M.R.B. Shaw (London:Penguin, 1963).

Jones, Michael (ed.) *The New Cambridge Medieval History*, vol. VI (Cambridge: Cambridge University Press, 2000).

Jussen, Bernhard. 'The King's Two Bodies Today', *Representations* 106(2009): 102–117.

Kamen, Henry. 'The Decline of Spain: A Historical Myth?', *Past and Present* 81(1978): 24–50.

Kaminsky, Howard. 'The Great Schism', in Michael Jones (ed.), *The New Cambridge Medieval History*, vol. VI (Cambridge: Cambridge University Press, 2000), pp. 674–696.

Kantorowicz, Ernst H. *The King's Two Bodies: A Study in Medieval Political Theology* (Princeton, NJ: Princeton University Press, 1957).

Kasten, Brigitte. 'Economic and Political Aspects of Leases in the Kingdom of the Franks during the Eight and Ninth Centuries: A Contribution to the Current Debate about Feudalism', in Sverre Bagge, M.H. Gelting and T. Lindkvist (eds), *Feudalism: New Landscapes of Debate* (Turnhout: Brepols, 2011), pp. 27–55.

Keegan, John. *The Mask of Command* (London: Jonathan Cape, 1987).

Keegan, John. *A History of Warfare* (London: Pimlico/New York: Vintage, 1994).

Kehew, Robert (ed.) 'Bertrand de Born', in *Lark in the Morning: The Verses of the Troubadours*, trans. Ezra Pound, W.D. Snodgrass and Robert Kehew (Chicago: University of Chicago Press, 2005).

Keller, Hagen. *Zwischen regionaler Begrenzung und universalem Horizont. Deutschland im Imperium der Salier und Staufer 1024 bis 1250, Propyläen Geschichte Deutschlands*, vol. I (Berlin: Propyläen, 1986).

Kempf, Friedrich. 'Das Problem der Christianitas im 12. und 13. Jahrhundert', *Historisches Jahrbuch* 79(1960): 104–123.

Kennedy, Paul. *The Rise and Fall of the Great Powers* (New York: Vintage, 1989).

Kersken, Norbert. *Geschichtsschreibung im Europa der,,nationes".Nationalgeschichtliche Gesamtdarstellungen im Mittelalter* (Cologne: Münstersche historische Forschungen, 1995).

Kissinger, Henry. *World Order: Reflections on the Character of Nations and the Course of History* (New York: Allen Lane, 2014).

Klassen, John. 'Hus, the Hussites and Bohemia', in Christopher Allmand (ed.), *The New Cambridge Medieval History*, vol. VII, *c.1415–c.1500* (Cambridge: Cambridge University Press, 1998), pp. 367–391.

Knudsen, Tim. 'Ministerialsystemet', in *Dansk forvaltningshistorie*, vol. I (Copenhagen: Jurist- og økonomiforbundets forlag, 2000), pp. 465–552.

Kolmer, Lothar (ed.) *Der Tod des Mächtigen. Kult und Kultur des Todes spätmittelalterlicher Herrscher* (Paderborn: Schönigh, 1997).

Kouri, E.I. 'The Reformation in Sweden and Finland', in E.I. Kouri and Jens Olesen (eds), *The Cambridge History of Scandinavia*, vol. II, *1520–1870* (Cambridge: Cambridge University Press, 2016). pp. 44–59.

Kouri, E.I. and Jens Olesen (eds) *The Cambridge History of Scandinavia*, vol. II, *1520–1870* (Cambridge: Cambridge University Press, 2016).

Koziol, Geoffrey. *Begging Pardon and Favour: Ritual and Political Order in Early Medieval France* (Ithaca, NY: Cornell University Press, 1992).

Kroener, Bernhard R. 'The Modern State and Military History in the Eighteenth Century', in Philippe Contamine (ed.), *War and Competition* (Oxford: Oxford University Press, 1984), pp. 195–220.

Krynen, Jacques. *L'empire du roi. Idées et croyances politiques en France, xi–xv siècle* (Paris: Gallimard, 1993).

Kunt, I. Metin. *The Sultan's Servants: The Transformation of Ottoman Provincial Government, 1550–1650* (New York: Columbia University Press, 1983).

Kunt, I. Metin. 'Turks in the Ottoman Imperial Palace', in Jeroen Duindam, *et al.*, *Royal Courts in Dynastic States and Empires: A Global Perspective* (Leiden: Brill, 2011), pp. 289–312.

Lachaud, Frédérique and Michael Penman (eds) *Making and Breaking the Rules: Succession in Medieval Europe, c.1000–c.1600* (Turnhout: Brepols, 2008).

Ladurie, Emmanuel Le Roy. *Montaillou, village occitan de 1294 à 1324* (Paris: Gallimard, 1975).

Ladurie, Emmanuel Le Roy. *The French Peasantry 1450–1660* (Aldershot: Scholar Press, 1987).

Ladurie, Emmanuel Le Roy. *The Ancient Regime: A History of France 1610–1774* (Oxford: Blackwell, 1996).

Lampert, *Annales*, in *Lamperti Monachi Hersfeldensis Opera*, ed. Oswald Holder-Egger, *Monumenta Germaniae historica. Scriptores rerum Germanicarum in usum scholarum* (Hannover, 1894), pp. 1–304.

Lang, Jacques, *François I* (Paris: Perrin, 2009).

Lange, C.C.A., Unger, C.R., *et al.* (eds) *Diplomatarium Norvegicum* (Christiania, 1849–).

Le Goff, Jacques. 'Les trois fonctions indo-européennes, l'histoire et l'Europe féodale', *Annales ESC* 34(1979): 1187–1215.

Le Goff, Jacques. 'Le Roi dans l'Occident médiéval: caractères originaux', in Anne Duggan (ed.), *Kings and Kingship in Medieval Europe* (Exeter: Short Run Press, 1993), pp. 1–40.

Le Goff, Jacques. *Saint Louis* (Paris: Gallimard, 1996).

Lenman, Bruce P. *Military Engineers and the Development of the Early-Modern State* (Dundee: Dundee University Press, 2013).

Levack, Brian P. *The Witch-Hunt in Early Modern Europe* (London: Longman, 1995).

L'Hermite-Leclerq, Paulette. 'L'ordre féodal (XI–XIIe siècles)', in Georges Duby and Michelle Perrot (eds), *Histoire des femmes*, vol. II, *Le moyen âge* (Paris: Plon, 1990), pp. 217–260.

Lieberman, Victor. [rev. of] 'Parthasarathi, Why Europe Grew Rich and Asia Did Not', *The English Historical Review* 128(2013): 1251–1254.

Lind, Gunner. *Hæren og magten i Danmark 1614–1662* (Odense: Odense Universitetsforlag, 1994).

Lind, Gunner. 'Den heroiske tid? Administrationen under den tidlige enevælde 1660–1720', in *Dansk forvaltningshistorie*, vol. I, *Stat, forvaltning og samfund fra middelalderen til 1901* (København: Jurist- og økonomiforbundets forlag, 2000), pp. 159–225.

Lind, Gunner. 'Den store krig' and 'Europæisk krig, europæisk fred', in Esben Albrectsen, Karl-Erik Frandsen and Gunner Lind, *Konger og krige 700–1648, Dansk udenrigshistorie*, vol. I (Copenhagen: Danmarks Nationalleksikon, 2001).

Lindegren, Jan. 'Men, Money and Means', in Philippe Contamine (ed.), *War and Competitions between States* (Oxford: Clarendon Press, 2000), pp. 129–162.

Lukes, Stephen. *Individualism* (Oxford: Blackwell, 1973).

Luscombe, David and Jonathan Riley-Smith (eds) *The New Cambridge Medieval History*, vol. IV.1 (Cambridge: Cambridge University Press, 1998).

MacCulloch, Diarmaid. *Reformation: Europe's House Divided, 1490–1700* (London: Penguin 2004).

Macfarlane, Alan. *The Origins of English Individualism: The Family, Property and Social Transition* (Oxford: Blackwell, 1978).

Machiavelli, Niccolò. *The Prince*, trans. Quentin Skinner and Russel Price (Cambridge: Cambridge University Press, 1988).

Machiavelli, Niccolò. *Florentine Histories*, trans. Laura F. Banfield and Harvey C. Mansfield Jr. (Princeton, NJ: Princeton University Press, 1990).

Macintyre, Stuart, *et al. The Oxford History of Historical Writing*, vol. IV *(1800–1945)* (Oxford: Oxford University Press, 2011).

MacKay, Angus. *Spain in the Middle Ages: From Frontier to Empire 1000–1500* (New York: St Martins Press, 1977).

Maddicott, John. *Simon de Montfort* (Cambridge: Cambridge University Press, 1994).

Maddicott, John. *The Origins of the English Parliament, 924–1327* (Oxford: Oxford University Press, 2010).

Maitland, Frederick William. *The Constitutional History of England* (Cambridge: Cambridge University Press, 1909).

Mandrou, Robert. *From Humanism to Science 1480–1700* (London: Penguin, 1978).

Mann, Michael. *The Sources of Power*, vol. I, *A History of Power from the Beginning to A.D. 1760* (Cambridge: Cambridge University Press, 2003 [orig. 1986]).

Marks, Robert. *The Origins of the Modern World: Fate and Fortune in the Rise of the West* (Lanham, MD: Rowman & Littlefield, 2007).

Martinez, Lauro. *Furies: War in Europe 1450–1700* (New York: Bloomsbury, 2014).

Mason, Haydn. 'Optimism, Progress and Philosophical History', in Mark Goldie and Robert Wokler (eds), *The Cambridge History of Eighteenth-Century Political Thought* (Cambridge: Cambridge University Press, 2006), pp. 172–194.

Mayer, Theodor. 'Die Ausbildung der Grundlagen des modernen deutschen Staates im hohen Mittelalter', in Hellmut Kämpf (ed.), *Herrschaft und Staat im Mittelalter, Wege der Forschung*, vol. 2 (Bad Homburg, 1956 [orig. 1939]), pp. 284–331.

McKitterick, Rosamond. *The New Cambridge Medieval History*, vol. II (Cambridge: Cambridge University Press, 2005).

McNeill, William H. *Venice, the Hinge of Europe 1081–1797* (Chicago: The University of Chicago Press, 1974).

McNeill, William H. *The Pursuit of Power: Technology, Armed Force, and Society since AD 1000* (Oxford: Blackwell, 1983).

Melve, Leidulf. *Inventing the Public Sphere: The Public Debate during the Investiture Contest (c. 1030–1122)*, vols I–II (Leiden: Brill, 2007).

Melve, Leidulf. 'Propagating Constitutional Reform in the Middle Ages: The Baronial Rebellion', in Jørn Øyrehagen Sunde (ed.), *Constitutionalism before 1789: Constitutional Arrangements from the High Middle Ages to the French Revolution* (Oslo: Pax, 2014), pp. 78–94.

Menache, Sophia. *Vox Dei: Communication in the Middle Ages* (New York: Oxford University Press, 1990).

Meyer, Jean. 'States, Roads, Armies, and the Organization of Space', in Philippe Contamine (ed.), *War and Competition between States* (Oxford: Clarendon Press, 2000), pp. 99–127.

Michaud, Claude, 'The Kingdoms of Central Europe in the Fourteenth Century', in Michael Jones (ed.), *The New Cambridge Medieval History, vol.* VI (Cambridge: Cambridge University Press, 2000), pp. 756–763.

Miller, William Ian. *Blood-Taking and Peace-Making: Feud, Law and Society in Saga Island* (Chicago: The University of Chicago Press, 1990).

Moeglin, Jean-Marie. 'Eduard III et les six bourgeois de Calais', *Revue Historique* 292. 2 (1994): 229–267.

Mokyr, Joel. *Culture of Growth: The Origins of the Modern Economy* (Princeton, NJ:Princeton University Press, 2016).

Moncrieff, Charles Kenneth (trans.) *Song of Roland* [EBook #391] Release Date: January, 1996.

Monod, Paul Kléber. *The Power of Kings: Monarchy and Religion in Europe, 1589–1715* (New Haven, CT: Yale University Press, 1999).

Moore, Barrington. *The Social Origins of Democracy and Dictatorship: Lord and Peasant in the Making of the Modern World* (Boston: Beacon Press, 1966).

Moore, R.I. *The European Revolution c. 970–1215* (Oxford: Blackwell, 2000).

Moore. R.I. *The War on Heresy: Faith and Power in Medieval Europe* (London: Profile Books, 2012).

Mörner, Magnus. *The Political and Economic Activities of the Jesuits in the La Plata Region: The Hapsburg Era* (Stockholm: Victor Pettersson, 1953).

Morrill, John. 'Conclusion: King-Killing in Perspective', in Robert von Friedeburg (ed.), *Murder and Monarchy: Regicide in European History, 1300–1800* (London: Palgrave Macmillan, 2005), pp. 293–299.

Morris, Ian. *Why the West Rules – for Now: The Patterns of History and What They Reveal about the Future* (London: Profile Books, 2011).

Morris, Ian. *War – What Is It Good For? The Role of Conflict in Civilisation, from Primates to Robots* (London: Profile Books, 2015).

Mousnier, Roland. *Peasant Uprisings in Seventeenth-Century France, Russia and China* (London: Allen and Unwin, 1971).

Mulryne, J.R., Maria Ines Aliverti and Anna Maria Testaverde. *Ceremonial Entries in Early Modern Europe: The Iconography of Power* (Farnham: Ashgate, 2015).

Muto, Giovanni. 'The Spanish System: Centre and Periphery', in Robert Bonney (ed.), *Economic Systems and State Finance* (Oxford: Oxford University Press, 1995), pp. 231–259.

Najemy, John M. 'Arti and Ordini' in Machiavelli's *Istorie Fiorentine*', in Sergio Bertelli and Gloria Ramakus (eds), *Essays Presented to Myron P. Gilmore*, vol. I (Florence: La nuova Italia editrice, 1978), pp. 161–191.

Najemy, John M. *A History of Florence, 1200–1575* (Oxford: Blackwell, 2006).

Nederman, Cary J. *John of Salisbury* (Tempe, AZ: Arizona State University, 2005).

Needham, Joseph. *The Grand Titration: Science and Society in East and West* (London: Allen & Unwin, 1969).

Nelson, Janet. 'Queens as Jezebels: The Careers of Brunhild and Balthild in Merovingian History', in Derek Baker (ed.) *Medieval Women* (Oxford: Blackwell, 1978), pp. 31–77.

Nelson, Janet. 'The Frankish Kingdoms, 814–898: The West', in Rosamund McKitterick (ed.), *The New Cambridge Medieval History*, vol. II (Cambridge: Cambridge University Press, 2005), pp. 110–141.

Nelson, Janet. 'Kingship and Royal Government', in Rosamund McKitterick (ed.), *The New Cambridge Medieval History*, vol. II (Cambridge: Cambridge University Press, 2005), pp. 383–430.

Nexon, Daniel H. *The Struggle for Power in Early Modern Europe: Religious Conflict, Dynastic Empires and International Change* (Princeton, NJ: Princeton University Press, 2009).

Oakley, Francis. *The Mortgage of the Past: Reshaping the Ancient Political Inheritance (1050–1300)* (New Haven, CT: Yale University Press, 2012).

Oakley, Francis. *The Watershed of Modern Politics: Law, Virtue, Kingship and Consent (1300–1650)* (New Haven, CT: Yale University Press, 2015).

Oakley-Brown, Liz and Louise J. Wilkinson (eds) *The Rituals and Rhetoric of Queenship: Medieval to Early Modern* (Dublin: Four Courts Press, 2009).

O'Brien, Karen. 'English Enlightenment Histories, 1750–c.1815', in José Rabasa, Masayuki Sato, Edoardo Tortarolo, and Daniel Woolf, *et al.* (eds), *The Oxford History of Historical Writing*, vol. III (Oxford: Oxford University Press, 2012), pp. 518–535.

Oexle, Otto Gerhard. 'Deutungsschemata der sozialen Wirklichkeit im früheren und hohen Mittelalter. Ein Beitrag zur Geschichte des Wissens', in Frantisek Graus (ed.), *Mentalitäten im Mittelalter: Methodische und inhaltliche Probleme* (Sigmaringen: Jan Thorbecke, 1987), pp. 65–117.

Olesen, Jens. 'Inter-Scandinavian Relations', in Knut Helle (ed.), *The Cambridge History of Scandinavia*, vol. I (Cambridge: Cambridge University Press, 2003), pp. 718–719.

Onnekink, David and Gijs Rommelse (eds) *Ideology and Foreign Policy in Early Modern Europe (1650–1750)* (Farnham: Ashgate, 2011).

Opačić, Zoe. 'The Sacred Topography of Medieval Prague', in Sæbjørg Walaker Nordeide and Stefan Brink (eds), *Sacred Sites and Holy Places: Exploring the Sacralisation of Landscape through Time and Space* (Turnhout: Brepols, 2013), pp. 252–281.

Ormond, W.M. 'The West European Monarchies in the Later Middle Ages', in Robert Bonney (ed.), *Economic Systems and State Finance* (Oxford: Oxford University Press, 1995), pp. 123–160.

O'Rourke, Kevin H., *et al.* 'Trade and Empire', in Stephen Broadberry and Kevin H. O'Rourke (eds), *The Cambridge Economic History of Modern Europe*, vol. 1, *1700–1870* (Cambridge: Cambridge University Press, 2010), pp. 98–121.

Osiander, Andreas. *The State System of Europe, 1640–1990* (Oxford: Clarendon Press, 1995).

Osterhammel, Jürgen. 'World History', in Axel Schneider, Daniel Woolf and Ian Hesketh (eds), *The Oxford History of Historical Writing*, vol. V (Oxford: Oxford University Press, 2011), pp. 93–112.

Østerud, Øyvind. 'State Formation', in Bertrand Badie, Dirk Berg-Schlosser and Leonard Morlino (eds), *International Encyclopedia of Political Science* (New York: Sage Publications, 2012).

Otto of Freising. [*Gesta Frederici*], *The Deeds of Frederick Barbarossa*, trans. Charles C. Mierow (Toronto: Toronto University Press, 1994) .

Parker, Geoffrey (ed.) *The Thirty Years' War* (London: Routledge, 1987).

Parker, Geoffrey. *The Military Revolution: Military Innovation and the Rise of the West, 1500–1800* (Cambridge: Cambridge University Press, 1988).

Parthasarathi, Prasannan. *Why Europe Grew Rich and Asia Did Not: Global Economic Divergence, 1600–1850* (Cambridge: Cambridge University Press, 2011).

Pennington, Kenneth. 'Law, Legislative Authority and Theories of Government, 1150–1300', in J.H. Burns (ed.), *The Cambridge History of Medieval Political Thought* (Cambridge: Cambridge University Press, 1988), pp. 424–453.

Peterson, Willard J. *The Cambridge History of China*, vol. 9.1, *The Ch'ing Empire to 1800* (Cambridge: Cambridge University Press, 2002).

Phillips, Mark. *Francesco Guicciardini: The Historian's Craft* (Toronto: University of Toronto Press, 1977).

Phillips, Mark. 'Machiavelli, Guicciardini and the Tradition of Vernacular Historiography in Florence', *The American Historical Review* 84(1979): 86–105.

Phillips, Mark. 'Barefoot Boy Makes Good: A Study of Machiavelli's Historiography', *Speculum* 59(1986): 585–605.

Phillips, Seymour. *Edward II* (New Haven, CT: Yale University Press, 2010).

Piketty, Thomas. *Le capital au XXIᵉ siècle* (Paris: Seuil, 2013).

Pincus, Steve. *1688: The First Modern Revolution* (New Haven, CT: Yale University Press, 2009).

Pinker, Steven. *The Better Angels of Our Nature* (London: Penguin, 2011).

Pinker, Steven. *Enlightenment Now: The Case for Reason, Science, Humanism and Progress* (New York: Viking, 2018).

Pitts, Vincent J. *Embezzlement and High Treason in Louis XIV's France: The Trial of Nicholas Fouquet* (Baltimore, MD: Johns Hopkins University Press, 2015).

Pognon, Edmond (ed.) *Les très riches heures du Duc de Berry: 15th-Century Manuscript* (Geneva: Liber-Minerva, 1979/83).

Pohl, Walter and Veronica Wieser (eds) *Der frühmittelalterliche Staat – Europäische Perspektiven* (Vienna: Österreichische Akademie der Wissenschaften, 2009).

Poly, Jean-Pierre and Éric Bounazel. *La mutation féodale, X–XII siècle* (Paris: Presses Universitaires de France, 1980).

Pomeranz, Kenneth. *The Great Divergence: China, Europe and the Making of the Modern World Economy* (Princeton, NJ: Princeton University Press, 2000).

Pomeranz, Kenneth. 'Ten Years After: Responses and Reconsiderations', *Historically Speaking* 12. 4(2011): 20–25.

Post, Gaines. *Studies in Medieval Legal Thought* (Princeton, NJ: Princeton University Press, 1964).

Postan, M.M., E.E. Rich and Edward Miller (eds) *The Cambridge Economic History of Europe, vol. III* (Cambridge: Cambridge University Press, 1963).

Prestwich, Michael. *Edward I* (New Haven, CT: Yale University Press, 1997).

Prestwich, Michael. *Plantagenet England, 1225–1360* (Oxford: Oxford University Press, 2005).

Quetel, Claude. 'Lettres de cachet et correctionnaires dans la généralité de Caen au XVIIIᵉ siècle', *Annales de Normandie* 28(1978): 127–159.

Rabasa, José, Masayuki Sato, Edoardo Tortarolo and Daniel Woolf, *et al.* (eds) *The Oxford History of Historical Writing*, vol. III (Oxford: Oxford University Press, 2012).

Rady, Martyn. 'Rethinking Jagiello Hungary (1490–1526)', *Central Europe* 3(2005): 3–18.

Redworth, Glyn and Ferdinand Checa. 'The Kingdoms of Spain. The Courts of the Spanish Habsburgs 1500–1700', in John Adamson (ed.), *The Princely Courts of Europe: Ritual, Politics and Culture Under the Ancien Regime, 1500–1750* (London: Weidenfeld and Nicholson, 1999), pp. 43–65.

Reinhard, Wolfgang (ed.) *Power Elites and State Building: The Origins of the Modern State in Europe* (Oxford: Oxford University Press, 1996).

Reinhard, Wolfgang. *Geschichte der Staatsgewalt. Eine vergleichende Verfassungsgeschichte Europas von den Anfangen bis zur Gegenwart* (Munich: Beck, 1999).

Reuter, Timothy. *Germany in the Early Middle Ages c. 800–1056* (London: Longman, 1991).

Reuter, Timothy. 'The Origins of the German Sonderweg?', in Anne Duggan (ed.), *Kings and Kingship in Medieval Europe* (Exeter: Short Run Press, 1993), pp. 179–211.

Reuter, Timothy. 'The Feudal Revolution', *Past and Present* 155(1997): 177–195.

Reyerson, Kathryn L. 'Commerce and Communications', in David Abulafia (ed.), *The New Cambridge Medieval History*, vol V (Cambridge: Cambridge University Press, 1999), pp. 50–70.

Reynolds, Susan. 'Social Mentalities and the Case of Medieval Scepticism', *Transactions of the Royal Historical Society VI Series* 1 (1991): 21–41.

Reynolds, Susan. *Fiefs and Vassals: The Medieval Evidence Reinterpreted* (Oxford: Clarendon Press, 1994).

Reynolds, Susan. 'There Were States in Medieval Europe: A Response to Rees Davies', *Journal of Historical Sociology* 16. 4(2003): 550–555.

Reynolds, Susan. 'Fiefs and Vassals after Twelve Years', in Sverre Bagge, M.H. Gelting and T. Lindkvist (eds), *Feudalism: New Landscapes of Debate* (Turnhout: Brepols, 2011), pp. 1–13.

Rian, Øystein. *Sensuren i Danmark-Norge. Vilkårene for offentlige ytringer 1536–1814* (Oslo: Universitetsforlaget, 2014).

Rian, Øystein. 'Centre and Periphery', in E.I. Kouri and Jens Olesen (eds), *The Cambridge History of Scandinavia*, vol. II, *1520–1870* (Cambridge: Cambridge University Press, 2016), pp. 392–415.

Rich, E.E. and C.H. Wilson (eds) *The Cambridge Economic History of Europe*, vol. V (Cambridge: Cambridge University Press, 1963).

Richter, Melvin. 'The Comparative Study of Regimes and Societies', in Mark Goldie and Robert Wokler (eds), *The Cambridge History of Eighteenth-Century Political Thought* (Cambridge: Cambridge University Press, 2006), pp. 147–171.

Riley, Patrick. 'Social Contract Theory and its Critics', in Mark Goldie and Robert Wokler (eds), *The Cambridge History of Eighteenth-Century Political Thought* (Cambridge: Cambridge University Press, 2006), pp. 347–375.

Riley-Smith, Jonathan. 'The Crusades 1095–1198', in David Luscombe and Jonathan Riley-Smith (eds), *The New Cambridge Medieval History*, vol. IV.1 (Cambridge: Cambridge University Press, 1998), pp. 534–563.

Roberts, Michael. *The Swedish Imperial Experience 1560–1719* (Cambridge: Cambridge University Press, 1979).

Roche, Daniel. 'Encyclopedias and the Diffusion of Knowledge', in Mark Goldie and Robert Wokler (eds), *The Cambridge History of Eighteenth-Century Political Thought* (Cambridge: Cambridge University Press, 2006), pp. 172–194.

Rodriguez-Salgado, Maria. 'The Habsburg-Valois Wars', in G.R. Elton (ed.), *The New Cambridge Modern History*, vol. II, *The Reformation 1520–1559* (Cambridge: Cambridge University Press, 1990), pp. 377–400.

Rogers, Clifford J. *War Cruel and Sharp: English Strategy under Edward III, 1337–1360* (Woodbridge: Boydell Press, 2000).

Rokkan, Stein. 'Dimensions of State-Formation and Nation-Building: A Possible Paradigm for Research on Variations within Europe', in Charles Tilly (ed.), *The Formation of National States in Western Europe* (Princeton, NJ: Princeton University Press, 1975), pp. 562–600.

Rosén, Jerker. *Svensk historia*, vol. I (Stockholm: Svenska bokförlaget/Bonniers, 1961).

Rowlands, Alison. 'Witchcraft and Gender in Early Modern Europe', in Brian P. Levick (ed.), *The Oxford Handbook of Witchcraft in Early Modern Europe and Colonial America* (Oxford: Oxford University Press, 2013), pp. 449–467.

Rowlands, Guy. *The Financial Decline of a Great Power: War, Influence, and Money in Louis XIV's France* (Oxford: Oxford University Press, 2012).

Ruiz, Teofilo. *A King Travels: Festive Traditions in Late Medieval and Early Modern Spain* (Princeton, NJ: Princeton University Press, 2012).

Ryrie, Alec. 'Moderation, Modernity and the Reformation', *Past and Present* 223(2014): 271–282.

Sallman, Jean-Michel. 'Sorcière', in Natalie Zemon Davis and Arlette Forge, *Histoire des femmes*, vol. III, *XVI–XVIIIe siècles* (Paris: Plon, 1991), pp. 455–467.

Saul, Nigel. *Richard II* (New Haven, CT: Yale University Press 1997).

Saxo Grammaticus. *Gesta Danorum: History of the Danes*, ed. Karsten Friis-Jensen, trans. Peter Fischer, vols I–II (Oxford: Oxford University Press, 2015).

Sayles, G.O. *The Medieval Foundations of England* (London: Methuen, 1966).

Scales, Len. *The Shaping of German Identity: Authority and Crisis, 1245–1414* (Cambridge: Cambridge University Press, 2012).

Schama, Simon. *The Embarrassment of Riches: An Interpretation of Dutch Culture in the Golden Age* (London: Fontana, 1988).

Schilling, Heinz. 'Reich-Staat und frühneuzeitliche Nation der Deutschen oder teilmodernisiertes Reichssystem: Überlegungen zu Charakter und Aktualität des Alten Reiches', *Historische Zeitschrift* 273(2001): 377–395.

Schmale, Wolfgang. '"Liberty is an Inestimable Thing": Some Unexpected "Laboratories" of Human Rights in France and Germany', in Janet Coleman (ed.), *The Individual in Political Theory and Practice* (Oxford: Oxford University Press, 1996), pp. 171–189.

Schmid, Karl. 'Das Problem der Unteilbarkeit des Reiches', in Karl Schmid (ed.), *Reich und Kirche vor dem Investiturstreit. Vorträge beim wissenschaftlichen Kollokvium aus Anlass des achtzichsten Geburtstags von Gerd Tellenbach* (Sigmaringen: Jan Thorbecke, 1985), pp. 1–15.

Schmidt, Georg. *Geschichte des Alten Reiches* (Munich: Beck, 1999).

Schmidt, Georg. 'Das frühneuzeitliche Reich: Komplementärer Staat und föderative Nation', *Historische Zeitschrift* 272(2001): 371–399.

Schmitt, Jean-Claude. *Le saint levrier. Guinefort, guérisseur d'enfants depuis le XIIIe siècle* (Paris: Flammarion, 1979).

Schneider, Axel, *et al.* (eds) *The Oxford History of Historical Writing*, vol. V (Oxford: Oxford University Press, 2011).

Schramm, Percy Ernst. 'Die Krönung in Deutschland bis zum Beginn des Salischen Hauses (1028)', *Zeitschrift der Savigny-Stiftung für Rechtsgeschichte. Kanonistische Abteilung* 55(1935): 184–332.

Schramm, Percy Ernst. *Der König von Frankreich*, vols I–II (Darmstadt: Wissenschaftliche Buchgesellschaft, 1960 [orig. 1939]).

Schramm, Percy Ernst. *Geschichte des englischen Königtums im Lichte der Krönung* (Darmstadt: Wissenschaftliche Buchgesellschaf, 1970 [orig. 1937]).

Schück, Herman. *Riksdagen genom tiderna* (Stockholm: Riksdagens jubileumsfond, 1992).

Schwarz Lausten, Martin. 'The Disintegration of the Medieval Church', in E.I. Kouri and Jens Olesen (eds), *The Cambridge History of Scandinavia*, vol. II (Cambridge: Cambridge University Press, 2016), pp. 19–28.

Scott, Tom. 'Germany and the Empire', in Christopher Allmand (ed.), The New Cambridge Medieval History, vol. VII, c.1415–c.1500 (Cambridge: Cambridge University Press, 1998), pp. 337–366.

Scribner, R.W. 'The Reformation Movements in Germany', in G.R. Elton (ed.), *The New Cambridge Modern History*, vol. II (Cambridge: Cambridge University Press, 1990), pp. 79–93.

Seip, Jens Arup. *Teorien om det opinionsstyrte enevelde* (Oslo: Universitetsforlaget, 1958).

Sennis, Antonio. *Cathars in Question* (York: York Medieval Press, 2016).

Service, Elman. *Primitive Social Organization* (New York: Random House, 1962).

Service, Elman. *Origins of State and Civilization* (New York: Norton, 1975).

Shagan, Ethan H. *The Rule of Moderation: Violence, Religion and the Politics of Restraint in Early Modern England* (Cambridge: Cambridge University Press, 2011).

Sharpe, J.A. and J.R. Dickinson. 'Revisiting the "Violence We Have Lost": Homicide in Seventeenth-Century Cheshire', *The English Historical Review* 131(2016): 293–323.

Skinner, Quentin. *The Foundation of Modern Political Thought*, vol. II (Cambridge: Cambridge University Press, 1977).

Skinner, Quentin. 'From the State of Princes to the Person of the State', in Quentin Skinner *Visions of Politics*, vol. II, *Renaissance Virtues* (Cambridge: Cambridge University Press, 2002), pp. 368–413.

Skinner, Quentin. *Visions of Politics*, vol. III, *Hobbes and Civil Science* (Cambridge: Cambridge University Press, 2002).

Smalley, Beryl. *The Study of the Bible in the Middle Ages* (Oxford: Blackwell, 1952).

Smith, Alan G.R. *The Emergence of a Nation State: The Commonwealth of England 1529–1660* (London: Longman, 1984).

Smith, Antony D. *Theories of Nationalism* (New York: Holmes and Meyer, 1983).

Smith, Antony D. *National Identity* (London: Penguin, 1991).

Sobel, Dava. *Galileo's Daughter: A Drama of Science, Faith and Love* (London: Fourth Estate, 1999).

Southern, R.W. *Medieval Humanism and Other Studies* (Oxford: Basil Blackwell, 1970).

Southern, R.W. *Western Society and the Church in the Middle Ages* (Harmondsworth: Penguin, 1970).

Southern, R.W. *Western Views of Islam in the Middle Ages* (Cambridge, MA: Harvard University Press, 1978).

Southern, R.W. *The Making of the Middle Ages* (London: Pimlico, 1993 [orig. 1953]).

Sowerby, Scott. *Making Toleration: The Repealers and the Glorious Revolution* (Cambridge, MA: Harvard University Press, 2013).

Spence, Jonathan. 'The K'ang-hsi Reign', in Willard J. Peterson (ed.), *The Cambridge History of China*, vol. 9.1 (Cambridge: Cambridge University Press, 2002), pp. 120–182.

Spruyt, Hendrik. *The Sovereign State and its Competitors* (Princeton, NJ: Princeton University Press, 1994).

Stafford, Pauline. 'Sons and Mothers: Family Politics in the Middle Ages', in Derek Baker (ed.), *Medieval Women* (Oxford: Blackwell, 1978), pp. 79–100.

Steensgaard, Niels. *Carracks, Caravans and Companies: The Structural Crisis in the European-Asian Trade in the Early 17th Century* (Copenhagen: Scandinavian Institute of Asian Studies, 1973).

Steensgaard, Niels. 'The Seventeenth Century Crisis', in Geoffrey Parker and Leslie M. Smith (eds), *The General Crisis of the Seventeenth Century* (London: Routledge, 1978).

Steensgaard, Niels. 'The Seventeenth Century Crisis and the Unity of Eurasian History', *Modern Asian Studies* 24(1990): 683–697.

Stollberg-Rilinger, Barbara. *The Emperor's Old Clothes: Constitutional History and the Symbolic Language of the Holy Roman Empire* (New York: Berghahn, 2015).

Stone, Lawrence. *The Causes of the English Revolution* (London: Routledge, 1972).

Stow, Kenneth R. 'The Church and the Jews', in David Abulafia (ed.), *The New Cambridge Medieval History*, vol. V (Cambridge: Cambridge University Press, 1995), pp. 204–219.

Strayer, Joseph. 'The Laicization of French and English Society in the Thirteenth Century', *Speculum* 15(1940): 76–86.

Strayer, Joseph. *On the Medieval Origins of the Modern State* (Princeton, NJ: Princeton University Press, 1970).

Strayer, Joseph. *The Reign of Philip the Fair* (Princeton, NJ: Princeton University Press, 1980).

Strickland, Matthew J. 'In coronam regiam iniuriam: The Barons' War and the Legal Status of Rebellion, 1264–1266', in Per Andersen, Mia Munster-Swendsen, and Helle Vogt (eds), *Law and Power in the Middle Ages. Proceedings of the Fourth Carlsberg Academy Conference on Medieval Legal History* (Copenhagen: DJOF Publishing, 2008), pp. 171–198.

Stürner, Wolfgang. *Friedrich II*, vol. II, *Der Kaiser* (Darmstadt: Wissenschaftliche Buchgesellschaft, 2003).

Sumption, Jonathan. *Trial by Battle: The Hundred Years War*, vol. I (London: Faber & Faber, 1990).

Sumption, Jonathan. *Trial by Fire: The Hundred Years War*, vol. II (London: Faber & Faber, 1999).

Supple, Barry. 'The Nature of Enterprise', in E.E. Rich and C.H. Wilson (eds), *The Cambridge Economic History of Europe*, vol. V (Cambridge: Cambridge University Press, 1963), pp. 394–461.

Tallett, Frank. *War and Society in Early Modern Europe, 1495–1715* (London: Routledge, 1992).

Taylor, Claire. *Heresy in Medieval France: Dualism in Aquitaine and the Agenais, 1000–1249* (Woodbridge: Boydell Press, 2005).

Taylor, Craig. *Chivalry and the Ideals of Knighthood in France during the Hundred Years War* (Cambridge: Cambridge University Press, 2013).

Tellenbach, Gerd. 'Die Unteilbarkeit des Reiches. Ein Beitrag zur Entstehungsgeschichte Deutschlands und Frankreich', *Historische Zeitschrift* 163(1941): 30–42.

't Hart, Marjolein. 'The United Provinces 1579–1806', in Richard Bonney (ed.) *The Rise of the Fiscal State in Europe c. 1200–1815* (Oxford: Oxford University Press, 1999), pp. 308–325.

The King's Mirror, trans. Laurence M. Larson (New York: Twayne, 1917).

Thietmar of Merseburg. *Ottonian Germany: The Chronicle of Thietmar of Merseburg*, trans. David Warner (Manchester: Manchester University Press, 2001).

Thomas, Hugh. *Golden Age: The Spanish Empire of Charles V* (London: Penguin, 2011).

Thomas, Hugh. *World without End: The Global Empire of Philip II* (London: Penguin, 2015).

Thomas, Keith. *Religion and the Decline of Magic* (New York: Charles Scribner's Sons, 1971).

Tierney, Brian. *The Crisis of Church and State 1050–1300* (Englewood Cliffs, NJ: Prentice Hall, 1964).

Tierney, Brian. *Origins of Papal Infallibility: A Study on the Concepts of Infallibility, Sovereignty and Tradition in the Middle Ages* (Leiden: Brill, 1972).

Tierney, Brian. *Religion, Law and the Growth of Constitutional Thought* (Cambridge: Cambridge University Press, 1982).

Tilly, Charles (ed.) *The Formation of National States in Western Europe* (Princeton, NJ: Princeton University Press, 1975).

Tilly, Charles. 'Food Supply and Public Order in Modern Europe', in Charles Tilly (ed.), *The Formation of National States in Western Europe* (Princeton, NJ: Princeton University Press, 1975), pp. 380–455.

Tilly, Charles. 'Reflections on the History of European State-Making', in Charles Tilly (ed.), *The Formation of National States in Western Europe* (Princeton, NJ: Princeton University Press, 1975), pp. 3–83.

Tilly, Charles. 'War Making and State Making as Organized Crime', in P.B. Evans, D. Rueschemeyer and T. Skocpol (eds), *Bringing the State Back in* (Cambridge: Cambridge University Press 1989), pp. 169–191.

Tilly, Charles. *Coercion, Capital and European States* (Cambridge, MA: Blackwell, 1990).

Tocqueville de, Alexis. *Democracy in America*, trans. George Lawrence (Glasgow: Fontana, 1968).

Treharne, R.F. and I.S. Sanders (eds) *Documents of the Baronial Movement of Reform and Rebellion* (Oxford: Oxford University Press, 1973).

Trevor-Roper, Hugh. 'Religion, the Reformation and Social Change', in Hugh Trevor-Roper, *The Crises of the Seventeenth Century* (London: Liberty Fund, 2001), pp. 1–43.

Trevor Roper, Hugh. 'The Crisis of the Seventeenth Century', in Hugh Trevor-Roper, *The Crisis of the Seventeenth Century* (London: Liberty Fund, 2001), pp. 44–81.

Trevor-Roper, Hugh. 'Cromwell and his Parliaments', in Hugh Trevor-Roper, *The Crisis of the Seventeenth Century* (London: Liberty Fund, 2001), pp. 317–358.

Tullberg, Jacob. 'Beyond Feudalism: Comparative Perspectives on the European Middle Ages' (Doctoral dissertation, Copenhagen, 2012).

Ullmann, Walter. *The Growth of Papal Government in the Middle Ages*, 3rd edn (London: Methuen, 1970).

Valente, Claire. *The Theory and Practice of Revolt in Medieval England* (Aldershot: Ashgate, 2003).

Vallance, Edward. *The Glorious Revolution: 1688 – Britain's Fight for Liberty* (London: Abacus, 2007).

Van der Wee, Herman. 'Monetary Credit and Banking Systems', in E.E. Rich and C.H. Wilson (eds), *The Cambridge Economic History of Europe*, vol. V (Cambridge: Cambridge University Press, 1963), pp. 290–392.

Van Engen, John. 'The Christian Middle Ages as an Historiographical Problem', *The American Historical Review* 91(1986): 519–552.

Van Engen, John. *Sisters and Brothers of the Common Life: The Devotio Moderna and the World of the Later Middle Ages* (Philadelphia, PA: The University of Pennsylvania Press, 2008).

Van Gelderen, Martin. 'Liberty, Civic Rights and Duties in Sixteenth-Century Europe and the Rise of the Dutch Republic', in Janet Coleman (ed.), *The Individual in Political Theory and Practice* (Oxford: Oxford University Press, 1996), pp. 99–122.

Van Zanden, Jan Luiten. 'The Rise and Decline of European Parliaments', *Economic History Review* 65:3 (2012): 835–861.

Vasari, Giorgio. *Lives of the Artists*, trans. Julia Bondanella and Peter Bondanella (Oxford: Oxford University Press, 1991).

Vauchez, André. *La sainteté en Occident aux derniers siècles du moyen âge* (Rome: École française, 1988).

Verbruggen, J.F.. *The Art of Warfare in Western Europe during the Middle Ages* (Woodbridge: Boydell Press, 1997).

Verhulst, Adriaan. 'Economic Organization', in Rosamund McKitterick (ed.), *The New Cambridge Medieval History*, vol. II (Cambridge: Cambridge University Press, 1995), pp. 481–509.

Vierhaus, Rudolf. *Staaten und Stände. Vom Westfälischen zum Hubertusburger Frieden 1648 bis 1763* (Frankfurt am Main: Propyläen, 1990).

Von Friedeburg, Robert (ed.) *Murder and Monarchy: Regicide in European History, 1300–1800* (London: Palgrave Macmillan, 2004).

Von Friedeburg, Robert. *Luther's Legacy: The Thirty Years War and the Modern Notion of 'State' in the Empire, 1530s to 1790s* (Cambridge: Cambridge University Press, 2016).

Vries, Peer. 'Global Economic History: A Survey', in Axel Schneider, *et al.* (eds), *The Oxford History of Historical Writing*, vol. V (Cambridge: Cambridge University Press, 2011), pp. 113–135.

Waley, Daniel. *The Italian City Republics* (Harlow: Longman, 1988).

Warner, Marina. *Joan of Arc*, 2nd edn (London: Vintage, 1991).

Watts, John. *Henry VI and the Politics of Kingship* (Cambridge: Cambridge University Press, 1996).

Watts, John. *The Making of Polities: Europe 1300–1500* (Cambridge: Cambridge University Press, 2009).

Weber, Max. *Die Protestantische Ethik und der Geist des Kapitalismus* (Eftstadt: Area, 2007 [orig. 1905]).

Weiler, Bjorn. *Kingship, Rebellion and Political Culture: England and Germany, c. 1215–c. 1250* (Basingstoke: Palgrave Macmillan, 2007).

Weinberg, Steven. *To Explain the World: The Discovery of Modern Science* (London: Allan Lane, 2015).

Weinfurter, Stefan. *Heinrich II. Herrscher am Ende der Zeiten* (Regensburg: Pustet, 1999).

Whaley, Joachim. *Germany and the Holy Roman Empire*, vols I–II (Oxford: Oxford University Press, 2012).

Wheatcroft, Andrew. *The Habsburgs: Embodying Empire* (London: Penguin, 1996).

White, Stephen D. 'Feuding and Peace-Making in the Touraine around the Year 1100', in Stephen D. White, *Feuding and Peace-Making in Eleventh-Century France*, vol. I (Aldershot: Ashgate, 2005), pp. 195–265.

Wickham, Chris. 'The Feudal Revolution', *Past and Present* 155(1997): 196–208.

Wickham, Chris. *Framing the Early Middle Ages: Europe and the Mediterranean, 400–800* (Oxford: Oxford University Press, 2005).

Wieland, Christian. *Nach der Fehde: Studien zur Integration von Adel und Rechtssystem am Beginn der Neuzeit: Bayern 1500 bis 1600* (Epfendorf: Bibliotheca Academica, 2014).

Wilcox, Donald. *The Development of Florentine Humanist Historiography in the 15th Century* (Cambridge: Cambridge University Press, 1969).

Wilson, Peter H. 'Still a Monstrosity? Some Reflections on Early Modern German Statehood', *The Historical Journal* 49. 2(2006): 565–576.

Wilson, Peter H. *The Thirty Years War* (Cambridge, MA: The Belknap Press of Harvard, 2009).

Wilson, Peter H. *The Holy Roman Empire: A Thousand Years of European History* (London: Penguin, 2017).

Winch, Donald. 'Scottish Political Economy', in Mark Goldie and Peter Wokler (eds), *The Cambridge History of Eighteenth-Century Political Thought* (Cambridge: Cambridge University Press, 2006), pp. 443–464.

Wipo, *Gesta Chuonradi*, in *Wiponis Opera*, ed. Harry Bresslau, *Monumenta Germaniae historica. Scriptores rerum Germanicarum in usum scholarum* 61, 3rd edn (Hannover: Hahn, 1915), pp. 1–62.

Wong, Roy Bin. *China Transformed: Historical Change and the Limits of European Experience* (Ithaca, NY: Cornell University Press, 1997).

Woodside, Alexander. 'The Chi'en-lung Reign', in Willard J. Peterson (ed.), *The Cambridge History of China*, vol. 9.1, *The Ch'ing Empire to 1800* (Cambridge: Cambridge University Press, 2002), pp. 230–309.

Worseley, Lucy. *Courtiers: The Secret History of the Georgian Court* (London: Faber and Faber, 2010).

Yarrow, Simon. 'Religion, Belief and Society', in J. Arnold (ed.), *The Oxford Handbook of Medieval Christianity* (Oxford: Oxford University Press, 2005), pp. 23–41.

Yule, Henry (ed. and trans.) *The Travels of Marco Polo.* (1903), revised by Henri Cordier (1920). = The Project Gutenberg EBook of *The Travels of Marco Polo* (2004).

Zamorsky, Adam. *Poland: A History* (London: William Collins, 2009).

Zmora, Hillay. *Monarchy, Aristocracy and the State in Europe, 1300–1800* (London: Routledge, 2001).

Zotz, Thomas. 'Carolingian Tradition and Ottonian-Salian Innovations: Comparative Observations on Palatine Policy in the Empire', in Anne Duggan (ed.), *Kings and Kingship in Medieval Europe* (Exeter: Short Run Press, 1993), pp. 69–100.

INDEX

P163-4 ! puritanisme
p225 pietrin

Printed in Great Britain
by Amazon